1963

Jenny

Man's Physical
and Spiritual Nature

FRANCIS J. COLLINGWOOD *Marquette University*

HOLT, RINEHART
AND WINSTON

NEW YORK

CHICAGO

SAN FRANCISCO

TORONTO

LONDON

Man's Physical
and Spiritual Nature

That men
may humbly seek
the will of God

$Preface$ ~ OUR INTENTION IS TO
give an exact analysis of man's biochemical, physiological, sensory,
intellectual, and appetitive activities in treating of human nature in
its physical aspects and in its spiritual ability to understand and to
choose freely. The biochemical and physiological activities are
treated briefly, concisely, and in the least technological manner
consistent with a clear understanding of how these activities are
the basis for conscious life. The larger portion of the book is
devoted to a consideration of the sensory, intellectual, and appetitive life of man.

Our order of procedure and our general method in explaining man's nature is consistent with the consideration of man
given in the *Summa of Theology* by St. Thomas Aquinas. The
physical examples used in St. Thomas' text are distracting to
readers having some acquaintance with contemporary science and
require research into medieval physics by those who wish to ex-
pound his text in detail. Therefore we have used contemporary
notions and terms throughout to avoid all unnecessary difficulty
in the understanding of man's physical and spiritual nature. Moreover, it has been possible for some time to bring to bear on the
understanding of man's physical nature a more detailed knowledge
of the chemical and physiological processes involved in human
life than Aquinas possessed. We have attempted to take advantage
of this knowledge, with the result, in our estimation, that it makes

available to the reader a much firmer understanding of the transcendence of conscious operations over merely physiological activities than he would be likely to obtain otherwise.

Controversies over notions that have been held to be true for many centuries (that man is responsible for his actions, that he can rise above his circumstances and overcome his misfortunes, that his happiness is not to be found in material possessions) have arisen of late because of new findings regarding the physical and chemical aspects of man. This is especially true where the investigations of sensory processes and of automatic response activities have revealed a similarity between the physiological apparatus involved in human behavior and that involved in the behavior of other animals. The knowledge of this physiological similarity, coupled with the positivistic approach to scientific problems in the realm of matter, has given rise to a view of man that blurs the essential distinctions between man's activities as a highly organized physiological unit and as an intellect exercising critical judgment. Such a view attributes the human acts of thinking and of acting selectively to complexes of nerve cells. This book explains the differences between organ-based activities and spiritual activities, and considers fully the scope of man's freedom and the natural immortality of his rational soul.

We believe that we have presented in this text sufficient evidence to vindicate man's definition as both animal and rational, to explain his predetermined chemical and physiological activities as inseparable from, and subservient to, his conscious activities, and to indicate what man's possession of life is intended to achieve.

The author is deeply indebted to James Reilly, Paul Byrne, and James Barrett for help in writing this book; also to Mary Arden Hauer for editing the manuscript and to Elaine Ptaszynski for typing. The Philosophy Department of Marquette University has graciously extended its help in the production of this book.

FRANCIS J. COLLINGWOOD
October, 1963

Contents ~

ix

Chapter 3——*The Physiology of Sensation*   55

Chapter 4——*Sensory Experience as Knowledge*   96

Chapter 5——*Abstraction and Hearsay Learning*   141

Chapter 6——*Judgment and Truth*   176

x   *Contents*

CHAPTER 1

Introduction ~ WHAT IS MAN? IS HE a mass of protoplasm, a sac of water with an interesting variety of chemicals reacting with one another therein; is he a fantastic piece of workmanship in bone, muscle, and nerve—a highpoint of evolution in the animal kingdom; is he a busy hedonist pursuing thrills until he is overtaken by disillusionment about the joyfulness of pleasure or by the exhaustion of the grave—a lonely battler against cruel fates; or is he a displaced person longing for his home but having an unsure sense of direction toward it, a mind immersed in the exigency of reasoning out its own nature and proper end? These answers are constantly being proposed in our day as the kind of answers that man can arrive at by concentrating on the evidence of biology and physiology, and by perusing the interpretations of various philosophies.

Although some of these answers have been opposed to others by interpretations of man that see him as animal and nothing more or as a spirit somehow concerned with a body, there is abundant evidence to show that the viewpoints expressed in these answers single out aspects of man's being that complement rather than oppose one another.

Any one of the characterizations of man listed above is incomplete because it is based on only part of the knowledge that has been attained of man. Thus one could claim that man is only a sac of chemical reagents by ignoring those animal characteristics that are not to be found in isolated cells of protoplasm; and one could claim that man is only animal by ignoring the rational characteristics of such human activities as science, art, and commerce. The important task which we hope to fulfill for the reader is to show that these various partial views concerning human nature do add up to a consistent whole, using them to present as complete a picture of man's physical and spiritual nature as is necessary to understand the kind of being that man is. Our aim of presenting a valid and reasonably complete account of man's nature rests upon the consideration of the best evidence generally available in biology and physiology as to the physical nature of man and the evidence available to any observer of human behavior as to the spiritual nature of man.

The Value of Self-knowledge

The instruction *Man, Know Thyself* has always been pertinent to the individual members of the human race. The knowledge that a man possesses regarding what it is to be a human being and his awareness of his personal strengths and weaknesses is invaluable to his success in life. He can use this information to determine which of his chances to participate in personal, social, and business endeavors are really opportunities for gain and which ones are invitations to disaster. Inasmuch as our daily life offers many occasions to participate in endeavors of this sort, the development of some experience to form the basis for practical judgments is inevitable. But the ability to make sound and rewarding judgments in practical affairs does not develop automatically. The necessity of daily participation in vital activities demands only that we form some basis for practical judgment; the development of prudence depends upon a good use of the knowledge of the nature of man in general and of our personal talents and vulnerabilities. Prudence is found in the exercis-

ing of some of our talents so that we develop our personal potentialities in such a way that we progress toward the possession
of what is best in a fulfilled human nature.

We cannot capitalize upon our talents, however, or avoid
being led from the path of true personal progress by our weaknesses unless we keep them in mind as we plan the various actions
by which our life goes on. To keep them in mind presupposes
some reflection, upon the nature of man and upon what our experience has revealed of the personal traits whereby we know
ourselves. The intention of this book is to present the reader
with an organized view of the evidence about the "kind of thing"
that a human agent is and at the same time to provide an occasion for reflection upon the diverse ways in which a human being
may develop. Such reflection amounts to an examination of our
use of intellect to discern what is truly best for us and of our use
of choice and intention in carrying out decisions arrived at in this
manner. In brief, such reflection is that examining of one's life
which is the mark of an agent who realizes that his future is
largely of his own making.

A critical examination of one's personal way of life—to
see how it measures up to what is possible to man according to
the kind of being he is—requires a knowledge of appetite and its
role in moving us to act, as well as a knowledge of what goals are
most suitable to fulfill our desire for happiness. This involves an
understanding of what knowledge itself is and of the distinction
between man's knowledge on the level of understanding and on
the level of the senses. The latter distinction is continually being
assailed in our day on the basis of the current understanding of
the similarity of man's anatomy and his neural processes to
those of other animals, as though man's nature had changed because some new information about the details of his physical and
sensory activities had been discovered in the last century. But
this long-standing, common sense notion of man as an intelligent animal, as a possessor of abstract and certain knowledge, is
vindicated more and more fully in each succeeding century by
the marvelous progress that he makes in all of the sciences by the
use of his nonanimal reasoning abilities. It is this common sense
understanding of man as a rational and voluntary agent that
is presupposed in free societies and which is the foundation of all
the "oughts" in the laws of political and religious societies. Con-

sequently we ought to be very cautious in accepting opinions about the nature of man that are based only on an understanding of the biochemistry and the physiology of man and that ignore the bases for the traditional distinction between the rational and nonrational animal. This is especially so since the chemical analysis of living processes and the physiology of man's neural processes do not bear directly upon the question of differences between man and animal, but upon their similarities.

There is no real difficulty in maintaining the distinction between human and nonhuman animals, as the ensuing chapters will prove. What does require a little effort in the beginning is the understanding of the various methods by which man may be analyzed. Such understanding is very important because it is largely on account of the misunderstanding of the limitations of various methods of analyzing things that the essential difference between rational and nonrational has been challenged. Consequently we shall consider the various methods of analysis next.

Methods of Investigation

In order to show what kind of study our philosophical analysis of man is, we will contrast it with a natural science and with arithmetic in such a way as to bring out what it has in common with these sciences and how it differs from both of them. In this way we will indicate what is required on the part of the reader in order to be fully aware of his role as an investigator of the nature and activities that are characteristic of human beings.

When a person embarks upon the study of a certain subject it is necessary for him to have some notion of what he is studying and from what viewpoint he is studying it; otherwise he will be hopelessly lost and will have to resort to committing the *important parts* to rote. In the science of biology, for example, one studies (among other things) the physical and chemical parts of bodies, their individual functions, and their interrelationships in living things. Also, it is necessary to know that the sliver of tissue on the microscope slide is (or was) part of a living thing, in order to correlate the significance of what is seen through the microscope with the nature of living things. Thus in learning biology one is required to associate the names and activities that

Man's Physical and Spiritual Nature

are being studied with *actual existents* and *actual processes,* and to see that things are and act in conformity with the explanation being given. The viewpoint used in this science includes that which pertains to the self-maintenance, growth, and reproductive processes of organisms and excludes all viewpoints (economic, social, and so forth) that are not relevant to these processes.

In contrast to the biological approach, in arithmetic the student is required to learn by rote the laws governing the manipulation of numbers. There is very little appeal to extramental reality, and then only as an occasion for manifesting a fact of numbers that is equally true of many groups of extramental things regardless of whether they have any chemical or biological similarities or not. In arithmetic, addition is merely the placing of successive units in an artificial class and does not involve the assimilation of one thing by another, as is the case in adding nutrients to an organism. Multiplication is not by division as in living procreation, but is merely a complex addition.

In the whole realm of mathematics, of course, there are much more sophisticated activities than simple addition and subtraction. These operations are used as examples to show that pure mathematics is primarily concerned with symbols; to the extent that the ordering that our minds can produce in a symbolic way can be simulated in things, mathematics is concerned with things. The viewpoint used by mathematics does not require us to understand what chemical characteristics distinguish one kind of naturally occurring thing from another in order that the symbols used to represent them may signify them. It suffices that the rules of manipulation of symbols in use at the moment be obeyed, and that free invention as to their possible handling be given full reign. Thus the viewpoint used by pure mathematics (nonpractical mathematics) differs considerably from that used in biology.

The comparison of biology and mathematics in the preceding paragraphs serves only as a means of showing the difference between considering living things and symbols and differences in viewpoint from which one and the same kind of thing may be considered (apples looked upon as fruit and then as *numbering seven*). This comparison is not at all adequate to define biology and mathematics or even to tell what any science is. A philosophical analysis of man, like mathematics, uses logical methods to present its deductions and does not experiment upon or manipulate things; both depend for progress upon free inquiry, as all sciences do. Philosophy, however, does not restrict itself to the domain of symbols as pure mathematics does, but seeks to comprehend the nature and causes of extramental as well as mental realities. Thus a philosophical analysis does appeal to experience of actually living bodies as biology does but goes one step further in analyzing the internal as well as the external facets of conscious activity.

In comparison to practical sciences like medicine and agriculture, a philosophical analysis of man is concerned with explaining what man is rather than with supplying the know-how to perform successful actions. (See also Appendix 1a.) Unlike the majority of sciences it is concerned with *the purpose* manifest in human activities as an indication of the kind of thing that man is, and not merely as a phenomenon of human activity. We all have heard someone say, in vindicating his actions or in condemning them, that "Life is just a series of chance encounters" or "Life is meant to be used in aiding others" to express what he believes the possession of life by men means. In so speaking the person is expressing his philosophy, his assessment of the evidence about man's purpose that he has accumulated and reflected upon.

Our aim here is to look over the evidence about the nature of man and to show that from it some conclusions can be drawn that are not mere opinions, nor mere justifications of certain ways of acting, but rather are necessarily true assessments of what the possession of life by men encompasses. This means that our analysis must go beyond the mere apprehension of data if we are to understand the data in terms of an explanation of why man acts at all, and of why he acts in the ways that are characteristic of man as distinct from other agents, both living and nonliving.

It should be apparent that the unifying factor in the philosophical assessment of man is not some one viewpoint limited to one aspect of man but rather the thing being considered, for several viewpoints of man are included in this analysis. We call this study *rational psychology* because it is man as a rational agent that we are directing our attention to; and we shall certainly consider his soul, as the term "psychology" (when taken literally) implies. Because man is one thing, a consideration of him as intelligent and voluntary involves a consideration of him as sentient and emotional. Understanding and deliberate choice in man presupposes sensory contact with things and feelings of attraction, repulsion, and the rest as matter for the exercise of choice. Similarly the consideration of soul as the vital principle in living things involves the consideration of matter both animate and inanimate, for it is in the contrasting of the activities found in animate matter with those found in inanimate matter that the function of soul becomes evident.

In our philosophic depiction of man we will use the generally accepted findings of other sciences, especially biology and physiology, in constructing our account of man's being as biochemical and as sensory-responsive to his environment. We do this to give the reader a fuller understanding of his physical nature which, in turn, provides a basis for a better understanding of exactly what is involved in the sensory processes by which he becomes informed of his environment, and of what is involved in the various motivations that prompt him to action. The data revealed by biology and physiology, however, take us just so far in understanding the kind of thing that man is; they need to be supplemented by an analysis of the contents of man's consciousness. There are two ways to analyze human consciousness: (1) to examine the overt manifestations of consciousness, namely, behavior; and (2) to reflect upon the various states of consciousness, an act we call "introspection." Introspection can be practiced by any rational animal and requires no measuring apparatus; it is the act of self-awareness whereby we discriminate the acts of our senses and our emotions, our understandings and desires. It is presumed in all other methods of analysis of which man is capable.

Introspection in Human Cognition

If a person seeks to answer a question about what he is thinking or what he is going to do, or about how he feels, he cannot find the answer by looking around him or even by examining his body. Although he may gaze at some particular thing in his immediate surroundings, his concentration is upon what he is thinking about. He is looking into his own mental activities, his own emotional states, in order to express what he is thinking and planning and how he feels. Only he can carry out this inner inspection of his consciousness and he must do it whenever he wishes to express accurately the contents of his awareness. (See also Appendix 1b.) Even the most strenuously objective report of an event, a situation, or an experiment is a report of the occurrence as it entered into the observer's awareness. What else is possible? In fact, to be objective customarily means to delete from our report of something those elements that may have colored our apprehension of that something. Thus to make a report objective presupposes an introspective operation of discriminating in our apprehension the actually-given in experience from the spontaneous correlation of it with past experience. Just as surely as we cannot have actual experience of anything unless it produces some change in our conscious state, so also we cannot express anything to ourselves or to another except by looking into our conscious state. There we find as the subject of our expression either the content of our apprehension or the apprehension itself, as in reporting that we witnessed an event without reporting what we witnessed. Consequently the analysis of behavior depends extensively upon an introspective correlation between conscious states and actions stemming from them. In brief, introspection is the only sure way of discriminating the contents of our conscious states and of distinguishing among the various conscious states themselves: seeing, hearing, remembering, freely imagining, and so on.

EXAMPLES OF INTROSPECTION

Thus when someone hesitates to leap a mud puddle because he not only sees the extent of the mud puddle, but also *estimates* that his jumping ability is barely adequate to traverse such a distance, he is looking at an objective situation and at an appraisal of his physical ability simultaneously. Inasmuch as the objective situation is unknowable except that it be present in his consciousness somehow, both the extent of the puddle and the ability to jump are present to the awareness represented by "I think I can make it." Such a judgment, when it arises from careful consideration, manifests the ability that each of us has of being aware of our being aware of things—introspection. This is not only looking at things, hearing them, and touching them, but also discerning that we are looking, hearing, and touching. By introspection our acts of discriminating the visible, audible, and otherwise sensory aspects of things become subjects for predication or for reflection upon their significance as indications of something to be enjoyed or to be noted for later reference.

Similarly when we wonder whether an *explanation* being proffered by a child as to his role as an innocent bystander in the recent demolition of a cake by the pet dog is quite objective on his part or is being colored by his fear of reprimand, we are looking into the degree of conformity between the present account of the action and what our past experience tells us is most probably the truth of the matter. This action is similar to the judgment about jumping the puddle, inasmuch as no expression of what we think could be made unless there were an awareness of the objective scene and an awareness of this awareness. This second awareness is a seeing not only of the objective situation, but also of that situation as conditioned by our apprehension of it (our apprehension may be obviously faulty, as when we "see" a dog-headed child because of the juxtaposition of the child's head and the dog's body) and as the basis for a judgment about its possible antecedents and about what action should be taken as a consequent of it.

Even our *feelings* of regret and of exultation, of blueness and of serenity, are conscious aspects of our being of which we can have an awareness. It is to this awareness that we refer when judging that "This is a bad time to tell me your troubles" or "This is a good time to unburden yourself because I feel so good I could stand anything." Thus we apprehend not only our physical being, but also our emotional state, and both of them as parts of aspects of our self that can serve as a basis for judging how we should commit ourselves with respect to the needs of other persons.

CONTRAST WITH MERE ATOMS

If an atom could talk it could tell us something of itself; if its parts could talk, they could tell us something of themselves and reveal things about the atom that the atom itself could not tell us. Nonrational animals and vegetables cannot talk as men do, but their actions signify much to us about their nature, which we can attempt to understand. In contrast, man is the unique member of physical creation who can not only manifest by his actions the most important elements of his conscious nature as other animals can, but can also reflect upon his actions and *use purely conventional signs to convey what he discerns objectively, how he feels, and what meaning things have for him.* No normal human being can fail to grasp the essential features of man's desiring, conflict-resolving, action-initiating, and achievement-enjoying nature by the simple act of being aware of what he personally is doing and why.

Man is atoms and his atoms do not talk, although *he* does. His atoms have parts that do not talk, although the activities of atoms and molecules are certainly involved in his talking. Like other animals man exercises conscious activities such as no mere atom or molecule can exercise taken by itself. But he excels all other animals in having the *unique privilege* as a *reflectively self-conscious* creature of being aware, and of being aware that he is aware, of other things as well as of his awareness itself. Although this self-awareness is personal and cannot actually be shared, the understanding of its contents, as of anything else, can be communicated and shared. In fact without introspection man would never be able to utter any intelligible sounds except those that function as natural signs of feelings (groans, sighs, and so forth) for he could never match up conventional signs as to their conformity or lack of conformity with his meanings.

INDISPENSABILITY AND LIMITATIONS OF INTROSPECTION

No one can say correctly that the hands on a clock indicate twenty minutes to five without presupposing an awareness of the appearance of the clock as that about which he is talking, although he actually talks only about the appearance of the clock. Without the awareness of the appearance of the clock there would be nothing to say about it, not even whether or not there was a clock, unless one were content to say that his attention to his surroundings did not reveal a clock. To say even that, however, would presuppose a looking at his own conscious state to see what was registering upon it. If the person says correctly that he did not see a clock ten minutes ago, he is using introspection regardless of any concomitant apprehension of what is present now in order to ascertain the content of his consciousness in the past.

This analysis of apprehension as having an indispensable introspective factor holds universally. Thus to say that an experimental animal has a cancerous tissue, or that the salt is dissolving in the water, is to state what we see to be the case for our act of apprehension. Firstly we see the cancerous tissue and the gradual diminishing of the amount of crystalline salt present; simultaneously or subsequently we express what we know we are seeing or have seen. If our expression should prove faulty, because of inattention or something of the sort, we detect the inaccuracy by comparing our apprehension to the expression of it, noting the lack of conformity. Thus *to be able to express what our senses have detected* and to check our statement against the apprehended facts *always presupposes introspection*.

When introspection is not being used to analyze the impressions that the things in our environment produce upon our senses, but rather to analyze the actions and interactions that take place within the realm where the senses, the imagination, and memory relate with one another, it is limited of course to those activities of which we can have a direct awareness. Thus we have to make semiconscious motivations and forgotten but nevertheless perception-influencing opinions (habits, suppressed desires, prejudices) more evident by drawing them fully into our introspective view. Also, whole regions of our physical self are hidden to our senses under ordinary conditions, and no amount of scanning of our sensory consciousness or of our feelings will reveal such regions to us. The flow of the blood, the normal activity of digestion, and the normal neural processes can be experienced only by making them apparent to sight and touch. When these activities malfunction however, they may produce effects of which we can be conscious. Thus one can be conscious of the pain produced by indigestion because it forcefully draws attention to itself. Furthermore, a person can be conscious of the location of the pain, of how it upsets his normal temperament, of how it distracts his reasoning processes, and so forth. There are also external signs of the existence of pain and of its location, of how it disturbs a person's attitude and vitiates his rational processes, so that all of these signs could be known without introspection by an observer who could recognize the signs. This is the method of analysis used by those who do not trust the verbal accounts of a person's experience and strive for accuracy in their analysis by measuring the various physical and physiological factors involved in sensation and behavior. But these external signs are meaningful to men primarily because someone has had the experiences of pain and has testified through his introspective discernment how the overt signs correlate with his feelings of pain. It is by common consent to the subjectively witnessed connection between pain and its external manifestations (and other feelings and their overt signs) that men use conventional signs, words, to stand for our otherwise incommunicable feelings. Thus introspection is presupposed in everyone who designates an intelligible connection between what he feels and an overt manifestation of this feeling that can be subjected to a measuring procedure.

Introspection, then, is the only direct method of analyzing our conscious activities. As for every human activity it will occasionally be in error, but we can use the same remedy for overcoming error here that is commonly used in the experimental analysis of anything. That is, we can repeat the introspections, just as the chemist repeats the running through of a reaction to be sure of all its essential characteristics by having them manifested over and over again. For example anyone can practice the act of putting together various visual aspects of things so as to be conscious of a visual pattern (a ten-funnelled ship, a four-head nail, for example) that has never occurred in his experience of his actual environment. In this way he can be sure that he does possess the ability to exercise creative imagination. That other men have this ability also is easily confirmed by conversing with them or even by testing their ability to imagine a nonexistent arrangement of sensory appearances.

Any fact that we accept as being correctly stated on the authority of an expert in the field of endeavor that the fact concerns is based upon his ability to correctly report the content of his awareness.[1] Hence the account of the physiology of man's nervous system that will be presented in Chapter 3 presupposes that hundreds of physiologists have confirmed one another's observations of nerve cells and of the fibers that connect those cells to one another, to the sensory organs, and to the muscles of the human body. But this confirmation by many observers is incidental to the initial act of each physiologist of being aware of his awareness of the appearances of things. The confirmation by many presupposes the accurate introspection by each scientist involved of what his senses reveal to him about the parts of the human nervous system. The repetition of observations is not required to overcome any essential defect in man's ability to apprehend. It is required in order to sort out the incidental features from the regularly occurring ones, that is, to distinguish the factors found in every human nervous system from the incidental aspects that are unnecessary for the understanding of what such a nerve system is and of how it functions. The common agreement that does occur among various men working in the same field attests to the regularity of nature, not only in the subject being investigated but also in the apprehensive activities of man.[2]

Introspection, as we expect the reader to practice it here, involves the evaluating for oneself of the analysis of man's makeup and activities that is presented verbally in this text: the examining of the evidence about man's activities and constitution to make sure that it is correctly apprehended and expressed, making sure that any conclusions drawn from such evidence really do follow from it. Thus, with the exceptions of large parts of Chapters 2 and 3, which are based upon the authority of biochemists and physiologists, our analysis of man relies upon evidence about his nature and activities that is available to each and every one of us through the simple act of reflecting about himself.

In stressing introspection we have not sufficiently emphasized that it is but one step in the apprehending process and that it presupposes the normal functioning of various senses. Thus introspection is not by any means the unique source of information about man, for we may consider other individuals besides ourselves and consider them as proper subjects for observation and analysis just as we do anything else that comes under the scrutiny of our senses. Of course in analyzing the way in which our senses are affected by things outside of us we are using introspection, but the contents of our sensations of things outside of us are legitimate information too. In fact, it is only through our senses that we do contact our environment in a knowing way and thus acquire the experience upon which our understanding of things and of man is based. In this way we acquire understanding from our experience of things rather than from accepting the explanations given by others merely on their own authority.

OUR USE OF TERMS

To understand is to know what something is or is doing in terms of existence, substance, quality, quantity, relation, and action. These are some of the most common terms in the human vocabulary (there are numerous synonyms for each one), and they correspond to quite elementary and easily communicated concepts.[3] More sophisticated notions are elaborated from these terms by combining and multiplying them, for example, a planet is a group (quantity) of inanimate (quality) chemical (quality) substances. In designating things it is usually required only that we point to some difference that can be easily recognized, such as sense qualities, shapes and sizes, or qualities that distinguish one way of acting from another. All terms that are more elaborate than the basic ones mentioned here are built up from such basic terms (by the method shown in Chapter 6) and definitions will be supplied wherever they seem to be desirable.

Our philosophic approach to the study of man, which is concerned primarily with giving the most intelligible and truest account of man that is humanly possible now, at the expense of excluding many interesting novelties, seeks to explain what man is and to prove conclusions about his nature in the most accessible terms. We start with what is evident to everyone, or supported by experiment, and then proceed to attempt the analysis of what is obscure in terms of what has already been understood.[4] Progress in philosophy, as in natural science, depends upon both new information and a better understanding of what has already been discovered. In the following chapters we attempt to present in contemporary language both reliable evidence and the conclusions that follow therefrom concerning the chemical, animal, and spiritual nature of man.

Limitation of Physical and Chemical Methods of Explanation ~

IF WE WERE TO AC-
complish the analysis of man by the methods in favor in contemporary physics and chemistry, we would know man as a
mass in motion and as a fantastically complex group of very
many chemical elements. This is a valid and scientific knowledge:
it is well attested to and is a causal rather than a superficial
knowledge. But living things are more than their chemical and
physical parts. Since this point is sometimes a matter of dispute,
we will illustrate how chemical and physical analyses have
their own, albeit complementary, viewpoints which do not include the aspect *living* within them. To consider a drop of
water as a mass in motion is to consider its shape and size, its
weight per unit size, and the force of gravitation exerted upon
it which is said to be the cause of its weight; it is to consider the
path of its motion as rectilinear or curvilinear, and its velocity
and acceleration as well as the force of its momentum. To consider it according to physics is to consider also its electromagnetic properties as a conductor of electric charges, as a transmitter of heat and as a reflector and refractor of light, as a

conductor of sounds and of many kinds of energy. In all of these considerations the drop of water is a relatively passive recipient and transmitter of the activities of other agents.

It is in its role as a specific kind of substance, having definite activities and definite constituent components, that water is studied by chemistry. This science sees it as a dissolving agent, composed of two elements that have different properties than does the water. There are other ways of understanding what water is. Geology considers the role of water in bringing about the present appearance of the surface of the earth; oceanography considers it as a home for aquatic living things, and studies its motions in the oceans and seas of the earth.

To consider the drop of water as part of a living organism is to see it as caught up in an organization that dominates its activities and uses the water to carry on its own proper life. Thus the water is moved about not only according to the laws of gravitation and chemical combination, but also according to the regular order of organic processes. It is broken down into its components which recombine to form, with other chemical elements, the highly complex proteins and fats necessary for the formation of the heterogeneous parts of the organism. Water enters into these combinations according to its innate natural tendencies, but it is put in position to do so by the organizing vital principle of the whole organic complex, which not only gives to the living thing whatever unity it has, but also orders the individual molecules of the living substances as to their place and function. This ordering is not effected entirely according to the laws of inert masses in motion even though these laws are involved, nor entirely according to the laws of chemical combination which are also involved, but according to a different set of laws: the biological laws of organic self-maintenance, growth, and procreation. As subject to these laws of action, the water has entered into a system that subsumes the water into its very being, involving it in operations that are more than merely physical and more than merely chemical.[5]

Consider the water that is contained in the organs of sensation of man. It underlies activities that transcend any purely physical or chemical actions as they are known by physics and chemistry. The act of discerning things is so closely dependent upon the organs of the sense that there can be no awareness without the organ's proper functioning; nevertheless the awareness is somehow more than the healthy functioning of the organ, for it is functioning as a part of the body even when we are not being made aware of something through it. This is easily illustrated. If we extend a hand to touch the surface of a desk, we do not by that action become aware of the flow of blood in the hand or of the exchange of cell life for the energy of the motion by which we move, for these processes are unconscious metabolic activities that are indispensable to the act of touching the desk and of our becoming aware of the presence of the desk as an object that our hand is contacting. These processes go on whether or not we are actually touching something *and being aware of it*. We do not exercise any deliberate control over these activities as physiological processes. But when we do direct our hand to touch this or that, the physiological processes subserve our intention to touch something. Physiology has nothing to say about what this intending is, nor what the awareness is by which we detect the touched thing, as we shall see in Chapter 3.

MEASUREMENT AND EXPERIMENT

The methods of investigative analysis (scientific research), which proceed by means of measurement, do not have the same authority in the philosophical analysis of man as they do in the sciences concerned with inorganic matter. It is true that man is a mass in motion and that he is a chemical system. But these aspects of man are not the ones that set him apart from the rest of creation. Rather they are aspects that are common to man and to the rest of matter. For every existing material (extended) thing is a mass in motion and has a specific chemical nature that can be analyzed by measurement and ferreted out to some extent by experiment. But how can such subjective aspects of man's being as his feeling when kissed by his child, or being drenched in a warm summer rain, be expressed in quantitative terms? The physical elements involved here can be measured in ingenious ways; but to measure something is not to say what it is unless our viewpoint is arbitrarily restricted to quantity, considered exclusively as extension. Man in his sensing, thinking, and desiring is not merely extended substance.

Experimental techniques do not reveal the essential inner

aspects of man as they do for molecules and atoms. There is a barrier to this method in that what man is aware of, both in his surroundings and in himself, is not observable to others except in its physical manifestations and symbolic expression. Both of these observations, however, are mere signs of the hidden reality. They are trustworthy signs, we have reason to believe, but the sign is not the whole story, although it gives information about what it signifies. A gasp of surprise indicates surprise, but not the elation *or* anger *or* fright of which it is a sign. Similarly a congratulatory phrase or a handshake is a sign of goodwill; but it does not tell what the real emotions of the person involved are, unless it happens to be the case that he is glad to congratulate or to meet the one to whom he offers the sign. The one sure way to know what a person intends is to elicit from him a true statement of his intention.

All-powerful as are quantitative analysis and experimental investigation of complexes into their parts, they fall short of being adequate to lead us to certain truth about man's nature as a conscious being, because they cannot adequately handle the all-important awareness and desirous factors in man's behavior. Nor is knowledge by physical analogy capable of giving an ingress into the whole of man's nature.[6] We understand many things about masses in motion, and we can apply the principles discovered by this analysis to man as a physical mass. We understand much about chemical action and reaction, and we can apply those principles to man as a chemical complex (although the supervening life principle modifies these principles considerably); but the analogy between physical activity and chemical activity is not adequate, because the living conscious activity of man is not encompassed by any analogy with nonliving things. An analysis by analogy is successful only to the extent that the analogate follows the model. When this is not the case, man must turn to other methods for a valid understanding of the thing in question. The best mechanical and chemical analogies to *human* life fall short of simulating sensory awareness, human thought, and human desiring, although they do throw some light on these activities.

APPENDIX 16

Man's Conscious Self-identity ~

IN MAN AND IN OTHER animals having a conscious memory not only a *specific* self-identity, but also a *known numerical* self-identity, is maintained throughout the continual process of metabolism. Man in particular has the ability figuratively to get outside of himself and to reflect upon his conduct, even when he is actively engaged in some particular type of conduct. One part of his conscious being is not only aware of what he is doing now, but can also recall similar conduct in the past and can pass a judgment upon the comparative fitness of what he is doing at present. By this part of his conscious being he can recall to his present consciousness the visual, tactile, auditory, and other sensory aspects of a long-past event and be assured that the same being involved in that past event is also recalling its circumstances now. These actions are not merely the recalling of the past and the comparing of it to the present. (Photographs and memory machines can do that also, and often more accurately than man can.) There is also an awareness in the person's consciousness of his personal self-identity throughout the interval of his conscious lifetime. He is more assured of this than he is of many of the details of the events that he recalls. In fact he can transcend the actual events of the past and present by being aware that there are such, without relating his attention necessarily to any definite one.

It is this awareness of his own conscious self-identity that man relies on in making judgments of fact concerning himself and in being assured of the objectivity of things and events external to himself. How else could he distinguish accurately between being conscious of the physical state of his being, and being aware of a similar physical state in a similar creature than by being quite certain of his conscious self-identity, and reasonably certain of the testimony that his conscious awareness gives him regarding his physical state? In short, it is because a person is quite certain about the starting point from which he proceeds to identify things as *self*, *state of self*, and *other than self* that he has a basis for discerning reality correctly.

It is only because this awareness of his conscious self-identity is a fact that a person can raise the question of how one proves that he is or is not fully conscious, dreaming, or suffering delusions. The person who begins his discourse by saying "Assuming that I am not now dreaming," may be confused as to whether or not he can prove that he is awake, but he knows quite certainly that it is he who is confused on this issue and that the issue concerns conscious states that he has experienced. The difficulty that such a person has arises from the fact that he is trying to bring evidence to bear on the very assessor of evidence itself. This cannot be done. The problem is similar to the one of the person who tries to prove that he exists. He cannot ask anyone to accept his statement of evidence without having them consent to the fact that he is presenting evidence for his existence and therefore must exist in order to be doing this. It is quite impossible successfully to call into question the conscious knowing activity that is presupposed to any act of calling into question. The conscious knowing activity is the starting point of all personal and probative knowledge; therefore no proof for or against it can be propounded that does not assume its existence.

CHAPTER 2

Living Activity and Soul ~ To BEGIN OUR EXPLA-
nation of man we shall analyze various kinds of natural activities
in order to see the basic difference between the activities of
inanimate natures and those activities characteristic of living
matter. Then we shall take note of a hierarchy among living
things according to which we distinguish the conscious from the
nonconscious and the rational from the merely animal. Finally,
we shall introduce the philosophic notion "form" and explain
the meaning of the term *"soul"* as used in the expression "The
soul is the form of the living body."

Nature and Natural Activity

Aristotle gave to the term *nature* a special emphasis
and a quite distinct signification that has suffered many vagaries,
but which is still quite useful in contemporary thought. For him
"nature" signified an intrinsic source of spontaneous activity in
agents acting in the physical world around us. Thus things con-

stituted by nature (as distinguished from those having their present shape and composition by art) have within themselves a principle such that they act when the proper conditions for acting are present and cease acting when the conditions for acting are no longer present. For example, when vapors of chlorine are passed over heated sodium, a crystalline white material is deposited. This deposit is ordinary table salt, which has originated from the spontaneous union of the sodium with the chlorine to form sodium chloride. If we could separate out the smallest particles of this white stuff, we would find them to be quite homogeneous with one another and each of these smallest particles would be found to have the same property of eliciting a taste of saltiness when placed in contact with a healthy human tongue. Thus the term "nature" applies equally well to the smallest particle of sodium, the smallest particle of chlorine, and the smallest particle of salt because each of these substances has an ability to act on its own in ways that indicate that they are not identical with one another. Much larger particles, such as a molecule of animal protein, can also be said to have a nature inasmuch as they have characteristic chemical and physiological activities by which they are distinguished from their chemical components and by which one type of animal protein is distinguished from others.

The Scope of the Term "Nature"

The term "nature" can be applied equally well to a single instance of a chemical element and to combinations of various elements when the combination has activities that are proper to it.[1] There are aggregates of chemical elements, however, that do not have any activities proper to them as such aggregates. For example, a stone that one might pick up from a beach will usually have a variety of chemical compounds existing alongside of one another, but these various compounds do not share one substantial nature of which they are parts acting in concert. Their being together in one lump is not a manifestation of any chemical affinity that they have for one another, but rather is the result of other agencies that have brought them together at the place where the stone was found. Such agencies are the motions of the waves that rolled the stone about on the beach and of the geologic forces that exerted pressure to form the stone and brought that particular group of chemicals together in the first place to be pressed into a stone. These agencies are said to be natural, and what they have produced is said to have come about by nature, but the stone is an accidental unity inasmuch as the various elements that make up the stone are not together because of some chemical affinity for each other. In short a group of natural things may so unite with one another as to have an essential unity, and one nature of the whole, or they may merely cohere by mechanical forces and have only a unity of place.

The use of the term "nature" does not imply any more than that we can distinguish in our experiences of our surroundings various things having different kinds of activity. Its use does not imply that we know explicitly the source of the activity by which sodium unites with chlorine, or that we know the basic elements of our universe and the reasons for their various combinations. "Nature" is a term that refers to those intrinsic sources of activity which are basically responsible for most of the varieties of action, reaction, and interaction which constitute the mobile aspect of our universe of matter.

THE WORLD OF INANIMATE NATURES

From the point of view that we are adopting in using the term "nature" to indicate the essential intrinsic source of activity in various kinds of agents, the world around us is the home of many different kinds of natures both animate and inanimate. Each kind of nature is possessed by a multitude of individual things having the same essential properties. Thus each kind of chemical compound has its own characteristic natural activities by which we classify it as differing in some way from other kinds of chemical compounds. The level of chemical complexity determines to a large degree the kind of natural properties that a thing will have. Thus carbon existing uncombined with other chemicals has certain properties, such as its ability to absorb noxious gases and to unite with oxygen in combustion, which it does not have as a component of plant starch or when it is exhaled by men in combination with oxygen as carbon dioxide. Properties that are found to be characteristic of compounds simply cease to exist when those compounds are broken down into their components; properties that formerly were not evident come into being when chemical union occurs. It matters not whether these inanimate chemical agents are brought together by human action or other agencies. The resulting natural activities are attributable to the components and their manner of union, rather than to the agency bringing them together. Man's act in synthesizing chemical natures merely makes use of natural properties already inherent in things and brings about chemical compositions to imitate those that occur naturally or brings about new ones that have not yet occurred in nature.

Besides the activities attributable to natural agents because of their distinct chemical natures, there are activities we describe simply as those of bodies having bulk and hence location. Thus stones rolling up against one another act upon each other according to their velocity and weight, even though they do not act upon one another chemically. Water running downhill or being evaporated into the atmosphere is being acted upon according to its location and susceptibility to gravitational attraction and to its being heated. We will call this type of activity, of mass as subject to motion, merely mechanical activity. This terminology is not altogether accurate, because correlations between the mass and the motions of subatomic particles and the chemical affinities of the atoms of which they are parts have been discovered. That is, what we are calling chemical activity may be rooted in the mechanical activity of atomic parts. We are not saying, however, that chemical and mechanical activities are essentially different, but that on the macroscopic level of analysis we apprehend differences between them. The difference consists in this: Every material activity involves mass in motion, but some of these activities do not result in a change of natural properties in that which is affected by the motion. As further examples, a diamond can be used to cut glass without uniting with the glass, and water freezing onto the branch of a tree can break the branch by adding a weight that the branch cannot support.

The inanimate parts of our universe in general give evidence of two kinds of activity, chemical union (which is sometimes accompanied by separation when one element separates another from a third in uniting with it) and mechanical displacement of mass. Man has isolated most of the sources of these two kinds of activity. That is, he has learned how to distinguish and classify many kinds of chemical compounds and he can in principle apply these methods to all of the chemical combinations yet to be discovered. Consequently many of the chemical and mechanical factors involved in a series of natural events can be discussed both in themselves and as involved in the series of events. For example, the spontaneous emission of radiant energy from chemical activity going on in our sun gives warmth to waters on the surface of the earth. This warming activity gives the energy needed to produce a change of physical state in some of the water from liquid to gaseous so that it rises into the atmosphere. The subsequent cooling of this water vapor in the atmosphere is accompanied by precipitation as water droplets acquire sufficient mass so that their weight pulls them down to the surface of the earth; there the water as a chemical agent enters into the metabolism of living things as an indispensable ingredient in the maintenance of life. Each of the agencies in this example is attributed quite definitely to its source, and we have no doubt about the correctness of the attribution even though there still remains much mystery about light, about gravitation, and about chemical action.

Although we can identify, and if need be, isolate in a physical way the sources of chemical activity and also see how some mechanical activities originate from chemical action, nevertheless much mystery also remains regarding the origins of the motions of the earth and the other planets around their axes, and of the motions of the planets around the sun. Despite the fact that men have noted these motions since the dawn of recorded civilization, we cannot ascribe them to any of the natural agents that we have discovered, in any but a conjectural manner. The world of inanimate natures is well understood in many aspects, but is still a mystery in many others. Nevertheless we have attained sufficient understanding to be able to set down the general characteristics of natural activity in inanimate things.

GENERAL CHARACTERISTICS OF INANIMATE AGENCY

The kinds of natural activities which have been discussed so far have three general characteristics whereby they are distinguished from artificially induced activities and from actions stemming from free choice. Thus natural activities are *self-*

originating, spontaneous, and *predetermined.* By self-origination we mean that the activity flows from the agent in question and is not induced in it by some extraneous agent. For example, the action whereby sodium links with chloride to form salt originates in one or both of the component elements and is not given to them by any third agent. That is, the source of action is in the chemical agents themselves. Since the action of a material agent presupposes something upon which it acts, there will be a corresponding receptivity and sometimes a reaction (in chemical union of two things) accompanying the action. If what is being acted upon is merely receptive, then it comes under the influence of the agent that is acting and it may be moved to partake of an activity other than its own natural activity as a result. This is an induced activity. For example, falling rain tends toward the center of the earth according as gravitational attraction induces it to go there. Winds, however, may blow the rain from this path, and man-made containers may catch it and arrest its motion. In these two instances the rain is being acted upon by a second mechanical force besides gravity which also moves it about in place and by one that puts a stop to its induced motion. Its passivity to mechanical forces, which can induce a large variety of motions and physical states in it, in no way alters the rain's natural ability to enter into chemical combination with any of the things susceptible to its activity. The reason it is not so acting is that proper conditions for such action are not present. The rain water must be in contact with that which it is to react with in order for its chemical activity to be exercised.

When the proper conditions for action are present, however, the action simply proceeds to its conclusion, unless something interferes with it. Thus it is said to be *spontaneous,* that is, does not occur at one time and then not at another although the prevailing conditions are the same. All that is required is that the conditions be right; the action inevitably occurs. Consequently we can look upon chemical agents as having innate tendencies to act and to react that are actualized spontaneously when the conditions are right. By contrast induced tendencies, such as the tendency to be moved toward centers of gravitational attraction, are present because of the activities of other agents. If such agents should cease to act, if the source of heat is removed from a container of water, for example, the induced activity ceases also.

The third general characteristic, *predetermination of activity*, is well attested to by the laws of mechanics and the laws of chemical reaction. These laws state what invariably happens when mechanical forces and chemical agents act. They state, for example, that heated sodium in the presence of gaseous chlorine (at normal pressure) will inevitably unite with it, unless some other agent interferes. Similarly, at normal temperature and pressure, stones will roll downhill unless impeded by something and the rays of sunlight striking a surface will always impart some warmth to it. In general the descriptions of the natural activities of the chemical elements tell us how these elements *always act in the same specific ways in the same circumstances*, and the understanding of the manner of acting characteristic of various mechanical forces enables us *to predict in general* the results of the action by each one of them.

Because of the regularity with which inanimate agents act according to their kind, we look upon them as being predetermined in their actions. Thus the only factors that change their way of acting are extrinsic to their physical being. Apart from these extraneous influences, which can interfere with, modify, or suppress an intrinsically originating spontaneous activity, there is no choice or decision as to how to act exercised by inanimate agents. To say that they are predetermined simply means that *by having a certain nature an agent is bound to act, when it acts, according to that specific nature.* The manner of acting is determined in advance of the action by the kind of thing that it is; thus the action is said to be *specifically predetermined.*

The notion of predetermination applies to all natures according to our understanding of nature as a relatively permanent principle of action. Consequently it applies to living natures which in common with all natures can be understood to have characteristics that endure as long as the possessor of a living nature endures.[2] Thus all trees have certain chemical elements in their makeup, and similarities of structure and vital activities, so that when we have learned these elements we can confidently expect to say in general how any given tree will sustain itself and carry on its other vital functions. We must distinguish, however, between the degree of predetermination in living things which admits of some variations because of the multiplicity of heterogeneous subagents involved in their vital activities and the absence of variation in such activities as the uniting of oxygen and hydrogen in the formation of water.[3] Consequently we will call the predetermination of inanimate agents, *strict predetermination*, and say that the activities of living things are *generally predetermined* by the kind of living thing that each one is.

Living Natures

Inanimate things are involved in joining together and separating out from one another and in emitting energy in various forms and in absorbing it. In general living things have similar activities, since they unite chemically with their environment and absorb energy from it, and generate energy within themselves and channel it into other vital activities. But living activities also differ sufficiently from those of inanimate agents so that we are quite justified in using the term "living" to distinguish one general class of natures from all others. Within this general classification there are striking differences, because nonsentient life has very little unpredetermination while sentient life has some degree of choice and rational life has some degree of freedom. One predetermined activity that is basic to every kind of material living thing is the chemical activity of metabolism. This is an exchange of various chemicals between the living thing and its environment. (See Appendix 2a.)

Exchange of Chemicals with the Environment

In the process of breathing, land animals exchange oxygen and carbon dioxide with the atmosphere, and they exchange proteins, fats, carbohydrates, and water with others parts of their environment which they consume as food. Green plants use up some of the carbon dioxide in the atmosphere and pass oxygen back to the atmosphere, where it becomes available to animals. They also take in chemicals as food from other parts of their environment. Animals in general maintain their supply of digestible materials by consuming other animals and plants, whereas most plants consume only inanimate things.[4] The animal metabol-

ism breaks down the foods in the digestive system into their constituent chemicals and then incorporates some of these chemicals
into living tissue.[5] The food, even if it is living when consumed,
does not give the life that it possesses to what consumes it. Rather
the food takes part in the self-maintaining activities of the living
substance by acting as fuel and raw material for tissue replacement. It is rendered inanimate in chemical decomposition and
then becomes living again when it is incorporated as part of a
thing that is already living. Thus some parts of food on being assimilated into the very physical being of the living thing become
living substance, serve as tissue in the organism, and are used up
to be replaced by other new materials; while other parts of food
are used in an energy-yielding manner to supply the energy for
vital processes, such as nerve impulsing and muscle contraction,
and are then eliminated as waste products.

The digestive processes of each kind of animal occur
regularly in the same way. Although there is mechanical activity involved in obtaining the food and getting it into the digestive system, the process of assimilating the food depends entirely
upon the spontaneous activities of the chemicals secreted by
the digestive system. Thus the chemical exchange occurring
in digestion is similar to that which occurs in the action and reaction of chemicals not involved in vital processes. It is spontaneous and predetermined, for it takes place whenever food is
presented to the digestive system and digestion regularly breaks
food down to the same kinds of components that are either automatically absorbed into the cycle of life-sustaining processes or
caste off as waste. Malfunctions can occur and variations in food
can call forth more response from one part of the digestive system than another, but in general the range of unpredetermination
in food utilization is small.

There are other predetermined activities involved in the
maintenance of animal life. The absorption of oxygen by the
blood that is in the lungs and the release of this same oxygen to
the individual cells of the body that are in need of it, the response
of nerve fibers to stimulus from outside of the body (as in seeing and hearing), and the contraction or relaxation response of
the muscles to nerve stimulus are examples of the spontaneous
activity of the chemicals within the body, upon which the func-

tioning and interaction of each of the bodily parts depends. The next chapter will consider nerve and muscle activity in some detail; here we will concentrate upon biochemical activity in general as a striking example of what it is to be living.

STABILITY IN THE FLUX
OF CHEMICAL EXCHANGE

When chlorine has united with sodium to form salt, it no longer exhibits the properties of free chlorine. In order to become a constituent of sodium chloride it had to cease acting as free chlorine. Similarly food, as we eat it and digest it, has to cease being fruit and meat and grain in order to become living tissue. Most chemical actions are accompanied by reactions on the part of what is being acted upon, so that both agent and reagent are affected.[6] But when living substance and food interact, although there are chemical modifications in the living thing, nevertheless the living thing retains its specific identity as the kind of living thing that it is. *The essential nature of the living thing is not lost in the action and reaction with its food,* whereas the natural properties of the chemical compounds that have been assimilated no longer exist in their entirety. Some of the properties simply disappear and the remainder are utilized in the vital activities necessary to maintain the living substance and to enable it to act as a nature in its own right. Consequently we conclude that the naturally occurring organic compounds have ceased to exist as such, that is, they have been destroyed and their components have been chemically absorbed by the living body.

From this purely chemical point of view the most striking characteristic of a living thing is that it is constantly in a state of change throughout the larger part of its whole physical being and yet it maintains its specific identity as a certain kind of thing as long as it is living. Thus, in spite of being an endless process of chemical changes in which a large number of chemical components pass into the body and eventually pass out of it, the living human body retains its identity as a specific kind of thing for as long as it lives.[7] The signal that what has been an organism is no longer living is that it no longer carries on activities proper to its nature and its chemical constituents begin to exert independent activity. Their natural properties, which have been subordinated to the life of the animal, begin to be manifested in the decomposition of tissues. The circulatory processes of the body, which have maintained a supply of the right chemicals in the right places, also cease; the domination of the living processes over the chemical constituents of the body as to their function and location is no longer present. The body's chemicals are no longer subservient to the organizing principle that dominated them even while depending upon them.[8]

SELF-INITIATED ACTIVITY

An obvious characteristic of living things, then, is the stable presence of their specific natures in spite of the ceaseless process of energy exchange with the environment. Nevertheless it is a fact that there are nonliving systems made up of many discrete parts that appear to act upon and with one another. For example, the parts of an atom act upon, and in concert with, one another. The planets of our solar system are also in continuous motion and depend upon the sun for their orbits. Since the activities of the components of such systems are predetermined by the nature of the components and by the unifying principle of each system, why are not such systems said to be living?[9] They have a physical unity that enables us to distinguish one kind of atom from another and one solar system from another. They do not appear to be in need of a continual supply of energy from outside of themselves and so are less needy of external support than are those chemical aggregates that continuously have to unite in a chemical way with their environment in order to survive.

Is there anything else to be noted about living things that indicates an irreducible difference between them and inanimate entities other than their constant need to change in order to remain specifically the same kind of thing? *Inanimate things* are sources of motion, but they *do not move themselves.* They simply act when conditions are right; they never move themselves to act. By contrast each living thing is capable of acting and ceasing to act in conjunction with internal states of need and repletion. Thus living things exhibit behavior toward their external environment and their behavior is determined not only by the kind of living thing that each is, but also by the presence and absence of things in their environment that can evoke a response from them. Although much behavior in living things is predetermined (tropisms in plants, reflex and automatic responses in animals) and therefore does not differ significantly from activities of inanimates in this respect, nevertheless it differs in another way from the ever-present tendencies to which we ascribe the actions of inanimate agents. Such tendencies in inanimate agents are present until actualized in union with a suitable chemical partner. The same tendency is not manifested again until some external agency disunites the components that had been united previously. In living things the tendencies arise within the living unit, are actualized by action issuing from within the living thing (behavior) bringing in parts of the environment, and arise again as the result of metabolism. There are other tendencies also that are brought to fulfillment within the living thing, but they have no overt manifestation and consequently cannot be called behavior. They, too, arise within the living thing as a result of metabolism and are directed partly to self-maintenance of the living nature, and partly to growth, in the physically immature, and partly to the overt actions that we call behavior.

In the foregoing considerations we see the basis for the comparison of living things with the cosmos as a whole. Within the inanimate universe only unlike things (unlike in chemical nature or in electrical charge, or in position, or in state of energy, and so forth) act upon one another and if everything in the universe were in every way identical with every other thing nothing would happen. Thus action occurs in the cosmos because of the heterogeneity within it. The living body is often called a microcosmos because of the heterogeneity of its parts and their operations which enables the body to carry on many functions entirely within itself. Like any system that effects an interchange of energy and work it receives fuel from outside of itself. But apart from this dependence upon its environment the living body is a self-contained system, which both maintains itself in existence and develops itself to a state of maturity by actions arising within and terminating within its physical being. This kind of activity that occurs within a being we call "immanent activity." It is found in both living and nonliving things. In living things, however, some immanent activities are initiated by one part of such a being beginning to act upon another part, and for this reason *self-motion* as well as *maintenance of specific identity* are characteristics that distinguish living things from all other material beings.

It is obvious now that the complexity of a living system such as the human body is more than the complexity of a large molecule whose constituent atoms are bound to one another by interatomic forces; it is the complexity of a large number of physical parts, each of which has its own physical nature and is made up of thousands of molecules having their own chemical properties. All of these constituents are formed into one coordinated system called a living substance. The word "substance" as used by philosophers refers to a unit that exists by itself rather than as an aspect of something else. Thus a human being is one substance even though he is possessed of very many physical parts each of which when isolated from the rest is capable of existing by itself as a substance. It is the existence as a unit of a specific kind having an intrinsic principle of limitation that determines its physical extent which is denominated by the term "substance." The fact that all of the parts of a living body are interconnected as parts of a whole and function as parts of the whole only when the whole functions, and are moved about physically within the whole in subordination to the needs of the whole, indicates that their natural chemical activities are made to serve the needs of the whole. Conversely, the whole living thing is the sum of the parts with their individual activities, plus the organization of the parts in a unified system that is capable of acting as one thing.

Our discourse so far has been concerned with general characteristics common to every living thing, for self-maintenance and growth are characteristic of single-celled life as well as of the most complex arrangement of cells organized into one substantial unit. But we need to examine a little more closely the process by which living things grow to maturity in order to see how strikingly different this activity is from that of inanimate agents. Living natures seem to get something for nothing as they develop from their earliest to their mature state. Whence come the limbs that gradually develop out of the mass of cells that is the human embryo? Whence come the tendencies that prompt us to do what is necessary for the perpetuation of life? Whence comes the ability to move ourselves about in space? At one time the presence of

Living Activity and Soul

a living nature is manifested by the splitting of cells as the fertilized ovum starts the process of multiplication by division; at another it is manifested by the detection of a natural enemy in the immediate surroundings and consequent flight or combat. What is so amazing here is not the ability of living things to derive the means of self-maintenance from the environment, but the ability of a living nature to push on to the mature stage from the primitive one. Of course there is predetermination here for the progeny is of the same kind as the parent, barring mutations in the hereditary factors, and barring malfunctions that distort living bodies from the pattern of the species. But this predetermination is so complex that it defies imagination. We can picture to ourselves the nucleus of the sodium atom and its orbiting electrons. Even if the picture we form does not conform to the basic components of the sodium atom exactly, nevertheless we can imagine a determinate arrangement of parts and the motions of those parts as something falling within human comprehension. But what visualization can depict the mastery that a fertilized ovum is going to exert over the chemicals out of which it is going to develop a mature living body? (See Appendix 2b.)

SELF-ACTUALIZATION

We can refer to the growth of a living thing as *self-actualization*, for it is to a large extent by its own activities that a living thing proceeds toward a state of greater complexity in structure and toward a wider range of activities. In other words the living thing gradually improves upon its primitive state by making its possibilities of development give way to the actual possession of a more complex structure and of more activities than it had to start with. That this is done unconsciously in the area of physiological development appears all the more marvelous to us human beings who know how difficult it is to make really complex and ingenious structures, even when we have the end clearly in view and a general notion of how to fit the materials to the achieving of that end.

The end in view in physiological development is precontained in the primitive state, not consciously (as far as we know), but in the form possessed by the materials organized in that primitive state. It is as though there were a set of blueprints there for the building of a mature animal and it is according to these that the living structure is made larger and more complex. Since there is no one to read the blueprints, however, the plan for building is present in a different form. It is present in the form of giant molecules whose structure apparently determines the pattern of growth. Exactly how they function has not yet been ascertained fully, but that they play a key role in determining that a group of living chemicals (a fertilized ovum, an embryo, and so on up the scale toward maturity) shall develop into a mature living thing of the same kind as its parent is well established. It is as though the old notion about a similarity's being transmitted in the manner in which a seal (little image) impresses its image upon a receptive surface is pretty close to being a correct description of the actual process. The image produced by a seal, however, is the reverse of the figure on the seal and therefore is not a replica of that figure. Therefore if we modify the analogy in that respect, we have some general notion of how the plan according to which living things build their mature selves can be present in an unconscious way.

There is also a conscious factor in the self-actualization process of some living beings. Although we cannot define consciousness in any of the terms appropriate to the physical description of things, we can know it by experiencing it in ourselves and we can attribute it to some other animals. The possession of consciousness enables an animal "to behave" toward things in its environment. That is, it enables the animal to be aware of the presence of things and to act according to this information. As a result of action, in those conscious animals that have memory, experience may be built up and play a role in the development of the conscious abilities themselves. Thus there are two distinct ways in which the environment can affect the growth of a conscious living being: by providing an adequate supply of the chemicals suitable for the health of the organism, or contrariwise, by failing to provide an adequate supply with resultant malnutrition in the organism, and by providing it with the means to obtain the experience whereby it becomes clever according to its kind. Predetermined ways of acting are involved in the overt activities of many conscious animals, or at least this seems to be the case in what are called "instinctive activities." For example, an animal's withdrawing its paw from a noxious contact is an unconditioned reflex act. Experience with this act tends to make an animal capable of profiting from experience to avoid such contacts consciously. Thus experience can complement predetermined modes of action.

In man there seems to be little innately predetermined behavior. The human infant responds to felt needs such as food deficit and water deficit, often in useless ways like crying or striking, even when there is no one present who can respond to these activities in a way suitable to his needs. But he certainly can learn by experience! This manner of achieving a broader scope for activities has a distinctly unpredetermined aspect to it. We learn how to satisfy our practical needs by trial and error. No child is predirected to consume only what is suitable to him, or to avoid all noxious contacts. Even verbal instruction and physical exemplification of how to do things have to be repeated to be effective. By comparison with other animals man is obviously the least predetermined in his overt activities. While this is a disadvantage in the early stages of his life, it becomes the basis in the gradually developing rational animal for the exercise of free choice.

The foregoing topics will be treated in detail in the chapters to follow. We have achieved the intention of the first part of this chapter, namely, to clearly distinguish the living from the inanimate and to indicate in a general way the characteristics peculiar to conscious living things. We can sum up what has been discussed in saying that a living nature endures through a flux of energy and materials into it, from which it builds its incomplete being to the stage of completeness customary to its kind of being. Living things have an openness about them not found in inanimate things; conscious animals have a further kind of openness whereby the environment becomes not part of their physical being but part of their conscious being. In man this openness far surpasses anything like it in nonhuman animals. It is where there is consciousness that self-determination in the sense of choice of a way of acting can be found, because it presupposes some awareness of the end to be obtained as a condition for using one means rather than another to unite with it. Thus a blind animal cannot direct its activities by sight. The larger the number of awarenesses the greater the possibility of self-determination, for each kind of awareness (visual, tactile, and so forth) brings to the conscious being information about possible goals for activity and information about various means of attaining them. For example, a dog may see the appearance, hear the sound, or smell the odor of another dog and thus detect the presence of a friend or an enemy; he may see an avenue of escape, or hear the voice of an ally who will protect him in case the enemy is one from whom he must flee.

The Openness Characteristic of Man's Nature

"I am a part of all that I have met," says Ulysses in the poem by Alfred Tennyson. This is a true indication not only of the limitless conscious receptivity of a human being to his surroundings, but also of his formation by the reception of knowledge. Man as a knower is open to a universe that is always tending to act on his senses and inform him of its many aspects, and through the use of language he can learn what has occurred in the past as well as what his fellow men are thinking, feeling, and intending in the present. He is less open in the deliberate formulating of his modes of action and goals of action, because the adoption of a way of doing things and of a concrete goal to be attained preclude other ways of acting and the attaining of goals opposed to the one in view. Thus he can be the receiver of many diverse sensations, can accumulate countless experiences of many different kinds, and can master several intellectual disciplines which will tend to complement one another as his factual acquaintance with the world leads to a broader and deeper grasp of *the what* and *the why* of things. In this way *he does become a part of all that he meets*. But in forming himself according to what he has experienced and understood he must be selective, and each selection cuts out a host of possible alternative ways to conduct himself. Even so by the possession of the ability to see goals as fulfillments of desire, as preferable from several viewpoints, and as attainable by a variety of means he always has a basic ability to determine some aspects of his future and thus remain open to the possibilities that come his way.

Each human being starts off as an individual with his own body and inherited tendencies. What he is at the first moment of life will largely determine his physical development as an individual living body. But while he is growing according to the inherent tendencies of his physical nature he is also exercising his capacities for experience, understanding, and action as he develops personally. This development as a rational individual constitutes the fulfillment of a human nature precisely as human. It is in his growth as a person, as a rational, self-reflecting, and in many ways self-determined individual that man has an unlimited scope for fulfillment of his potentialities. Of course all individuals have not had and do not have the same opportunities for experience, understanding, and deliberate action but each human individual is like every other one inasmuch as his nature as a person is such that it can possibly be developed in a variety of ways.

Our intent here is not to explain in detail all that is involved in the development of a human person—that will be considered in Chapters 4 to 10—but to show man at the top of the hierarchy of the variety of natures of which we can have direct experience. The individual self-determined activities of men, posited to satisfy their personal desires, show an unending variety that is not found in the activities of any other material being. These activities—artistic, practical, knowledge-seeking and the like—attest to man's superior degree of self-determination and self-satisfaction. They reveal an openness in man's nature, an insatiability characteristic of man alone, for no other animal has this unending capacity. Man's perfectibility in his knowing and desiring not only far surpasses that of any other material being, but also surpasses even the human ability to satisfy it. Man is never fully satisfied. He wants ever more variety in his entertainment, ever greater perfection in his activities to subjugate matter, ever greater satisfaction for his desire to know what things are. He is the unfulfilled creature who seeks constantly to fulfill desires that are boundless in scope. His is an open nature whose joy consists in attaining the fulfillment possible to him. As Ulysses further says in Tennyson's poem: "Yet all experience is an arch wherethro' / Gleams that untraveled world, whose margin fades / For ever and for ever when I move." Man's open nature cannot circumscribe the whole of experience or of knowledge. Whatever he attains points the way to more and still more.

The Organic Whole and Its Organization

The presupposition underlying any attempt to explain something is that where a phenomenon exhibits an obvious dependence upon something else for its existence, arrangement, or activity, the explanation will reveal some aspect of the something else involved. If this is not done, the so-called explanation is only a superficial description of how things happen to be, without any explanation of why this is so. Every worthwhile explanation goes beyond mere sensory appearances to discover what accounts for them: to discover what their antecedents really are, to foresee what future developments they may signify, and to assign specific agents for specific activities.

INVISIBLE EXPLANATORY FACTORS

The assigning of reasons for what is so, however, is a venture mankind has learned to undertake cautiously.[10] Many events that appear to have a connection with one another turn out on closer inspection and upon experiment to have just happened to occur simultaneously. The human mind has often balked at assigning causes that cannot be seen or felt or heard, although their effects can be seen and felt and sometimes heard. The denial of gravitational force, of valence bonds, of electromagnetic fields because they cannot be seen would be considered a foolhardy thing by a physical scientist, for without these elements of explanation a great deal of physical, chemical, and electrical activity cannot be understood.

To assign a name to these invisible factors in material activity is not to pretend to understand them; we only point to them as explanatory factors that must be included in our account of things because we know they are involved. But there are reasons for an attitude of disbelief in the invisible. One obvious reason, *that men have often invented pure fictions to cover up their ignorance*, need not be discussed. More important is the attitude toward imponderables that has arisen because of the concentration upon measuring and testing methods of analysis in the various natural sciences. This emphasis has led many minds to reject any factors that cannot be measured or tested.

The use of quantitative methods of analysis leaves out of consideration not only factors that are incidental to the measurements and calculations, but also most of those factors that are always associated with extension (quantity, as an aspect of things, is their being extended) but which are qualitative and immediately perceptible to the senses. For example, the formula, "Force equals mass times acceleration," $F = Ma$, abstracts from all of the appearances of things having mass and from all the differences in the specific nature of those things having mass. Also this formula abstracts from all the possible kinds of force that could be involved in causing acceleration in the various masses to which the formula applies. All mathematical formulas that are useful in the sciences of matter, of necessity because they are mathematical, necessarily abstract from all of the features of actual beings, except those that can be measured or can in some way be definitely located in space.

The process of deliberately deleting the qualitative factors from consideration enables us to apprehend easily the quantitative aspects in themselves. For example, to count the apples in a basket we do not need to perceive every shade of color on every part of each surface, or to be aware of every sound that the apples make when moved. It suffices for counting that we can discern by the sense of touch each discrete quantity by its internal continuity and by its discontinuity from other quantities, or that by the sense of sight we discern the limits of the extension of each apple by contrasting their outwardly curved, colored surfaces.

This dispensability of qualities in the act of counting or of any other kind of measuring must be compensated for by the inclusion of these same qualities in giving the whole account of a material being. Thus it can be meaningful to consider a man or a fox as mere extended matter, as tonnage on an elevator or as consumers of available food. But in accounting for the whole being of the man or the fox their tonnage and consumption of food are just a few aspects of their being and do not indicate their specific differences. Similarly, the analysis of living composites in terms of their quantitative constituents only is not the whole account of their actuality.[11]

The stress on quantitative analysis, although it tends to suppress as irrelevant many qualitative factors in material being, does not do away with the necessity of admitting the existence of *invisible* but *measurable* forces. For example, the elevator shaft and the elevator car are the visible components of an elevator. The upward motion of the car is caused by the force exerted by the cable's being wound around the drum by the electric motor. If there were no motor, there would be no motion. The downward motion is caused by the weight of the car. If it had no weight it would not move down the shaft. Having weight is nothing other than the tendency to move to the center of the earth.

The motion downward is just as real as the motion upward; therefore there must be a real cause of the motion downward just as there is of the motion upward. The cable and the drum on which it is wound by the action of the motor are the immediate causes of the motion upward. The principal cause, in the sense that it is the source of motion, is the electromagnetic force of the electricity that powers the motor. The cause of the motion downward is a gravitational force attracting the mass of the car to the center of the earth. These two forces are equally real and equally invisible, but their effects can be measured; from this the strength of the forces can be gauged. Names are given to these forces even though they cannot be seen in themselves and their natures are relatively unknown. To leave them out of the explanation of how the elevator car is moved would amount to describing its up and down path without giving any reason why it moves.

The Notion of Form as Organizing Principle

The invisible factors in material reality are more numerous than the few just mentioned. To illustrate, take the explanation of the differences in chemical properties of the various elements offered by contemporary chemists. They hold that the difference between the specific properties of carbon and oxygen is due to the difference in the number of their orbital electrons and nuclear protons.[12] Carbon has six orbital electrons and six nuclear protons, while oxygen has eight of each. These constitutive differences which are manifested numerically are accounted for by some factor in the composition of these elements. If the components are identical and differ only in number and arrangement, then this difference is accounted for by something that causes the arrangements to be as they are. The difference between carbon and oxygen, according to this account, is a difference in the way they are formed. To account for this arrangement of parts, which is accompanied by properties specific to carbon and oxygen, we use the term *essential form* to indicate a factor in the atom of carbon and in the atom of oxygen, respectively, that makes each the kind of element it is.

By contrast, an incidental or accidental form does not figure in the determining of a thing's specific nature. Thus to be an animal is to be sentient, and the possession of sensory abilities stems from its being the kind of thing that an animal is. On the other hand, to be a trifle larger than other members of a species or to be slightly crippled is to differ from other members of the species in incidental ways, insofar as the quantitative form is different and the form proper to a limb is absent. Every actual thing possesses a form; this is true of even the most infinitesimal of particles and the most fundamental stuff out of which things are constituted. Let us suppose, for the sake of illustration, that man has discovered an ultimate building block out of which every extended being is composed. Whether it be an immutable extended something, an infinitesimal particle, or simply a flux of energy, some formative principle will be required to explain why things that are constituted of this basic building block really differ from one another. It is required in order to explain why the parts of a whole are of the kind they are when they exist by themselves and also to explain why the whole is the kind of thing it is, since the activities of the whole as a self-existing (substantial) unit are other than the activities proper to the parts when they are separated. Form is the inseparable and therefore immeasurable (and to some extent invisible) factor in material being which satisfies the requirements of such an explanation.

Every individual thing made of parts has those parts organized into a system; this organization determines that the thing be of a certain kind. Thus a molecule of limestone ($CaCO_3$, calcium carbonate) is an organization of calcium, carbon, and oxygen. It received this organization as the shell of a living marine organism and was deposited as a chalky substance when the organism died. As inert chalk the limestone is no longer organized as part of the organism, but it does remain under the organizing principle by which the calcium, carbon, and oxygen are united in the specific way characteristic of calcium carbonate. The influence of gravity tends to keep the limestone in one place on the surface of the earth and under the influence of the activity of the other molecules surrounding it. Whatever happens to the limestone in the future will be in accord with what its chemical and physical properties permit and in accord with whatever acts upon it. At any given moment, however, the limestone is an organization of parts having its own unity as a discrete molecular substance and having its own characteristic properties arising from its components and their organization. The form arises from the interaction of inanimate chemicals and is not separate or separable from the composite as long as it remains the kind of thing it is.

The greatest misunderstanding of the notion of form seems to arise from the necessity of talking about forms apart from the composite of which they are an inseparable, substantial part. The form is an essential part of that of which it is the form in the sense that it comes into being along with the coming together of the parts whose combination produces a different kind of being, as evidenced by its having properties other than those manifested by the components.

The Notion of the Soul

The term "soul" has been used for many centuries to indicate the organizing principle in living things. This term is used because of the actual differences between the activities of a man or any living thing and the activities of any inanimate thing. In light of our preceding discussion of chemical activity both within the living thing and apart from it, we can now make the notion of soul fairly explicit by identifying it with the notion of form. Thus we define "soul" as the *one form, of all the forms present in this complex substance formed of billions of chemical atoms, that accounts for the substance's being living and being one substance of a specific kind.*

Not only is every chemical complex, which has activities proper to it as a whole, something other than the sum of its parts, but even an individual molecule that is not chemically united to anything else has a dynamic as well as a static aspect. We can distinguish the dynamic aspect, which is manifested in the activities that a nature puts forth when the conditions are right, from the merely-existing-as-a-quantity aspect of every material being. The static aspect of a material thing is its being extended, so that it has each of its physical parts alongside of, and touching, some other of its physical parts. From this merely visual point of view, man and other animals and a solitary molecule have different quantitative forms. Especially from the dynamic point of view, however, do they specifically differ from one another, as the activities they share with other members of their kind clearly indicate. This is the case even though a man and a fox are formed of similar molecules that act according to their chemical natures.[13] In sum where there are differences in beings made of the same materials, *forms* account for those differences. The difference in general between the living and the nonliving is indicated by the use of the term "soul" to designate the one specific substantial form of a living thing.[14]

THE HUMAN SOUL

Our concern in this book is primarily with the human soul and its activities. We distinguish the possessor of a human soul from a mere animal and a mere plant by the activities that he performs, which they do not. Many animals besides man have lungs, a throat, a mouth, and the other necessary physical parts for forming distinctive sounds. But man alone has developed alphabets, that is, static line figures which stand for the various ways that he can manipulate his breath to convey intelligible sounds. Other animals communicate with one another, and man can imitate some of their signals (animal calls), but animals do not show any ability to convey *abstract notions* (such as "being" and "living" and "organic") as man does when he uses general terms. Although the use of language and the wonderful gains that human progress has achieved as a result of communication are the most striking overt signs of what is proper to man, all of the differences between man as an open nature and other animals are to be attributed to him because of his formative principle. The possession of these differences is indicated by the term "rational" in the customary definition of man.

The interconnection of soul and body in man has often been misunderstood and carelessly expressed. We need to point out some of these misinterpretations, lest the reader acquire them himself. It is not correct to say that the soul is in the body as a quantitative part is within a whole, for the physical parts of man are what they are because of his living form. Thus the action of the heart and of the lungs is indispensable to the continuing act of living; these organs are truly called sources of life, inasmuch as they pump the blood with its oxygen to where it is needed and indeed even supply the blood with that oxygen. But they are not the principle of life in the sense of their being the soul; rather they are what they are and do what they do because the soul is present. Nor is the soul to be thought of as something apart from the body as the fuel in a gasoline engine is something other than the engine itself, even though it moves it. For the engine is the kind of machine it is, and is able to use the fuel, because of the way in which its parts are put together to function as one unit. It is only on this basis of comparison, of one whole composite to another, that the human body can correctly be considered an analogue of a machine that derives motion from its fuel. Analogies, however, take us just so far in understanding something that we cannot apprehend directly, and by its very definition the substantial form of any substance cannot be separated from it so as to be apprehended directly.

The best way to understand the soul is as a vital organizing principle that contains all the parts of the body and causes them to be formed as they are and to function as they do as parts of an organized whole. Some persons have felt constrained to insist that all soul activity in man and in animals is a function of the body, in much the same way that the burning of oxygen is an activity of ignited dry wood. The activity of the soul is not merely spontaneous chemical activity; such basic human activities as conscious apprehension and a desire for absent goods cannot be attributed to the human body as chemical activities for they do not have a chemical description, but only as activities that bespeak living. Other persons have objected that the presence of the soul should manifest itself to such an extent that the energy contributed by the soul could be distinguished from that contributed by the chemical release of energy. But this demand could only be made of human activities that are apart from the body, for all bodily activities are simultaneously living and chemical.

The above objection, however, does demand a clarification of the connection that exists between form and nature. The nature of a substantial being is not its form, but rather the composite of form and materials when these two elements are considered as an inseparable natural unity and as an agent. The form determines that a substance shall be of a certain kind, but the form is completed by the materials of which it is the form. Consequently it is actually existing only when it is the form of some actually existing substance. Thus *form* is a part of the substantial whole, whereas *nature* is the whole conceived from the point of view of its being active. It is the substance acting as a nature that consumes energy. The form is the principle of the substance's actuality, that it be the kind of thing it is; the fully constituted substance is the principle of all of the physical activity that it manifests.

In further reply to this objection that the presence of soul should manifest itself by the expenditure of other than chemical energy, we must note that intellectual apprehension, judgment, and reasoning are activities of a purely spiritual kind, as we shall show. Although they are so dependent upon the activities of the senses that they cannot be studied in complete isolation from the senses in any experimental manner, nevertheless we can be sure that there is no energy involved in their activities as powers that operate independently of bodily parts.[15]

Man, then, is formed as a rational animal by a thoroughgoing principle of formation and activity, which is called the human soul. It is our task to attempt to analyze and explain man's distinctively human nature by considering the activities that are indicative of his nature. Man is distinctive because of the kind and extent of his knowledge, and the kind and range of his desires; therefore we shall concentrate upon these two aspects of human nature. Since the desire for food, for instance, which arises from within, is ineffective apart from the knowledge of how to satisfy it, we shall consider knowledge as in some way prior to other activities and to be a cause and a regulator of those activities. In our states of obvious awareness we know that the sensory apprehension of an apple precedes the remembering of similar or different apples and precedes the understanding of an apple as a substance or a fruit. For this reason it seems fitting to begin our analysis with the activities of the senses.

In the next chapter we shall present the physiology of the senses, not as a prelude to studying them in a medical way, but as a means of understanding how very intimately the living activities discussed in this chapter are bound up with the chemical and electrical properties of matter. This conforms with our aim, in elaborating a philosophical picture of man, to give as complete a picture as possible of man's normal activities. The lesser abilities of the senses are subservient to the spiritual activities, and the chemical processes in their turn serve the sensory knowing and appetitive activities. It is from this viewpoint that we shall treat the physiology of the senses to show the material basis of conscious sensory awareness.

APPENDIX 2a

Photosynthesis ~ THE SUBSTANCE
called chlorophyll, which is involved in photosynthesis (synthesis by the use of light), is a complex molecule found inside all chloroplasts. It is chlorophyll that uses the energy of absorbed sunlight to split water molecules into hydrogen and oxygen atoms. The oxygen is released, while the hydrogen is used in various chemical processes whose end product is sugar.

The red corpuscles present in the blood of animals are similar to green chloroplasts, but they cannot synthesize carbohydrates. The red cells contain hemoglobin, the chemical formula of which is similar to that of chlorophyll. Hemoglobin takes oxygen from the lungs and gives it up to the tissues of the body for use in their activities. The plant, on the other hand, uses the sugar produced by photosynthesis to make fats, proteins, and other carbohydrates that are the foods of animals.

The process of photosynthesis, as it is understood at present, requires six molecules of water from the plant's supply, which is obtained from the soil, and six molecules of carbon dioxide from the air. In the presence of sunlight, molecules of a three-carbon-atom, sugarlike compound are synthesized, and then this compound is transformed by the plant into *glucose*. A formula for the material exchange involved is $6CO_2 + 6H_2O \rightarrow C_6H_{12}O_6 + 6O_2$. The actual chemical activities are much more complex than this formula indicates.

Some of the glucose in plants is used to carry on the activity of combining atmospheric nitrogen and oxygen into nitrates and ammonia by a series of chemical steps. These compounds are linked with the products of photosynthesis to form amino acids, the immediate building blocks of protein. Proteins are an indispensable part of human food; they are broken down by digestion into amino acids, which are carried throughout the body to the various tissues. These tissues are in a constant state of change as they incorporate the ingested amino acids and use them up.

Plants are the essential food for the maintenance of most animal life—some animals feed on plants and others feed on animals that feed on plants. Some animals, like man, are omnivorous. Without plant life, animal life, as we know it, would not have food to nourish it or oxygen with which to breathe. Without sunlight there would be no green plants.

APPENDIX 26

Synthesis of the Living from the Nonliving ~ NEW BEINGS RESULT from the combining of different chemical elements, and existing complex substances are destroyed when their chemical parts separate. It is only natural, therefore, to expect that man would attempt to synthesize living things by bringing together in chemical combination, under controlled experimental conditions, the components of living things that have been discovered through chemical analysis.

In the natural process of forming living things, a living part of the living substance separates off and carries on its own living activities as an independent individual. But living substance is composed of the same chemical elements as nonliving substance, although the molecules forming the living substance of organisms are very complex indeed by comparison with those occurring elsewhere in nature. Therefore, why not break down the protein of a living thing into its basic constituents and identify them on the basis of their chemical properties, and then try to synthesize the same kind of living protein from these constituents? Theoretically, the mere combining of the proper proportions of the elements should give the same chemical structure as that of the living organism, and respiration might take place in the result. That is, the newly synthesized chemical organization would perhaps exchange chemicals spontaneously with the environment in order to obtain the energy to maintain itself.

A great deal of research in contemporary biology is concerned with a problem of this sort—the attempt to discover how one living creature succeeds in passing on its nature to its progeny. Working on the fact that a multicelled organism, such as a fruit fly, is a complex of cells that grew from a parent cell, researchers are attempting to discover how one cell could contain within it all of the information necessary to direct its activities of growth in size and complexity, and how it could receive this information from the living organism from which it arose.[16]

For a cell to reproduce itself by splitting, it must duplicate its own specific nature through the forming of a second nucleus from the original one, before the splitting off of the daughter cell takes place.[17] Otherwise, the splitting would simply reduce the bulk of the original cell and only the part containing the nucleus would be living. This duplication of the cell's own nuclear nature within the confines of the cell membrane has engrossed researchers for the last half-century. The results of this research have been quite fruitful in isolating the factors that are involved in the transmission of specific traits from parent to offspring. It is this transmission that perpetuates the species of living things so that microbes come from microbes and sweet peas from sweet peas. Some traits are heritable and some are not. By experimentation it has been found that the heritable traits actually transmitted from parent to progeny are uniquely associated with that part of the nucleus of the cell called the *chromosome*, and with as yet unisolated factors of the chromosome called *genes*.[18] These genes are now understood to be the physical factors that determine how the cell in which they are located shall develop. One set of genes determines that the cell shall develop into a microbe; another set determines that the cell shall develop into a mosquito.

When offspring appear with physical traits that are markedly different from those of the parent, and when these new traits breed true in succeeding generations, a *mutation* of the genes is said to have occurred. The fact that the new trait is just

Synthesis of Living from Nonliving   *51*

as invariable in successive generations as its absence was in prior generations seems to indicate that it stems from the same factors (the genes) as does the specific characteristics of the nature itself.

The attempt to isolate the controlling factor by separating it physically from the rest of the cell has been partially successful, and from the cell nucleus a type of inanimate substance has been obtained which is called nucleic acid to indicate its origin. When a similar substance was derived from the cell, but apparently from outside the nucleus, it was named ribonucleic acid, RNA, to distinguish it from the first kind, DNA.[19] The molecules of these acids have been found to be very large and are described as being long chains of lesser units, *nucleotides*. An ingenious use of the method of X-ray diffraction has revealed that the DNA molecule is a well-ordered set of nucleotides arranged as an original string of nucleotides with a second string running parallel to it and having its nucleotides joined to the first set. The two parallel strings are helical in shape, like a coiled spring.

The constituents of DNA taken from any living cell are the same no matter what the animal to which the cell belonged. It seems probable, therefore, that the various arrangements of the constituents of various samples of DNA explain which hereditary factors will be transmitted. Since the number of the possible arrangements of all the atoms in a DNA molecule is in the billions, it is feasible to account for the thousands of varieties of living things by various arrangements of the nucleotide components of DNA. Moreover, a theory now exists as to how the DNA in a parent cell produces a replica of itself before the cell splits in two. Let us forget the helical shape for a moment and consider the DNA molecule as though it were a ladder. The rungs are the nucleotides, but they are not symmetrical as are the rungs of a ladder. Imagine each rung with one length notched and the remaining length smooth, the dissimilar parts being unequal in length. Also consider each rung to be somewhat different from every other rung in the number of notches each has and in the length of the smooth part. Then imagine the ladder's being unzipped, in a zigzag fashion, along the line marking off the dissimilar parts of each successive rung and the two halves rotating away from one another. When this imaginary splitting occurs in

Man's Physical and Spiritual Nature

the DNA molecule imagine that the two halves then make for themselves, out of the materials surrounding them in the cell, a complementary set of nucleotides; that is, they fashion from raw materials a new side of the ladder, exactly like the one that separated off, to replace it. Everything will eventually be the same as before except that there will be two exactly alike DNA molecules where before there was only one, and the supply of raw materials in the cell will have been somewhat decreased.

One fact of evidence that lends much weight to the above theory is that when a virus infects a living cell it does so by usurping the materials of the cell to form numberless replicas of itself. In so doing it perpetuates its kind and destroys the host cell. But a virus when isolated has the appearance of an inert chemical; in fact, free RNA isolated from tobacco mosaic virus can infect tobacco leaves by itself. This shows that the rest of the component of the virus was not essential for the specific RNA to replicate itself. Also, some enzymes have been discovered that, when placed in a supply of nucleotides, synthesize some kinds of RNA and DNA. These synthetics do not have the nucleotide arrangements of any RNA or DNA isolated from living cells. But who knows whether man's ingenuity can duplicate such arrangements and synthesize a self-replicating molecule that would be indistinguishable from a similar one derived from a living organism?

Life is only from life has long been accepted as an axiom, and even now no notable success has been achieved in producing a living organism from inorganic materials. Yet in theory there is nothing against the possibility of discovering the right combination of materials and their organic arrangement, and then bringing this into actual being. The agent that has been able to do this has so far been a living thing acting according to its own physical nature. Perhaps man, by making use of his understanding of living processes, can duplicate in an artificial way what living natures accomplish in their way and produce some primitive type of living organism.

It is a very large step from the synthesis of a self-replicating molecule or of a primitive living organism to the synthesis of a conscious animal. Yet animals have inherited conscious traits that are usually called instinctive behavior. If these traits are transmitted by DNA or some other substance like it, then possibilities of human control of the heritable traits of animal life are not inconceivable.

It should be pointed out, however, that man as a rational and voluntary being does not display inherited traits in his rational and voluntary activities, because each human individual starts from scratch in the acquisition of intellectual knowledge and in the development of his ability to choose among alternatives by his estimation of their values, as we will show in later chapters. In these activities, what the individual learns and what he wills to accomplish depend much more upon him as an individual than upon any other factor in the development of these abilities, as we shall also show. Wisdom and virtue and political opinions are not inherited genetically, although they may be fostered by parents in their offspring. Thus there is no possibility that human control over genetic materials will ever directly menace or benefit the spiritual part of man's nature.[20] This control, however, may prove to be a boon in remedying the disorders that now cripple the use of these powers in those who suffer organic malfunctions of the cerebral apparatus.

CHAPTER 3

The Physiology of Sensation ~

IN THIS CHAPTER WE carry one step further the analysis of the physical aspects of man's nature begun in the preceding chapter by going beyond the chemical point of view to see how the various physical parts of the body act upon, and are acted upon, by one another. From this point of view man does not resemble the chemicals in a beaker—the protoplasm of individual cells (see Appendix 3a)— rather, he has the appearance of a machine at work. The description of how the nerves, muscles, bones, and specific organs of the human body interact is quite similar to a description of the parts of a machine in action. There is a special value in the physiological approach from the medical point of view, for a knowledge of the location of the various parts of the body and of their interaction facilitates man's attempts to remedy bodily malfunctions. From our point of view here, the value of the physiological approach will be to deepen the reader's genuine knowledge of man's physical nature, and in the analysis of the human peripheral and central nerve systems, to show how closely man's conscious activities are bound up with the physical and chemical activities of these systems. In this way we shall prevent the reader from erroneously identifying sensory consciousness with physiological activity and from forming incorrect notions as to the manner in which sensory consciousness depends upon physical and biochemical activity. At the same time we shall give the reader exactly the same physiological facts that are often used as a basis for denying that man has a rational intelligence and a free spiritual nature. The reader will thus be able to see that such denials have no merit.

Dangers of the One-Sided Approach

The two main aspects of sensory activity, the physical-chemical aspect and the knowing aspect are quite inseparable in fact, but they *are* separable in thought. Hence no error need arise in considering the sensory processes from the physiological point of view presented in this chapter and from the point of view of their cognitional attainment given in the following chapter. Nevertheless, two errors have persistently plagued man's attempt to understand the functioning of the senses. On the one hand, some accounts represent the conscious activities as being quite independent of the physiological ones, as though man were conscious of things quite apart from any activities going on in his body. On the other hand, it is fashionable in some contemporary treatments of sensation to consider consciousness as merely a physical function of the brain cells. This position of attributing awareness to matter goes back many centuries, but it has become especially noticeable since the advent of positivist attitudes in the natural sciences.

Each of these views, which are contrary to well-known facts, illustrates a pernicious error that has vitiated many human attempts to give a scientific account of things. This is the error of *giving an explanation that accounts for some factors* of the object under consideration *but denies the relevance or even the existence of others*. Thus those who reduce all conscious activities to functions of matter ignore the immaterial nature of human thought, which is manifested in a science like mathematics; while those who cannot see how the body can be involved in knowing ignore the strict curtailment in our sensory awareness that follows the malfunction of those specialized parts of the human body called sense organs. We hope to avoid this error by considering nerve activity and conscious sensing separately in order to understand them better, while at the same time never losing sight of their actual inseparability.

The Human Body and Its Nerve Systems

The use of chemical analogies that helped us in understanding the nature of living and of soul in Chapter 2 must now be replaced by a different kind of basic analogate. Thus, although the nerve apparatus of a living thing is a complex of many chemical compounds, we shall consider it for the moment merely as the physical link in an activity-coordinating system.[1]

Afferent-Efferent Circuits and Stimulus-Response

Let us imagine that telephone wires run from all of the skin areas of the human body and from the internal organs of the body, except those in the head, to the spinal column inside the spine. The wires run up the spinal cord, which passes through the center of the vertebrae to the brain in the head. Electrical impulses passing along such wires could carry information from the skin areas about the temperature of what is touching the skin and about pressures being exerted upon it. From the internal organs the wires could carry information about the functions of such organs in the metabolic processes and in the other activities required for self-maintenance of the body physically.

There are no actual telephone wires in the body, of course, but there is an interconnecting system of nerve fibers running from the areas mentioned, which underlie information-receiving and muscular activity. The nerves running from the skin areas and the internal organs to the spinal cord, which carry impulses *toward* this communications center, are called *afferent nerves*. There are also *efferent nerves* carrying impulses *from* the spinal cord to the muscles of the body and to the internal organs, which are highly specialized groups of smooth muscles. These nerves move the muscles and organs to action. An alteration in the physical condition of the skin (increase in warmth or cold, or the application of sharp or heavy pressure, for example) is productive of an activity in the afferent nerves that elicits a response from the nerve center. Thus an activity in some of the efferent nerves causes the muscles of certain limbs to act, so that the limbs move toward the cause of the alteration when the effect seems desirable, and away from it if the effect seems noxious. For example, the heat from a hot iron is a noxious stimulus that causes flexion of the arm muscles to withdraw the arm from the proximity of the iron. But a sensation of welcome coolness on the same arm when extended into a shady area on a hot day will produce a muscular action that may take the person's whole body out of the scorching sun.

The afferent-efferent process of the nerves can be viewed in a very simplified way as a stimulus, S, and a response, R. A *stimulus* to the nerve endings in the skin, for example, produces what we will call an *impulse*. This impulse is a chemical-electrical activity within the nerve fibers, which travels the length of a nerve network (several fibers joined end to end) into the spinal cord from which a similar impulse originates along an efferent-nerve network. The efferent impulse produces an activity (contraction and relaxation in muscles) in the part of the body upon which the network terminates. This activity is called the *response*.

The Interconnection of Nerve Centers

The picture of neural connections just presented represents connections with only two of the nerve centers, the spinal cord and the brain. Actually, we can locate three areas in the human body that function as the principal receivers and transmitters of nerve impulses from many different parts of the body. (There are still other nerve centers, but they are more limited in their connections and function.) The third is an area that runs alongside of the spine on the ventral side (toward the abdomen). This area is the center of the *autonomic* (nonvoluntary) nerve system, which is primarily concerned with regulating the activities of the internal organs of the body and of the glands that secrete the chemicals necessary for many vital activities. Since we do not exercise any voluntary control over these activities, such as we exert over our activities of sensing and moving and speaking, they are said to be nonvoluntary activities served by a nonvoluntary nerve system. The brain not only regulates some of the activities carried on by the spinal column (reflex activities), but also receives impulses underlying sensation; it is the center for many other physiological functions that underlie our conscious and voluntary actions.

The three nerve centers are connected to one another by nerve fibers, by which they interact with one another. For example, an unexpected pin prick on the finger can cause a person unthinkingly (reflexly) to withdraw his finger from the noxious stimulus. But the same person can consciously suppress this reflex tendency, which is produced by the spinal column, and deliberately hold his finger to the offending pin. The interconnection of the sensory nerve system and the autonomic nerve system can be clearly seen when we consider that a feeling of fright upon seeing something startling can cause a speeding of the heart beat and other reactions in the internal organs.

In every description, some elements are basic and must be understood at the outset. Our explanations are then built up from these elements. *Quantity* (shape, size, and so forth) and *quality* (texture, composition, and so forth), *action*, and *passion* are basic factors that can be detected by human sensation; as such they form a basis for an explanation of what is known primarily by the human senses. Therefore we shall begin our description of nerve activity by distinguishing the appearance and the activities of the various parts of the human nervous system. (For further details, see Appendix 3b.)

The Neural Components

An individual nerve cell is called a *neuron;* the fibers are called *axons* and *dendrites*, depending on the direction in which they conduct nerve impulses. A neuron has a nucleus surrounded by cytoplasm. The cytoplasm, however, extends some distance from the cell body in small tubelike extensions, which are called nerve processes. One of these processes, the axon, is usually longer than the others and transmits impulses away from the neuron. Most neurons have only one axon. The other processes extending from the cell body are usually short in comparison with the axon; because they branch out in numerous directions they are called dendrites. Dendrites conduct impulses to the cell body.

The end of the axon distant from the cell body terminates in small branches that resemble dendrites. When these end processes of the axon terminate upon the dendrites of another cell or upon the body of another cell, they are capable of transmitting an impulse to the other cell. These areas of proximity are called *synapses*. It is known that chemical activity at the termini of an axon is followed by activity in the dendrites and the cell body,[2] apparently triggered by the small end processes extending from the axon onto the dendrites and cell body. Although the direction of transmission is from dendrites to cell body to axon, experiments have shown that the nerve fiber can conduct impulses in either direction.

Since conduction can be in either direction, it is thought that the nature of the synapse itself explains why nerve impulses are propagated across the synapse in one direction only, from axon to dendrites to cell body. The synapse is looked upon as a regulating factor which determines the pathway for an impulse that shuns possible pathways on one occasion and uses them on another.

The Artificial Stimulus of Nerves

Much of what is known about nerve activity has been discovered by experiments using electrical stimuli.[3] The preference for this method of investigating nerve phenomena stems from the fact that of all the activities that can elicit nerve activity (cutting, crushing, heating, and applying natural stimuli to stimulus receptors), the passing of electric currents and the detecting of differences in electrical potential can be controlled and measured most easily and accurately. Moreover, there are naturally occurring differences of electrical potential between various parts of the body and between various parts of the nervous system.[4]

Whenever an instrument intervenes between the senses of the observer and the object of observation, it is possible that an *artifact* may be produced. An artifact is an aspect of the observation of an object that is caused by the use of an instrument or reagents; it is not really a part of the normal state of the object. The immobility and coloration of fixed and dyed tissues is an example of an artifact. The investigator using instruments on the object of his observations must carefully distinguish artificial from natural phenomena; this is especially the case in investigating bioelectrical phenomena. In the account we are about to give of electrical measurement and what it reveals, we believe that the findings indicate properties of neural conduction that are present by natural causes.

ELECTRICAL FACTORS IN NERVE CONDUCTION

When a nerve fiber is not conducting an impulse, no voltage difference can be detected by very fine electrodes placed at different positions on its surface. But when the electrodes are in contact and the fiber is made to conduct an impulse, the point through which the impulse is passing will register a negative potential, compared to other points on the fiber. This kind of negative potential flows along the fiber and appears to be a physical component of the nerve impulse, or at least an accompaniment of the nerve impulse. Its speed varies for different nerve fibers from 100 meters per second for a large fiber enveloped by a sheath in mammals to less than two meters per second in small unsheathed fibers in some cold blooded animals.

When a nerve fiber is stimulated artificially by passing an electric current along it from one electrode to another, further characteristics of nerve conduction become evident. The stimulus to the nerve comes with the onset and cessation of the current flow. There are minimum voltages and minimum durations of current flow for each type of fiber, so that stimuli of lesser voltage or shorter durations are insufficient to trigger a nerve impulse. Such stimuli are said to be subliminal, because they are below the threshold (*limen*) required to activate the nerve. There are limens for natural stimuli also.

Once the nerve has been aroused so that an impulse begins in it, the stimulus is no longer required because the impulse is self-propagating and the rate of conduction is not slowed as the impulse travels farther from the source of origin. This means that a very intense stimulus and a very rapid application of stimuli do not produce any increase in the intensity or rate of travel of the nerve impulse in a single fiber. Therefore, where many fibers of one nerve are acted upon by a stimulus, a greater intensity (a bright light or a loud sound) may activate more nerve fibers than a lesser intensity (a weak light or a low sound), and in this way the magnitude is registered in nerve activity. These characteristics of nerve conduction are summed up in the "all-or-none" law, which states that a stimulus sufficient to produce a response in a nerve will produce the maximum response of which the nerve is capable. That is, in reacting to a stimulus the nerve conducts at its best or not at all.

It follows that a nerve impulse is not simply an electric current flowing the length of the nerve, because currents are attenuated by the medium they flow through and consequently have a diminishing strength the farther they travel.[5] But because the impulse produced by natural excitation reveals voltage changes on the surface of the nerve membrane, the probability that the impulse may be an electrochemical kind of activity can be entertained seriously.

A nerve fiber or cell must rest after pulsing before it can react to a second stimulus. This period of rest, when the fiber or cell is quite unresponsive to stimulation, is called the *absolute refractory* (unresponsive) *period*, which averages about one millisecond for a mammalian nerve.[6] Therefore nerve fibers in man cannot be stimulated with a frequency greater than 1000 times per second. This rules out any transmission of light stimuli and of sound stimuli above 1000 vibrations per second by having the nerve fiber transmit impulses at the same frequency as that of the impinging stimulus.

The foregoing discussion is the customary way of talking about nerve conduction as manifested in artificial stimulation and motor response. The complete explanation of what a nerve impulse is in terms of chemistry and physics has yet to be discovered. What accompanies nerve conduction in terms of the subjective factors of conscious imagery, remembered experience, and consciously exercised motor activity is reasonably clear, but precisely how these factors are connected with the physical and chemical activities is not understood at all. Of this we are quite certain—if the physico-chemical activity is suppressed or the organ (receptor, nerve connection, and synapsing area in the spine or brain) impaired, the conscious activity does not take place.

The physical pathways of nerve conduction have been charted reasonably well in all parts of the human nervous system, except the brain where the complexity of the neural connections is so great as almost to defy the imagination. Yet even in the human brain many paths of nerve conduction have been traced, and many areas of the brain's outer surface (the *cortex*) have been found to be associated with specific sensory and motor activities. In order to see how this nerve conduction takes place, we shall consider briefly the physiology of nerve conduction.

The Physiological Functioning of Nerves

THE REFLEX ARC

A neuronic and synaptic chain linking a receptor to an effector is one of the basic operating parts of the nervous system. The term *reflex arc* is applied to an ideal instance of this operation, in which the chain is represented by the smallest number of neurons required to explain the activity. See Figure 1.

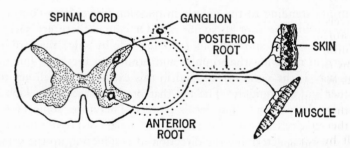

Figure 1   Diagram of a spinal reflex arc, showing a receptor neuron in an extravertebral ganglion. (From C. H. Best and N. B. Taylor, *The Living Body*, 4th ed. New York: Holt, Rinehart and Winston, 1958)

The stimulus to the skin is followed by an impulse along the dendrites of the receptor neuron through the receptor cell body, which is located in the dorsal ganglion in the spinal nerve, near the spine. The impulse travels along the axon of this receptor neuron to the synapse with the dendrites of another receptor neuron in the dorsal gray matter of the spinal cord, and thence to the dendrites of the motor neuron located in the ventral horn of the gray matter. The effector neurons send an impulse over their axons to the effector organ, which as a consequence is activated. This activity is called a "reflex," to indicate that the stimulus triggers an innate response automatically without any conscious mediation's being involved. Mediation *can* be involved, however, as in our previous example with the pricking of a pin. In many instances there is simply a stimulus followed immediately by a response. The blinking of the eye when a potentially injurious object approaches it closely is an example of a reflex activity without any intervening mediation. The number of neurons involved in a reflex arc is usually more than two, but for the sake of simplicity we shall consider a reflex arc in which only two neurons are involved.[7]

The *patellar tendon reflex*, which is caused by tapping the tendon just below the kneecap (*patella*), is an example of an actual two-neuron reflex path. The tap stretches the extensor muscle on the front of the thigh, thus setting up a nerve activity that travels to the spinal cord, where through a synapse it affects the motor neuron in the ventral gray matter. The axon of the motor neuron extending to the muscle in question moves it to contract, thus causing the foot to swing out. Of course there are several sets of dendrites and neurons (running side by side) that are involved in receiving the stimulus and producing the kick, but the pathway is the same for all, and in this example they all act together and act quickly. The tap that produces the reflex kick is felt by the person whose leg is tapped. Therefore, some of the nerve activity that is transmitted to the spinal cord passes through synapses that determine the direction of conduction up the spinal cord to the sensory centers of the brain. Also, as the muscle that has been tapped contracts and pulls the leg straight, a message to the flexor type of muscles that bend the leg back causes them to relax, so that the extensor muscles can be effective. This part of the message has an *inhibiting* action, for it does not stimulate the flexor muscles to act, but rather prevents their opposing the extensor muscles. This ability to direct the course of the impulse and to produce relaxation rather than contraction is thought to reside in the synapse.

The coordination that exists in the interaction of the

nervous system is a marvelous example of the self-maintenance that was mentioned in a previous chapter as a characteristic of living activity. For instance, a stimulus over a large area, such as when one bumps into a solid object that contacts chest, stomach, arm, thigh, and knee, is followed by dozens of reflex actions that maintain the person's balance, remove him a little distance back from the offending object, and may produce a yelp of surprise. The stubbing of the end of one's small toe can produce just about the same results, although the area stimulated is only a fraction of that stimulated in the first instance. The result produced by a stimulus is proportionate not only to the body area, but also to the importance to the person of reacting to the stimulus in such a manner as to preserve his well-being.

In man the activities initiated by his will use many of the same neural pathways as those used in reflex activities. Contemporary theory about neural conduction believes that the dendrites of the effector neuron are potentially connected to a multitude of sources that can cause the neuron to impulse. The connections are said to be potential because some possible pathways are not used every time the effector neuron in the spinal column impulses. Which connections are actually made depends upon the prime origin of the stimulus and the activity of the synapses, which can inhibit conduction as well as facilitate it. When a person deliberately rubs his chin because he sees a foreign substance upon it, the prime origin of the rubbing action is a decision to act, which is made effective by efferent impulses from the brain to the motor neurons involved in moving the hand and arm. The same person's hand can be reflexively withdrawn from a hot object. Similarly, a gasp can be quite deliberate, or it can also be produced reflexively by a state of fright.

Thus we see that the impulse that flows along the axon of the effector neuron can originate in any of half a dozen locations in the brain, in the skin, or in another muscle. It can be instigated by an external stimulus, an internal stimulus acting upon a muscle, or by our decision to act now and in this manner. No matter what the origin of the stimulus is, the nerve impulse that produces activity in the motor apparatus always passes along the same efferent path in reaching that motor apparatus from the spine. This route is called the final common path of the nerve impulse. When the impulses from two different sources tend to move along this final common path to produce conflicting kinds of activity, one action takes place and the other is repressed.[8]

Innate reflex actions integrate the actions of the parts of the body that are spatially distant from one another and evoke reactions toward externally occurring stimuli that are valuable to the body as a whole. Such activity could not be carried out with the unfailing consistency required of it, were man to act only by his conscious perception of needs. Thus *unconditioned reflex activity*, as distinct from *conditioned* (or learned) *reflex activity*, carries on many functions that are essential to life, such as the immediate withdrawal from harm, and the stimulation and depression of various visceral activities, for example, which are normally executed without conscious interference. On the other hand, consciously directed activities have a wider range of purpose than do reflex actions. Some of these, the gathering of food, the forming of shelters, and the avoiding of insuperable dangers are every bit as essential as some reflex activities. But in man many other conscious activities are not essential in this manner; rather, they are directed to pursuits that are pleasurable. Many voluntarily performed acts are not means to any further end, but are ends in themselves. (Examples of these activities will be given in Chapters 7 and 8.)

There is a slight similarity between reflex activities and habitual actions in man, inasmuch as each type of activity follows a characteristic mode of action whenever it occurs. Truly habitual modes of action, however, are not innately predetermined as unconditioned reflexes are. They are consciously engendered in most cases (except when they grow into being through inattention, as in the case of intemperance) and by repetition of action in all cases. (Intellectual habits are not modes of action, for thought is not action in the way that the motion of effectors is. The genesis of such habits will be considered later.) Thus the similarity of habitual actions to stimulus-response (*S-R*) activity is quite superficial, and any attempt to explain habits resulting from choice in man as basically stimulus-response automatisms is foredoomed.[9]

SUMMATION

In our foregoing analysis of nerve systems in man, we have briefly described the nervous system and have shown that experimental analysis of nerve conduction indicates that this process appears to be an electrochemical one occurring unconsciously in much the same manner in all parts of all nervous systems. The reflex arc, an ideal instance of stimulus and response, illustrated the kind of neural activity that is involved in actual stimulus and response in animals. Its manner of occurrence and the obvious differences between reflex and voluntary activity have been indicated.

To complete our sketch of the physiological analysis of human sensing and acting, we need to see briefly what is involved in muscular movement and then to examine the physical and chemical aspects of the sensory processes in more detail.

Muscle Movement

The basic distinction in the appearance of muscles is between the *striated* muscles, which are usually connected to bones, and the *unstriated* muscles, which are usually found as the walls of visceral organs.[10]

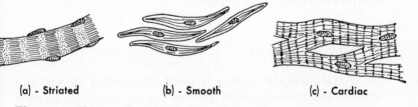

(a) - Striated   **(b) - Smooth**   **(c) - Cardiac**

Figure 2   Types of muscle cells. (From M. A. Wenger, F. N. Jones, and M. H. Jones, *Physiological Psychology*. New York: Holt, Rinehart and Winston, 1956)

The striated muscles are named for the alternating light and dark stripes that the microscope reveals on their surface. The unstriated muscles have no such surface appearance; they are also called smooth muscles because they are flat, whereas the striated muscles are oval in shape. The biceps of the upper arm is a good example of the oval shape of striated muscle, and stomach muscles are characteristically smooth muscles. Muscle consists of threadlike fibers of diameters ranging from one to one-hundredth of a millimeter and from a few millimeters to several centimeters in length. Great numbers of these fibers are grouped together and are surrounded by connective tissue to form muscle bundles. Groups of these muscle bundles form a muscle; that is, a muscle is a group of muscle bundles forming a unit that is attached at its ends to another muscle, or to the skin, or to bones. Muscular activity is accomplished by the tensing and relaxing of the threadlike fibers.[11]

Effector neurons act upon the muscle fibers through the tips of their axons. Chemical changes occur in this stimulation of the muscle, and a change in electrical potential at the tip of the axon and in the muscle fiber can be recorded as the nerve impulse produces contraction in the muscle. When the contraction produces a shortening of the muscle, some motion in the body results, for some bones or tissues are moved by the shortening. But there can also be muscular activity without shortening of the muscle, as when the extended arm is maintained motionless against a weight held in the hand. Similarly the extensor muscles of the leg by their tension enable a person to stand still in an upright posture. Much of the physiology of muscle has been discovered, but our concern here is only to note how muscles act as effectors moved by nerve impulses.

Sensory Receptors

Of particular interest in our understanding of man as a sentient and rational animal are the sensory receptors through which comes all the knowledge that man has of his universe. They use afferent nerve connections. All nerve endings that can be designated as sensory receptors are selective as to the stimuli by which they can be moved, except the pain receptors which are stimulated by a variety of noxious stimuli (heat, cutting, heavy pressure, and so forth). Various ways of indicating this selectivity have been sanctioned by continuous usage; we shall explain the two most common nomenclatures in contemporary usage as an introduction to the discussion of sensation itself.

The "ceptor" terminology, widely used in physiological circles, designates the various locations of the stimulus receptors.[12] *Exteroceptors* are receivers of stimuli from that part of the nonself universe that is external to the body. *Interoceptors* are receivers of stimuli from that part of the nonself universe which is contained within the body; they are involved in the digestive activities of the alimentary canal. *Proprioceptors* are receivers of stimuli from the skeletal muscles and bones and from various internal organs. Much of this stimulus and response activity is unconscious, but the action and interaction of skeletal muscles and tendons does impinge on consciousness to some extent and gives information about the extent of, and the status of, the physical self. This division of receptors overlaps a bit in the area where the external environment is becoming the internal nonself. Thus by taste and smell (classed as exteroceptors or interoceptors) we can be aware of flavors and odors of food yet to be consumed, as well as of food that is being consumed. In fact, by taste and smell we can detect many objects (metals by taste, chlorine by smell, for example) that we never put into our digestive system. Except for this overlapping, the classification by position of the stimulus is acceptable enough.

In order to be more specific about the exteroceptors, it is necessary to classify the stimuli receptors according to the nature of the stimuli they receive. Thus we have a *light* receptor, the eye; a *sound* receptor, the ear; *chemical* receptors, the tongue and the olfactory apparatus in the nose; *tactile* receptors, the warm and cold spots and the light contact and deep-seated pressure receptors; and *pain* receptors. There is also a distinction between *distance* receptors (*telereceptors*), such as the eye, the ear, and the olfactory membrane, which are in *mediated contact* with an object, and receptors that detect only the source of stimulus in *immediate contact* with them. An alternate name for sensory receptor is *sensor*.

A method of distinguishing the senses as *external* and *internal* has been in vogue for many centuries. The basis for this distinction lies in the fact that some physiological acts underlying sensation occur only in the brain, while others involve both the brain and other neural units external to the brain. For example, imagination and memory depend on the eye and the other sensory receptors for receiving information, but the act of remembering past experiences and of imagining a two-headed nail do not involve any of the sensory receptor organs. In contrast, sight and hearing depend upon both the brain and the eye or the ear, respectively. Thus the term "external sense" is applicable to the five senses that are classed as exteroceptors, while the term "internal sense" applies to sensory activities that are distinct from those of the exteroceptors and confined to the region of the brain. In this classification the proprioceptors, if they are to be included at all, will have to be classified as external senses responsive to touch.

We shall now discuss the physical and chemical aspects of receptor activity in order to indicate the physical basis for distinct conscious sensations. Since the tactile senses are the simplest to describe, we shall discuss them first; and then in the order of complexity, the chemical senses, hearing, the vestibular sense, and finally sight.

The neuronal process that extends from the receptor neuron, which is located just outside of the spine, to the skin is more like an axon than the dendrites that we have already described, for it is long and single like the axon that extends from the cell body into the spinal column.[13] (See Figure 1.) At its peripheral end the receptor neuron has a specialized protoplasmic structure, or it may branch out into several unsheathed nerve fibrils, some of which are the receptors for painful stimuli in pain-registering nerves; others are receptors for warmth and cold stimuli in warmth- and cold-reporting nerves, respectively. The various receptors with connections going back to the spine, travel in groups from the skin surface and form the peripheral part of one spinal nerve. There are 31 spinal nerves that send fibers to innervate the skin of the body. Thus the skin surface has 31 skin areas (dermatomes), which are served by 31 spinal nerves. Each of these nerve trunks contains a multitude of nerve fibers: some serve tactile reception, others conduct impulses from other sensory receptors in the muscles, and many of the fibers conduct efferently to muscles and tendons.

Sensation by Immediate Contact

PRESSURE, TEMPERATURE, AND PAIN SENSES

There are several different kinds of tactile receptor located in the skin at various depths that detect warmth and cold and different pressures of touch. The sensations arising from the stimulation of these receptors make us aware of temperature and pressure on the surface of the body. The temperature senses can easily be stimulated by applying warmth and cold to small areas of the skin. When this is done systematically, it is evident that the receptor organs for warmth and the receptor organs for cold are localized so that only certain skin spots respond to warmth, and different ones respond to cold.[14] The parts of the body having surface hair, and the surface hairs themselves, are sensitive to light touch when it is applied reasonably quickly, so as to produce slight deformity of the skin and bending of the hairs. At the root of the hair is a nerve ending that encircles the follicle in which the hair is rooted. The bending of the hair and also the application of light pressure on the skin close to the hair stimulate this receptor. There are many other specialized nerve endings in the skin, as well as naked nerve fibrils which simply come to an end below the surface of the skin. Some of these nerve endings detect the application of heavy pressure and some detect painful stimuli. There are receptors responsive to pressure in the visceral organs, also. The adequate stimulus in pressure detection is deformation of the tissue containing the receptors.

Pain is produced in the skin areas in various ways—by pricking the skin, by stretching it excessively, by pinching it, and by applying excessive warmth, to name a few. We cannot name the exact stimulus for pain because we do not know what common factor of these various noxious stimuli causes them all to produce sensations of pain. The pain receptors (nociceptors) not only respond to many kinds of stimulus, but are located in other places as well as the skin—we certainly feel pain in our muscles and have stomach aches, headaches, and so forth. Also, pain regularly elicits avertive action where this action is beneficial, whereas the other tactile sensations are merely informative as often as they are motivational. Because the nerve endings that respond to painful stimuli are widespread throughout the body and respond to different painful stimuli in different parts of the body (some visceral organs do not react to cutting and pinching), it is impossible as yet to assign the various nociceptors accurately, but we do know with certainty that the unsheathed nerve fibrils in the skin are responsive primarily to painful stimuli.

PROPRIOCEPTION

The tactile receptors, when described collectively, are called *somesthetic*, in contrast to the *kinesthetic* senses which detect motion that occurs in the muscles, tendons, and joints. The term "proprioceptor" applied to receptors of stimuli from these parts of the body indicates that the information received originates from one's own (proper) physical equipment. Sensations from muscle, tendon, and joint are relayed over neuronal circuits just as other sensations are, but they obtrude on consciousness to such a slight degree that we have to concentrate on them deliberately in order to notice them as distinct sensations. Nevertheless, we are fully and intimately aware of the position and direction of movement of our limbs (normally), for we unerringly direct them from one position with respect to the body trunk to a different one.

Kinesthesis is the group of senses that makes us aware of the motion and position of various muscles and bones without our using sight for that purpose. Thus a person sitting down at a desk can move his feet and locate them in a comfortable position without having to look to see where they are. Just as the nerves responsible for muscle contraction make direct contact with the muscles and tendons, so a set of afferent fibers runs from the muscles and tendons to the central nervous system; eventually some of the fibers run to conscious centers within the brain.

The manner in which the motion of joints is reported is not yet understood except that certain receptors for deep-seated pressure occur abundantly near bone joints. The sensations from muscle contraction and extension impinge so little on consciousness that we are not aware of them; perhaps they do not register there at all. We do, however, have conscious control over many of our muscles—most of our awareness of muscle motion and limb position comes from nerves that report on the tendons and the joints. The soreness of overused muscles is not a kinesthetic but a pain sensation.

The Chemical Senses

Both taste and smell appear to be stimulated by chemicals in solution (gaseous molecules that stimulate the sense of smell do so only when they dissolve in the moisture of the olfactory membrane), but the exact manner of stimulation is not understood at all. Thus the name "chemical sense" is used, but this could turn out to be a misnomer when the details of the nature of gustation and olfaction become known. There is no taste of substances that do not dissolve in saliva, and yet many soluble substances will not elicit the sensation of taste. Furthermore, most substances that dissolve in saliva or the mucus surrounding the olfactory receptor apparatus are more soluble at higher temperatures, but they are not uniformly more stimulating to taste or smell at higher temperatures. For example, the amount of salt that savors hot food often proves to be too much for the same food as it cools, because the sensitivity of taste to salt is increased as the temperature of the food falls from hot to warm. In brief, we know nothing about the specific quality in things that evokes the sensation of taste.

The same confusing situation is present when one attempts to state what is the adequate stimulus for smell and to describe how it stimulates. Thus most chemical *elements* (the halogens and a few others are exceptions) do not cause sensations of smell, but many *compounds,* especially organic ones, have a pronounced effect on the olfactory receptor. Pain receptors and other touch receptors are often stimulated at the same time as the taste and smell receptors, so that objective control of stimuli is difficult and makes precise experiment impossible.

Although tastes are classified as sweet, sour, bitter, and salty, there is no standard classification for smells. But the range of smells is quite large in man. In rodents the sense of smell is exceedingly well developed, and the portion of the brain devoted to receiving smell stimuli is relatively large, while in the human brain the portion devoted to smell is comparatively small.

The sensory pathways for smell are different from those

for taste. Although the two senses often cooperate in experiencing delightful sensations from food, it is possible to suppress the activity of one and thus isolate the proper activity of the other. Furthermore, the receptors for taste are taste buds in the top surface and edges of the tongue, while the olfactory receptor is located quite high up in the nose and can be stimulated only by substances making contact there. For all of these reasons, and because the stimuli receptors in each case are physiologically different, it is accurate to classify taste and smell as distinct senses.

The receptors for taste are the taste buds, which are much like small flower buds. Groups of taste cells make up the interior of the taste buds. These taste cells send small sensory hairlike processes to form a bundle issuing a very short distance through the tip of the taste bud. The buds differ a little in size, but not otherwise. The buds on the tip of the tongue detect sweet stimuli, those on the side edges detect sour stimuli, those at the back of the tongue detect bitter stimuli, and salt stimuli appear to be effective with all taste buds. The center of the tongue's surface has no taste buds and consequently detects no stimuli. The burning sensations of hot liquids and hot pepper, and the slick feeling of oil in the mouth, are due to the stimulation of pain and touch receptors.

The receptors for smell are located in an olfactory membrane that is small in size and located high up in, and on both sides of, the nasal cavity. Ordinarily the air drawn in through the nose in breathing crosses only the lower part of the olfactory membrane, so that a sniff is required to concentrate the stimulating particles over the whole membrane and give a stronger sensation of smell. The olfactory cells in the membrane are tipped with hairs. It is not known whether these hairs can trigger a nerve impulse or whether the stimulus must penetrate to the cells buried within the membrane.

Sensation by Mediated Contact

Both hearing and sight are distance senses, for although stimuli contact them directly, the sensations are information about sources of stimuli that are practically always located some distance away from the organs of hearing and sight.

The Ear

The part of the ear that we can easily see is the *outer ear*, which is made up of cartilage and skin lying alongside the head and a funnel leading into the skull that is stopped up at its inner end by the eardrum. In addition to the outer ear, there is a *middle* and an *inner* ear. The middle ear is a small chamber beginning at the eardrum. Three bones traverse it serially: the hammer (*malleus*), one end of which is joined to the eardrum; the anvil (*incus*) with one end forming a movable joint with the head of the hammer; and the stirrup (*stapes*), joined to the other end of the anvil by one end and to the wall of the inner ear by the other.

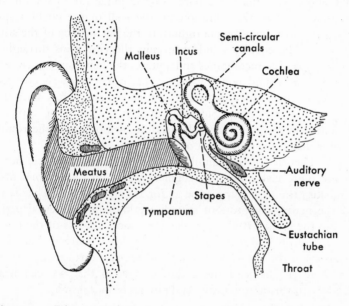

Figure 3 Diagram of the human ear with partial view of semicircular canals. (From M. A. Wenger, F. N. Jones, and M. H. Jones, *Physiological Psychology*. New York: Holt, Rinehart and Winston, 1956)

In the inner ear are located the organs for hearing and the semicircular canals for equilibrium.

The middle ear is connected by a narrow canal (*Eusta-*

chian tube) to the back part of the nose. This allows air to pass in and out of the middle ear to equalize the pressure on both sides of the eardrum. The organ containing the sensory sound receptors is the snail's shell (*cochlea*) in the inner ear. The cochlea looks like a snail's shell because it is formed of a coil that makes two and three quarters turns around a central bony column. It is filled with a fluid whose motion stimulates the sensory hair cells of the *organ of Corti,* a sensory receptor located on a membrane inside the cochlea.

Sound waves are ordinarily transmitted through the atmosphere into the external ear where they contact the eardrum, which is a membrane stretched across the inner end of the outer ear. This membrane vibrates with the frequency of the sound wave and moves the three bones of the inner ear in unison, so that they transmit the vibrations to the wall of the cochlea and through an oval window contiguous to the flat surface of the stirrup. Inside the cochlea a fluid transmits the vibrations through a couple of flexible membranes and agitates the hairs on the sensory cells. A small round window below the oval window is covered by a flexible membrane that moves out and in alternately with the vibrations of the stirrup. Since the fluid in the ear is incompressible and is in a closed space, the flexible membrane of the round window makes the movement of this fluid possible.[15]

Theories of the stimulus and impulse connection in hearing are quite elaborate and technical; since no one theory predominates, the case is the same as for taste and smell. That is to say, the neural receptors of stimuli are known, the neural pathways in the brain have been discovered, and the parts of the brain involved in discrimination of pitch have been mapped; but how vibrations of the atmosphere and their physical qualities are transmitted by the hairs of the auditory cells so that we can hear sounds with various intensities and pitches is not known.

THE VESTIBULAR APPARATUS

The auditory apparatus is contained within the bone of the skull. The innermost part of this cavity in the skull contains the cochlea, or inner ear. This part of the cavity is called the *labyrinth* to indicate that it has many small paths running through the bone and connecting with one another. Three of these bony

Man's Physical and Spiritual Nature

pathways are filled by semicircular membranes full of a lymphatic fluid. These semicircular canals are situated at different angles to one another so that any motion of the head in any plane will move the lymphatic fluid in at least one canal. Each canal terminates both of its ends in a membranous sac (the *utricle*) in an oval hollow in the bone which is called the *vestibule* (to the labyrinth). The sense involved is named the *vestibular sense* from the position of the sensory apparatus involved. There are several areas in the vestibular apparatus where sensory hairs are stimulated by the motion of the lymphatic fluid.

The stimulation of one of these specialized receptors by changing the position of the head results in changes in the tension of muscles of the body, so as to adjust the position of the body to maintain its usual upright posture against the pull of gravity and against any other force tending to move it off its center of equilibrium. No conscious sensation is connected with the stimulation of the vestibular apparatus, and the actions produced as a result of stimulus are entirely reflex in nature. But we can be conscious of dizziness and nausea when the vestibular apparatus is stimulated by the rapid twirling of the body or by the motion of a boat at sea. The vestibular sense is usefully at work for a skier moving sideways across a slope because it makes him lean toward the slope at the proper angle to keep himself from falling over and down the hill. Also, the tensing of the muscles, the spreading apart of the feet, and the outswinging of the arms of a person landing from a jump are prompted to some extent by the vestibular sense. Apart from such examples as these the vestibular sense quietly and unobtrusively performs its task of affecting the tension of limb muscles to compensate for movements that tend to throw us off balance.

THE EYE

The adult eye is about one inch in diameter and appears as though it were constructed of five-sixths of one sphere fronted by one-sixth of a smaller sphere (the cornea). The spot in the center of the front of the eye is the *pupil*, which admits light rays into the eye where they travel through one body of liquid, the *aqueous humor*, then through the *lens* and through a second liquid, the *vitreous humor*, to strike the *retina* which lies on the inside of the back and side walls of the eyeball. The pupil is surrounded circularly by the multicolored *iris*, and both are covered by the translucent *cornea*. The retina is an area of rodlike and conelike nerve endings whose nerve processes and connections with other neurons lie on top of these nerve endings.

Seeing occurs when light passes through the pupil and the lens and then penetrates the overlying layers of nerve fibers to excite the *rods* and *cones*. The nerve fibers that lead from the

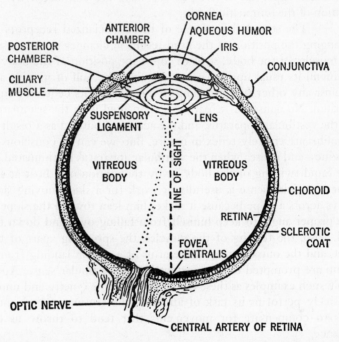

Figure 4 Horizontal section through the eyeball. (From C. H. Best and N. B. Taylor, *The Living Body*, 4th ed. New York: Holt, Rinehart and Winston, 1958)

rods and cones synapse several times before they group to join a nerve bundle called the *optic nerve*, which passes out of the eyeball at a spot in the back wall. Since this spot has no rods or cones, it is a blind spot.[16] Close beside the blind spot is a yellow spot that is more susceptible to light than any other in the retina. Since this yellow spot is a depression in the retina, it is called the central

Man's Physical and Spiritual Nature

pit (*fovea centralis*). The central pit is overlaid by a thinner layer of nerve processes than any other part of the retina, which contributes in part to its great sensitivity to light.

When a person focuses upon a single object, the light from the object is focused by the lens down to a very small bundle of rays that falls directly upon the central pit in each eye. This pit is the area of most accurate and most sensitive vision for brightly illuminated and for colored objects. Vision in the rest of the retina is poor in comparison with foveal vision.[17] In man the central pit has many cones but has few rods, whereas the rest of the retina is liberally supplied with rods. This fact supports the explanation of vision which holds that the cones are used when vision takes place in bright light, and for the reception of color, while the rods are much more sensitive to light and therefore respond when illumination is dim. Thus rod vision is restricted to black, white, and gray.[18]

The Mechanics of Vision

The cornea is the translucent part of a tough, fibrous, elastic container that is the outermost layer of the eye and preserves its shape. Light passes through the cornea and the fluid behind it before traversing the pupil to strike the lens. The lens is about one-third inch in diameter, with both of its faces convex. The lens is held in position, a little distance behind the pupil, by ligaments, which by contracting can stretch the lens to make it less convex, and by relaxing allow the tension within the lens itself to contract to make its surfaces more convex. In this way light from a distant object and from a near object can be focused equally well.[19]

The iris is a diaphragm lying between the cornea and the lens. It is a set of two muscle fibers. One of these fibers on contracting diminishes the opening in the center of the iris, while the other by contracting enlarges it. Thus the human eye adapts itself to various degrees of illumination by contracting the pupil in bright light and expanding it in dim light.

Another means of light adaptation, which is more chemical than physical in nature, is the effect of a pigment occuring in the rods—visual purple (*rhodopsin*). When rhodopsin is present in sufficient amounts, the rods are quite sensitive to light and function well in dim light. But bright light quickly bleaches the purple pigment and makes the rods so much less sensitive that vision becomes an activity of the cones alone. In dim illumination and in darkness the pigment is automatically resynthesized; its presense in the rods restores them to a state of high sensitivity. This is a clear indication of the role that chemical activity plays in vision.[20]

Thus we have seen that one aspect of human vision is the photochemical process in the rods of the retina. The intensity of this process depends upon the quantity of light projected upon the retina. Actually there are two quantitative factors involved: the intensity of the light that stimulates the retina and the duration of the stimulation. Since the intensity of illumination varies according to the area reflecting light to the eye, a small object the same distance from the eye as a large one may not reflect enough light to stimulate the eye, whereas the larger surface reflecting more light will be visible. Very minute intensities of light striking the retina can arouse a sensation. Theoretically a healthy eye that has become adapted to darkness can detect the smallest amount of light energy that a source can emit. The retina is estimated to be 3000 times more sensitive than a very fast photographic film.

When the retina is stimulated by light, electrical changes occur in the retina and in the optic nerve, which can be detected and measured in the usual way. These electrical phenomena indicate that the nerve conduction involved in vision has an electrochemical aspect, as have all the other sensory processes that we have explained. The frequency of impulsing increases as the intensity of the stimulus (illumination) increases in vision, just about as it does in the other sensations. (See Appendix 3c for a discussion of color vision.)

Conclusion

The discoveries made by the science of physiology about the interconnectedness of all of the living parts of the human body (fluids such as the blood and the cerebrospinal fluid contain living cells but are not themselves living) reveal how closely integrated are the various parts of the body. This closeness exists

Man's Physical and Spiritual Nature

not only for cooperation with the biochemical activities that are the life of the cells and tissues, but also for the execution of voluntary actions.

Although some attempt has been made in textbooks of popular psychology to pooh-pooh the term *voluntary* as being inaccurate or to ignore the voluntary activities of men by deliberately omitting any discussion of them, the facts of man's voluntary and rational activity are easily ascertained by anyone who reflects upon his own actions.[21] Can we not walk when we will to and talk when we so desire, and deliberately ignore the most pressing physical needs because we choose to do so? We cannot carry out any physical activity without the cooperation of the muscles and therefore not without the cooperation of the motor nerves. When is this cooperation ever lacking in a normally functioning human body? It simply never is lacking. The efferent nerves impulse and contract and relax muscles not only when they act reflexly, but also when we want them to do so.

Some accounts of nerve conduction use such terms as "message" and "information" in connection with the impulse that travels along the nerve, and such terms as "decision" and "choice" in connection with synaptic activity. The similarity between a verbal communications system and the over-all neural afferent-efferent activity has already been discussed, and the mysterious action of the synapses in transmitting impulses selectively has been noted. But these are not conscious activities. They are on a par with the chemical activities of metabolism to the extent that nerve conduction and chemical activity are predetermined by the nature of a nerve cell and fiber, and the kind of process that metabolism is.

Consciousness is not a function of any known part of the human body, although the functions of some parts of the brain are indispensable to consciousness. We, as living animals, are conscious; but no neuron, no synapse, no nerve tract, no part of the cortex as a chemical or physical entity is conscious. It is the individual person who is conscious, and the neural processes serve his conscious activities, not vice versa. Thus we note that the activity of neural processes is not made known to us in our conscious activities but has been discovered through experiments performed upon the nerve apparatus. What we are conscious of is that part of our internal and external environment that produces impulsing in the sensory nerves and those motions of our bodily parts that produce impulses in similar nerves. We have learned by experimental procedures that it is impulses in the nerves serving effectors that result in the release of chemical agents, which act upon muscle tissue to make it contract or relax. In innate reflex activities the nerves are acting in a predetermined manner according to their makeup and organization. These same efferent nerves (at least in the final common path), acting in their predetermined mode of activity, are made to serve our desires. Of this fact we are more certain than we are of any explanation as to how the nerves accomplish what they do.

Our introduction of information from physiology, however, has not led us to a negative conclusion about the interaction of the sense organs and the stimuli that produce impulses in the nerves serving them. Quite the contrary. Every person can be aware that his sense impressions bring him into contact with his environment. The physiology of the human nervous system confirms this fact on the microscopic level and indicates to some extent how it is so. The implications of this contact were well expressed by Aristotle: *The sense in act is the sensible in act.* By *sensible* he meant such aspects of our environment as the hardness, the sharpness, or the wetness of something contacting our body, as well as sound waves agitating our eardrums and reflected light impinging upon our eyes. Such sensibles are *in act* or actually existing, since they are capable of being sensed by us when they are actually acting upon our sensory receptors. By *sense* Aristotle meant not only the receptors that we have been discussing in detail, but also the activity proper to each kind of receptor when viewed as residing in that receptor, whether sensation is actually taking place or not. By *sense in act* he meant the sensation actually occurring so that both organ and awareness are involved. Aristotle's statement then can be understood to mean that when we are aware of our environment, something of that environment is actually present in the sense. Since for a physical thing to be actually present is for it to be present physically, according to Aristotle something of our environment is physically present in the organs of sense; this presence is accompanied by awareness, to the extent that we actually sense something only when some aspect of our environment adequately stimulates our sense receptors.

Man's Physical and Spiritual Nature

Modern science and technology have made clear to us that the environment we sense is just as actually present in our bodies as is the part of our environment that we digest. The mass of a small stone in the palm of one's hand produces a distortion of the nerve cells specialized for pressure detection, just as it produces distortion in the molecular arrangement constituting the surface of a jelly dessert or any other nonliving colloidal solid. But the difference in the reception of this distortion-causing pressure is obvious to us who are alive—we feel the pressure, but the jelly dessert does not give any indication of feeling.

In this chapter we have tried to show the reader how certain he can be in concluding that what he sees, hears, feels, and senses in any way is truly present, actually, in the organs he uses for sensing. Reflected electromagnetic radiations are in the retina; sound waves are in the cochlea; chemicals are in the mouth and the nose; and mass (as pressure) and heat are in the somatic cells and the sensory receptors located there.

In truth then, the sensible as it actually exists is actually in the sense that is actually sensing. How it arrives there has been explained, but the connection between what the sensible does upon arrival and what happens subsequently in the neuronal circuits of the central nervous system is hardly understood. We have discussed the physical nerve system that integrates the reflex actions of diverse parts of the body for the benefit of the physical man as a whole and also serves as an indispensable physical component in man's awareness of his body and his environment. In the next chapter we shall turn our attention to the other aspect of sensory action—the consciously apprehensive—wherein something in our environment is present to our conscious self as an object of knowledge.

APPENDIX 3a

Protoplasm ~ PROTOPLASM EXISTS
in either of two colloidal states: the sol or the gel. Colloids are
liquids that contain dispersed particles. The particles are not actually dissolved, and although they are invisible to us, they are
quite large in comparison with monatomic molecules. The size of
colloidal particles is between one ten-thousandth and one mil-
lionth of a millimeter in diameter. Colloidal suspensions are so
named because those that occur naturally are sticky, like weak
glue. To imagine the appearance of protoplasm, one may picture
the gelatin often used for desserts as it progresses from the state
of a highly mobile liquid when first mixed with hot water to
stages of lesser and lesser mobility until a gel is formed. Protoplasm can change from sol to gel and back again to sol as it engages in various living activities.

The use of the term "protoplasm" is a mere convenience
that must not be allowed to hide the fact that *cellular stuff* is quite
heterogeneous—it contains many kinds of substance. When analyzed chemically the constitutents of protoplasm are, approximately: water, 80 percent; proteins, 15 percent; fats, 3 percent;

carbohydrates, 1 percent; and inorganic salts of sodium, potassium, calcium, iron, and so forth, 1 percent. Water is the simplest substance present, as its chemical formula, H_2O, indicates. Carbohydrates are so named because they generally contain carbon atoms linked to hydrogen and oxygen atoms, combined in the same ratio as in water. For example, $C_6H_{12}O_6$ is the formula for glucose, the sugar that supplies energy for the work performed by human muscles. Fats contain carbon, hydrogen, and oxygen, but these elements are not linked in the same way they are in the carbohydrates. The proteins differ in that they are composed of carbon, hydrogen, oxygen, nitrogen, and frequently sulphur. When compared to all other molecules, protein molecules are giants; their size is partially a result of their being present in colloidal suspension rather than in solution. For example, hemoglobin, a protein that occurs in our red blood corpuscles, has a chemical formula, $C_{3032}H_{4816}O_{872}N_{782}S_8F_4$, indicating a total of 9512 atoms in each molecule. Other protein molecules contain millions of atoms.

The various chemical activities of animal and plant life are protoplasmic activities because the cells constituting the bodies of living things are composed of protoplasm. These cells engage in many kinds of activities. The protoplasm inside the cell streams around the nucleus; in some cells even the nucleus has a measurable rotation. There is also electrical activity in all cells, with voltages that can be measured. These voltages are diverse and range from a difference in potential from one side of a neuron to another to a rapid stream of impulses along a nerve cell to the brain. A tissue cell can have a voltage difference of 50 millivolts from one side of its cell wall to the other.

APPENDIX 3b

Development from the Cell in Amoeba and Man ~ WE HAVE TALKED OF

cells in Appendix 2b as the basic units of living substance containing the nucleus, which is the means of transmitting the nature of a given species from one individual to his progeny. Here we shall consider the cell as a self-maintaining living system possessing the characteristics that, in larger animals, are embodied in their neural systems.

The microscope reveals that all different tissues and organs of the human body are composed of cells, which vary considerably in shape and structure. They do have some characteristics in common, of course, because they are all composed of protoplasm (Appendix 3a). Since protoplasm is relatively colorless, it has to be stained by dyes in order for the interior parts to be made visible under the optical microscope.[22] Individual cells carry on living activity within themselves and also contribute to the life of the whole animal when they are part of one.

A cell is a mass of protoplasm surrounding a nucleus, the entire mass being contained by an outer cell membrane. This membrane varies in mobility from comparative stability in the cells comprising our skin to the absolute fluidity of single-celled animals like the amoeba, an easily understood example of a typical cell.

THE AMOEBA

The living activities of the amoeba illustrate the living activities of single cells within a body, and at the same time, the activities of the complex of cells that constitute a body. The amoeba is about 0.25 millimeters in length, of irregular shape, and

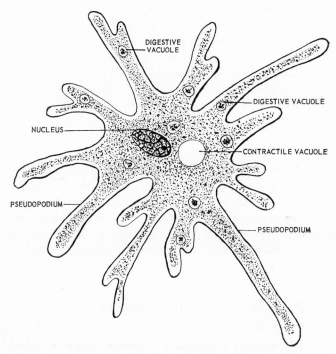

Figure 5   An amoeba. (From C. H. Best and N. B. Taylor, *The Human Body*, 4th ed. New York: Holt, Rinehart and Winston, 1963)

almost colorless. It has a central part, called the *nucleus*, which is shaped like a little globe and is more viscous than the rest of the cell. The nucleus can be stained by dyes so that it stands out from the protoplasm surrounding it. This surrounding protoplasm is the *cytoplasm* (cell plasm). The cytoplasm and the nucleus are both protoplasm, but they are separated by a nuclear membrane. Each has a different function in the continuance of life.

Within the cytoplasm are clear bubbles, called *vacuoles*, which aid in the assimilation of food and the elimination of waste products. The food vacuole serves as a temporary stomach; it is a kind of food container in which digestive fluids render the contained food available for metabolism. As the digested fats, sugars, starches, and proteins of the ingested food are absorbed, the vacuole decreases in size until it is large enough to contain only the waste materials that are subsequently passed out. The digested materials are built up into protoplasm, some to be used for growth and some for movement. Respiration in the amoeba involves the use of oxygen (dissolved in water) and the release of carbon dioxide, just as it does in higher animals.

The amoeba moves by putting out little feet (*pseudopodia.*). Several may spread out simultaneously. They may arise at any point on the surface of the cell and extend in various directions. One of several pseudopodia going in the same direction will appear to win priority over the others and the rest of the cytoplasm will flow into the leading foot, carrying the nucleus along, which causes the whole cell to move. This movement can take the animal away from unpleasantness, it can result in the capture of other organisms, and it can place the amoeba over a bit of food which it then proceeds to surround with a vacuole and ingest. Often the amoeba's food is mixed with nonfood; the cell simply ingests the food and then moves away from the nonfood.

RESPONSIVENESS AND REPRODUCTION IN AMOEBA

The amoeba responds to different stimuli in much the same manner as higher animals do. Sometimes it will ingest any animal or plant that it can, but when confronted with several species of food, it selects certain types and avoids others. The amoeba definitely discriminates between contact with a glass rod, or a needle, and contact with food, retreating from the former but attempting to engulf and ingest the latter. The amoeba also reacts negatively to chemicals like salt and sugar by moving away.

Thus we can see that a definite *stimulus* and *response* kind of activity, which can discriminate between various stimuli and respond in different ways, is present in the amoeba. This stimulus and response activity is a combination of two basic physiological factors—contractility and irritability. An amoeba when stimulated will usually contract and send out a stream or streams of itself on the opposite side from that on which it was irritated. It then flows into these false feet, thus moving away from the irritation. The stimulus-receiving apparatus and the con- tracting apparatus are not physically differentiated so that they can be definitely singled out: the amoeba's body as a whole both receives, and reacts to, a stimulus.

The bodies of higher animals have specialized parts to serve the various functions that are served by the unspecialized body of the amoeba. Thus in higher animals some of the cells have a special structure and chemical composition that equip them to take on specialized functions as receivers of stimulations (such as the eye and the ear, which are specialized to receive the actions of the visible and the sounding elements of the external environment) and as effectors of contractions (muscle fibers, which produce motion by contraction).

Most of the cells produced by a mature multicellular or- ganism are used for replacing cells depleted in the activity of liv- ing. These cells are called *somatic* (body) *cells*. Some of the re- maining cells are called *germ cells* because their function is to en- gage in the reproduction of a new organism.

In the amoeba, reproduction takes place in less than half an hour at ordinary temperatures. The nucleus divides into two parts, each of which appropriates some of the available cyto- plasm, thus forming new daughter cells. Under ideal conditions these new cells grow to maturity in approximately one day. Mul- ticellular animals like man were originally single-celled growing from a single cell by a process of multiplication much like that by which the daughter cells of the amoeba are formed. Thus from a single cell the multicellular organism became many cells that co- hered to one another. All of the organic parts of man were even- tually built in this way from raw materials.

Development of the Human Neural System

The reproduction of human beings requires two kinds of germ cell, the *ovum* and the *spermatozoon*. It involves the contact of the nucleus of the ovum, supplied by the female, with the male-produced spermatozoon after the spermatozoon has penetrated the surface of the ovum. The ovum that has thus been fertilized then divides into two cells, each of which in turn divide into two more, and so on, to produce the billions of cells that constitute the infant body. It is in this process that the DNA molecules exercise their marvelous function of directing the growth and differentiation of the multiplying cells to produce an embryonic human body. Thus, somehow, the fertilized ovum contains within itself the pattern of cell division that will result in the shape and internal structure of a human body.

Complex as the process is, it is possible to follow the first steps in the multiplication of cells and their differentiation into the three layers from which all of the various parts of the body develop. The initial products of multiplication cling together, forming a ball. Within this tiny ball a spherical cavity develops in the middle of the mass of cells. But even as the cavity is forming, the cell mass is elongating and the spherical cavity is beginning to collapse inward. Also, the cells that had become differentiated in being separated by the inner cavity now come to lie alongside of one another, but remain differentiated. In the human embryo a third layer forms where the first two layers meet. These three layers are the *ectoderm* (outer layer), *mesoderm* (middle layer), and *endoderm* (inner layer). While the sides of the cavity are collapsing inward to form this triple layer of cells, the whole elongated string of cell layers turns about an imaginary center so that its ends meet to enclose a new cavity. Thus a new ball with walls three layers thick is formed around a cavity in the center— the digestive cavity which enables the embryo to contain its own food supply.

As the cells of the embryo continue to multiply, all of the different parts of the human body develop from three layers of cells. From the outer layer the epidermis, the nervous systems, and the sense organs take shape. The respiratory system, the liver, the pancreas, and the lining of the digestive system gradually emerge from the inner layer. The skeleton, the muscles, the connective tissue, the heart and blood vessels, and the excretory and reproductive systems develop from the middle layer.

The spinal cord grows inside the developing spine and becomes differentiated into an outer white layer (white matter) and a central gray layer (gray matter). In the very center of the cord is a hollow through which the spinal fluid flows. Since the spinal cord is quite long in comparison with its width, the gray matter is best thought of as a gray column running the length of the spine and into the lower part of the brain. The white matter from this point of view is a white column also running the length of the spine and surrounding the gray column.

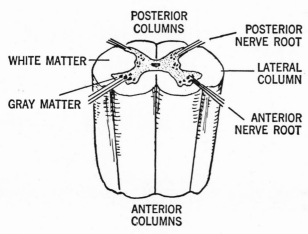

Figure 6   A section of the spinal cord with central gray matter. (From C. H. Best and N. B. Taylor, *The Living Body*, 4th ed. New York: Holt, Rinehart and Winston, 1958)

The gray column is composed of nerve cells and tissues that hold them in place. The white column comprises many nerve fibers which proceed from the nerve cells and communicate with other nerve cells at different levels of the spinal cord and with the brain. The part of the spinal cord closest to a person's back is the posterior section, in which sensory nerves from the sense organs join with the nerve cells of the gray matter. The forward section of the spinal cord is called the anterior part, and from the nerve cells located here arise long fibers that run to the muscles and, when necessary, stimulate them to contract and relax. The nerves connected to the dorsal section of the gray matter join together to form a bundle and depart from the spinal cord through openings in the vertebral column. The nerves leaving the ventral portion of the gray matter leave in a bundle, also. These two bundles join a short distance from the spine to form a spinal nerve. This bundle of nerve fibers travels alongside muscles and around bones to reach the part of the body for which they are destined. The afferent fibers innervate skin and sensory receptors; the efferent fibers, muscles and organs.

APPENDIX 3c

Color
and
Color Vision ~ WHENEVER A RAY OF

light passes through a lens, where it is focused, the appearance of the object carried by the light ray is inverted. Thus visual appearances falling on the human retina are upside down when compared to the position of the object as determined by touch, but we usually *see* the object in the same position in space as touch indicates—right side up. Somehow, then, we correct for the upside-down position of the visual image on the retina.

The same kind of correction also takes place automatically in our sensing of sizes. The image of the smallest visible speck of matter in high illumination is approximately one-ten thousandth of an inch in diameter, but we could never see a speck as small as the retinal image. Conversely, the extent and some of the detail of a scene covering several dozen miles, for example, the horizon seen in good illumination or a countryside as seen from an airplane, can register on the human retina, stimulating an area of less than a square inch. Regardless of the size of the retinal impression, we tend to see things, when viewing conditions are excellent, in the size that measuring instruments indicate they possess.

In the detection of color we also accommodate to some degree, for colors we see in surfaces are really reflections from the light that strikes the surfaces. Thus the color of an object as seen depends upon the color of the light that falls upon it. An object appears red to us in sunlight because it absorbs all color, but red will appear black in green light because it will absorb green and not reflect any light. The prevailing theory on colored surfaces holds that any surface that appears colored in sunlight does so because it absorbs some part of sunlight and reflects the rest. Since sunlight passed through a clear prism can be broken up into the colors red, orange, yellow, green, blue, and violet, these colors must somehow be contained in colorless sunlight. The sky appears blue, even though sunlight manifests no color until it strikes something, because small dust particles and gas molecules whose diameters approach the wavelength of the blue end of the spectrum scatter the blue wavelength in the atmosphere, thus giving it a blue appearance.

Since black is the visual appearance resulting from the absence of color and white is the visual appearance resulting from the combining of all colors into a colorless light, black and white are not usually counted as colors. Any white light from the sun or some other source may be colored by passing it through a transparent but colored medium; the medium reflects some colors and lets others pass through. This is the principle on which light filters are based.

The colors that result from the scattering of white light passed through a prism can be brought together by a convex lens to form a beam of white light. White light can also be produced by combining the three primary colors: red, green, and blue. In fact, all other colors can be produced by combinations of the primary colors. This principle can be illustrated by using a red, a green, and a blue light and directing the lights to one spot on a white screen. When red and green coincide on the screen yellow is produced; blue and green together produce cyan blue; and all three primary colors falling on the same spot produce white.

One contemporary theory as to the discrimination of color by human sight holds that there are three kinds of cones in the retina, each kind reacting to a specific primary color and all of

Man's Physical and Spiritual Nature

them reacting equally to white light. In this explanation the seeing of blue results from the stimulation of the blue receptors only, and the seeing of yellow from the stimulation of the red and green receptors. No proof of this explanation has been given, but experiment has revealed areas in the retina that are selectively responsive to the four physiologically unique colors (that do not change under varying conditions of observation): blue, red, yellow, and green. The largest area is responsive to blue but not to the other colors; the smallest area, around the fovea centralis, is responsive to green. Thus when a group of colored disks are brought slowly into the peripheral field of vision toward the line of sight straight ahead, the blue disk will be visible first and the green last. There are other visual phenomena, however, that cannot be explained by this theory, and there are other theories of color vision. No one theory has received any significant degree of confirmation.

CHAPTER 4

Sensory Experience as Knowledge

IN THIS CHAPTER WE shall treat the senses as purveyors of information that is always determinate and never universal. We learned in the previous chapter that there is a great deal about the physicochemical operations of the senses that is not yet understood. This condition of ignorance also applies to a discussion of the conscious experiencing of things. But, just as in the last chapter so also in this one—a coherent account of the activity of the senses will be given even though much mystery still remains.

We shall select *consciousness* as our indefinable term and use *awareness* as a synonym for it. Then, in order to be precise, we must distinguish sensory awareness as that which is concerned only with the concrete and the determinate from the intellectual awareness of the concrete and determinate as given in the representations that the senses form of things and from the intellectual awareness of the common aspects of things sharing the same nature. Sensation, sensory activity, sensory experiencing, and sensory awareness are synonymous expressions used to indicate an awareness of something definite and recognizable by any one of the human senses. We shall call such definite things, which are recognizable by sight and hearing and the rest of the human senses *sensibles*. Intellectual awareness extends to the same things as the senses do but its manner of apprehension is different, because the intellect sees also what is common in things while the senses apprehend things only as singulars. The intellect can also judge and reason about things, whereas the senses detect only their appearances. This intellectual ability, to transcend the limitations of the senses while depending upon them for information, will be considered in Chapter 5.

Sensation as a Center of Controversy

Conscious sensory activity has been the subject of controversy in the past, it is the subject of considerable controversy now, and it will probably continue to be a controversial topic in the future. The three main facts underlying this controversy are:

1. Sensation is man's only direct contact with his nonself world and with his physical self.
2. Intellectual consciousness has no specific organ (as sight has, for example) through which it operates.
3. Intellectual judgments are firmly connected with, and therefore often confused with, sensory cognitions.

These facts are the basis of controversy inasmuch as:

1. Some men deny that there is a nonself world, and some deny the existence of any other aspect of self than the one involved in awareness.
2. Some men maintain that consciousness is merely a biochemical activity and nothing else.
3. Some men consider the term "intellect" to stand for a pious fiction invented when man had no knowledge of the physiology of the sensory activities.

Let us illustrate briefly how easily controversy can arise over some aspect of apprehension. Suppose that our friend X claims that the classroom window is open. We challenge him to prove it. He says that he can see that it is so.

"How do you know that the window is actually as you see it?", we challenge. He thrusts his hand out through the opening, and then says, "Surely this is proof." "How do you know that things actually are as your sense of touch reports them to be?", we ask. "Well," he replies, "there was no sound of impact as my hand was thrust through the opening and there is nothing present for anyone to taste or to smell. Since all five senses corroborate one another on the window's being open, I feel sure that it is."

We claim that corroboration of one sense by another is comforting, but what if it turns out that each one is mistaken? What we desire is a proof that any one sense, or each sense by itself, reports events as they actually are.

After some reflection, Friend X claims that to desire such a proof is to ask for the impossible. The proof would have to be made known to us through our senses, and a further proof that our senses apprehend the first proof correctly would be required, and so on indefinitely. Moreover, if any witness, human or nonhuman, assured us of the infallibility of our cognitive acts, his message would also be subject to the same conditions that originally led to our demanding proof—the proof would have to be communicated to one of the very senses whose reliability was being called into question.

Friend X continues, "A person must start with the evidence revealed to his senses; when he is in doubt he can test his apprehension of this evidence by consulting with other men.[1] Since awareness begins in seeing, hearing, touching, and so on, and is of what is seen, heard, touched, and otherwise sensed, no other state of awareness can be expected to be superior to this primary one so as to pass judgment upon it. In brief, no proof of anything can be accomplished without assuming the reliability and objectivity of our primary acts of awareness."

"But surely," we reply, "our explanation of the physiology of sensory activity is proof that all sensation arises within the living body and terminates therein. Even if the stimuli are real and do originate outside the body, they do not enter into the body, for the stimulus is received by the sense receptor and does not go any farther into the body as light or sound. The nerve impulse accompanying the reception of stimulus arises in the end organ of the nerve and has characteristics common to all nerve impulses. Therefore, it does not reflect any specificity of the stimulus that gave rise to it. How then can you be so fool-hardy as to maintain that activity arising and terminating in the body can be informative of something that is not the body. How can you insist that there is actually a window when we have shown that there is nothing in sensation other then set responses to stimulation of the receptors?"

The argument of Friend X *forces us to admit that we cannot prove that there are stimulus receptors* because our only argument as to their existence is that we sense them. If we argue that we can accurately measure the stimulus applied and trace nerve conduction from the receptor to a certain area of the brain, his reply is inescapable: "Measurement presupposes the existence of the measuring instrument, the measured thing, and the one who *reads off* the measurement so that it can be understood. Also, the nerve pathway and the brain are known to us only through our act of seeing or otherwise sensing them, so that any discussion of them presupposes sensory awareness of their actual being."

We are forced to admit that since his open window cannot be proven to exist then we must be consistent and realize that our physiological description of nerve conduction cannot be proven to correspond to any actuality either.

The argument is at an impasse because it is now apparent that no question can be raised as to the existence of any object of sensation, including one's own physical being, without presupposing the existence and knowledge value of sensation itself. But we cannot prove in any manner that sensation is or is not adequate by anything prior to it in our experience for there *is* nothing prior to it in our experience.

An alternative way of arguing in attempting to deny the objectivity of what our senses are aware of is to maintain that *colors and sounds do not really exist*, although there is some objective reality that acts as a stimulus for the sense receptors. An example follows:

P. "Is it not true that what appears to sight to be redness in the skin of an apple is nothing other than the way our nervous system reacts to being stimulated by reflected light? To put it more succinctly, do you not admit that there is no actual color in surfaces?"

Q. "There is no color for any other receiver than a living eye, just as there is no sound for any other receiver than a living auditory system, but there is electromagnetic radiation which impinges upon the eye and there is vibration of the atmosphere which impinges upon the ear. The person who knows these physical descriptions in terms of what instruments reveal to our senses does not see electromagnetic radiation or hear vibrations of the atmosphere except as color and sound, respectively."

P. "Does this not amount to saying that there is actually no color, that color is a subjective way of interpreting certain wavelengths of electromagnetic radiation?"

Q. "I deny that there is any interpretation here because human beings testify that they see many things as colored without having to interpret what they see at all. Physiological science testifies that color (including black and white) is the only adequate stimulus to the retina of the human eye. In fact it is only by interpretation, of what occurs when colorless sunlight is refracted by a prism into the colors that we ordinarily associate with things, that we have been able to identify the visible spectrum with a portion of the whole range of electromagnetic radiation. To describe these activities in themselves, and as productive of impulsing in a sensory nerve, and also as that which the sight sees, is to describe one set of activities from three points of view. There is no error involved in this."

P. "Surely what we sense as color is nothing more than reflected light rays of a certain wavelength, so that the color we see depends upon which wavelengths are reflected by a surface."

Q. "Yes."

P. "Moreover, since we see only the rays that are reflected, does it not follow that they are not part of the surface of the seen object but rather something that the surface does not possess at all? After all, it is the rays that the surface does not absorb that are reflected and thus make it visible. Also, the neurons, fibers, and synapses that conduct impulses to the central nervous system do not take on the color that strikes the cones but simply relay the stimulus in the same manner

Man's Physical and Spiritual Nature

as do the nerve fibers and synapses connected to the organ of Corti in the cochlea. In short, it really is an interpretation, although an automatic one, that fails only in clear-cut cases such as color blindness, the reasons for which are not understood." [2]

Q. "Although color blindness and other deficiencies in the eye and its nerve processes prove that there is a very definite physical dimension to sight, does it not also prove that the receptor for normal vision is highly specialized to detect color although the nerve conduction that results from it, and the concomitant cerebral activity, are no different in kind than that resulting from stimulation of the hair cells in the organ of Corti or in the vestibular apparatus? Furthermore, since the retina does not become the color of what is seen nor does the neural pathway or the white and gray matters of the brain, does it not follow that the *conscious reception* of the colored appearances of objects is *not merely a physiological activity?* Does it not *prove* that the sensory, conscious awareness of both self and nonself, which is the primary fact of all investigation of cognition, is based upon, but is quite different from, the physical and chemical exchange of energy with the environment that is characteristic of vegetative life?

"As for the color attributed to surfaces, the color of the light originally falling upon them makes a great difference as to how the surface will appear to us—different surfaces absorb different colors and therefore also reflect different colors. If a surface is bathed in a color that it entirely absorbs, the surface will not reflect any color; whereas if it is bathed in sunlight, the surface will probably absorb some components of white light and reflect the remainder. All that we say in asserting that the skin of this apple is green is that the colors reflected by the apple's skin, which make us aware of its presence, size, and shape, are called green, and that this fact results from the selective absorption by the skin of the other electromagnetic radiations falling upon it in sunlight. One could say that the surface of the apple is a green reflecting surface to be more exact, but that differs little from saying that sight sees the apple as green. Obviously there is no reflection of green in the absence of light, so that no one can hold that the surface of the apple is green by itself. Nevertheless, some property of the surface of the apple absorbs all of the colors except the ones that it reflects. Therefore it is not necessary, nor in any way useful, to foresake the names imposed upon the appearance of things, for the appearances are still the appearances." [3]

This debate could be prolonged by examining electromagnetic radiation in detail up to the point where we must admit that we have as yet no precise knowledge of how it stimulates the rods and cones. Even if we discover the method of stimulation in the future, the knowledge thus gained will not contradict the facts that are most evident to us now. Therefore our sample debates have not only illustrated typical differences of viewpoint, but, as all well-intentioned debates should, they have served to reveal some preliminary facts about sensory awareness: (1) that we must accept conscious sensation of both self and nonself as primary indemonstrable factors in all cognition and (2) that sensible objects can be expected to be described in different ways according as they are apprehended by the unaided senses or by instruments. As a consequence we see that of the prime positions in the controversy over sense knowledge, the first is quite untenable and the second ignores the fact that no explanation in biochemical or physiological terms has ever been given of sensory awareness.

More will be said on these points as the chapter develops; the indispensability of intellect as an explanatory factor in human knowing will be considered in detail in the next chapter. We shall proceed now to analyze sensory awareness not only as a phenomenon that can be observed of other people—something quite diverse from, and objective to, our personal self; but also as an activity that each person carries on within himself.

Conscious Sensory Powers

Any notion that we use to analyze our sensory knowing precisely as sensory knowing is necessarily going to be a notion from the content of consciousness itself. We possess no means of introducing any measuring or experimenting tool into consciousness in any other way than by being conscious of it, and this is to possess it not as a practical instrument but as an object of awareness. When we direct our attention to consciousness, we are no longer dealing with what can be calculated and physically manipulated. We cannot locate our consciousness in a precise place at a precise time so as to measure it. We have departed from the solid and the ponderable completely, because there is no length, no breadth, no depth to our sensory awareness of a solid book. We have only an *awareness* of the length, the breadth, and the depth of the actual book.

The parts of the nerve apparatus involved in sense consciousness have physical properties, but not consciousness itself.[4] It is possible physically to isolate and excise one single neuron, but it is not possible physically to isolate or to excise one single visual, auditory, or other sensory apprehension. As a sign of our inability to understand the interconnection of the conscious and the physiological parts of sensory awareness, we note that all experiments upon conscious factors in sensation depend upon information from the subject as to when and to what extent he is aware of the controlled stimulus.[5]

Proper Sensibles

Some basic definitions of the factors involved in consciousness should help the reader to understand more fully the conscious activities about to be discussed. By the term *sensible* we mean everything that can be detected by sensation. An apple, as a colored object, is a sensible for sight and a frog's croak is a sensible for hearing. There is a division among sensibles inasmuch as some, the *proper sensibles*, are known first and without the mediation of any other sensible, while other sensibles are known only through the mediation of the proper sensibles. Thus the colors reflected by the apple are received immediately by the eye after being transmitted through the space between the apple and the eye. Color is all that is received because there is no adequate stimulus for sight other than reflected light and direct light.[6] But by means of that set of colors the apple can be distinguished from other things near it. Thus the leaves of a tree are a lighter green, and the trunk a darker green, than the apple.

The example just given illustrates the primary function of each sense, namely, the detection of the existence and appearance of the proper sensibles presented to it. Thus by sight we judge that there are two greens present in our environment and that they differ from one another in their degrees of greenness. This is not a reflexive judgment in which the sense is aware of conforming to the sensible. Rather it is an act of discrimination in which sight distinguishes various hues (shades) of color and intensities of hue, hearing detects various pitches and loudness of sound, and so on for the other senses. Thus the sensory judgment by which each sense discriminates the characteristics of its proper sensible is a person's primary contact with an object of sense consciousness. Figuratively speaking, it is the door through which all information about his physical self and his physical environment enters into his awareness. The proper sensible is completely defined when to the notion of its being the aspect of an object that is first detected by a sense we add that it is primary to all other sensed aspects of things, because they are known only by means of proper sensibles. Although the proper sensibles for sight and hearing are indefinitely numerous variations of colors and sounds, so much so that no person ever expects to sense all of them, nevertheless there are many other aspects of sensibles that are *sensed* by means of the proper sensibles and many things that are *understood* by means of the proper sensibles.

To illustrate, through color differences we can become aware of the distance location and the movement of apples on a tree, of the unity and yet the individual separateness of all the apples on one tree, of the fragility of an apple when crushed by a stone, of the strength of the tree trunk when buffeted by the wind, and so on. Among the many notions detected by color differences there is an essential division based upon the distinction between what is actually sensible and what is not.

COMMON SENSIBLES

That which is directly sensible but which is not a proper sensible is called a *common sensible*. The name "common sensible" indicates that certain sensible aspects of material objects are detected by more than one sense. Thus the size of an apple can be both seen and felt. But the name "common sensible" fails to indicate a more important fact about such sensibles, namely, that they are known only by means of the proper sensible aspects of things. Thus the size of an apple is detected by contrasting the colors of the apple with the colors that surround it, and by contrasting the feeling of the texture of the skin of the apple with the nonresistance of the air surrounding it. Because these common sensibles are known in a secondary way, by means of the proper sensibles, they are not discriminated by the senses with the same accuracy as the proper sensibles. To illustrate, our awareness of the presence of a white stone in our hand is not a difficult matter to ascertain, but the quantitative aspects of the stone, its size and weight, are difficult to apprise correctly by means of the proper sensibles without the aid of measuring instruments. In other words, when we judge (in a fully conscious state) that the stone is white and is pressing upon our hand, we are judging correctly, but when we judge that the stone in our hand is a little larger or smaller than the one on the ground, or that it is heavier or lighter than the other one, we are not assured of the correctness of these judgments until we have actually measured the stones for size and weight. In brief, *common sensibles can easily be misjudged* if we do not include standards of measurements in our appraisal. The fact that common sensibles can be known directly by measurement indicates that they represent the quantitative aspects of the material world.[7]

Accidental Sensibles

That which is not actually sensible in things but which is signified by its sensible aspects is called an *accidental sensible*, because a judgment of the identity of something can be made from its appearance. Thus a moving shape in the distance can be judged to be a man or a bear from its general form and upright posture. Obviously such judgments can be very tenuous indeed when the appearances are only remotely connected with the nature of the thing (size as being indicative of man or bear, or a statue or mirror image of either) and when the appearances are apprehended under unfavorable sensory conditions. Nevertheless, judgments about accidental sensibles can be quite accurate when the appearance used is an excellent sign of what it is an appearance of. For instance, a picture on a television receiver is an excellent sign that picture transmission is taking place somewhere; ripples on a watery surface are a sign that something is producing motion there; the release of heat in a chemical beaker is a sign that a chemical reaction is taking place, and so on.

The point to be noted about accidental sensibles and common sensibles is that the senses apprehend only their proper sensibles directly and the common sensibles mediately, and it is by means of these apprehensions that the judgments regarding the other sensibles are made. Some other judge (the intellect which will be discussed in detail later, in Chapter 5) is responsible for seeing the necessity of using standards in the exact apprehension of the quantitative aspects of the sensible and for discerning the factors involved in material being that are not discerned by the senses at all. Thus the third point of controversy listed under "Sensation as a Center of Controversy" at the beginning of this chapter, is seen to be untenable once the limitations of the senses and the scope of human apprehension are analyzed critically. To assert that there is an awareness of that which directly affects each exteroceptor, and yet to deny that there is a different kind of awareness that passes judgment on the appearances and natures of those causes of exteroceptor activity, is to fly in the face of the facts that man measures things and that man seeks constantly to know their nature.

The reason why the common sensibles are not grouped with the accidental sensibles, even though both are apprehended accurately only by acts of judgment, is that the common sensibles *do* make a difference in the sensing of the proper sensibles, whereas the accidental sensibles *do not*. Thus a large red surface appears differently to sight than does a small one, but it makes no difference to sight whether a red surface belongs to a real apple or a wax one. Furthermore, the senses discriminate between a large and a small quantity, a moving and a motionless body, and so on for the other common sensibles; it is for their *accurate* discrimination that arbitrary quantitative standards were initiated.

As far as practical usefulness is concerned, a knowledge of the common sensibles and the accidental sensibles is more important than an awareness of the proper sensibles. Of course, the quantities, the motions, and the natural qualities we make practical use of are detected only through the proper sensibles; therefore the proper sensibles are indispensable to human knowing.

But apart from the aesthetic value of beautiful colors and sounds it is the knowledge of what an object can be used for that is paramount in our animal life, and the knowledge of what something *is* (over and above its being a locus of appearances) that is of primary importance in our speculative life.

We may note here a certain irony about man's situation as a knower—the things that are of most interest to him, the fundamental elements in things and the knowledge of how to control his environment, are the most difficult for him to apprehend correctly. The history of practical and speculative science has been in large part the history of man's constant striving to overcome his inability to ascertain accurately the common sensible aspects of matter and the nature of things. The first-mentioned inability has yielded in large degree to man's ingenuity in devising and using instruments to measure exactly, and to manipulate, matter and energy. The second inability has diminished somewhat as experimental science has grown, but man still does not have an exhaustive knowledge of the nature of anything.

A table has been prepared to facilitate the reader's understanding of senses and sensibles. The usual five senses and the proprioceptors are listed as external senses, together with a physical description of the stimuli and an indication of the proper, common, and accidental sensibles. Since the internal senses do not lend themselves to this physiological method of analysis, they are not listed.

In the following numbered paragraphs we add more detail regarding sensibles in the table on page 108.

1. Each proper sensible has several variables, as well as varieties, so that there is a variety of colors in addition to more and less intense hues. Size and shape are not included as common sensibles under smell and taste, because although it is possible for one to roughly estimate sizes and shapes by smell and taste alone, it is not usual to do so. Sight and touch are much easier to employ for this purpose.

2. The motion listed as a common sensible for the sight, hearing, smell, taste, touch, and pain senses may be motion of the self or motion of another object indifferently, whereas motion detected through the vestibular sense and kinesthesis (sense of movement and position) is primarily motion of the self.

3. The common sensibles listed are basically those of

TABLE OF SENSES AND SENSIBILITIES
External Senses

SENSES	STIMULI	PROPER SENSIBLES	COMMON SENSIBLES	ACCIDENTAL SENSIBLES
Sight	Electromagnetic radiations of wavelengths from 800 to 300 millimicrons, received by rods and cones	Color, including black and white	Motion, size, shape, rest, multiplicity, and unity	coin, man, tree, apple, conflict. Thought as manifested by a purposeful structure
Hearing	Expansion and contraction of a compressible medium in contact with the eardrum or accessory organ	Sound of the object sensed	Motion, rest, multiplicity, and unity	Riot, collision. Thought as signified by words
Smell	Chemical properties of substances in contact with the olfactory membrane	Odors of the object sensed	Motion, rest, multiplicity, and unity	Candy, fruit, beverages
Taste	Chemical properties of substances in contact with taste buds	Flavors of the object sensed	Motion, rest, multiplicity, and unity	Candy, fruit, beverages
Touch	Light and heavy pressure produced by external contact, warmth and cold by external contact	Contact, pressures, and warmth-coldness	Motion, size, shape, rest, multiplicity, and unity	Weapon, sympathy, kind of cloth

Man's Physical and Spiritual Nature

SENSES	STIMULI	PROPER SENSIBLES	COMMON SENSIBLES	ACCIDENTAL SENSIBLES
Kinesthesis	Motion in muscles, tendons, and joints	Movement of bodily parts with respect to one another	Motion, rest, and multiplicity	The physical self
Vestibular sense	Motion or change of motion of head alone and of body as a whole as affecting position of head	Nothing apprehended that can be recognized as peculiar to the arousing of this sense. The movement that activates this sense apprehended by kinesthesis. Reponse a reflex one	Motion	The physical self
Pain sense	Multiple stimuli, such as heavy or sharp contact, excess cold and warmth, and cutting	Pain	Motion, size, and shape (of painful object), rest, and multiplicity	The physical self

Aristotle's text with substitution of multiplicity for number (Ross translation), because number as an intellectual grouping of units is not a sensible. The list may appear to be incomplete, since location can be discerned by all of the five senses. Aristotle considered the common sensibles in a rather offhand manner (*De Anima* III 1, 425a, 15-17) whereas St. Thomas listed them as being reducible to quantity (*S.T.*, I, 78, 3, ad2), which they obviously are. Since extension, and therefore location, are as inseparable from quantity as are size and shape, but the detection of size and shape presupposes an awareness of location, it may be that he did not think it necessary to list location separately.[8]

4. Aristotle encountered some difficulty in assigning a proper sensible for touch (*De Anima* II, 11, 422b 16ff.). The

Sensory Experience as Knowledge

genus for the various kinds of touch could be called macroscopic contact to distinguish it from molecular contact in smelling and tasting and from the microscopic size of light waves or particles involved in retinal stimulation. But then this would not exclude the contact made by air involved in hearing. It seems more fitting to assign pressure, warmth, and cold as the proper sensibles for touch and to leave the question open as to whether it is better to save the usual sense of the word "touch" and assign three objects of its awareness, or to list the warmth sense and the cold sense as two more senses over and above touch.

5. The accidental sensibles listed simply give an indication of what is meant. The lists are not at all complete, and more could easily be supplied for sight and hearing as well as for the other senses. Of course, the proper and common sensibles as things that are understood are included among the accidental sensibles.

6. The vestibular sense might be disqualified as a sense since we have no conscious discrimination through it, but it does discriminate changes of position and of motion.

Extent of Sensory Organs

On the basis of distinct stimuli and nerve pathways, physiology distinguishes the various senses. In an attempt to explain these differences further some investigators allege that the ultimate basis of the distinction between hearing and seeing and the other senses is in the different locations in the brain where the afferent pathways from the various receptors terminate. Such a theory ignores the specificity of the receptors. It is true that light touch, taste, smell and the vestibular sense, and hearing all have hair cells as their receptors, but these hair cells are quite specific as to which stimuli they will react to. The hairs of a person's arm react to simple contact; but the hair cells of the cochlea and the vestibular apparatus are within fluid systems, which transmit the touch to them, and cannot be acted upon by direct contact with external stimuli. The hair cells in the taste buds and the olfactory membrane detect as flavors and odors only chemicals in solution that touch the hair cells. For the sense of sight there are no hair cells, only the rods and cones.

This diversity of receptor organs would be pointless if

the only distinction between sensations were the area of the brain involved. Actually there is a greater difference among the various kinds of stimuli receptors than there is among the structures of the various cells in the brain. It has been found in every science that difference in form is accompanied by a difference in activity. Thus the heart can act as a pump for the blood because of the kind of muscle it is. So, too, the eye can react to color because it is a certain kind of receptor, but the ear cannot be stimulated by light. The question as to what physical organ will be involved in any sensation can be answered in this way: The receptor cannot engage in conscious activity unless its natural connections in the central nervous system are intact; there also cannot be any conscious sensation through a defective receptor. Therefore at least the receptor and its afferent connections to the central nervous system are the organ.[9]

Distinction of Powers

Physiological data are basically physical and chemical; as such they throw no light upon the conscious part of conscious activities. For this reason physiological data can only be used indirectly to distinguish the various kinds of conscious activities in which man engages. An analysis of cortical structure shows physiological differences in various areas, but none of these differences is very marked. The functions of these areas are discovered by tracing various afferent and efferent nerves from one area to another of the central nervous system and to distinct parts of the body. The route taken, and the function of the part of the body wherein the nerve terminates, may give a hint as to the function of the part of the cortex involved. The function of these areas can also be discovered by interfering with normal cortical operations and by seeing what effects are produced thereby. Experiments of this kind, however, presuppose that the difference between apprehending for the first time and remembering something that has been apprehended before, is easily recognizable. That is to say, the distinction of various ways of being aware must precede any discussion as to which parts of the human body are involved in the awareness. Therefore, since no criterion extrinsic to consciousness can be used to distinguish one conscious act from another, some criterion from within consciousness must be adopted for this purpose.

Some of the difficulties involved in distinguishing the various external senses have already been discussed. But there are other difficulties in assigning the number and precise roles of the internal senses because their activities are usually so closely connected in time as to be temporally inseparable.[10] We must therefore construct the basis for distinguishing various kinds of conscious activity before we can discuss the internal senses in more detail.

Since we are going to speak of individual sense powers or sense faculties, it is necessary to anticipate the immediate criticism of those who consider "faculty" to be a spurious notion. Let us consider one such opinion: "Also the psychologist has no faith in the doctrine of "faculties" or packaged units of generosity, truthfulness, talkativeness, or friendliness, partly because physiological studies of brain activity fail to demonstrate such isolated functions." [11]

This use of the term "faculty" does not agree with our usage. The difficulty stems from the misconception of a perfectly valid notion and the past use of the notion in contexts where it did not apply. The valid notion is that of a distinct activity: Seeing is not hearing, and walking is not reasoning.

DEFINITION OF POWER

Seeing, walking, and reasoning are activities as distinct from one another as receiving information is different from acting upon it and as both of them differ from turning over ideas in one's mind. In the first case the person is being acted upon by his environment; in the second he is acting upon the environment; and in the third case only his thoughts are involved. Therefore the activities just mentioned cannot reasonably be said to be identical. But the person who acts in these different ways is one and the same person acting in three different ways simultaneously. To indicate that these abilities reside in one person we use the term "power," which means simply *the ability to do something*. Thus one person can act in various ways; that is, one person has several powers.

The term "faculty" has been used with several meanings,

one of which is identical to our meaning of power. Thus the "faculty of speech" means the ability to speak and the "faculty of sight" means the ability to see. Sometimes the term "faculty" is used to indicate not only the ability to be exercised, but also the organ of the body through which it occurs. Thus the "faculty of sight" could be taken to mean the eye and its physiological processes as well as the ability to see. By using only the terms "organ" and "power" here, we shall avoid the ambiguity of "faculty."

So-called Faculties as Dispositions

Some powers have the characteristic that they may be used in various ways, as one may walk quickly or slowly. A tendency to use a power consistently in a certain way, always to seek a reason for holding an opinion, for example, is called a *disposition*. Dispositions come into being usually from our desiring that we shall act in such and such a way. Thus the "faculties" mentioned in the quotation above are mere dispositions to act in one way rather than another. "Generosity" is a disposition to allow the use of one's own goods by others, "truthfulness" is a tendency to make our speech conform with our correct thought, "talkativeness" is a tendency to use our powers of speech excessively, "friendliness" is a tendency to take an interest in others. Who can deny that there are such dispositions in many persons? To expect to locate such dispositions physiologically is akin to looking for little pictures in the brain. No one should believe in a "faculty" psychology that talks of dispositions as being packaged units, any more than one should accept a psychology that attempts to explain man but refuses to distinguish the various powers by which he acts. The dispositions in question can easily be seen to be results of the act of the will, but only by those who are willing to distinguish the will from the lesser powers that are moved by it.[12]

Power and Object

What is it about powers that has led to their rejection as genuine elements of explanation by some psychologists? Apparently it is the diversity of ways of acting on the part of some powers that raises the question as to whether one or several powers are involved. For example, man's ability to see can attain to everything in the universe that can reflect light to the eye. In the realm of visibles there are large and small visibles, fast and slow visibles; bright and dull, green and red, old and young, and painful and happy visibles. We do not posit different senses of sight for the large and the small, and for the other varieties of visibles because they all come under one sense They are visible no matter what else they may be. There is no difficulty, then, in describing the object of the power of sight as the visible. By *object* of an apprehensive power we mean that of which it is conscious in its act of apprehension. A further distinction can be made between the *material object* of an apprehensive power, *the thing as a whole that is known;* and the *formal object, the aspect of the thing by which it is known.* Thus a singing bird is a material object for both sight and hearing, but its visible aspect is a formal object for sight alone and its song is known only to hearing. Hence the basis for distinguishing various powers is the distinction of various formal aspects. These formal aspects are called proper sensibles when reference is to the external senses; in other instances they are simply called formal objects.

Our task now is to attempt to discern the formal objects of the internal senses. We shall distinguish the internal from the external senses and each internal sense from the other on the basis of irreducible differences in their acts of discrimination, keeping in mind that no sense power can make a reflexive judgment—a judgment about its own act. By using these two criteria we shall distinguish *an ability to retain the sensory impressions* discriminated by the external senses and *an ability to retain the temporal orientation of some events* that we have experienced. Further analysis will lead to positing *an ability to discriminate the suitable from the unsuitable* in our environment and also a sensory awareness *that discriminates the acts of each external and internal sense except its own*—a general power of sensory consciousness.

The Internal Senses

THE IMAGINATION

In direct sensation the receptor end organs are acted upon by the stimuli adequate to move them. Apprehension results if we are attentive to this act of our environment upon us. The apprehension of one visual area precludes the simultaneous apprehension of an entirely different one located elsewhere. Thus the engagement of our attention upon the visible objects in front of us excludes the possibility of our seeing what is going on two yards directly behind us at the same time. If we switch our attention and our gaze to some other area, we no longer actually see the first one.[13] Although the number of scenes that sight can discriminate successively is endless, sight (or any external sense), when functioning normally, can never reproduce in itself a visual impression received once before. The only way that such a sensation can be repeated is by having the original visibles confront sight once again. In brief, sight does not retain impressions. The same limitation applies to all of the external senses, because the sense is in act only when the sensible is actually present.

Although the individual external sense does not retain its impression of the sensible, we can at will retain our impression of some sensibles or recall them to our attention when the actual sensibles are no longer present. Thus we can often remember the visible sensed sensible, as we once sensed it, but not by means of the sense that actually discriminated it. Anyone can be aware of the continuity between an actually sensed visible and the memory of it. For example, engage in a game of checkers and close your eyes to visualize the future moves that you will make. The checkerboard actually seen and the one visualized when the eyes are closed are identical for all practical purposes of locating the colored squares and the disks on them. The remembered checkerboard is continuous with the one actually seen, so much so that it seems necessary to hold that the actual seeing of the one is the cause of our remembering it.[14] This seems especially reasonable when we consider that our identification of a presently viewed object as one that was viewed in the past requires a pretty close similarity between the object viewed in the past and our memory of it. We can never reproduce the actual union with the sensible to confirm that our memory is exact, however, for that union is irretrievably in the past.

Nevertheless our conscious awareness clearly distinguishes between the actually being seen visible and the remembered one. For if a person is fully conscious, not daydreaming or dreaming at night, he has no illusion that the *image* which he recalls, or simply retains as actual seeing ceases, is anything but an image. Although this transition from actually seeing to merely retaining an image of the sensibles as seen often passes unnoticed, it implies a necessary distinction between the power that apprehends the sensible and the one that retains our impression of it. Each power can be acting simultaneously with respect to numerically different sensibles, as when we compare the color and size of the checkerboard in front of us with a larger one that we previously used in another city. Or, to illustrate further, the elaboration of a very large, approximately circular, dark green apple in the imagination, by comparison with which the scrubby cooking apple on the table is markedly inferior, is an activity that may be prompted by our having seen the cooking apple, but it certainly is not modeled upon the appearance of the cooking apple. Thus the human imagination is a memory power by which we can *retain our sensory impressions of things* as the direct senses actually discriminated them, or *consider something* that was previously apprehended but which is *quite different from what is actually present*, or *make up something* that is as similar or as dissimilar to what has been sensed as one pleases to make it. The formal object of imagination is the sensible not actually present, that is, the sensible as an *image;* its activity is the retention of the sights, sounds, tastes, and so forth, that we have sensed. Thus the word "image" in this context is used to stand for memories of the audible, the gustatory, the tangible, and the olfactory, as well as the visual.

The term *imagination* was probably used originally to indicate that this sense power is concerned with mere *images* of reality; whereas sight, hearing, and the other direct senses are concerned with the actual things of which they discriminate the sensible aspects. But if there is the continuity between the actual sensing and the image produced in the imagination that we have asserted does exist, then the image in the imagination can serve just as well as the actual appearance of a thing as a means of knowing something about it. Thus the images in the imagination serve not only as a means of recalling and identifying singular things—they can also furnish a basis for detecting what is common and enduring in sensible things.

The direct senses cannot of themselves make the past present to us, but the imagination can provide the retained impressions upon which we depend for apprehension of a temporal continuity in the appearances of things. This continuity enables us to know which features are common to several things and thus to recognize kinds of things by their appearances. It is in this way that we can distinguish varieties of things by the impressions they make upon our senses: eggs from oranges, stones from berries, and so on. In this matter we do not need to know in a definitive way what an egg is or what an orange is (both can be defined as containers of living seeds carrying on the work of propagating a species). It suffices that we can recognize them as distinct for practical purposes. The sensible aspects of things are *signs* of what they mean to us in a practical way, and can also be signs of what they are in themselves to our intellect. The hardness of the stone to the teeth and its relative insolubility in saliva are signs of its inedibility; while the softness, taste, and nonharmfulness of the oranges and berries are signs of their edibility. These practical signs are sufficient to enable us to recognize the items in question. Other animals use such signs, too. This indicates an essential role played by the imagination in the preservation of life: the recognition of food in the present depends to some extent upon memory of past experience, which records many signs of what is useful and what is harmful in our environment.[15] In fact, one *may even define the imagination as a storehouse of signs*. It is from these signs of the usefulness of things that our practical knowledge of things develops, as we shall see in Chapter 6.

CREATIVE IMAGINATION

By *creative imagination* we mean the imagination as a producer of appearances we have not experienced, although we have experienced the elements out of which these new appearances are made. The designer of the settings of a stage play uses his imagination to create a scene. The fiction writer imagines the sequences necessary to develop the plot of his story; the surgeon imagines new techniques to reach the difficult part of an organ to correct a disorder. In these examples the materials being used by the imagination have been garnered from previous experience; the creator in each case is rearranging them tentatively to see if they will accommodate his intentions. Thus in his imagination he can perform activities that he cannot afford to undertake in reality until he sees what the result will probably be.

Anything that can be adequately represented by a *determinate* image can be stored by the imagination. Thus it is a storehouse not only of naturally occurring appearances, but also of conventional signs, for these are quite determinate. Such conventional signs are the letters of the alphabet, and all combinations of them in language; chemical and mathematical formulas; and the like. Because the meanings of these conventional signs are quite often the subject of debate, they can hardly be said to be determined strictly. But the symbols are quite determinate, for they are sensible signs of meanings. As the retainer of conventional signs, the imagination comes under the direct control of the intellect because when the conventional symbols are used they are arranged according to some meaning that they can express and not according to natural appearances. For example, if a person wishes to express his understanding of the function of food in maintaining life, he must recall the necessary words as he speaks them, and the words he uses will have conventional meanings. Thus the movement of his thought in detailing the function of food is paralleled by the imaginative activity of recalling in the desired sequence the conventional terms that are to be orally expressed or written. In brief, then, the function of the imagination as a storehouse of signs is to store both natural and conventional signs.

The versatility of the imagination as an instrument for expressing our thoughts and for solving problems presented in symbolic form is quite obvious. The imagining of words to be spoken or written is a synthesis of combinations of conventional symbols that may not have existed in that form previously for the person involved. The working out of a solution to a mathematical or a chemical problem by manipulating scientific symbols is a replication on the sensory level of the actual manipulation on the physical level of the things symbolized. In a similar manner the average person may plan the parts of a future action. But in this activity the person is projecting his being into the future by picturing the goal to be achieved and picturing his possession of it.

The imagination, then, is a sense of the past and of the future, but it does not master the temporal aspects of reality by itself alone, as we shall explain shortly. Since the imagination has such a diversity of functions—recalling, creating, problem-solving, and projecting into the future—should we not distinguish different powers for these operations? This is not necessary, because all of these actions are concerned with making us aware now of determinate images that are formed according to something that has occurred or will occur in our experience. However, there is another multiplicity involved in remembering what we have seen, heard, touched, and so on. It is the same multiplicity of formal aspects that led to our distinguishing a multiplicity of external senses. Should there not be a distinct memory for each one of these external senses, since their proper sensibles both are discriminated separately from each other and also can be recalled separately from each other? We take as evidence for our position that only one sense need be posited for atemporal sensory recall the fact that we can recall the visual, olfactory, and gustatory impressions of a satisfying steak as three impressions of one thing in one single act of remembering. It is the aspect of satisfying in our remembered experience of the steak which, because it has no visible or other proper sensible aspects, requires the distinction of another sense to account for it. Thus the specific activity that differentiates the imagination from the direct senses is its concern with what is not actually present[16]—it differs from the other internal senses in that it merely stores impressions.

Temporal Memory

There are several determinate relationships that cannot be represented by any proper or common sensibles, and hence the imagination cannot be aware of them. The first of these relationships is the time factor associated with material things. If we accept a philosophical definition of time, the numbering or measurement of change according as it is successive and continuous, then there must be some explanation of how we are made aware of time. Clock and calender time are measures of earthly and lunar motions; we can become aware of these instruments by sight, and of their meaning by intellectual understanding. But these presuppose that we have some awareness of duration; otherwise we could not refer their measurements to anything. We are aware of the duration of an act of direct sensation because the duration is an inseparable element of the stimulus activity and of our awareness. But when it comes to remembering the duration of a sensory experience or placing it in the past, the image of what was experienced is of no help. If we gaze at an apple for 30 seconds (a comparatively long time), we increase our apprehension of details somewhat over the period of time, but the image by which we remember the apple can be recalled and appreciated in a second or two. The 30-second duration of the original sensation cannot be imagined, but it can be remembered. There seems to be no alternative but to posit a sense power with a concern for the temporal aspects of things.

Since we retain very many experiences without any deliberate effort, noticing them only when some occasion arises for recalling them, it seems most probable that the imagination retains as images every sensible ever sensed. Its storing of impressions is intimately based upon the neural processes that never fail to occur when stimulus is adequate. It seems impossible, therefore, that by an external sense we should be clearly aware of a sensed sensible without this sensed sensible's being recorded by our imagination. But we cannot easily recall to mind experiences that made very little impression on us. In fact, of the multitude of sensory experiences a person has in one day, there are many that he could not recall at all.[17] If we say to X, "Tell me exactly what you were doing at one minute after nine o'clock last Saturday morning," he is likely to reply, "I don't know." If we can relate to X exactly what he was doing at the stated moment, there is still only a slight chance that X will recall it. Let us suppose that, during the specified minute X was trying to write a letter to his mother. He cast his glance around the room occasionally, registering the colors and shapes that his gaze encountered but paying little attention to them. He could not recall any of those visual appearances later as being the content of his consciousness at the specified moment, because they made an insufficient impression on him to be retained in a definite temporal sequence. He could recall writing the letter and the general time of day from our reminder of his actions, but the appearances of his surroundings and even the contents of his letter might escape him unless he accompanied us to the particular room and reread the letter. But upon doing that he would probably recall them quite well as being located in a definite period of his past.

All sensations have a very definite location in the calendar and clock measurement of time, but some of them obviously are not as firmly located in our temporal awareness as others. No one, philosopher or physiologist, has been able to claim success in explaining how the identification of the "pastness" of past experience is retained. Nevertheless, one relationship between the memory of temporal aspects of experience and the characteristics of what is being sensed is evident: Those experiences involving a distinct value for us personally are retained and firmly located in the time sequence. (See Note 22.) Such values as the *necessity* of consuming this food to ward off starvation and of using this piece of clothing to ward off the painfulness of the winter's cold, the *usefulness* of saving this food for later and the *pleasurableness* of tasting this drink are not capable of being represented in an image, as their abstract form of expression indicates. The events that proved to be useful and necessary, however, involved sensibles whose appearances could be easily retained. That these appearances were more easily remembered than the thousands of others apprehended in the *recent past* suggests that their *connection with a valuable experience* is the basis for their being easily remembered.

The same connection between the discrimination of value for us personally in some sensed part of our environment and our ability to recall a past event is found when we consider our *distant past*. Events that at the moment are located indiscriminately in our distant past can be located according to clock and calendar time if the events were sufficiently impressive at the time they occurred. Thus X can easily recall that there was an occasion in his life when he nearly drowned and that he avoided death by his own strenuous efforts, which took him to shallow water. He usually tells of this incident as happening in his early youth, no exact date being remembered until he deliberately sets out to find it by connecting it up with other remembered events of his past life. By comparing the dates of these events he eventually locates the date of the near-drowning. We call this process of connecting past events in a definite temporal sequence *reminiscence*. No one reminisces to recall quite unimportant events.

Even older persons who have retired from active life and spend much of their time reminiscing dwell mainly on details of the past that were impressive in their own estimation at the time. Thus thousands of sensed details of our past experience are never recalled, because they made little impression at the time of their apprehension and they have not acquired any further significance with the passage of time.

We have posited two powers whose activity is to present to our present awareness the appearances and the temporal location of events that are not actually present: that which retains sensed sensibles as mere impressions we have called the *imagination;* the other we call temporal *memory.* Thus the recalling of images as an aid to understanding or as the occasion for talking about something not present involves the imagination as the power that *presents the sensible scene.* Even if that sensible scene is a freely imagined one, a triangular path of light having the sun the moon and the earth as its three points, it can embody some value for the person imagining it and thus be the subject of instant recall on a later occasion. Its value may stem from its usefulness in the act of abstracting, or of creating, or of embodying a meaning. In these instances the sensible scene is valuable to our intellectual activity. This aspect of the temporal memory and of the imagination will be treated in detail in Chapter 5. The temporal memory is involved in another kind of activity wherein it serves the sense appetites and the will. This aspect will be treated in Chapters 7 and 8. Our present treatment of the temporal memory has been to show it as one of the internal senses involved in retaining in a temporal sequence those events of our experience that impressed us.

THE GENERAL POWER OF SENSE

The term *sensus communis,* which has been in usage for centuries to designate the common root of the other senses, means *common sense* when translated from Latin. But in our times "common sense" is the name given to the human prudence that is based upon the most obvious information about our environment. Therefore we shall use a name that appears to us to characterize suitably the special nature of this sense—*the general power of sense.* The attention of this sense power is directed to the activity of the other senses except the vestibular sense. One of its activities becomes obvious when we consider, that although we detect the coldness of an ice cube by touch and its whiteness by sight, we can still identify the object felt as the object seen. Since we cannot see warmth and cold, nor feel color, we must possess an ability to know these two sensibles under some higher formality, a sense that can know both sensibles simultaneously and yet as sensibly diverse. It might seem that we can easily make this identification by seeing that our hand is touching the ice. But in fact all that we see is the juxtaposition of the hand and the ice. The awareness that the hand is indeed being cooled by contact with the ice is proper to the sense of touch. The identification that it is the same thing which is white and which is cold can only be made by an awareness that encompasses both of these proper sensibles. The case is similar for identifying by sight the source of a sound. What hearing discriminates is greater and lesser sounds; sight is used by our general power of sense to detect the location of the sound with the maximum intensity. Since sight is not aware of sound and does not of itself communicate with hearing, only our ability to be aware of both of these sensibles simultaneously can identify a visible as the source of the sound. Often our identification of the sources of several sensible impressions is merely an inference based on past experience. In such cases we make use of signs to come to conclusions. Regarding such inferences we should note that sensible impressions cannot be true or false for they are effects of the sensibles upon us, but our inferences can be false for they are judgments.

The person rapt up in the sound of music can become impervious to all scenes registering upon his retina and to most touch stimuli. This is manifested by his not responding to gentle visual and tactile stimuli; he cannot even recall them when he is aroused from his concentration on the music. In other words, although the sense organs for sight and touch were being acted upon, our music lover was not paying attention to them. There is a definite distinction between looking at something and actually seeing it, and between listening to sounds and actually hearing them. That distinction is between our fully conscious presence to the sense in question and our concentration upon the act of some other sense which makes us inattentive to the first one. In brief, the general power of sense is to some extent capable of greater and lesser attention to the activities of the other senses.

Conversely we can distinguish between the presence of a sensible and the absence of it to any of the external senses as well as between the activity and nonactivity of the imagination, memory, and cogitative senses. Thus anyone can be aware, by hearing, of the presence of a sound and, by consciousness of not hearing, of its absence; likewise for the other sensibles. Similarly we can distinguish between an actual seeing of something and an imaginary or remembered seeing of something. Because this ability to distinguish the being of an actual visible from the being of an imagined or remembered visible depends upon our degree of consciousness (we do not easily make this discrimination when we are semiconscious in sleep), some authors tend to use *consciousness* as a synonym for *sensus communis*. As long as this use of the term "consciousness" is restricted to sensory consciousness, and as long as it means no more than the act of awareness of the general power of sense, the name is acceptable. There is an intellectual awareness also in the human acts of apprehension which must not be confused with sensory activity.

Let us recapitulate what we know of the general faculty of sense and fill in any omissions in describing its activities. Functioning as our awareness of the various acts of the other senses, this general faculty discriminates between the presence of a sensed sensible and the absence of one in an external sense. It also distinguishes actually-being-sensed sensibles from merely imagined or remembered sensibles. Furthermore, by it we can discriminate normal and accurate functioning of a sense from such malapprehensions as occur when a visual scene is too bright or too dim, or when a sound is too loud or too soft or too shrill for accurate sensory apprehension. The general faculty of sense is physiologically distinct from the external senses inasmuch as it uses no external receptor end organ, for the injury or destruction of any one of the exteroceptors deprives it of information but does not affect its normal activity with the sensation remaining. Furthermore, it is directly affected by injury to the brain even though the receptor organs of the external senses are not physically affected thereby. The organ of the general faculty of sense is apparently the brain or some part thereof.

As the indispensable awareness necessary for sifting various sensations of one object (the cold and grayness of the ice cube) and simultaneous sensations from diverse objects, the general faculty of sense is that by which we identify the sensible appearances that go together in the imagination's representation of a complex of sensibles. Thus, to remember the smell, the appearance, the taste of a certain food is to retain three sensible aspects of one item as being proper to that one item. Since these aspects were apprehended diversely, it must be the general power of sense that identifies the common locus in reality of the impressions recalled by the imagination. All identification of a common source of aspects which are apprehended by diverse external senses is made by the common power of sense, because the proper senses are so limited in their scope of apprehension that they cannot be aware of one another's proper sensible.

We have treated some of the internal senses in the order of increasing difficulty (from our viewpoint), and so have left the most difficult to the last—the sense power concerned with the concrete sensorily based values of things and actions to the individual person. Some writers explaining this sense have pointed to the activities of nonhuman animals that aspire to goals that are suitable for the animal. Such actions, they say, imply that the animal possesses a knowledge of those goals as attainable by following a set of series of actions. They use this sensory ability in nonhuman animals as an analogue of a similar sense power in man. But we know very little about the conscious activities of nonhuman animals. Therefore, to argue that because animals have a sense power for knowledge of concrete goals man must also have a similar sense power is to argue from what is somewhat obscure to us to what can be made evident by reflection upon our everyday human activities. Experimental techniques are throwing some light on what the nonhuman animal acquires by learning, and the determination as to what sensory information may be assumed to be innate in a given species of animal seems to be a task for that kind of investigation. Our arguments as to the existence and nature of the cogitative sense will be based upon evidence available to everyone.

THE NEED OF EXPERIENCE

Two persons attempting to build a garage will have quite different success if the first is a good carpenter and the second is a complete novice in all manual arts. If the carpenter takes pity on the fumbling novice and tells him explicitly how to perform each act involved in the construction, the novice may then *understand* what to do but may nevertheless still make a very unsatisfactory structure. The ingredient the novice lacks, which is wellnigh impossible to pass on to him by mere words, is the skill that comes with practice, that is, with the kind of participation called *experience*. His senses and his understanding are involved when he listens to the carpenter, and he may even make use of intellectual experience in translating the carpenter's terms into ones that are more familiar to himself. The experience that he needs for acquiring the skill of carpentry, however, is one in which he is involved as a physical agent. It is a committing of his physical capacities to doing something or making something. No activities of this kind can be carried out apart from the use of our senses in directing and observing the results of our activities. Moreover, the results of the activities cannot escape falling under our opinion that the actions done or the things made are suitable to the desires that prompted us to them. Although opinions are expressions of intellectual activity, there is something akin to them on the sensory level accompanying many of our activities as we assess what suits us physically in what we are doing, as well as what is unsuitable and to be avoided. Thus, in guiding one's hand in holding nails being struck and in holding a board that is being cut, there is a constant estimating of the position of the hand, the paths of the tools as they are being used, the near misses, the suitableness of withdrawing the hand because its support is no longer necessary, and so on. Over a period of time a person who keeps repeating one kind of activity develops a "feel" for what is the most suitable way in his estimation to execute that activity. The skill he develops depends upon that judgment of what is best—an estimation that cannot be transmitted to another by mere words. It is gained only by experience—physical involvement in doings and makings—and can be decreased or lost by lack of use. It is not merely a motor habit; it is the sensory accompaniment of motor habits that accumulated as the habit was developed and that serves as a ready reference in giving advice to others concerning the skill in question, and in projecting one's own actions successfully toward the end for which the skill is used.

Different kinds of experience can serve as a basis for different skills. Experience of itself, however, will not automatically produce skill in anyone. There must be the continual desire to improve the making or doing involved, for it is quite possible to repeat actions over and over again without improving their efficiency. In such an instance no "feeling" for the task is developed, and this lack of know-how is a part of our awareness of our physical being. Although no skills are innate in man (although many of the desires that give rise to motor skills are innate), some persons seem to have a natural aptitude for one skill or another, or even for several different skills, so that they require much less experience to become proficient than do others not so endowed. But having only an aptitude conferred by nature is not sufficient for skillful making and doing; the details to be mastered by practical activity must be supplied by sensory experience. Furthermore, in order to progress toward skill one must profit by his mistakes and successes: by eliminating or modifying unsuccessful actions and repeating and improving successful ones. Thus what is presupposed in developing a commercial skill is also presupposed in every suitably successful human doing and making.

THE COGITATIVE POWER

On the intellectual level we call assimilated experience a *habit of science* or a *habit of opinion*, according as the intellect achieves certitude in its understanding, or only probability. These habits will be investigated later. More basic in the knowing process is the sensory experience upon which each human being bases his doings and makings. The term *cogitative power* indicates that the kind of sensory evaluation man uses in initiating or furthering the course of an activity is acquired by a comparison process (cogitating) in which the result of one way of doing something is seen to be more in accord with what was desired than are alternative methods. For it is as a result of acting and of assessing the consequences of our actions that we develop a sensory ability to distinguish the suitable from the unsuitable in our ways of acting and of being acted upon. Thus we learn (and remember) that bumping (action) into hard or sharp things is usually painful and that being warmed by the sun (being acted upon) is desirable when temperatures are moderate, and undesirable when temperatures are very high. It is the discriminating of the way the sun actually warmed us and the accompanying well-being that we experienced that we attribute to this sensory power. By it we assess the suitability of present and past experiences and use this information to guide us in our future actions. Cogitative sense is not concerned with *what it is to be comfortable* or *what it is to be frustrated* but with *actually being comfortable* and with *actually failing to fulfill a felt need.*

Thus from desires comes a tendency to satisfy them, and from acting upon this tendency and evaluating the results (the discerning of whether or not the goal of the action was attained, and if so, what satisfaction it yielded) comes the experience necessary to satisfy future desires to the needed degree of fulfillment. (Cf. Chapter 7 for many detailed examples.)

This activity of the cogitative sense is called *estimating,* that is, the assessing of the achieved or probable results of some action. It is the activity of estimating the probability that a certain set of actions will attain a definite end. The end may have a negative characteristic—it may be the avoidance of something noxious or deadly, rather than the positive attainment of some enjoyable good. Thus a man who works with deadly materials governs his actions according to a strong tendency to preserve his own well-being as he works. That there is more involved here than mere observation is obvious when we consider that the terms "suitable" and "unsuitable," which designate the formality in things that this sense discriminates, imply the physical self as that for which a doing or a receiving of activity is suitable. In other words the desirous self is involved—the person as moved by desires to satisfy such physical needs as the need for food and drink, the need for muscular activity (recreation), the need to avoid discomfort and to attain a comfortable environment. In order to estimate what is suitable to one's physical self that state of that self (how we feel) must be known, as well as what actions proved to be suitable with respect to that state in the past.

The cogitative sense is also called the *particular reason,* because the practical information we store as sensory experience is obtained by comparing past successful actions with present possible ones and the term "reason" indicates the power to compare various known aspects of things. By his particular reason man not only profits from his individual past experience in constantly positing actions to satisfy his needs, but he can also put understood patterns of action into effect by cognizing in a concrete situation the various elements that he has understood in an intellectual, and therefore general, manner. Thus, to tell a small child to "close a door" may be ineffectual, because his notion of closing something has been limited to putting tops on jars and putting his lips together; whereas to tell a more mature person to "pick the smallest orange in the basket" is to ask him to recognize differences in size as an interpretation of "smallest," to interpret "orange" as distinct from other kinds of fruit in the basket, and to interpret "pick" as a lifting operation.

Because of its function in discerning what matters to us physically in that which falls under the direct senses, it is to the cogitative sense that we attribute the discernment of all of that information which is stored by temporal memory. As a sign that this is the case we can try to recall something from the past in which we are not physically or at least emotionally (directly or vicariously, as when we relate the experiences of others to ourselves) involved, but in vain. That which is worth remembering, of the countless things and events that we experience, is what affects us in more than a merely cognitive way. Thus no proper or common sensible, considered in itself, has any greater or lesser importance for us except in terms of what we desire. Hence we posit the cogitative sense to discriminate the more and the less valuable, the necessary and the valueless, in the operable factors of our environment. As a result any person who has lived long enough to be able to do for himself in any way has some estimations of what to do in most situations, in order to better himself by acting to acquire something or to avoid something undesirable. This ability does not imply that each person understands the natures of the things involved in his pursuits and avoidances, but only that he can discriminate desire-satisfying activities from fruitless ones. Furthermore, we call this power *particular reason* to indicate that it is invaluable in interpreting how abstract formulas, statements of fact, or statements of actions to be undertaken are to be interpreted and applied in concrete situations. Since such interpretations are made by each person in every situation that demands both action and the understanding of the situation, there can be no doubt about the existence of this power.

The presupposition that underlies the whole preceding deduction is that what one power alone discriminates is proper to that power. Furthermore, this discrimination cannot be known by any other power except one whose formal viewpoint is distinctly more encompassing so that it not only knows what is apprehended in the act of another power, but knows other things, too. Of necessity, then, our analysis began with the most obvious distinctions between the external senses and proceeded to a hierarchy of powers in which these senses are the least knowing ones because they are determined so strictly in their scope to the proper sensibles. But as we distinguish powers higher in the hierarchy, the very fact that the higher powers cognize several lesser viewpoints simultaneously is a distinct difficulty in our assignment of objects to powers. Because we had to resort to reflection and argument in order to discern the four internal senses, those who believe that only overt evidence of a distinction is reliable find the positing of the general power of sense and the cogitative sense difficult to accept. Yet, despite this difficulty the facts remain that man is *one agent acting in a multiplicity of diverse ways* and *a patient receiving stimuli in many modes of reception.* No other account of man than one that distinguishes various abilities within him is adequate to these facts.

We shall now consider the intentional aspect of sensing, that is, the representational aspect, in order to see what kind of activity sensing is.

Sensation as Intentional Union

The term *perception* is widely used today to refer to the act of discriminating the sensory aspects of our universe. Some authors oppose perception to sensation as the being aware of the present sensible (in terms of what the sensible is and in terms of the memories of it that spring into our consciousness upon viewing the sensible), as opposed to the mere reception of stimuli in the end organs. But there is no such thing as a mere reception of stimuli in the end organs, unless it be when the person is semi-conscious in sleep or rapt up in some matter that makes him impervious to the stimulus. In both of these cases, however, no awareness is present. We prefer to consider "sensation" and "perception" as synonyms for the whole act of conscious discrimination of the presence and appearance of a sensible to a sense. The distinction between discriminating some present sensibles and *recognizing* them as similar to what was sensed previously, or as being signs of a certain nature, or as signifying the possibility of some worthwhile action is a distinction between the acts of the external senses by themselves and the acts of the external and internal senses in conjunction. Each kind of act is equally a sensory act although the second is more complete. The term perception may have a distinct meaning from mere sensation when applied to this more complete kind of act. But in everyday parlance this distinction is not adhered to; consequently we will attempt to be so explicit in the ensuing exposition of sensory activity as to avoid all confusion to the reader regarding the aspect of sensation in question.

The specific nature of an agent determines the kind of effect the agent will produce in the subject that it acts upon. Thus a warming agent will warm what it contacts; a dissolving agent will dissolve some substances put in contact with it; and a hard material will deform and even crush living flesh. On the side of that which is acted upon, there are determinants modifying the effect of an action. Thus a sheet of asbestos will be warmed only a trifle by the flame of a gas burner, whereas the same flame will make a sheet of copper quickly become too warm to touch with the uncovered hand; salt will dissolve rapidly in water, but glass will not be affected by water; and a steel-pointed stylus will crush soft materials, but not diamonds.

The first-mentioned of the two aspects of activity and passivity is expressed in saying that *agents act according to their natures,* according to their physical makeup and special abilities. The second aspect is expressed in saying that whatever receives action upon itself from another, by its own nature and conditions of existence determines both how the activity will be received and to what extent it will be received. This act of determining on the part of the patient the reception of the effect produced by an agent, has been expressed for centuries in a concise Latin formula:

Quidquid recipitur, recipitur modo recipientis, which says literally that *what is received, is received in the manner of the receiver.*[18]

Two-Fold Effect of Stimulus

The principle set down in the preceding section is very useful in analyzing sensory activity, for there are two diverse modes of the reception of stimuli: *the physical* and *the intentional.* The light that produces an image in a mirror is received in a physical way only, for the mirror gives no evidence of having any power of awareness. But the mirror image can be used by someone as a means of seeing that of which it is the image, by means of the image. *The detection of images requires the presence of an original and a reflected copy, and the realization that the original does have the texture, parts, and location that it appears to have and that the reflection only appears to have them.* Light reflected from a surface produces a light pattern on the retina of the human eye, but the person whose retina is thus stimulated does not *see* an image; rather he becomes *aware* of the colored surface. The nature of the one who *sees* is not the same as the purely chemical nature of the mirror. The mirror does not know the sensible whose image it reflects, but the human stimulus-receiver is aware of the existence and appearance of the sensible that is stimulating his sense of sight. Obviously it is by means of what is in the retina that the person sees, because when the retina stimulus is absent, the seen sensible is absent, too. Let us suppose that the visible is an apple; we shall call this something of the apple in the retina a representation of the apple. The visible is the patterning of the colors not absorbed by the surface of the apple, and as such it is *representative* of the surface of the apple. But in our act of seeing we never see color patterns in the retina. We do see the visual aspects of surfaces that reflect light to the eye; we can confirm that the seen thing is located where we see it by the sense of touch.[19] Thus one effect of the visual stimulus is to trigger off a chain of physiological activities; the other effect is to specify what our act of seeing reveals to us. We shall now consider each sort of receptivity in detail.

The Physical Reception of Stimulus

The discussion of the physiology of the various extero-ceptors and of nerve conduction to the central nervous system made it clear that in sound detection, for example, something physical is continuously present from the point of contact of a sound wave on the tympanum to the termination of the auditory impulse in the brain. The organ of hearing is transmitting impulses over the nerve network connecting the ear to the brain when a person is actually hearing; during a silence the ear is not conducting in the same way. In the activity of nerve impulsing, chemical changes occur; energy is consumed with the consequent minute release of heat from the nerves. The chemical constitution of the nerve is changed during the impulse, but is quickly restored so as to permit another impulse to be transmitted. This kind of change is called an *alteration*, because although some aspect of the nerve is altered, it is not changed so completely that it becomes another kind of tissue or just lifeless chemicals.

Any kind of chemical change in a nonliving assemblage of chemicals, however, usually changes the nature of the assemblage and gives rise to new properties at the expense of some of those previously possessed by the assemblage. Therefore the dissociation of a molecule of water into atoms of hydrogen and oxygen is accompanied by a radical change from the non-combustion-supporting property of water to the combustion-supporting activity of the free oxygen. The atoms liberated by this dissociation do not naturally return to associate with one another. If they are to recombine, some agent must capture and bring them together under the proper conditions. By contrast the restoration of the chemical constitution of the receptor organ and the sensory nerve occurs without fail as long as the organism is alive and healthy. Therefore we must posit the presence of living activity here to explain the reversal of polarity within the nerve, and the source of living activity as well, the soul.

In hearing, then, occurs one of those biochemical activities, discussed in Chapter 2, that are integrated into the action and interaction of the other parts of the body. Such activity is just as much dominated by the human soul as are the usual metabolic processes underlying all physical self-maintenance of the body. In each of these distinct activities subordinated to the life of the whole man, there are aspects resulting from the spontaneous activity of the natures of the chemicals involved, and activities, dominating the spontaneous ones, that are characteristic of living matter and are never found apart from it.[20] For both kinds of activities, we posit just one organizing principle, the presence of the soul.

The power of the soul, introduced earlier in this chapter to distinguish various sensory activities from one another, is also invoked here to explain the nonchemical and yet spontaneous apprehension of aspects of our environment and of ourselves. It depends upon the biochemical activity of the organ and accounts for the presence of a sensed sensible *in our awareness*.

Consider this example. The cornea transplanted successfully from one human eye to another is maintained as a living part of the body by the soul of the person who receives it.[21] The soul needs only an adequate instrument for its activity; an adequate instrument for the sensory activity of seeing is one that can receive reflected and direct light and respond to it. The parts of the eye are adequate because the human soul is present there, integrating the activity of the parts and subordinating these chemical and physical activities to its own sensory act of being aware of some sensible.

The Conscious Reception of Stimulus

In understanding the activities of the senses an error commonly occurs when we think of the representations and "images" as though they were static, whereas they are in fact operations of the powers being described. Thus the awareness of the static appearance of a marble statue is *seeing*, and so on for the other sensibles. This activity of the direct senses is the origin of the remembering activity of the imagination. No little pictures are being transferred around in the peripheral and central nervous systems. The act of seeing visible appearances cannot itself be seen; we can only see, and reason about it, as we have been doing throughout this chapter. The sense powers, while differing from one another in some respects, have this in common—*their operation is productive of an awareness, but not of physical images*. The so-called images are only our awareness; they cease to exist as actually present to us when we cease to be aware of the actual sensibles (or of the sensed sensibles in remembering).

Experiments upon the human nervous system and the brain do not reveal anything with an appearance similar to what we actually see and hear around us because the act of being aware of our surroundings is to some extent nonmaterial. The appearances are in our awareness, but just as consciousness cannot be analyzed in itself by any measuring instrument, so also the images in our consciousness cannot be detected by any mechanical probe or recorder. They simply are not material in the same manner as are the mirror image and the light pattern in the retina. The sensory impressions are quite definite and determinate, and so are the concrete entities of which they are representations. But by comparison with colored surfaces and vibrating bodies, and the like, our conscious impressions of these surfaces and the sound-producers are quite immaterial, although not with the immateriality of a concept. They are immaterial to the extent that they have no physical qualities, no color, and no vibrations, although they are representations of such qualities. Unlike concrete things they cannot be located as being definitely here or there; they can be located as being present in the knower now, or as absent from him now. But only *he* can be directly aware of their presence or absence, because no observer of the sensing subject can detect the content of conscious sensing. Even when some sensible is present now, however, it cannot be identified with any part of the sense organ or with any of the multiplicity of activities in the end organ, the affector chain, and the central nervous system. What we are sure of is that malfunctions of this complex neural apparatus vitiates, and may even prevent, our conscious acts of apprehension; artificial stimulation of parts of the cerebral cortex can be accompanied by the spontaneous recall of past experiences.[22] All that we can conclude from this meager evidence is that the act of being aware of some sensible is a nonphysical, nonchemical, and therefore nonmaterial activity on the part of a power whose operation is absolutely bound up with the physiological activities of the nervous system.

Since nonhuman animals are conscious and act according to their awareness of things in their environment, we assume that their conscious activities have the same general characteristics as ours. No images are revealed upon dissection of animal brains, nor do their actions normally lead them to act toward illusions. Rather, animals respond to concrete actual sensibles around them. We deduce therefore that in all sentient activity that has been investigated by man there is a physical reception of physical stimuli and a simultaneous nonphysical reception of the stimuli in the animal's consciousness.

The difference in the modes of reception accounts for the fact that one stimulus produces differing impressions. Thus the colored surface is present on the retina in a physical way by the reflected light, the hardness of a nail is present in the hand by its pressure upon the hand which is representative of its hardness, and the vibrations of a tuning fork are present in the ear after having traveled through the medium that transmitted them. Simultaneous with these physical presences we are aware of the colored surface, the hard surface, and the sound of the fork. These sensibles then are received both physically and as sensed sensibles. As physical sensibles they occupy the sensory end organs and thereby specify the act of the individual sense, so that we see that visible whose colored surface is reflected in the retina and feel the hardness of that nail which is in our hand, and so on.

To indicate the function of that physical aspect of an actual sensible whose presence in our sensory end organs is accompanied by an awareness of the actual sensible itself, we say that it has *intentional existence* in us. Its intentionality is its ability to represent the actuality of that of which it is a physical aspect. Thus we use the term "intentional" in saying that the colored surface of a book is present in our awareness, not physically but intentionally; that is, by something of itself that is representative of itself. Stimuli are present only physically and not intentionally in unconscious reflex activities; but they are present both physically and intentionally in consciousness and in consciously directed activities. In brief, the physical aspect of sensible objects that is present in a physical way in the sense organs is present intentionally in consciousness.

A quite revealing sign of the difference in the physical and the conscious reception of the sensed thing may be found in the quite different reactions of various persons to the same kind of stimulus. Thus, of two persons watching a power shovel excavate for a tunnel, the one used to doing hard labor for his wages will marvel at the strength and capacity of the shovel,

while the engineer will be calculating the amount of earth removed in a given time period to see if the actual working is keeping up to his schedule. A third person, a painter for example,
will be registering disgust at the unseemliness of the gaping hole
produced by the mechanical monster. Each of these persons is
seeing approximately the same physical scene, and yet their very
act of viewing it is so influenced by the accumulated experience
of their respective professions that each one sees it as something
the others are totally unaware of. This could not be the case if
there were only a physical, and therefore quite determinate, reception of the stimuli. But it *is* the case, because in the conscious reception of the stimuli the person is aware not only of the thing as
it actually appears (to a greater or lesser extent, depending upon
how objective he is being), but also of many of his past experiences that influence his reception of what is present to his senses.
Thus the condition of the receiver always determines what he
perceives in the sensed sensible. The reception of concrete
objects into consciousness in a representational way indicates the
kind of immaterial operation that is proper to a sense power.

Sensing is an activity in which the appearances, the surface phenomena of material things, take up residence in our consciousness for a short period of time. Aristotle's short descriptive
phrase apropos of the union of the sense and the sensible is worth
considering once again: *The sense in act is the sensible in act.*
The phrase "in act" is contrasted with the phrase "in potency"
to indicate the difference between *what is* and *what is merely
able to be.* The eye covered by the eyelid is not actually seeing; it is merely able to see, whereas the uncovered eye cannot
fail to register the light stimuli being reflected to it. We may fail
to be conscious of what is registering upon the eye because of inattention, but if we attend to what is represented there, we can
see just about whatever we choose to look upon. Therefore, actual seeing depends upon the presence of something actually visible and upon our choice of what shall be concentrated upon.

Two-fold Passivity of the Senses

Since it is incapable of apprehending unless a stimulus
is present to the sense organ, an external sense power is said to be
initially passive. *A passive power is one that must be acted upon*

in order that it perform its own proper act, and a sense power is moved from not sensing to sensing by the sensible aspect of reality to which it attains in the very act of sensing. This sensible aspect is also the specifying cause of sensing, for the sense cannot be aware (normally) of anything except what is actually present to it. An external sense only acts, then, when a sensible is present and the sensible determines what can be sensed at that moment by the exercise of the sense. There is a *physical union* between the stimulus and the end organ of the sense, accompanied by an *intentional union* between the sensible aspect of the thing and the consciousness of the person who is sensing. Therefore the end organ and the stimulus are actually one by a physical union, while the consciousness is one intentionally with the sensible aspect of the object of which the person is aware. In seeing the colored surface of an apple the pattern of light that is the visibility of the apple's surface is transmitted to the retina. In the retina this pattern of light is received physically by the rods and cones, and intentionally by the power of sight, so that the sense possesses the colored surface to the extent that it is visible without possessing the actual surface physically at all. Thus *the sense in the act of sensing is the sensible.* However, the eye does not become the apple's surface nor does the ear become the tuning fork in a physical way. These sensibles retain their existential status as being other than the eye and the ear, respectively. Consequently this precision must be included in our definition of sensation. *Sensation is becoming the sensible determinately, as other.*

Regarding the presence of the sensible there can be no error in our judgment unless there is a physical defect in the organ or the nervous system or brain. Similarly, since the singular characteristics of the sensed object move the sense to its act of discriminating hues and intensities in color, and pitches and intensities in sound, and so on, there will be no error in discrimination unless there is a physical defect involved. In short, how can there be anything in the awareness of an external sense other than that which the environment places physically in the end organ of each sense? A sense power is initially passive, and in being moved to act, its act is simultaneously specified in every detail by the sensible that moves it.

Although our senses register the aspects of sensibles faithfully, many a slip can occur in communicating the contents of our sensations to others. Thus a certain amount of "coloring" (modifying to suit some preformed notion) occurs because of past experience and personal viewpoints in exercising the senses. Also, words do not accurately describe the singular details of things, so that attempts to make words fit this purpose cannot be as successful as the impression obtained by presenting the actual sensible itself for scrutiny. Furthermore, our universe is one of constant change, and as the conditions of the one sensing and of the thing sensed vary, so do our impressions, although not so much that we cannot recognize similarities and differences with what was sensed in the past. Minute changes are very difficult to express, however. Try to describe the weathering that has taken place in a stone during a summertime of wind and rain, or the change in appearance of a page of a book as it ages from month to month. Quadrillions of other details in sensed things beggar description, even though they can be discriminated by animal senses at the time of the actual sensing.

Continuity of the Act of Sensing

The immediate result of the act of an external sense is the presence in the consciousness of some aspect of a material thing. There are other senses involved in the storing of apprehended aspects of things and in discerning individual values of elements in the environment and of actions toward or away from them. Many senses are involved, but their activities are continuous with one another because there is no subject matter for remembering unless there is something being apprehended and there is nothing from which to derive experience unless the relevant factors of some event are present in consciousness. This does not mean that some sensible must actually be present for the imagination and temporal memory to be moved to operate. Our desires can move these other internal senses just as well as an actually present sensible can. In fact, when one is asked to write a theme or solve a practical problem he usually searches through his past experience for relevant information and recalls the stored images concerned with this information simultaneously, or conjures up suitable images out of the storehouse that is the imagination. In this activity of recalling images as being relevant to past experience, and in conjuring up images that do not represent in all

Sensory Experience as Knowledge   139

sensed aspects any past experience, it is our wish to do so that is the moving cause.

If we look upon the action of the stimulus as an activity starting from the material object, specifying the apprehension of one sense and thus the exact impression that imagination shall retain of the source of the stimulus, we can understand the continuity of the activity of the senses in one direction, the afferent one. Another continuity of sensory activity starts from an idea to be realized in some concrete circumstance and terminates in the realization of that concrete scene's existence by an external sense. A meaning that we have understood about sounds or textures is validated by our sense of hearing or our sense of touch, and no imaginary validation or recalled experience has quite the conviction of the actual sensing. Thus the senses are not only unique judges of the existence and characteristics of material things, but they also are the judges that confirm our intellectual deductions about the presence and reality of material being.

There is then an efferent line of activity in which the actions of the various sense are to some extent directed. The origin of this efferent chain of activities is twofold. One source is our desires, which determine what we shall attend to and what we shall do (treated in detail in Chapters 7 and 8). The other source is the intellect, the human ability to go beyond the limitations of the senses in examining sensory evidence and experience according to its own inclinations to turn up new signs of the natures of things. In the next two chapters we shall attempt to analyze all of the activities of this nonanimal power that accounts for the purely human activities of men, their pursuit of sciences and arts, their cultivation of beliefs, and their communication through language.

CHAPTER 5

Abstraction and Hearsay Learning

~ IN CHAPTER 4 THE determinate aspect of our sensory awareness and accumulated sensory experience was manifested. When we hear, we do not hear sound in general; we always hear a very definite sound. Similarly, we never see a color in general; we always see a very definite hue and intensity of some definite color. In brief, there are no sensibles that are not quite definite, and each one is complete in countless details. Just examine a blade of grass and note all of the details of the surface and the edges. Put it under a simple magnifying glass and the number of irregularities along the edges that become visible is surprising, although not nearly as large as the number seen when the appearance of the grass is magnified in a powerful microscope. But it is not necessary to see all of the minute details in order to see the size, shape, color, and location of a blade of grass. The features that are visible to unaided vision in sunlight are sufficient for its recognition and location in space.

The Recognition of Commonness among Singulars

When we look closely at blades of grass in order to compare them, we see that their details vary. Each blade differs in length, in breadth, and in thickness. Some have rougher edges than others and their coloration is not uniform. Nevertheless, we experience no difficulty in classifying these items as being instances of the same kind of thing. Thus, although our senses can attain only to the macroscopic details, we are not restricted to knowing just the sensed details of each blade. We can be aware also of the *similarity* among the blades of grass in that they have such details, in spite of the difference in the actual details themselves. More simply, we know that being grass is not entirely a matter of differing details, for there are some factors that each blade has in the same way that each other blade has them. It is the *similarity in their possessing certain characteristics*, rather than any exact conformity between the characteristics possessed, that enables us to classify them as being of the same kind.

This ability of ours to transcend the differences in the details of things, and thus to see their similarities, is also manifest in our use of language. Note how the term "grass" can be used to name all of the varieties of lawn grass by pointing to something that they all have in common, even though the various varieties do have special differences among them and each individual blade has its singular details. The other common nouns have the same ability to signify what is common to many by leaving out the details that are peculiar to a special subgroup or to some individual. Thus the name "dog" applies equally to Great Dane and to Cocker Spaniel. It does so because it can be used in a similar way of each type of dog and not exclusively of any one type or any one individual dog.

Since language is merely an expression of thought, we must go beyond language to thought in order to see what is involved in thinking. This activity enables us to talk about the characteristics that things have in common even though the physical being of each material thing is proper to itself and therefore is not actually shared by any other material thing. That we do have this ability to talk about what is common to many no one doubts. But some persons do doubt that the indifference of common nouns to many of the details of actual things signifies a property of intellectual knowledge. Thus today, even as in the time of the pre-Socratic philosophers, there are men who question the existence and nature of the human intellect. They give as the reason for their attitude their belief that there is no difference between sensory apprehension and what is called "intellectual understanding." They hold the opinion that because the imagination can have general images, therefore common nouns signify these sense images. With a view to overcoming this skeptical attitude we shall develop this chapter by evaluating the kind of facts stated at the opening of the chapter and by showing that their explanation is not to be found in the acts of any sense or any combination of senses. For the sake of clarity the full extent of intellectual operations will not be given in this chapter; the acts of judging and reasoning will be treated in Chapter 6. In this chapter we shall consider the human act of understanding, that is, the act of obtaining a grasp of the meanings of things. The signification of "meaning" will become clear through our use of the term in various contexts. Meaning is too basic in intellectual activity to be defined by means of an activity more basic than understanding.

In general, to understand something is to go through human experience of the appearances and activities of things to discover something of their enduring natures and to learn how they are interrelated. There are two ways in which a person may obtain understanding by his own efforts. The one, called *abstraction*, will be treated in this chapter; the other, called *reasoning*, will be treated in the next chapter. There is another way of achieving an understanding of things: by accepting the explanations offered by other persons in the absence of evidence for the correctness of their explanations. We call this learning by hearing (or reading) what another person has to say, or more simply, *hearsay learning*. Since the ability to appreciate hearsay information presupposes both sensory experience and some understanding of things, we shall consider knowledge acquired by personal discovery first and hearsay knowledge later.

Abstraction from the Singular to the Common

The usual method of advancing beyond the information obtained by sense impressions is to note characteristics that are common to many things and to consider them apart from those many things in order to understand the characteristics themselves. This act of apprehension is called *abstraction*. It is not merely the considering of the sensory impressions of the imagination apart from the objects of which they are impressions but a consideration, for example, of what it is *to be* colored and shaped and *to have* activities of a certain kind.

EXPERIENCE AND ABSTRACTION

In order to form a complete picture of the beginning of intellectual knowledge, let us make an imaginary trip from the sensible object through the external senses in direct contact with nonself material things and through the internal senses into the intellect.[1] Since visible sized things are made of invisibly small components, perhaps we should begin our analysis with them so that we shall be treating the most basic stuff in things. That is the aim of many physical sciences. But if we start with the most minute aspect of a blade of grass that our best microscope detects, we are still somewhat removed from the smallest entity there is. Therefore our choice of a starting point is quite arbitrary. If we begin with the smallest aspect that an optical microscope reveals or the smallest one evident to unaided vision, our starting point is equally arbitrary and therefore no more necessary than the first one as far as explaining knowing is concerned. In fact, all actualities about which man knows in an experiential way must be proportioned to his senses, for he has had to invent instruments to make "subvisibles" visible and "inaudibles" audible. Therefore the question of what size of object to start with is resolved by the demand of each sense for a stimulus that is adequate to move it normally, that is, one that is physically discriminable with accuracy by any sense being discussed. In any instance of understanding we have the same problem of explaining how that which appears to the unaided senses, or to the senses using an instrument, is understood. Size is a common sensible aspect of things that

Man's Physical and Spiritual Nature

makes a difference in the appearance of what we are aware of, but makes relatively little difference in *how* we understand the thing having size. Therefore it is more convenient to start with naturally occurring wholes that are perceivable on the macroscopic level and to explain how these are understood. The explanation will hold for other things of whatever size as long as they are known by abstraction.

The surface of an apple is sensed by us through sight and touch; sight apprehending the definite color, size, and shape of the apple and touch detecting its texture, solidity, size, and shape. Thus we are simultaneously conscious of the many determinate sensible characteristics of the apple's surface known by different senses, and we can remember them fairly accurately if we try to do so. Let us suppose that it is the first apple we have experienced. It will make the same impression as will any novelty to which we direct our attention, and we shall apprise the apple and its parts (including the stem) by their color, size, shape, hardness, weight, and perhaps by some other sensible qualities. We shall then have a fairly rich experience of the apple by combining the information yielded by both sight and touch. By biting into the apple or by cutting it apart into many pieces we can obtain further impressions about it. All of the impressions gained in this way are proper to the one apple in question.

If another apple, of a different kind, is brought to our attention, our experience of it will be similar to our experience of the first one in some details, but not in others. The two apples will have this in common: They are colored shapes having weight and solidity. Their having stems, cores, seeds, and flesh is also a common trait. Now, for the sake of simplicity in our illustration, let us suppose that there were only two apples that we could ever experience. We could grasp from our experience that all the members of this class have the same kind of constitutive parts, and although their actual sizes, shapes, colors, and weights are different, they are similar to one another in *the having* of size, shape, color, and weight (as most material things have) and especially in having the same kind of constitutive parts.

Let us assume that we were the first to call these objects "apples" and then had to explain to someone else who had never experienced an apple what an apple is. We would say that by "apple" we mean a solid having parts that are physically differentiated from one another to such an extent that we can indicate them as a central part (core), a peripheral part (skin), and a third part different in texture and appearance from these two and lying between them (flesh). (From further experience of the being of apples other common traits would become evident, such as their being fruit, their chemical composition, and so forth.) We could have said this much even if we had experienced only one apple. In that case we could also have learned that it was edible, in retrospect, upon our feeling of well-being after having eaten it. All that the simple experiencing of two apples adds to our knowledge of one apple is that the shape of the whole apple and its taste, firmness, and coloration are rather variable. By cutting up and looking at a thousand apples of every known variety, we add to our knowledge of these varying incidental features but do not detect any more characteristics common to all apples. Our experience of one apple told us the physical facts about one apple, and our experience of two of them showed us which aspects the two had in common. Thus we are able to say what we mean by "apple" by stating the little that we understand of its physical (as contrasted with chemical) makeup. However, we leave out the details that differ from apple to apple and attribute only their common characteristics to them.[2]

No Sense Image Is Truly General

Although we can form a sensory impression of the aspects common to all apples, based upon some actual experience of them, the image is not truly general inasmuch as its details must be determinate. It is general in representing features which all apples have, but it is not truly representative of the varieties of sizes, shapes, tastes, and so on. In fact, if the image were taken as representative of the size, shape, and taste of every apple, it would clearly be a false representation of the singular details of most apples. A representation of all apples must be indeterminate as to singular details, for it is in these minutiae that apples differ from one another. Since every sense image is what it is because of the appearances of sensibles, every sense image is replete with incidental details and no one sense image can represent the members of a species by their incidental differences. However, any complete apprehension of those aspects of an apple accessible to the human senses automatically captures what is common to each apple, as apple. But as *this* apple each one differs from the rest. Consequently any such apprehension can serve to illustrate what is common to all apples and in this sense it can be called a *general sense image*. For if it is of an apple it has those characteristics that are distinctive of the kind of thing that an apple is and consequently can be used as an instance of them. General images of sensibles are useful for illustrating what we mean (a picture is reputedly worth a thousand words), but they are not necessary for every abstraction because our experience of sensibles usually retains many examples of each species of sensible, sufficient to manifest some traits common to the members of a class.

There can be no sensory impression of a nonspecific class such as "the class of living things" or "the class of material things," because of the great indeterminacy of these notions. We can define "living" as self-moving, and we can define "material" as being extended so as to have distinguishable parts, but there is no single image that can include all of the species of living things or all the species of material things. In fact, general sensory images are limited to individuals, for example, to trees as having roots, trunks, and branches (depicted vaguely), and to trees as being coniferous or deciduous (with more detail) and to their varieties. Yet even a picture of a pine can be general only in the sense that it has what every pine has; for it has its own singular details that other pines do not share. Sensory images are determinate in the very details that are absent from definitions; therefore they cannot be equated with meanings as are definitions. Thus one of the obvious differences between sense knowledge and intellectual knowledge is the determinateness of all sensory apprehension and memory, while the understanding of the common traits of things has to be indeterminate in order to be common. Even the experience accumulated by the memory for the cogitative power, although acquired by comparison and the detection of the most valuable from among many experiences, is nevertheless a determinate kind of knowledge. It probably involves the forming of general sensory images as a guide in projecting future actions, but such images are determinate, as has been explained.

Let us sum up what we have established so far about nonsensory knowing in man. Man's ability to go beyond the proper and common sensibles in the very act of making use of them as a means of knowing what is common to several things is called the *intellect*. Its primary operation, the discovering of what things have in common, commences with the abstraction of some characteristic (or characteristics) from the object presented in sensory experience. In this activity the intellect attains to what the senses know of things and discerns some of the common qualitative factors in the sensory appearances of things.

The term "intellect" may have been imposed to indicate the ability of this human power to peer into the experience we have of sensibles and to read there (*intelligere*) far more than the senses can ever be aware of. For such is the first act of this marvelous power in obtaining an understanding of sensible things. When we use intellect to examine our experience of sensibles to note what characteristics they have in common, we see that for the sensibles in question to be the *kind* of things they are involves the possession of certain characteristics, or conversely, that the possession of certain characteristics is why they are what they are. We do this, for example, when we recognize that *to be* visible is *to be* reflecting light. No sense power understands what it means to be visible, for no sense power distinguishes *to be* and *to have* in the appearances of things.

Erroneous Notion of Abstraction

A naive approach to abstraction views it as setting aside what is incidental to the nature of something and concentrating on what is left. But this is impossible in the beginning of human knowledge—how can we know in advance which aspects of any sensible object are common and which are not? If the particular size of an apple and its exact coloration, shape, and taste are not found in all apples of the same species, then these characteristics are properly said to be incidental to this kind of apple. That sensibles vary somewhat from apple to apple is known only by observing these particular sensibles. If, by impossible hypothesis, such particular appearances could be set aside from an individual apple, nothing would remain for the senses to grasp. The characteristics that we understand to be common to many individuals exist as common only in our thought of them. Abstraction, then, is not the setting aside of anything, either physically, sensorially, or mentally. To abstract is to grasp the notion of apples as having size from the having sizes of these apples, of their having color from the being colored of these apples, and of their having flavor from the tasting of these flavors.

The intellect is involved in the expression of the judgment by which we indicate what we mean by "apple," and therefore in the recognition of the similarity of the appearances. Its grasp of what is similar in the two apples, however, is expressed in saying that *to have* stem, skin, flesh, a core, and a curved colored surface is common to apples. Thus the intellect grasps that which is similar in the apples through what the senses reveal, but it grasps the similarity as *a way of being* of things rather than as a mere similarity in appearances. When expressing what it has thus grasped, the intellect describes a *being, having* such and such characteristics.

Interrelation of Powers in Abstraction

What is the relation of the intellect to the sense powers in this act of abstraction? The sense powers report the textures, sounds, appearances, and activities of things, nothing more. These aspects of things, however, reflect a pattern that the intellect can discern because it knows what the senses know, as known by them, but from a wider viewpoint. The intellect views things as kinds of being that differ, as far as the senses are concerned, in their sensory aspects, but it sees a commonness in these aspects and thus detects *kinds* of things. The senses, of course, also detect commonness in things, but their discrimination is restricted to proper sensibles and the endless variety of these sensibles—the hues of color, pitches and qualities of sounds, textures and degrees of warmth and cold, sweet and sour tastes, and the many varieties of smell.

All of these sensibles are but signs of the kinds of things that possess them, so that the senses report reliably many aspects of experience that they themselves do not discriminate. For instance, sight senses patterns of light and variations of hue and intensity, but it knows nothing of what a pattern is, or what a variation is. Only a power that can know the acts of the external senses, not only knowing what they know but also their manner of operation, can detect in the sensibly apprehended sensibles similarities and differences in the very details that make a difference to the senses themselves. This power can apprehend what it is to be colored, to be sounding, to be physically contacted, and the rest. In short, the whole analysis of sensation given in the preceding chapter could not be made by any sense power, because although some senses discriminate the sensible that is sensed by an external sense as the specifier of the activity of that sense, no sense power can reflect upon itself. For this reason we call the intellect a higher power—it can look upon the activities of the various senses and know the particular object of each as the formality of a *kind of being*, and can view the initial passivity and consequent activity of the senses as *modes of being* of powers.

DEFINITION IS OF THE COMMON

That the intellect does apprehend things in quite a different manner than the senses do is further evident when we consider what we mean by a general term such as "fruit." This term signifies apples, oranges, pears, peaches, figs, dates, and so on, by what they have in common, namely, that they are seed containers of woody plants whose meat is edible. (We use this definition, by origin and usefulness, to indicate two more viewpoints from which common traits can be detected.) Since the meaning is assigned by us, it is definitive for us of all things having the characteristics by which we define fruit. Things not having these characteristics are not fruit from our viewpoint and things having them but not being otherwise similar to the species already classified as fruit are nevertheless fruit. Thus strawberries have seeds on their surfaces and differ in this from apples and the rest, but they are correctly classified as fruit.

If our definition is faulty, we shall know it when we experience something that has all the characteristics of our definition but does not have some other aspect in common with the fruits we have classified. This will mean that we have overlooked something. Thus a nut is a seed container of a woody plant, but brazils, pecans, almonds, filberts, and peanuts, to mention a few, do not have juicy meats as do the larger fruits. We can arbitrarily bar nuts from the class we have defined as fruit by including softness and juiciness of the flesh in our definition of fruit, or we can leave the definition as it is and include nuts as a kind of dry fruit. In any case, definition involves stating only the common traits, never the individual ones.

THE COMMONEST COMMON NOTIONS

The abstract notions of widest application are *being*, *quality*, and *extension*. Being signifies actuality of any kind and only the actual is directly sensible. As our discussion of sensation showed, every sensible thing is sensed as an extended quality; by means of these qualities the quantitative aspects of material things can be known. Thus the possible objects of direct intellectual knowledge are all material beings, for material being and extended thing are synonymous. At present human knowledge of the quantitative aspects of things ranges from the thickness of a spider's thread down to the diameter of a hydrogen nucleus and up to the unimaginable diameters of galaxies and the distances between them. In every area of investigation the detection of the presence of material reality is by the senses or by some instrument that can ultimately register on them. The reasonably exact analysis of material reality is by measurement of the quantitative aspects of things and by calculation with them. Thus the proper and common sensibles are man's instruments for the intellectual penetration of reality; and its abstract designations, "quality" and "quantity," are the widest in extension after "being" and are therefore the most common notions that we can use in classifying the appearances of material things.

There are other abstractions quite as universal as the notions of extension and quality, but these abstractions are usually not as widely used since they are more proper to the intellectual analysis of material being than to the cognizing of appearances. Thus, the notions of being composed of parts and of being movable and otherwise changeable are true of every material being encountered in the experience of man, regardless of how these beings agree or differ in appearance and nature. But the majority of the notions we have obtained by abstraction are less universal than these.

It is not necessary to list all of the notions that the human intellect has obtained by abstraction from human experience of reality, for all of our intellectual stock in trade is based in some way on human experience but differs from that experience as the general differs from the singular. When we perform conscious acts of abstraction, both the singular and the common aspects of reality are simultaneously present to us through the consciously active direct senses and/or the internal senses. Thus in matters offering little difficulty the direct senses, imagination, and intellect will cooperate simultaneously in an act of understanding. For a person advanced beyond infancy there will be things given in direct sensation that cannot fail to be identified in part with some previous experience. Hence notions such as *a thing by itself* (substance) and *part or aspect of a thing* (moving or stationary; glossy or dull; hard or soft; and so on) are so basic in experience and thought that they are hardly ever defined. What we mean by them is immediately clear upon reference to the experience in which they are given.

ABSTRACTION REQUIRES EFFORT

While the aforementioned abstractions occur almost without our being aware of them, the enlargement of one's understanding depends greatly upon individual effort and talent, for there is a conflict between the limited viewpoints of the senses and the richness of being of sensible things. The intellect's task, as a power seeking to find rest in the possession of certain knowledge, is not only to sift experience ever more thoroughly but also to overcome the limitations of the senses and to encompass the richness of relationships and implications in the being of things.

If we contrast things, *experience*, and *understanding* for richness of content, obviously things are the richest because no man has ever experienced the fullness of being of even the simplest or the smallest material thing. Experience ranks next in its richness of the sensory detail that the direct senses and the instruments used to extend their range can receive. In the last place ranks the human intellect, both individual and corporate. It is obvious that no individual person can understand all that is contained in his sensory experience; the fact that man's corporate endeavor to understand his universe is still continuing also indicates that there is much of being that has not been encompassed by human understanding.

Because of the richness of detail in the sensible things that we encounter, it is usually necessary to know more than two instances of a particular kind of thing (our example of the two apples relied on the reader's wide experience) to give us enough experience to realize what is common to the species. We often do not pay attention to the common characteristics of our experiences at the time they occur, because our interest is directed to quite practical matters. But we can usually recall past experience when we wish to do so and can examine it for information recorded there, even though we did not advert to it at the time of the sensation. For example, a person who smokes is able, upon reflection, to assure himself that the smoke from his tobacco always rose up in the air as did the smoke from tobacco being smoked by others. From this it is an easy step to form a judgment about this common sensible aspect of smoke (its motion) and to attribute "being something that rises in the air from burning tobacco" to "being smoke from tobacco." More simply, he could say that tobacco smoke is a visible something that rises up in the air from burning tobacco.

The person might analyze his experience a little further and see that in all of his experiences the smoke arose in curves and curls, that the motion of the colored gas never followed a straight line. What he obtains from his experience depends upon what he is seeking, for one person may see a commonness where another person does not. Thus any person reflecting upon the details of the tobacco smoke could recognize something common to all such smoke, namely, that it is a visible something; or he could go further and note the direction and path of its motion; or he could go even further and seek to find out why smoke moves as it does and what it has in common with other gases. Whether a person thinks about tobacco smoke at all, and whether he perseveres until he understands it in terms of its causes, depends very much upon what effort he exerts and his personal aptitude for such discovery.

Abstraction, of course, is not restricted to the realm of natural observation. Anything that can be discriminated by the senses can yield evidence for the formation of a common notion. A very fruitful method of discovery is to divide an object of investigation into smaller parts—division will always reveal something about the composition of the whole. This method is used very extensively by contemporary physics and other sciences that use physical principles in their explanations. In our previous example of the apple, the removing of the skin is one method of arriving at a crude notion of the dimension of depth by the use of visual appearances. By simply viewing the apple at a distance from the eye as a plane figure we get the notion of bidimensionality; by penetrating beyond the surface, we grasp the notion of tridimensionality. The notion of material *substance* as a solid quantity could arise in the same experience.[3] In each case the notions of bidimensionality and tridimensionality, as well as of quantitative substantiality, are given by visual impressions even though sight does not *understand* what it is to be a plane or a solid or a substance.

Although abstraction is a simple act on the part of the intellect, which either understands something from experiencing it or simply fails to grasp what is distinctive about it, there are further aspects of abstraction that must be treated in detail in order that the exact nature of intellectual knowledge be understood fully.

Abstraction from the Changing to the Enduring

WHAT ENDURES?

In the sensible things we are seeking to know there are aspects that endure for the span of time that the sensible thing itself exists. These aspects are the common aspects, for to be truly common to many the characteristics must endure as long as their subjects do; otherwise commonness would exist among them at one time and not at another, and understanding by class notions would then be impossible. The detection of what is common precedes the assurance of the lastingness of such characteristics, which must first be singled out before we can assay whether or not they are enduring. But what can be said to be enduring in the sensible realm of endless change? No apple or apple tree endures for very long, and inanimate things are also subject to change. The transmutation of copper to zinc accomplished in the laboratory shows that the transmutation of radioactive materials to lead is not the only instance of metals' changing their natures. In fact, a theory with some supporting evidence states the possibility that every other element developed from hydrogen by the grouping of hydrogen atoms with the concomitant rearranging of the subatomic particles. If this is so, it would mean that all of the various chemical natures achieved the natural properties they now have by being synthesized from less complex natures. In that case a molecule that is now copper may (theoretically, at least) later become zinc by a natural process. Of course, since a change in natural properties is involved here, the same molecule is not really copper and then zinc, but at any rate many of the same electrons and protons will be present in the copper and in the zinc. How, then, can anything be said to be enduring over and above its basic components—the nuclei, the electrons, and the fields of force—if everything composed of them is quite changeable?

At the least, an electron can be said to endure as an electron for the period of time during which it possesses the mass and charge by which it is defined. If, as a physical theory suggests, the electron can be expended so that its mass and charge are converted to work, it nevertheless is identifiable as an electron up to the moment of its conversion. If we assume that the basic unit of matter is a kind of energy that has solidity and mass at one time but not at another, then its nature as pure energy endures as long as it has that form. Thus, for a material nature, to be enduring can only mean *to possess the characteristics that identify it as a certain kind of nature for as long as it is that kind of nature.* This statement will hold true whether we consider a quite basic element of the universe, such as the hydrogen atom, or a very complex entity like man. All are material, are composed of parts, and are therefore changeable.

In our analysis in the preceding paragraph we considered only the elements involved in processes, not the processes themselves. But that which endures is not necessarily some component factor that remains self-identical in the changing of complex things, although this is the case with the chemical elements when considered in and by themselves.[4] The enduring aspect can be a certain order in change that is indicative of a specific kind of nature. Thus in the changes that occur in apple trees, the regular recurrence of leafing, budding, fruit-bearing, and leaf-shedding indicate what kind of thing it is. What endures over the centuries is this sequence in change. Mutations, which produce new strains or even new species, testify simultaneously to the regularity of natural agents in their activities and to the existence of random events that can modify or completely alter the properties of a nature.[5] Constancy may also be found in the constitution of things, as evidenced by their definitions; for example, table sugar has a definite chemical definition as does each of the organic compounds whose analysis is given in textbooks of chemistry.

The "enduring" in things, then, is found in their activities, which indicate the kind of thing each is, as well as in their composition. The term "enduring," however, is always used relatively of things, because it is being applied to natures that are material and changeable, which come to be and later pass out of existence. The enduring characteristics of things are indicative of the natures which the succession of members of a species perpetuates. It is in this sense that we speak of the vegetative nature and the animal nature and the nature of a fox, to distinguish what is regularly the case from incidental variations. In nonliving things man has not sufficiently observed the transmutation of elements to find anything akin to the perpetuation of species in living things. Thus classes of nonliving things are established solely by commonness of properties and of composition (especially in chemistry and chemistry-based sciences), for an inanimate nature perdures through time by remaining numerically the same nature, even when subsumed by the form of some composite into which it enters.[6] Living natures endure by changing; nonliving natures endure by remaining the same.

THE ATEMPORALITY OF INTELLECTUAL KNOWLEDGE

The material universe is the spatially extended, quality-possessing environment that surrounds each individual for an immeasurable distance in every direction. Its duration is measured by man, who calls this measure *time*. We have just explained how the enduring in material things is conditioned by time: The living have their spans of duration measured by time while the duration of the nonliving is the basis for the measure called "time." Our senses suffer the attrition of time (metaphorically speaking) in the aging of their organs and they are just as strictly limited to the

Man's Physical and Spiritual Nature

here-and-now and there-and-then conditions of knowing as are material things in their act of existence. In brief, the senses know the appearances of things as located definitely in time and place. Only the imagination in the act of presenting an image that does not correspond to any combination of parts that ever did exist in our experience escapes being limited to a definite time. But even so, the parts that fit into such a combination were apprehended at definite times and in definite locations. The imagination has no awareness of time, however, nor have any of the external senses, because time is not an appearance and does not have an appearance.

Our intellectual grasp of time is based upon our apprehension of the duration of things, and especially upon the characteristic of pastness in that duration, for time is noted in succession rather than in the present now. Thus our intellectual notion of time is based upon the apprehension of a sense power, but it is not obtained by the abstraction of the "common element in many instances," any more than is our knowledge of color as the proper sensible for sight and our knowledge of sound as the proper sensible for hearing. For, if these starting points of all knowledge could only be apprehended by a discursive process of sorting among several instances of seeing and hearing to detect the most common notion in each, what could be detected in these instances as a basis for the comparison? We could not compare one kind of nonknowing with another as the starting point for all of our human understanding. If we reflect upon what happens when we return to full consciousness from sleep, we can see in this analogue of the first moment of understanding that there may be a little confusion as to whether something is actually being sensed, merely being imagined, or is being relived from the past; but there is no confusion between the audible, the visible, and the tactile aspects of things in the understanding of our sensory awareness. If the intellect did not know the acts of these powers as actually apprehending the sensory aspects of matter, where would it obtain information about their proper objects? The intellect needs to know this in order to discern the commonness in things of the same kind, for that commonness is known only by means of the apprehended sensibles. Thus we must conclude that our intellectual awareness of time is no more and no less direct than the awareness of the act of memory that assures us of the pastness of a recalled scene and of the future possible success of a projected action.[7]

Once the intellect has attained its initial understanding of the apprehending acts of the senses and of what is present in them it considers what it has apprehended not according to the limitations of the senses but according to its own mode of being as a higher power whose act of cognition extends beyond the merely local and temporal instances of any being that has actually been experienced to all possible instances of such being. In this way the intellect can generalize about the proper objects of the senses and can conclude that the discerning of color and sound, and so forth, are cognitive activities common to many kinds of animals. It is thus, too, that any nature or property can be considered apart from the actual possessors of that nature or property. For example, our understanding that being a good conductor of electricity is a physical property of copper, is obtained from the experimental observation of a finite number of instances of actually finding this property in samples of copper, or by accepting in good faith the words of those who say that it is so. Once the understanding is obtained, it is no longer restricted to any of the instances that have actually been observed; however, it is the common bond uniting all of those instances intelligibly. Although all of those instances may be remembered disparately on the same level (and only on the sense level can their multiplicity actually be cognized, because the intellect in its act of abstracting from the singular to the common does not retain the details whereby the instances differ), they are considered indiscriminately in one understanding of a natural attribute of copper.

We may include all of the instances explicitly in an act of predicating universally, but this is an entirely different matter, of the expression of our understanding, involving factors that are not relevant to the act of understanding per se. Now even if all copper should change to zinc, or even if copper were a purely imaginary metal invented by someone, the understanding of copper as a metal with the property of conducting electricity would be quite correct. Since copper does actually exist materially, our understanding of it extends to all instances of metal with the physical constitution and properties that we designate by the name "copper," whether we have actually experienced them or not. All of the instances of this occurrence in the past and all future ones are thus understood, although not discriminated numerically, by the one act of understanding what it is to have the physical constitution and the properties designated by the term "copper."

The human intellect in its act of understanding some characteristic or property as being common to things of a certain kind is therefore not bound to consider the object of its understanding in any definite time and place. This does not mean that it always considers the objects of its understanding as though they were not located in time and place. The intellect simply is atemporal in its act of considering the abiding characteristic or property of some nature. If the intellect failed to grasp notions atemporally there would be no continuity or progress in human knowledge, for all progress would involve the repetition of all the temporal details of all the personal experiences by which matter was effectively handled in the past. Such repetition is obviously impossible, and as we have seen, the content of experience is communicable by words but the experience itself is absolutely incommunicable.

The enduring in thought is not conditioned by time, as are reality and sensation; it endures unchangeably because it is apart from time. The facts of physical reality are the facts in time but they are understood in an absolute way, such that the temporal aspects are omitted as irrelevant to understanding the enduring natural characteristics common to members of a class. The atemporality of intellectual knowledge, as well as the common-to-many representation that understanding-by-abstraction yields, are both due to the kind of knowing power that the intellect is. Just as all material existents are located in time, so too there is no physical entity that actually shares its being. The commonness comes into our knowledge in the act of understanding that, for example, to be man is the same for Jack as it is for Bill as it is for Jim and for the rest of mankind. In brief, it is because of the nature of the human intellect that human knowledge has the characteristics of generality and atemporality that it does have.

We have seen that sense knowledge is to some extent devoid of the characteristics found everywhere and always in material being. Thus the senses possess an awareness of the sensible as it appears at a definite time and in a definite place. After the actual sensing is accomplished, however, imagination and memory retain the sensed sensible as a remembered something with no restrictions that the remembering must take place where and when the actual sensing occurred. The scene remembered must be located exactly in the time and place of its occurrence, though, if the question of the location of the actuality that it depicts is raised. The intellect transcends the limitations of the sense memories in considering aspects of the sensed objects, irrespective of any location in time and place they may happen to have.

This intellectual ability is put to use in a kind of abstraction that is called "quantitative abstraction." The intellectual operation involved in this kind of abstraction has been much discussed in the past by philosophers and mathematicians. Although contemporary mathematics has developed from various starting points, all of which are useful to some extent, the question of the absolute foundations of mathematics is still posed as a problem to be solved, much as the question of a universal mathematics that would contain all specific branches of mathematics within it was posed in the Platonic and Aristotelian periods of Greek philosophy. We shall attempt to avoid leading the reader astray in talking of the intellectual operation regarding mathematicals by staying as close to easily confirmed evidence as possible.

ABSTRACTION AND MATHEMATICALS

A pseudoproblem dealt with in a previous part of this chapter concerned the starting point in the explanation of abstraction processes. The problem was stated as one of deciding what size of material being should be considered in explaining how we achieve understanding of the environment. In the ensuing discussion it was pointed out that size is a common sensible that is quite relevant to the appearance of a thing, but which has little relevance in the explanation of the understanding of the qualities that are the proper objects of the external senses. Nevertheless, the quantitative aspects of things are extremely important in the practical activities of manipulating matter to suit our desires. For example the number and size of objects, as well as their shape, is quite relevant to how they can be moved and to how many can be placed in a given container.

Apart from practical interest in the quantitative aspects

of things there is a speculative question to be considered: whether the quantitative appearances of things can be defined. Formulated differently the same question is: Can we discover any aspects that are common to several material beings precisely as having their physical parts extended in space? In order to visualize quantities as mere physical extensions, we need to simplify our sensory impressions by leaving out everything not relevant to their being considered as physical extensions. In effect this means leaving out the proper sensible qualities by which the quantities were detected, to as great an extent as possible. Thus if we start by trying to visualize the shape of an apple, we can subtract from our sensory apprehensions of apple the taste and smell and sound of its being eaten. We cannot subtract color completely, however, for the prime condition of actually seeing or of merely visualizing some quantity is that it be visible. But we need not visualize the colors actually occurring in the surface of some apples; any non-distracting color will do quite well for identifying the shapes of quantity. Similarly all of the tangible aspects of the actual apple can be subtracted, except the rigidity necessary to maintain the shape.

When the imagined shape has been simplified by subtracting irrelevant details, we next have the problem of comparing such shapes for common characteristics. Between two apples thus stripped of sense qualities we can observe that their shapes are tridimensional and their surfaces differ somewhat in their extent of curvature in various parts. Tridimensionality is a feature of every solid and can be defined and considered as common to all actual solids. As an attempt to distinguish kinds of curved surfaces, we might posit a definition of the straight as a basis for distinguishing the curved as a departure from straight. If we define straight according to how we arrived at it, we call it the noncurved. This definition is in fact a negation, and thus unacceptable. If we then look to experience to find some model for our notion of noncurved, we can find one in the rays of sunlight that bathe our earth. We can define a ray of this light as a cube having four straight sides several million miles in length and having ends very minute in area. In order to reduce this figure to the simplest one that will fulfill our sensorially intuited notion of "straight," we can subtract the dimension of depth by leaving only one side several million miles in length. We thus visualize a long plane surface of slight breadth. If we subtract the breadth completely, we then have nothing to visualize; therefore we must reduce the breadth to the absolute minimum visualizable so that we have the minimum extension required to represent our sensorially intuited "straight."

So much for the manipulation of the imagination in trying to arrive at the elements of quantitative shapes. Note how easy it was to formulate the notion of straight from curved by negation but that the action of negating in the image present in the imagination is both involved and difficult to execute. By "negating" in the imagination's image we mean the subtraction of certain visualized aspects, which is tantamount to denying that they belong to the visualized figure. We use this device often in our intellectual attempt to solve problems, that is, we often form the negation of some positive notion, posit this as an imaginable entity, and then try to imagine the entity. A famous example is the negating of the notion that through a given point on a plane there can be only one straight line parallel to a given straight line. The working out of such a negation led to the inventing of geometries different from Euclidean geometry.

We now consider the possibility of defining "the straight" as it is visualized in the imagination. We can attempt to duplicate the process of arriving at "straight" in the imagination by defining cube and then subtracting dimensions in our definition. By deleting the notion of depth our definition is reduced to being that of a rectangular plane. By deleting breadth it is reduced to saying that "straight" is extension in one dimension only. There is nothing self-contradictory in such a definition, although we cannot visualize "straight" as it is thus defined because the minimum requirement quantitatively for visualization is that what is visualized be an area. This is not a difficulty in speculative knowledge, since the intellect's manner of considering things does not demand that they actually be located in time and place. In fact all artistic devising, whether of quantitative factors or not, takes place in the imagination under direction of some cognitive power, such as the cogitative in projecting future actions and the intellect in visualizing meanings (assessing the adequacy of the general sense image to the meaning that it is meant to convey). It is to the purely quantitative (minimally qualitative) constructions in the imagination that we apply the term *mathematical* primarily. Thus we can visualize triangles with straight (minimal breadth) lines for sides, and many other plane and solid figures apart from the quantities that actually exist. These mathematicals are not completely abstract since they exist in the imagination, but they are *partially abstract* by comparison with the shapes of actually existing quantities. We cannot draw straight lines because actual quantities are too uneven, but we *can* approximate them in our imagination—this is sufficient basis for our definitions.

As existing in their definitions the triangles and the other figures can be called *completely abstract mathematicals*. As the elaboration of mathematics proceeded historically, it became increasingly clear that reference to actual existents as the occasion for defining mathematicals diminished to minimal importance. Thus in the development of what we call the natural numbers it was only necessary to have some quantity as the subject for enumeration. The size or shape of each quantity did not matter; it only mattered that the quantity could be considered as discrete, that is, as separate or separable from other quantities. The attempt to model geometric figures upon actual shapes occurring in nature persisted for many centuries after the compiling of the *Elements* by Euclid. Mathematicians gradually came to realize, however, that what they were doing in imitating natural shapes could be done just as well by assuming various elementary quantities as having a minimum of determinate characteristics (the x used in elementary algebra, for example) and then forming all conceivable arrangements of these quantities, among which would be the figures that they had been copying from natural things. Thus contemporary mathematics as a speculative discipline involves the free inventing of combinations and interrelationships among the parts of continuous quantities and among discrete quantities. The notion of these quantities is arrived at by a process of *subtraction* similar to the one involved in imagining a straight line. The *abstraction from singular to common* is usually unnoticed because in the mathematics dealing with abstract quantities, such as the shapes analyzed in geometry and the sets used in set theory, what is discovered about the *type* of mathematical involved is often discovered from just one instance of it. There are very few sense qualities involved in the grasping or inventing of these mathematicals, and consequently the distracting and obscuring factors are at a minimum.

Mathematicals have a practical usefulness to the extent that they can be used to order matter and to calculate the results beforehand. Thus mathematics is indispensable in physical science and commerce, which consider things largely from a quantitative point of view, and also in many trades and arts that are concerned with the production of effects in matter involving the manipulation of quantities. Mathematics considered as the knowledge of completely abstract mathematicals has great precision because of its abstraction; considered as knowledge by means of imagined forms (geometry) it is less precise, as we have seen. But in both instances the precision is greater than any to which we can attain in the measuring and manipulating of actual quantities. Thus we can imagine a circle with perfectly circular circumference, but we can only approximate this perfect circularity in assigning a circular shape to actual matter. Similarly, we can divide four into two twos in thought and by the use of symbols in our imagination. But when we attempt to divide a two-pound cake of soap exactly into two one-pound portions, we can never know if we have succeeded or not. If we use a scale that registers only pounds and does not measure fractions of pounds, then our portions could be unequal by several ounces without our knowing it. Using a scale registering only ounces, we could be off by several fractions of an ounce in our measurement. If we use a scale registering billionths of an ounce, we could be in error by a ten-billionth of an ounce. Therefore, although we can easily obtain perfect precision symbolically in the imagination's representation of the division of the soap ($2 = 1$ and 1), and we can easily understand what one pound is (an arbitrary and approximately invariable unit of mass defined in some practical manner such as "the mass of a piece of platinum preserved in the Standards Office in London"), we can never be sure that any other mass is exactly equal to the standard pound. The mathematicals that can be imagined and those that can only be defined can serve as models for the ordering of matter; that ordering approximates the precision of the mathematicals according as human ingenuity devises ever finer means of discriminating quantity.

Insofar as mathematicals are a model for imposing order and regularity on matter, they have a practical usefulness and are a means of attaining a knowledge of matter that could not otherwise be obtained. In fact, they can supply the very form by which some material entities are apprehended. Thus by applying the notion of spherical shape to the imagination's representation of our planet earth, many men were able to interpret the sinking of a ship from sight as it passed the horizon, and the circular shape of the shadow cast by the earth on the moon in a lunar eclipse, to mean that the earth was spherical in shape. Later explorations verified these deductions. Such intuiting of mathematical relationships (quantitative ones) between phenomena, and their verification or falsification, are commonplace in contemporary physical science.

We have dealt with only two kinds of abstraction, one in which the intellect garners notions of what is common to all material things and to various species of material things as represented by the senses; the other in which quantity is treated as though quantity itself were a substantial existent, and the parts, properties, and interrelationships of quantities are also considered. The method of determining what is common to singulars represented in the senses is the same in both of these kinds of abstraction, although it was stressed more in the first kind. The two kinds of abstraction differ in the formal viewpoint involved. This viewpoint is the *sensorially qualitative* in what we call "physical abstraction," and the *imaginationally quantitative* in the second. Thus "abstraction" means to know what is common among singular instances of qualitative being and of quantified being. If we but reflect upon the many aspects of qualitative being treated in chemistry, and upon the multifarious developments within mathematics, we can see that abstraction is an initial activity on the part of the intellect, which is followed by thinking about the notions of various kinds of being attained by abstraction. It is by intellection of the acts of the sense powers in sensing and by abstraction from the multiplicity of incidental details in the sensory awareness of singular things that the intellect gets its start in comprehending being. Its progress from there is discussed in Chapter 6.

There is some question as to whether the two kinds of abstraction we have described in detail are the only kinds. Within each kind are as many different abstractions as there are formal viewpoints adopted by the various physical and mathematical and mathematico-physical sciences.[8] It is also possible to discern some common traits among the less common (but nevertheless common) notions obtained by the first two kinds of abstraction. One consideration of logic is to see what is common among the various kinds of classification that the intellect makes—and thus it distinguishes genus from species. Similarly metaphysics considers aspects that are common to all finite being, no matter what kind it is, and arrives at notions such as potency and act. We shall not treat of these abstractions in this work, since our intention is to explain the characteristic operations of the intellect, and the two kinds of abstraction we have analyzed are sufficiently illustrative of this act of the intellect.[9]

Man obtains much information about himself and his universe through actual experience. Our analysis of the manner in which the intellect can receive information, however, has indicated that, when experience is expressed as a meaning, then that meaning can be communicated to other persons by words even though the experience itself is quite incommunicable. Thus some words are representative of meanings, since we coin them to stand for what we have both experienced and understood. Other words, such as proper names and words used to designate mere recognition of a difference rather than a knowledge of what that difference really is, are less meaningful but are nevertheless a means of communication. We must investigate this method of communicating because the manner in which mere configurations of lines (written words) and mere combinations of sounds (spoken words) can take the place of sensory apprehension and accumulated experience is a part of exploring all of the ways by which the human intellect is informed.

Each human being's experiences, feelings, and desires are personal and therefore not directly communicable. By the use of words, however, he can evoke in the consciousness of another person not only memories and imaginings of events, but also an understanding of what experiences, feelings, and desires are. There is nothing in man's experience that cannot be spoken of and thereby communicated to some extent. The simplest sensations, the strongest emotions, the most esoteric beliefs, and the most evident facts can all be expressed in whole or in part by words. Any person whose experience is limited by unfortunate circumstances can range the surface of our globe and the depths of space in his imagination, once he has mastered the use of words and has ready access to the records of the experiences and thoughts of others.

Hearsay Learning

WORDS AS SIGNS TO A RATIONAL MIND

The ability to use words is proper to rational beings and is not shared in any degree by the other inhabitants of the earth. Other creatures of the earth do have means of communication, though, some of which have been discovered and interpreted by man. But no use of words has been discovered in such communications; they are restricted entirely to the use of natural signs.[10] Comparative experiments have been made on the learning ability of normal human children and infant simians, which showed that progress was comparable for the simian and the child until the latter began to grasp the meanings of words. From that point on, the human being manifested his rational nature by completely outstripping the simian in all activities depending upon the ability to associate words, actions, or things. One ought not to conclude from such comparisons that man has some marvelous sense power to apprehend language, and that if the simian could only develop such a power, he could easily compete with man in all human endeavors. Many attempts based upon such a faulty assumption have been made in educating animals and have persistently come to naught. The reason for this failure is that the difference between the mere sentiency possessed by brutes and the rational intelligence of man cannot be bridged. Man's rational intelligence is an innate power presupposed to the acquiring of a skill like the mastery of language.

The sensory apparatus involved in man's use of words is considerable. Although the written and the spoken word of the same spelling have the same meaning, their use requires learned skills for different powers. These skills are acquired by repetition, whereas the detecting of meaningful sounds seems to be as spontaneous as the hearing of any sound. In the latter case, however, there is an acquired skill in distinguishing the conventionally meaningful sounds from those having merely a natural signification, but the human person starts acquiring this skill so early in life that he tends to overlook it. Thus the use of words in communication depends upon acquired habits of seeing, hearing, sound-making, and hand-moving. These habits are closely related, for the writing of a word one hears involves not only the understanding of its meaning, but also the visualizing of its letters and the motor skill of putting them legibly upon paper. All of the sensory skills involved should be classed as habits of the power called imagination, since we have assigned all acts of mere reproduction of sensed sensibles to this power. The motor skill would be assigned primarily to the muscles of the hand and arms, the agents forming the legible marks on paper. Since writing is a voluntarily acquired activity rather than a reflex one, its source as a representation of something is in the imagination where judgment as to how well the written marks correspond to the desired ones is based. Because they are deliberately formed, all of these habits ultimately have a rational source. They differ from other habits inasmuch as they are concerned with meanings as signified by conventional symbols. Therefore these habits come under the direction of the intellect in a special way, for the intellect alone apprehends meanings and knows how to code them into symbols that express meaning.[11]

One distinction in the use of words must be noted here to indicate our appraisal of an opinion that reduces all words to signifying only what can be detected by the senses. The distinction is between words that signify what can be sensed and words that signify what can never be sensed. For a term to have a signification means that it has a meaning. A term's having a meaning denotes that it is being used as a sign of the understanding of something. Thus the distinction between terms according as they do or do not represent sensibles is basically a distinction between kinds of understanding. If a term is used for which there is no corresponding understanding, then that term can be said to signify nothing or to be an invalid term. Thus "wordless speech" and "dry wetness" are nonsensical, but "sky" and "orange" easily evoke understanding because they can be located in our sensible experience. "Man" and "nation" also evoke understanding. But there is a difference in the signification of the latter, for they simultaneously signify both that to which one can point and that to which one can never point. Man's shape and distinctive physical features can be pointed to; his temperament, memory, beliefs,

Man's Physical and Spiritual Nature

and awareness of obligation cannot be sensed. One can point to the human elements that constitute a nation, but their convictions and the determination to follow them cannot be located in space. Thus it is manifestly impossible to hold that all words are validated by an appeal to sensory information alone. Words have come into existence as men decided to make use of them for expressing their thoughts, and just as rational thought transcends the limitations of mere sensory experience so many words in the language of civilized groups signify meanings that cannot be validated by any sensory experience.

LEARNING THROUGH WORDS

Some terms, then, do signify what we have experienced, while some signify notions that we have arrived at through reflection upon what we have experienced. Terms are useful because they enable men to communicate rapidly and precisely without their having to resort to pictures or to any other kind of reproduction of the actual things being discussed. The manner in which terms, sense images, and thoughts are interconnected is still a subject of investigation, but some aspects of their relatedness can easily be grasped. We have already seen the dependence of the intellect upon sensory experience for the obtaining of an understanding of things. Therefore the recall of some previous act of understanding may be accompanied by the recall of the sensory experience upon which it was based or the recall of some part of that experience. Conversely, the reoccurrence in the present of events experienced in the past is the occasion for understanding these events in the same manner as previously. Conventional terms, however, can take the place of the actual presence of things as a basis for the act of understanding. Such understanding is not achieved through abstraction nor through direct intellectual awareness of the apprehensive acts of individual external senses. It is achieved by the recognition of the meaning of words and the acceptance of that meaning as possibly being informative about things. Thus, "blueness" and "sky" are discriminated by sensory experience. That the sky has a blue appearance because of the way in which dust particles in the air affect the sunlight passing through the earth's atmosphere can be understood simply by knowing the meaning of the terms and of their arrangement in the explanatory statement. Moreover one can understand this statement without imagining "sky" or "dust" or "light," although usually some activity of the imagination over and above the retaining of conventional symbols accompanies thinking. Thus the presence of actually existing sensibles or of our remembered experience of them is required for our initial acts of understanding, but whatever can be learned in terms of these basic acts of understanding can be learned by reference to them alone without any reliance upon sensory information. In the previous example, blueness can be understood to be a quality affecting sight directly, while dust can be understood to be small particles of matter and sunlight to be energy radiated from a source distant from the earth. The refraction of sunlight by dust particles can be understood as the selective bending and scattering from a straight-line path of part of the radiated energy.

There are other examples of understanding in which there is no possibility of referring to an actual or remembered sensible because the understanding is far removed from sensibles. Thus "emergencies are occasions for calling upon clear thinking" expresses a judgment about an understanding that is not tied to any given sensory experience; and "Classification is useful for any attempt at definition" is a judgment about understanding to which nothing in sensory experience can ever correspond. From these examples it is now evident that learning can take place solely by the comprehension of the meaning attached to conventional symbols, provided they are based upon meanings that have been grasped from experience of things, of sensory activities or of the acts of the intellect itself.

Some characteristics are peculiar to the act of learning from the words used by others when contrasted with the act of learning from experience. We shall consider them now, along with the characteristics the two methods of learning have in common.

LEARNING FROM STATEMENTS OF OTHERS

No one can accumulate more than a very small part of all of the experience that the human race as a whole has obtained, and sensory experience can only be shared (in a limited way) when those who share it experience the same sensibles and are in much the same subjective condition (two people enjoying the same sunrise, for example). Therefore an individual man's knowledge of the world about him would be as limited as that of a nonrational animal if he could not communicate by words. Furthermore, no advance in the understanding of our universe would be possible if each new generation were unable to communicate by words the knowledge learned by previous generations. If such were our unfortunate condition there would be no history and no science, no profiting from past mistakes and no satisfactory answers to the recurring questions about the natures of things.

Thus man in relation to all the possible knowledge of all things is much like our solar universe in relation to the rest of the heavenly universe. Just as our small part of the heavens is separated by vast stretches of comparatively empty space from the rest of the heavens, so each individual human being is prevented from experiencing the larger part of what is knowable about our earth and heavens because of his location in only one of millions of places at any given time and in a comparatively short period of the vastness of time. Yet, to accumulate the experience necessary for the understanding of some one physical nature requires the attention of the person seeking such knowledge in a definite part of his environment and over varying periods of time. For example, to discriminate the appearances of some sensible does not require much time or concentration, but to detect the characteristics peculiar to "apple" as distinct from "pear" and to generalize to the notion of fruit as "edible seed-container" require both time for observation and the intellectual act of discerning the common elements revealed by observation. It is obvious, then, that just as physical distance is a barrier to our seeing clearly what the rest of the heavens are like, so physical and temporal distance restrict each human being's actual experience to the small portion of all reality that he can actually observe.

Man as a *specific kind of knowing creature* runs into barriers of time and distance also; for there are things that are difficult to observe not only because they are beyond the range of human vision in distance, but also because they are too small to be discriminated by human sight. Furthermore, many knowable aspects of reality happened when men were not present to observe them and in areas where man could not observe them (for instance, on the ocean floor or on the surfaces of most planets). Individual men have sought to overcome these limitations to their knowing by the use of three methods that have become characteristic of the knowing activities of the human species. Thus it is by virtue of *man's ability to draw inferences* from present evidence about the state of the universe and its contents in the past and in the future, and about its hidden factors in the present, that he is called scientific. Similarly *his ability to devise instruments* to extend the range of his senses is a testimony to his rational ability to adapt means to ends. The universally obvious sign of man's intelligence is *his use of words for communication,* for words are the ordinary means of expressing our reasoned deductions. Whereas many persons do not engage in experimental investigations such as those undertaken by contemporary physical sciences, everyone can benefit from such investigations when their nature and results are communicated by words. The use of words thus enables us to communicate our experiences and thoughts to one another, not only as a means of exchanging facts and opinions but also as an important means of learning.

Each human child develops a practical understanding of the appearances and events that occur often in his conscious experience, so that he acts towards them in a manner satisfactory to himself. He gradually enlarges this understanding by his own activities and has it enlarged by others when he learns to interpret their words. It may be true that *most* of a child's interests are quite practical, but this does not stifle his interest in seeking to find out what things are. As we have shown, the indispensable element from which rational understanding begins is sensory experience, and an awareness of *what things are* is involved in the awareness of *what things are for.* These two aspects of human knowledge develop together, but they are not identical. The cultivated human desire for practical knowledge leads man to discover the uses of things, irrespective of what they are over and above their being objects of use; while the pursuer of speculative knowledge uses information of a practical nature to the extent that it helps in ferreting out the ultimate constituents and causes of our universe. Each member of the human race, possessed of normally functioning powers, is capable of great progress in the acquisition of both kinds of information, so much so that we can compare the human intellect to a writing tablet that is so extensive that there is no obvious limit to how much can be inscribed on it.

The Aristotelian analogy between a blank writing surface and the human intellect is a good illustration of the unprejudiced attitude of the human mind toward its first information. It also shows the unlimited scope of this power, which can know not only the acts of the sense powers and all that these acts discriminate, but can also go far beyond the range of the senses by the invention of instruments and by acts of reasoning. The endlessness of the intellect's desire for information is manifested in youth by our delight in novelties, and in the mature person of intellectual attainments, by his simultaneous grasp of some part of his chosen field of study and his glimpse of the many aspects yet to be explored. More homely signs of the human intellect's constant interest in information are found in our alertness to conversations, even those not directed to us; in our attention to all kinds of writing, signs, and doodle marks made by others, even torn up messages that have to be assembled in order to be read; and in the obvious fondness of many literate human beings for reading books, newspapers, pamphlets, and so forth. Of course there are many motives behind our various word-apprehending activities. But even so, these activities manifest the nature of our intellect as an omnivorous assimilator of information.

We need to distinguish the various ways in which the intellect can handle the information received verbally in order to distinguish information that can be related to some experience from information that is merely matter for belief. If someone describes to us a series of events in which he took part, we can usually review the events he describes by appealing to our imagination and memory. If he is recounting a tale of his own prowess and exaggerates too much, our belief balks at accepting an account of events that our own experience tells us is highly improbable. This act of checking a verbal account against what our personal experience indicates to be possible and probable applies to any kind of information as long as it fulfills the prerequisite of being related to some human experience. However, if the verbal account refers to an experience we have never had, or if we have never had a similar experience, we can only try to piece together some factors from our own experience in order to substantiate in a sensory way what we are being told.

Abstraction and Hearsay Learning   173

Because of the readiness of the intellect to receive information, we have a tendency to accept whatever can be understood and to assimilate it with what has already been understood. Thus, information that is based solely on authority of others can find just as ready acceptance as that based on personal experience. *Hearsay information* comes from many sources, from parents and teachers and textbooks. All of these sources are generally quite trustworthy because they are directed to the welfare of those whom they instruct. Even so, some statements that we accept on the authority of such benevolent instructors may be found to be at odds with experience. The parental chiding that "Smoking will stunt your growth" runs counter to the fact that the child being warned has a ten-year-old friend who smokes and who is almost six feet tall. Statements made in a general way, that "Tulips bloom early in the spring" for example, may be contradicted in several instances because the ideal conditions for blooming did not prevail. Thus statements made with the best of intentions must sometimes be modified by the hearer to account for the facts of experience.

Argumentative textbooks and argumentative persons are not usually accepted with the same quiescence with which we accept statements from those instructing us in a purely informative way. The reason for this is that argument goes further than does mere exposition—it proceeds from what is easily cognized to what is deduced therefrom—and we are reluctant to accept conclusions casually put forth by others until we have tested them carefully in our own thought at our leisure. Argument attempts to gain convictions about both understandings and beliefs, for beliefs are to actions what proofs are to progress in probing the hidden factors in our universe.[12] We act according as we believe our actions will attain future goals, and we make progress in the science of what is not yet evident to us by establishing irrefutable proofs that lead us toward that knowledge.

The brief analysis of hearsay information just given, while revealing its importance as the most common means contemporary man uses to enlarge his store of information, also points to a difficulty in its acceptance—hearsay information may be reliable or it may be incorrect. When we plan to use hearsay information as a guide for our activities, the truth or falsity of that information can mean success or failure in the venture. There-

Man's Physical and Spiritual Nature

fore it is necessary for each person to exercise discretion with respect to the source and probable correctness of hearsay information. That is, a man must make his own decisions as to the meanings embodied in his own experience and as to the reliability of the information imported to him by others. All acts of decision as to what is the nature of a thing and as to whether information is true or false are acts of the intellect judging. This act of judging is not in fact separate from the act of seeing what is common to many singulars, but we have concentrated upon the attaining of information in this chapter to make the rather complex activities of the intellect easier to understand. In the next chapter we shall consider the intellectual act of judgment and all that it involves.

CHAPTER 6

Judgment and Truth ~ OUR SENSE OF SIGHT

in cognizing visible sensibles discriminates hues of color and intensities of illumination—it is therefore the proper judge of these matters.[1] Our sight's ability to discriminate in this way can be known to us intellectually if we simply pay attention to its activity and thus distinguish the seeing from the seen, as was done in Chapters 3 and 4. It should be noted, however, that our sight itself does not reflect upon its own activity. Sight knows the visible, but it does not know seeing. Even the act of carefully examining the excised organs of sight yields to sight only hues, sizes, shapes, and motions of the parts of the organs. The case is the same for the other direct senses, since by them we grasp only their proper sensible and some common sensibles. Our senses do not discriminate between what is being sensed and the act of sensing. In short, none of our senses comprehends its own act.

The All-knowing Intellect

By contrast, intellectually we understand both the sensed thing and the sensation of it. For this reason we can correct sensory impressions that do not accurately represent the way things really are. Thus we *see* a straight stick that is partially immersed in water as being bent at the water line and *understand* that in this case the visual impression does not represent the stick as it actually exists, because the water is bending the rays of light by which we see the stick. Similarly we can correct words that we misspelled as we wrote them down on paper by making a critical comparison of the way the words do appear with the way they ought to appear. The remembering of words and their meaning is a joint action of the imagination and the intellect; the intellect's role as the power that understands the activity of this sense power and directs it is quite obvious.

The scrutiny of the human intellect extends even to its own activities. Thus the researcher looking for significance in the results of his experiments, and reading the accounts of similar experiments performed by others, is quite conscious that he is searching *his own understanding* for clues to the essential activities of some nature and that he is reading an account of *the understanding achieved by the intellects of investigators* who conducted similar experiments. Besides these activities of abstraction and understanding, and of considering hearsay information, our awareness extends to our acts of judging about the mode of existence of something whose meaning we have grasped, and to our acts of reasoning and of assembling words to express what we think. In short, the human intellect is a *self-reflexive* power that knows things, their appearances, and their manner of existence, and also knows its own acts of apprehending and judging by which it knows them.

In this chapter we shall see that it is because the intellect has the tremendous ability to permeate all of reality, even its own acts, that it can exercise a *critical judgment* as to how well representations of things correspond with the actual things, and as to how well actual human activities correspond with what they ought to be. Such a power as this has the ability not only to make judgments and to determine the truth and falsity of its own judgments, but also to be critical of those made by other intellects. *Intellect is indeed the supreme knowing power in man.* In the first part of this chapter we shall consider the acts by which we add to those elementary notions about things that are the beginnings of intellectual knowledge, and then proceed to a discussion of the intellect as a critical power capable of forming judgments of truth.

The act of the human intellect by which we build up our rudimentary apprehensions of material being is called *composition*. The act by which we separate in thought notions of the attributes of things that do not exist together in reality is called *division*. Since these acts are presupposed in all judgments of truth and falsity, it is to these acts that we shall now direct our attention.

Composition and Division

The intellectual act of abstraction consists in concentrating on some aspect of the subject being studied so that it may be singled out and understood, both in itself and as an aspect of that subject. The richness of being of everything occurring in nature, and the limited apprehension characteristic of the acts of the senses, guarantee that no single act of abstraction will reveal the whole intelligibility of any material thing. Therefore many acts of abstraction are possible upon any subject matter under consideration, and many are necessary in order to circumscribe its intelligibility under any one formality. Thus, to understand oxygen adequately in its role as part of the atmosphere, quite a lot of information about its production by plants and its fixation by animal respiration and by fire is required. This, however, is only a small part of the possible knowledge about oxygen; consequently, although its role as an atmospheric gas can be understood under that viewpoint quite correctly, there are other viewpoints from which oxygen can be studied successfully. For example, oxygen is studied as a component of metallic oxides and of water. Some of these partial viewpoints can be (and have been) coalesced into one formal viewpoint of oxygen as a chemical element in all of its occurrences and activities. This viewpoint when extended to all such elements is the study of matter that we call chemistry. Such knowledge is acquired through compositions in which new information is added to what has already been acquired about a subject. As an indication of this, one may examine a textbook in inorganic chemistry and note how one's knowledge of the subject is increased from quite elementary notions by the constant addition of new notions that are combined with those already grasped.

CONTINUITY IN LEARNING

In order that some continuity be maintained between the thing or kind of thing being investigated and what is being learned of it, something in thought must stand for the actual thing or kind of thing; this something is added to successively as more and more is learned about it. Since the most common aspect of all things apprehensible by the human intellect is that of "being actual" or "actually being" (however one may choose to express it), the notion of "being-something-actual" is logically the basic concept to which additions can be made as knowledge becomes more complete. The much-quoted statement of St. Thomas, *Primo in intellectu cadit ens*, points to the relatively indeterminate notion of *ens* as the focal point for the addition of knowledge in our attempt to elaborate concepts that are adequate understandings of things. This notion of being is the least determinate of all notions; consequently it is the most elementary understanding we can have of every thing and every kind of thing. It signifies their actuality as possessing existence in some way. What else could be first in the intellect, since only what is actual is knowable directly?

We do not mean that we always, or even very often, use the notion of being in its naked simplicity as that to which we add further determining notions in elaborating a concept adequate to some kind of thing. The island universe of the child's experience contains a multitude of familiar things. In learning their names, as well as what they are (distinguishing in both names and understandings that some are very common and applicable to nearly everything, while many others are restricted to only a few things or only to one thing), he accumulates most of the basic notions that can serve to identify the thing about which he is learning and to which he can add new notions as he discovers them. Thus the child enlarges his island of knowledge by discovering different kinds of familiar things (different kinds of food, of toys, of trees, and so forth) and by discovering new relationships among familiar things. In this process the same basic notions are used over and over again as the starting points in the process of learning something new. In the act of analyzing a developed understanding of something into its most common parts, however, we logically end up with the notion of being as the most common and the least determinate.

COMPOSITION AS MERE ADDITION

The act of adding new notes to those that already identify a nature or thing about which we are thinking is *composition*. It is usually accompanied by a verbal composition in the imagination. Thus to the notion of "being a solid" we add the notion of "being fruit" to produce a nondefinitive notion that adequately represents some aspects common to all apples. Similarly, we add the notions of comparative smallness and of the possession of an electrical charge to the notion of mass in rapid motion in an attempt to form an adequate understanding of an atomic particle.

Since we can join in thought any notions that are not mutually contradictory, the multiplicity of different compositions possible is limited only by the condition that self-contradictory compositions do not make sense. Thus one can understand the meaning of "Mountains are edible" and "Sparrows are good swimmers," and judge that these compositions do not correspond to the actual combinations of things and characteristics they are supposed to describe, for the attributes do not belong to the subject. However, we cannot understand "Mountains are nonmountains" or "Birds are nonbirds," because these compositions are self-contradictory. We cannot make sense out of statements that say that an attribute simultaneously does and does not belong to a subject. All compositions other than self-contradictory ones can be understood by the intellect; they can be entertained as representations in thought that possibly do conform to the combination of aspects that exist together in things.

COMPOSITION AND THE SENSES

Although the intellect is the power that enables us to go beyond the mere appearances of things and to detect common natures, relationships, and interdependencies among things, it is not restricted in its acts of composition to thinking about common natures and relations. The intellect can also encompass in its judgments all singular aspects of things, to the extent that they are the proper and common objects of the various senses. Thus the imagination, which spontaneously records the sensed aspects of the present sensible, and also the cogitative and its memory may enter into the act of composing with a singular subject. The compositions, "This pen is truly green" and "That stroke of luck befell me once before," involve the intellect and the imagination, and the intellect and the memory, respectively, as well as the external senses.

Further, the same singular topic may be involved in a long series of compositions that add more and more information about the topic. For example, by using the name of a friend as the subject of a series of attributive propositions we may attribute to him each event of his life. This constitutes a multiplicity both considerable in extent and incomplete as long as he lives—a multiplicity of rememberings on the sensory level subserving a multiplicity of understandings on the intellectual level. Although a remembered sequence of events is usually remembered as the sequence actually occurred in time, once its beginning has been recalled; nevertheless composition, which attributes the remembered experience to a definite subject, is exclusively an intellectual act inasmuch as no sense power is aware of the notions of "being" or "having," and these two notions are involved in every act of composition.[2] Thus to judge that an apple is red is to assert that it *exists* with a red appearance, or equivalently that it has redness. Even in compositions that involve absolute identity, as "This is Sam" and "Triangle is a three-sided polygon," the notion of identity in being and identity in meaning is a notion of how two ways of considering something exist as coinciding with one another. Therefore, although composition involves the acts of the external and internal senses, it is basically an intellectual act.

The act of composition correctly performed adds to our knowledge. It is a means of expanding both our experience of material being, for there are additions to our sensory apprehension of one and the same thing or kind of thing on the sensory level, and also our understanding of various natures and genera of being. The mere act of understanding what something is, however, or of what a term means, does not indicate which meanings or which terms should be brought together in composition except when the meanings are known necessarily to involve one another. Thus the understanding of "rational" and "animal," or of "straight line" and "three-sided plane figure," yields no clue that these sets of notions can be combined to give a correct understanding of man and triangle, whereas the understanding of "animal" necessarily involves "substance" and "living" as part of its meaning. For "Animals are living substances" is a composition about which there can be no doubt of correctness, once "animal" is understood. Accordingly as the intellect increases its apprehension of material being and understanding of the interconnectedness of things, it learns of more necessary implicit connections between terms and can express them in compositions the correctness of which is beyond question. For example, man is a rational animal, triangle is a three rectilinear-sided plane figure. That these compositions be known to be correct, however, presupposes the critical discrimination by the intellect of the degree of conformity between composition in the intellect and the actual manner of existence of things. This critical judgment will be examined in detail further on in this chapter.

DIVISION AND NEGATION

When we are abstracting some common attribute from our experience of sensibles, many other aspects of our experience are simply left out of consideration by the very act of discerning what is common. Thus in noting the physical constitution of several apples that have been cut open to reveal their cores and seeds, we cannot simultaneously note the number of seeds in a core, the slight variations in seed shape, and the fragility of the meat of the apple. The act of counting the number of seeds in a core prevents our making a detailed examination of the vagaries in shape of each seed, and likewise prevents us from systematically testing the texture of the meat of the apple. Therefore, to the extent that we cannot grasp all of these aspects of the apples simultaneously, we fix on some aspects and ignore the rest at that moment. This division of our attention does not necessarily involve any intellectual act of denying or negating an attribute of a subject. In the attempt, however, to distinguish among all of the known aspects of a thing—elements that are truly common to a nature from those that are incidental—explicit separating off of the incidental aspects is necessary by a judgment that such aspects are not to be included in the definition. Such negation does not appear in the definition. Thus in determining the nature of citric acid by extracting it from the pulp of citrus fruits, we concentrate on determining the chemical formula and deliberately exclude all considerations about fruit that are not relevant to this determination.

The quite explicit *act of negation*, then, is found in the denying of some aspect of a subject. In the statement, "John is not here," the act of being in some designated location is explicitly divided off from all of the singular characteristics that can be correctly attributed to John now. This intellectual act of negation does not achieve the same correspondence between thought and reality that composition does. When composition is correct, there is a genuine addition to the known aspects of the subject of the composition, so that the degree of completeness of the correspondence between the knowledge and the whole actuality of the thing increases. But correct judgments of negation do not increase the degree of correspondence of the knowledge of the subject to the actuality of the subject, because there are no negations that actually exist in nature.

Negations are exclusively intellectual acts in which attributes are explicitly excluded from what is meant by the subject, and modes of existence are excluded as being proper indications of how the subject exists. No sense power is capable of apprehending by means of negations. Thus sight does not discriminate a color as "not red," but as green or yellow or some other definite hue. The imagination does not so much negate or divide off breadth from a line as reduce it to the minimum size imaginable. The breadth thus subtracted is left out of consideration altogether. In intellectual negation, though, the feature divided off frequently remains as a content of our apprehension (except in the aforementioned instance of searching for a positive attribution); for we define "line" as dimension in one direction (without breadth), but we define "straight" as not curved.[3] The imagination does engage in many acts of composition, as in imagining a golden apple, but it does not have any capacity to represent negations or nonbeing in any other way than by combinations of symbols. Its manipulation of sensory aspects to depict desired scenes involves some selection, and therefore avoidance (a kind of division). What is avoided is not capable of being imagined as something negated, it can only be imagined as discrete from something else, or be left out of the contents of the present activity of the imagination altogether.

The *negation* involved in our intellectual acts of identifying things is *indicative of a limitation* in our ability to apprehend intellectually, because all of the things presented to us on the level of magnitude that enables our senses to operate correctly are positive and definite. Thus to call one kind of curved surface or line irregular is to admit our inability to find the formulas properly descriptive of such curves. Some of this reliance upon negations in the forming of our understanding is quite temporary, since what is known by negation now may be known in an act of composition later when the proper classification or correlation is learned. Thus an animal described as similar to a rabbit in appearance, but not as large as the rabbits we remember, may later be identified as a brown squirrel. In this instance the negative designation, "not as large as a rabbit," gave place to the positive notion of "the size of a brown squirrel." *In intellectual acts other than mere apprehension the use of negations is not a sign of imperfection;* it is rather a sure sign of the intellect's ability to transcend the limitations of the senses in distinguishing and expressing the true and the false.

PRIOR KNOWLEDGE AS CATEGORIES

Both composition and division depend upon prior knowledge, as the meaning of the terms expressing this intellectual activity clearly indicate. What is this prior knowledge? In elaborating an understanding, prior knowledge is some notion corresponding to that element in the thing which allows us to discriminate it as a possible object of intellectual understanding. Thus it may be merely a visible something or a touch-stimulating something, according to the way that we become aware of it. Now, this manner of identifying the object is truly intellectual and is truly an understanding (although very minimal), but we recognize that this very limited way of identifying a thing is not at all adequate to the encompassing of the actual intelligibility that it will yield if we concentrate on it. Accordingly, we naturally (if our interest is caught) sort out from our previous understanding notions brought together in thought to represent this kind of thing before us. This process involves the use of notions that are quite stable as elements in our understanding of things and for which there is an easily grasped terminology usually obtained in late infancy and early childhood. We mentioned these notions briefly earlier in connection with the child's enlarging of his universe of knowledge; we mention them again now to indicate clearly what is presupposed by all acts of composition and division. Those notions that are basic in communications we call *categories* in order to indicate their usefulness as a basis for classifying many of the things we experience. We mean such notions as "the green," "the loud," and "the bitter," all of which apply to many things and are themselves classifiable in the category, sensible quality, in the mind of the person who knows this category.

If our previous analysis of intellect is correct, then its primary acts of apprehension consist in discerning what is common in our sensory experience of various sensibles. It is impossible to analyze the temporally first acts of our own intellect or of another person's intellect, because we cannot locate them. Whether or not these first acts are accompanied by the use of symbols in the imagination to stand for what is understood is a problem incapable of solution, because the expression of what we understand and of what we imagine is based upon the manipulation of words and therefore presupposes their presence in the imagination. It is obvious, however, that the initial learning of words depends upon grasping in a sensory and experiential way that which the word names or signifies.

Once our fledgling intellect has formed its own notions of what things are and has associated words with these notions (whether correctly or incorrectly does not matter, because the erroneous use of words in communication will elicit correction), it unhesitatingly fits many things met for the first time into categories that have already been formed. Thus a two-year-old child may call margarine and butter by the name "cheese" because of the similarity in appearance and use. The learning of the correct names and the distinctive features of these various foods corrects the misapprehension and enlarges the understanding while supplying new categories for the classifying of various foods. Once a few general categories have been learned, ever so many things met with in experience can be classified by them with varying degrees of complexity, depending on how many categories are used; conversely, all complex expressions of what we understand can be separated into less complex ones, and ultimately, into some expressions that stand for simple elements of human experience.

Categories Resulting from Abstraction

That the human intellect makes use of categories in its constant assimilation of the knowable universe may seem to be a mere dogmatic assertion, despite the fact that we have grounded this notion in experiences common to everyone. Therefore we shall make two further points about their use in order to make the role of categories in human knowledge as clear as possible. First, the very act of knowing what is common to many necessarily results in a notion that classifies many things by some common characteristic, or characteristics. Thus the simple act of noting that all of the objects impressing themselves upon one's visual awareness at this moment are visible and three-dimensioned, establishes three categories into which hundreds, perhaps even thousands, of things fit according as they are visible and/or three-dimensional.

Now, since the characteristic act of the intellect in understanding is not to tarry with singulars as the senses do (although it knows them as the senses know them) but to note the aspects that are similar in various things, it is impossible for the intellect to note such similarities without seeing the characteristics thus noted as being several instances of the same kind of thing, that is, as members of the same class. The very act of abstraction produces one notion that may be considered absolutely in itself without reference to any sensible, but it may also be considered as a category into which all of the singular sensibles on which it is based may be fitted as being of that kind. The categories mentioned by Aristotle in his *Organon* were set down as being logically prior, in the sense that they were the most universal classes terminating the act of breaking down an expression into its simpler parts. Such categories are useful when one wishes to be quite exact in his use of terms. Also, whenever one attempts to define or classify some element of experience these categories are useful starting points, because their meaning is easily grasped from experience. But one need not refer to them in ordinary acts of cognition, for there are as many categories in a person's thought as there are common notions; these notions seldom need to be resolved into their logically simplest elements.

The second point concerns the way in which we retain the knowledge of the various things we have understood by what they have in common with one another. Once a person has formed a notion to which he attaches the name "thing" (meaning a "that" which exists in its own right), and one to which he attaches the notion "color," and so on for the other categories, he can think of what he means by "thing" and "color" and the rest without any reference to the actual things and colors from which he obtained the notions. Also, although in apprising the essential characteristics of some nature our intellect may proceed step by step to add one notion to another, it does not recall its understanding of that nature by adding one notion to another over again as it did in the initial act of cognition. In other words, a remarkable feature of the act of composition is that it does not leave us with an assemblage of meanings showing evidence of the concept's growth through composition. The notion in our thought corresponding to the actuality of the thing understood is a unit of understanding, in which several parts that were apprehended separately on various occasions are considered all together under the one dominant feature by which the intellect is now understanding the thing. Even though one aspect of the understood essence may be dominant in one instance, this dominance does not of itself suppress, hide, or exclude any of the other intelligible features of the nature in question; rather, it includes them as actually understood and therefore as part of the intelligibility of the aspect under consideration at the moment. However, in concentrating upon or constantly remembering something by one aspect of it we may come to forget the others.

There are also aspects of the being-understood nature that are not yet understood; these potentially intelligible factors in the being in question are also included in the intellect's understanding, but as potentially intelligible actualities rather than as fully understood ones. For example, anyone can be aware that a leaf of a tree is a disposable appendage of the tree, whose shape is one means of distinguishing one kind of tree from the other. This understanding is of *what leaves are*, and is incomplete. To it may be added the notion that the process of photosynthesis occurs in the leaf and that this process is indispensable to the life of the tree. The understanding has been enlarged by the addition of understood aspects of the leaf's activity; yet that very understanding includes still other aspects that are not yet fully understood. Thus, how the energy of the sun is utilized in photosynthesis, and why the chlorophyll in the chloroplasts is green, are not fully understood. In spite of a multiplicity of actually understood and potentially intelligible factors in this knowledge of leaf, the understanding of leaf is a unity for when we are asked to explain leaves, we consider the whole unit of understanding. But since it cannot be expressed by one simple statement, we choose some one aspect and proceed to explain it and the involvement of the other factors with it. Another sign of the unity of understanding is evident in the resolution of the problem of how various aspects of a nature are related to one another, because the resolution at one stroke ties together a multiplicity of factors, thus giving them an understood unity.

Our intellect thus has functions apart from the acts of considering singulars as the senses apprehend them and of abstracting from experience. We often reflect upon that which already has been grasped in some way so as to delight in its beauty or excellence; or in order to see if the seeds of solution to a problem lie hidden in the statement of the problem; or to see if there is some wider basis of explanation that will be generic to several more specific explanations, as Newton's law of gravitation is descriptive of both terrestrial motions and planetary motions. There are other reasons for deliberating over what has been understood, especially in matters pertaining to actions to be performed where the selection of the best means to attain a desired end makes all the difference between attaining the end well or poorly, or not at all. Moreover, the necessity of reconciling nonidentical, or even conflicting, statements on a given topic requires thought.

As we have already mentioned it is possible to join any meaning to any subject being thought of, as long as there is no known contradiction involved. This fact raises the question of how we know which meanings go together and which do not in our attempt to represent things in our thought as they actually exist. How do we get assurance that the meanings of the subjects to which we assign them are correctly understood? Can we know with *certainty* and achieve *truth*, or not? To answer these questions as clearly as possible, we shall first examine the kind of judgments that are an indispensable part of our living activity because they are involved in each of our actions—practical judgments. From the analysis of these judgments we can discover what judgment is, and then apply this information to the analysis of knowledge obtained for its own sake in order to see how truth and falsity come to exist with respect to it.

Practical Truth and Falsity

Practical knowledge is that which enables us to carry out activities successfully. It is a knowledge of what can be done to things; the criterion of its correctness is the success, partial or total, or lack of success of the actions guided by it. The child's island universe of knowledge is predominantly practical knowledge at first, since it is directly subordinated to satisfying needs. But the wonder as to *what things are* is partially satisfied by practical knowledge, for a cup is what holds milk or water, and milk and water are what satisfy hunger and thirst. As the child progresses in knowledge he substantially increases his practical information and also becomes wary of incorrect information. He learns that many liquids are not good to drink and that many actions, such as striking hard objects or touching hot objects, have very undesirable consequences. In short, each one of us learns some practical truths about the things in his environment.

PRACTICAL KNOWLEDGE

Practical truth is found in the judgment made by a person that some of his past actions and the results of those actions conformed to his desires and hence were truly practical. With respect to present and future actions, this person can be guided by the success of past actions and by the failure of other actions to attain the desired end in deciding which means will assuredly attain to the desired end. Thus he can drink milk in the expectation that his thirst will be lessened. The test of this proposed action is the actual drinking of the milk; when this has been done a decision as to whether the milk did in fact lessen his thirst can be made. As long as the decision concerns a completed action, it is easy to compare the desired result with the achieved result and to decide whether they conform in all particulars or not.

When the decision as to the success of the action concerns an action going on, or one projected for the future, the basis for the comparison is not the same. In the first instance all the details are unchangeably fixed (there is no changing the past), whereas in the second instance the details are known only tentatively because they come under our control in varying degrees and are not fixed unchangeably until the action is completed. In the first instance we can tell ourselves that the action fulfilled our desire, in the second instance we can tell ourselves that the action will *quite probably, probably,* or *merely possibly,* fulfill our desire according as our past experience enables us to judge about the degree of control that we have over the various factors involved. To put the matter succinctly, we can say that practical judgments as to past events are quite certain when we have a sure knowledge of what was desired and of what happened; practical judgments as to present and future events are necessarily tentative.

High and Low Expectancies in Practical Knowledge

There are areas of experience in which the accuracy of practical judgments is quite high and others in which it is quite low. In the common-sense universe of everyday experience a person posits hundreds of actions—dressing, eating, moving about a room—with a minimum of concern that they may not be successful. This common-sense universe is called such because each person knows with a knowledge that he shares with most other persons he meets that certain actions are sensible (reasonable), while others are foolish. The range of activities covered by this accepted knowledge of how to act depends upon the sophistication of the group possessing it. Thus every reasonable person in American society knows enough to avoid the shock of powerful electric currents, to avoid being hit by a heavy vehicle, to move on the correct side of the road in traffic, and so forth; and every sensible human being knows the need of appeasing thirst, hunger, tiredness, and the like. In groups of people that have some special interest in common there are further utterly reasonable notions shared by all of the members of a group. Thus bankers are agreed that lending money to a bad risk is foolish, and merchants that a dissatisfied customer is not likely to return with his business.

The reason for the common agreement in these areas of activity is that familiarity with the activities in question has assured us of their regularity and consequent dependability. This familiarity has enabled us to know more about the kinds of things our customary actions deal with than a casual encounter would reveal. In practical matters, the better our knowledge of the things lying within our power, so that we can control where they shall be and how they shall operate, the greater practical control we have over them. Success in understanding how to manipulate familiar objects to make them serve our desires engenders an expectancy as to what will or will not happen as we use these objects in the future. For example, as a result of using ordinary porcelain drinking cups and heavy plastic cups over a period of time, a person learns to expect that the porcelain cup will chip or shatter when dropped on the floor, while the less fragile plastic cup will not.

When our activities depart from quite familiar realms of operation, we do not have the knowledge to ensure successful action and have to try out various actions to learn what is required to make them successful. Thus the young child, who has come to expect acquiescence to many of his demands for loving attention from his parents, learns through painfully unsuccessful experience that such demands make little or no impression upon other children of his own age. The parent can see the child's universe of experience and practical knowledge enlarging, and can note the accompanying change in the child's personality, as he learns a new way of acting toward a new kind of being, one who is not committed to loving him. This learning process may be painful but nevertheless it can be successful as the child learns how to act toward others in ways compatible with his desires. He can achieve a practical knowledge which gives him a high expectancy that his actions toward others will produce the results that he desires or he may fail to achieve this and have only a low expectancy that what he wants to happen will happen.

High expectancy depends upon knowledge of what factors are involved in having one's own way and upon the individual person's ability to dominate or otherwise bend those factors to the serving of his purpose. There are areas of human activity, in which the possibility of successful action is strongly modified by the number of factors involved over which man has little or no control. To use a homely example, the driving of an automobile to a chosen destination involves a knowledge of the operation of the vehicle and a knowledge of the path to the destination. This knowledge is easily acquired and put to use; but human foresight cannot detect all of the factors that may prevent the success of the journey, sudden deterioration of the road, impact with an uncontrolled vehicle, or a disastrous lapse of judgment. Even an alert person who travels the same route daily in a vehicle faces the possibility of being overtaken by an irregularity, because all of the circumstances of his journey are not known to him nor are within his control.

From the preceding discussion it is evident that practical truth, the knowledge that a certain action definitely will achieve a result in conformity with what is desired, depends upon how well we understand the action and the things it involves. The amount of knowledge required varies in proportion to the number of factors involved in the action and the degree of difficulty in getting them to conform to our desire. In many areas of practical activity our assurance about these factors is so great, that if an action misses its calculated end, we never doubt the efficacy of the action but look to see what element involved is not as it should be. For example, the wiping of a window with a cloth having a cleaning agent will undoubtedly remove some of the dirt from its surface. If the window becomes dirtier as we wipe, we do not doubt the efficacy of wiping but, instead, examine the folds of the cloth to discover the hitherto unseen clump of dirt that is smearing the window. Thus although there is an area of everyday experience in which each person makes thoroughly competent judgments with ease, nevertheless from time to time an occasion arises that requires an appraisal of why things are not as we are accustomed to find them. The statement, "Wiping the window with the cloth will clean it," turns out to be a false statement on one occasion, because the desired result did not come from the actions directed to produce it. The appraisal seeks the reason for the failure; upon discovering it we see that our original practical statement is still correct, provided that no other factors enter into the action.

JUDGMENT OF PRACTICAL TRUTH

The act of appraising the difference between what was intended and what actually happened is not so difficult for past actions, as we have seen, but it *is* a challenge for presently being executed and projected future actions because the various parts and circumstances of the act must be foreseen. Yet, a careful appraisal is possible by anyone who wants to expend the necessary energy. The appraisal requires a consideration of all the things involved in the action and all the relevant circumstances, and the weighing of the probability of their occurring as desired. The habit of doing this is called *prudence* (discussed in Chapter 9). As a result of considering the action required to attain an end we make a judgment as to its probable effectiveness, and then choose to posit it or not. The judgment is nothing more, and nothing less, than saying to oneself that this will work. Thus *a practical judgment is the saying to oneself that an action will attain its aim, or that it will not.*

The notion of *conformity* is involved in practical judgment inasmuch as the judgment pronounces upon the conformity of the proposed or already performed action to an action that exists only in the imagination and thought, but which unerringly attains the end sought. For example, an athletic person needs to jump a 15-foot-wide hole in the ground; from experience in jumping he estimates the speed and height necessary to arc to the opposite side of the hole. He notes that the ground is very muddy and judges that he cannot possibly attain the necessary speed while running through the mud. He wisely decides not to try to jump and to seek some other way of crossing the hole. His decision is based upon his judgment that the speed that he could attain by running in the mud would not conform to the speed he knew to be necessary to carry him across the hole. On the other hand, a person lacking athletic experience might make the attempt without knowing the requirements for success in this venture; he would fall in the hole.

Judgments of Singulars and of Existence

Speculative Judgments about Singulars

The elements of practical judgment are a knowledge of what is required to carry out an action successfully and a knowledge of the availability and possibility of control of those requirements. Similar elements of judgment, namely, the forming of a standard of comparison and a subsequent noting of any conformity or disconformity with it, appear when the intellect is concerned not with an action to be done but with saying to itself what something is. Thus to say that "This road is wet" is to say that what it is to be a road and what it is to be wet actually exist together as something that sight is aware of now. For such a judgment to be possible there must already be some knowledge of what a road is and what wetness is. This poses a problem, however. Is not the knowledge of what wetness is obtained by an act of judgment? If so, what knowledge is prior to it and how was it obtained if not as the result of judgment? In other words does the requirement of prior knowledge for any casual act of judgment lead to an endless regress of prior knowledges?

This question brings us back to our previous point about the infant's island universe of experience and practical knowledge. There "green" is what he is looking at now and so is "shovel." Later he learns to associate slightly different hues with the class name "green" and to know shovel through its purpose rather than by its shape alone. But, strictly on the sensory level, the act of discriminating colors by the sense of sight is repeated over and over again. The colors of an infant's surroundings are impressed upon his eyes even before he can discriminate them, and he can discriminate them for a long time before he learns their names. Thus his act of recognizing a present color is in terms of an already long association with colors. This constantly repeated discrimination of colors goes on for as long as a person has the use of his normal sight. Thus throughout a person's entire life as a fully conscious being he has a well-developed memory (varying of course from individual to individual) of hues and contrasts by which judgment upon a present sensible can be made. Since the external sense merely apprehends and does not remember or reflect upon its own act, and since whatever judges about two things must know both of them, any judgment about past and present colors is made by the intellect in view of what sight is discriminating now and of what memory recalls of past visual sensations. The same account of judgment regarding proper sensibles holds for the other external senses, namely, that the intellect in knowing the act of the external sense and the act of internal senses in re-presenting a sensible sensed in the past can judge as to their conformity or lack of it.

This operation of our intellect does not usurp the autonomy of our external senses, for it is obvious that the intellect by itself is powerless to know any sensible. Furthermore, that which informs the external sense is the appearance of the material thing; its stimulus activity obeys the laws of physical action which cannot be interfered with by any act of human thought. The act of the intellect does affect the operation of some of the internal senses however, as we discovered in Chapter 4. Thus the imagination and the cogitative power are not only moved by the external senses, but also by the intellect. They serve in reporting the appearances of things and also in translating ideas into determinate replicas of our understanding in the imagination, as well as into definite physical actions.

The intellect's certitude with respect to the existence and proper sensible characteristics of singulars is comparable to the certitude of our practical knowledge about actions that we repeat constantly in the course of our daily lives. In fact, our knowledge originates in the senses, whose cognitive act is initiated and specified by the actually existing sensible, so that for a sense to be aware is for the sensible to be present to it. Hence in knowing the acts of the senses the intellect is mediately aware of the initial source of all knowledge. That our intellect does not know singulars immediately limits its contact with actually existing singulars, only to the extent that we know them intellectually through the formality of the five external senses; consequently we may be led astray if a sense organ is defective. By intellect we transcend the limitations of the external senses, however, as already explained in Chapter 5. Thus we can overcome occasional defects in sense organs by comparing the present awareness of the sensible to the customary one and then seeking out the reason for the variation. Also a person can overcome a permanent defect in a sense organ by first becoming aware of the deficiency in communicating with other persons and then making allowances for it, that is, in the future he simply accommodates himself to the defect. A person who is hard of hearing can detect his difficulty in conversation with others and a person with defective vision could learn this by testing his discrimination of hues with that of others. Persons who do not discover such defects are limited in their apprehension of reality; this limitation is not of itself a source of error, however, for the apprehensions are incomplete in comparison with those of persons having normal senses but they are not necessarily false ones.

Summarily, man in judging about singulars according to their proper sensible aspects uses his accumulated sensory experience of sensibles as a criterion against which to judge presently-being-apprehended sensibles as conforming or not conforming to some proper sensible already apprehended. If recall is exact the judgment is correct, if recall is defective judgment is likely to err; such errors are difficult to rectify because many singulars change in their sensible details with time. The intellect's primary concern in understanding, however, is to discover what kind of thing something is. This knowledge is usually based upon a multiplicity of experiences, as well as the evidence actually present to the senses at the moment, so that a misplaced detail very often is of no importance.

EXISTENCE AS KNOWN BY THE INTELLECT

A judgment concerning that which is present in our awareness may be required as to the existence or nonexistence of something. The way in which something exists is called its *mode of existence*. Thus the pencil on the desk is said to have *real material existence* while a pencil existing only in the imagination is said to have a *merely imaginary existence*. The external senses and the internal senses, especially the general power of sense, are the detectors of these two kinds of objects of knowledge, but the distinctions they discriminate do not extend formally to modes of existence.[4] Thus it is by what we see that we distinguish a painted scene from a real scene; but the very notion of existence does not coincide with any proper or common sensible, or with any of the objects of the internal senses. It is reserved to the intellect alone to distinguish various modes of existence and to attribute them to various existents. We do this by using the criterion of *actually-moving-an-external-sense* to distinguish the really materially existent from the merely imaginary and the criterion of *being incapable-of-being-cognized-by-any-sense* to distinguish the *intelligibly real only* from the materially real and the merely imaginary modes of existence.

This ability on the part of the intellect to discern various modes of existence is not exercised apart from its act of knowing what things are, because it is impossible to attribute a mode of existence to nothing. The quiddity content of thought is distinguishable from the mode of existence by the act of considering one and the same quiddity as materially real, then as merely imaginary, and finally as merely an understood thing. It is but a step further for the intellect to consider quiddities and modes of existence separately (something that no sense power can do); it is thus that the familiar distinction between what a thing is, and whether and how it exists, is made.

Just as the gradual increase in the child's universe of practical knowledge is accompanied by the growth of a critical attitude and ability to distinguish the easily accomplished from the difficult or impossible to accomplish, so the growth of our intellectual knowledge-for-its-own-sake is accompanied by the gradually developing realization that the truth of a judgment as to what something is necessarily entails a knowledge of the mode of existence possessed by the quiddity being judged. To answer "What is it?" by saying that it is merely a figment of the imagination or that it is something real (meaning that it exists apart from being imagined or thought about) is as legitimate a reply as saying that it is a color or a figure. Of course, such an answer does not distinguish the quidditative components of the thing in question, but it can certainly be equally as relevant as that information. For example, it is more relevant to know that a threat to one's life is imaginary than to know the singular details of the threat. It is also very relevant in discussing atomic particles to know whether any particular one actually exists or whether it is merely a hypothetical entity posited as a possible explanation of some as yet unresolved problem.

These various modes of existence are explicitly considered in practical judgments as to what worked in the past, what is likely to work in the as yet nonexistent future, and what is merely a dream that can never be put into effect. It is the explicit considering of these actions in themselves apart from their existence as actual or possible or impossible that marks *the first fledging of human intellect as a critical power*. When this ability has been developed in a fully conscious way, our intellect possesses the means of passing a critical judgment upon actions; upon its own acts of apprehension, composition, and division; and also upon its act of drawing conclusions and of realizing whether they bear upon material, imaginary, or purely mental existents. As a person develops the use of his intellect as an instrument for discerning what is actually the case from what is not, he also develops the ability to discern the truth value of many of the statements made by others by referring them to his own knowledge of what is possible, impossible, or improbable. The possession and use of the intellect as a power to judge critically in the many ways just mentioned is of such great importance to the individual human being and to human kind as a whole that we shall now proceed to analyze it in detail.

Knowing Critically

The development of a critical attitude by the intellect varies greatly from one person to another, depending upon temperament, environment, and education. Even in those who possess a well-developed critical judgment, its use is strongly modified by personal feelings. In fact, as we shall see in the succeeding chapters, man's dispositions, habits, and desires exert a powerful influence upon the use of his cognitive powers. Therefore, for the sake of clarity we shall consider the growth of man's critical attitude in the use of his intellect separately from its involvement with his passions. The growth of our awareness of this critical ability personally is paralleled by a gradual growth in Western man's awareness and use of it in his various corporate efforts to better his state of being and of knowledge.

Many of the notions that form the basis for our customary way of talking about things are so much a part of our language that we seldom advert to them; but the acceptance of such notions as cause and effect, and necessity and contingency, without knowing exactly what they are based upon, is dangerous in that we use these notions constantly and can quite easily be in error regarding them. In order to show the importance of these notions and of the other notions required as a basis for exercising critical judgment, we shall show how they arose gradually out of human experience and curiosity during the early stages of Western civilization, and how they gradually appear in each individual's experience of the world about him. Finally we shall examine typical occasions for the exercise of this intellectual ability. The remainder of this chapter, therefore, will be devoted to considering *the notion of proof* that attempts to satisfy the demand for certitude in human knowing, *the apparatus of scientific knowledge* which is involved in both corporate and personal knowledge with certitude, and *the exercise of critical judgment in daily affairs*.

THE DESIRE FOR PROOF

In the growth of Western civilization there was a strong contrast between the attitude toward human knowing in the period prior to the sixth century B.C. and in the subsequent four centuries, which coincide with great developments in mathematics, science, and philosophy among the Greeks.[5] In the prescientific era a well-developed practical knowledge existed among the inhabitants of the banks of the Nile and those living in and adjacent to the Fertile Crescent along the Tigris and Euphrates Rivers. Their codes of law indicate a critical attitude as to what did and did not conform to the will of the rulers. Number systems and some computational mathematics were used in building, in reckoning prices, and so on. Systems of belief were built up to explain the origin of the universe and its final destiny, and special societies were organized around these beliefs. There were also systems of belief about man and about what was good for him, which were based upon clearly understood truths about the needs of his nature; these beliefs and truths formed the basis for the mores of these civilizations. Renegades who did not accept the mores and the laws based upon them were punished. Human activities in those days had a strongly practical intent; consequently the notion of certitude in knowledge was on the level we have already discussed in our analysis of practical knowledge and practical truth.

The notion of science, and the notion of proof upon which science is based, are scarcely adumbrated in the earlier civilizations, whereas the stress given to the notion of proof and the general acceptance of its desirability is one of the striking characteristics of the sophisticated Greek discussion of the universe and its intelligibility. There had been conflicting accounts of what the world was all about in earlier civilizations, but the notion of trying to prove one account as true in order to put all doubts to rest is a product of the eras immediately preceding, coinciding with, and closely following the lifetime of Socrates. Within that few centuries of human history, from the time of Thales to the time of Archimedes, the basic problems of obtaining human knowledge about the nature of the universe and the things in it, and of having a guarantee that this knowledge was everlastingly true, were discussed and brilliant attempts to solve these problems were made.

Proof in Mathematics

We shall consider the notion of proof as it was developed in mathematics first, because the early mathematics of the Greeks is not difficult to follow and the abstractness of mathematical considerations facilitates comprehension. The Egyptian and Mesopotamian civilizations contained in their computational mathematics a value for the ratio of the circumference of a circle to its diameter, which was roughly the number three. Thus $\pi = 3 \pm$ was accepted as a good enough ratio for practical purposes; the question of the exact value of π was considered to be a practical matter of the degree of precision one needed in measuring and building. The necessity of considering the quantitative factors in the environment was met by the use of symbols and formulas for calculation that were adequate to the desires of those who used them. The wide scope of quantitative analysis in everyday commerce, and the certainty about quantitative factors given by measurement, made a mathematics of natural quantities a very useful kind of practical knowledge. It is not surprising, then, that groups of men in various early societies should have concentrated their attention upon the natural numbers and upon the simple figures, which gave primitive arithmetic and geometry their practical usefulness, as having a special ability to reveal the hidden facets of nature.

The group of men among the Greeks who gained most notice for their interest in numbers and figures considered as entities apart from their practical utility, were called the Pythagoreans, after Pythagoras, their leader. At first the Pythagoreans were not so much concerned with proofs because they were bemused by the properties of various natural numbers and figures. The interest in mathematics as a study in which the proof or disproof of formulas and the possibility of constructions were paramount concerns, however, grew steadily. The problem of squaring the circle, that is, of finding an exact value for π, became a general topic of discussion, along with the problem of trisecting an angle and other problems of similar difficulty. This growth of interest represented a development from a largely practical interest in mathematics to an interest in mathematical entities for the sake of knowledge alone. The explanation of the development of Greek mathematics is a book-size undertaking in itself, but the notion of proof as it developed there is not hard to explain.

Examples of Practical Proof

One way to prove that something can be accomplished is to accomplish it. The first Greek mathematicians used only a compass and a straight-edge, but nevertheless they made many ingenious constructions as *proof* that what had been entertained as a mere possibility could actually be achieved. Thus to answer the question "Can a straight line be drawn perpendicular to a given straight line?" in a practical manner, is to set down a method whereby anyone who wishes to do so can construct the perpendicular. *The actual construction is proof of the statement proposing the possibility of the construction.* Similarly to find two numbers whose product is 81 is actually to multiply 9 by 9 or 3 by 27 as a practical proof that the problem of finding such numbers can be solved. In the numerical proof we can see that two sets of numbers satisfy the requirement; this gives rise to the notion that a statement may be proved in more than one way. We can also see the *everlastingness* of the proof, as long as the numbers never change their values. From these two examples it follows not only that different factors may be used to prove one and the same statement, but also that the elements used in the proof should not be subject to variation if the proof is to stand forever.

THE PRESUPPOSITIONS TO PROOF

The multiplicity of ways of proving a statement to be true reinforce the intellect's certitude concerning the statement. The proofs, though, are only as stable as the elements out of which they are constructed. The Greek mathematicians realized that the elements of proof had to be guaranteed in some acceptable manner, because an endless regress in proving one set of notions by a prior set would render proof impossible. Thus one of the basic requirements for the proving of a statement is that *the means by which it is being proved shall not stand in need of proof.* An indication of this need is easily seen in the first part of Euclid's *Elements* (of mathematics), where certain things are set down as not being subject to debate. Thus it is *postulated* in that work that "A straight line can be drawn from any point to any point" and that "A circle may be described with any center and at any distance from that center." From these two, of the five postulates set down by Euclid, certain other statements about circles and their parts can be proved.

In nonmathematical matters the notion of proof developed along lines similar to those in mathematics. (Whether the notion of proof embodied in Greek mathematics was borrowed from nonmathematical thought, or vice versa, or whether both avenues of thought developed independently alongside one another, has not been firmly established.) The stable beginning from which something was to be deduced with certainty was similar to the postulate but different in its subject matter and *in its dependence upon experience.* Thus the statement, "Some things change," is not postulated. Rather, it is based upon experience and is a statement of what human experience indicates about ourselves and our surroundings. Similarly the statement "Some things come into being by human actions and some do not" is an expression of common human experience. These statements are similar to postulates in that they do not require any proof. They differ inasmuch as they conform to the facts of experience, whereas the statements about lines and circles are about ideal beings that cannot be sensed.

It is evident from this analysis that in attempting to prove statements about our physical world we will need to start with statements about what is evident to everyone in order to prove something to everyone, and with statements that are evident to anyone who is well versed in a certain area of experience (agriculture, for example) in order to prove something about that area of experience. In all areas of proof, if the accuracy of the basic statements that are assumed without proof are in fact open to question, then whatever is shown to follow from these statements is likewise subject to doubt.

The need for unquestionable statements as the basis of proof for something that follows from these statements imposes a further need: The use of terms whose meanings are unambiguous. Thus in Euclid's *Elements* definitions of point, line, straight line, angle, figure, circle, and so forth, are given in the beginning of Book One along with the postulates. A point is defined as "that which has no part" and the extremities of a line are defined as "points"; "line" is defined as "length without breadth." Any attempt to define "part," "extremity," and "breadth" would have involved the assumption that they were not easily understood but that a clear understanding of the meanings of the words existed by which they could be defined. The natural stopping place for this regress to prior terms and meanings would be at a meaning with which no one could reasonably disagree.

In the previous chapter we showed that in mathematics the agreement obtained about starting points does not have any necessary connection with existing material things, even though plane geometry as codified by Euclid seems to have used naturally occurring things as models and is quite definitely based upon imaginable entities. Euclid, however, did fulfill the requirement for having unchangeable starting points for his proofs by providing definitions. There is the same need for stability in the means of producing proof in the analysis of nonmathematical matters. In this realm, though, there is a minimum of arbitrariness, for the statements of fact upon which any proof are based must conform to the natures of things that are quite definite.

Arbitrariness can be found in the naming of things, natures, connections, and relationships; but there is no arbitrariness in the natures, natural operations, and dependencies of things. Consequently the final reference for the meaning of a term signifying a naturally occurring thing is the actual thing itself.

PROOF BY CONNECTEDNESS

The very notion of proof itself, as distinct from the requirements for the basic premises, is based upon the connectedness of things. For example, the perpendicularity of a line is connected to the space-encompassing nature of a right angle. It is because they are connected that the construction of a perpendicular involves the constructing of a right angle. Similarly, the actuality of a plane rectilinear triangle involves the encompassing of an angular space equal to that of two right angles. Only the construction of a short line is required, parallel to the base of the triangle, through the vertex of the triangle, to enable the proof to go forward by means of the properties of a transverse to two parallel lines. Other kinds of connectedness are involved in mathematical relationships, such as greater and lesser, factor of, sum of, and the like, which are capable of being used as means of proof.

In nonmathematical considerations of natural things man has discovered some kinds of connectedness enabling him to say that because of one thing another thing is necessarily so, or is very likely to be so. Thus if two things are discovered to be connected so that when one occurs the other must have preceded it or must follow from it, this knowledge of the connection gives assurance about the sequence.[6] This is easily seen in practical matters where a knowledge of what is most likely to happen gives the possessor of this knowledge an opportunity to capitalize on it. For instance, if a tiller of the soil knew that warm weather and rainfall were to occur regularly throughout the coming spring, he could safely put his seeds in the ground earlier than usual without any fear that they would rot or dry up. In this way he could assure himself of a sufficiently long growing season for his crop to reach full maturity.

One way to attempt to gain the knowledge needed to predict the weather would be to record the kind of weather that preceded the advent of spring over a number of years and search that record for any regularity of occurrence of favorable spring weather for planting and any regularity in the kind of winter weather preceding it. If such a connection were discovered, then a possible sign of a favorable spring for early planting would be available. The record could also indicate what kind of winter was usually followed by a poor season for the farmer. A better method would be to discern not only the signs of impending warm and cold and dry and wet spells, but also the actual factors whose presence at a given time determines what the weather will be at a future time. This method of analyzing natural occurrences is preferable because it gives a better understanding. To understand the actual factors of some occurrence is to eliminate any ambiguity that may exist in the mere signs considered by themselves.

THE SPECULATIVE REALM OF INVESTIGATION

In this example of attempting to obtain assurance about what will happen, the elements that influence the success or failure of the farmer's crop-raising activities are known to some extent, but they are not within his control. This situation is different from that presented in our analysis of everyday practical activities with things whose location and actions are to some extent dominated by us. Consequently the farmer can examine the factors involved in producing favorable or unfavorable spring weather, but he cannot as yet exert any influence upon those factors. In brief, he can examine them as *matters* of vital concern *beyond his control*. This attitude of interest, without ability to control, is expressed in the term *speculative* (from *speculari*, to look at), which can be used to describe our interest in, and knowledge of, things that cannot be affected by us.

The term "speculative" is applicable in a sense to all of our knowledge of what things are, for although man can synthesize many new things by combining already existing ones, he does not have in his control the causing of any nature that it be as it is. He can only discover what properties natural things have and then make use of them. When an experiment in transmuting one metal into another is successful, man has not determined the natures of the individual metals by causing electrons, protons, neutrons, and the other subvisible factors involved to be what they are; he has merely modified the order among these parts, or removed or added parts. The distinction between the speculative and the practical in knowledge is useful, however, for the knowledge by which we can successfully order matter and utilize its properties for our own ends is grounded in the possibility of our performing activities; whereas speculative knowledge is grounded in our ability to abstract, to make correct compositions and divisions, and to reason validly to conclusions.

There are many subjects of investigation in which we have no ability to exert control and therefore cannot gain the information that having control of material activities can give us. For example, the past is beyond our interference so that we can only conjecture about how things might have turned out if something had been otherwise than it was. Similarly there are many areas of investigation, such as the weather and planetary motion, where man can not yet exercise any control over the factors involved. He can only observe and reason about them.[7] Nevertheless he has a vital interest in them because the various things and happenings that make up the present also predetermine the future.

In attempting to know the future, and in attempting to know that part of the past history of the universe that has not been recorded by any human agency, man must resort to the use of intellectual analysis of evidence without having any possibility of applying practical proofs to the results of his analysis. In other words, man cannot manipulate the past and future as he can manipulate numbers, figures, and all kinds of mathematicals in order to see what is possible or impossible. He must rely upon his intellectual ability to discern unquestionable starting points for the reasoning process, to discern correctly the various kinds of connectedness that exist among things and events, and to reason validly from evidence to conclusion. As a result of man's continued efforts to find certain knowledge about things over which he exercises no control, an apparatus for analyzing evidence has come into use, one that is presupposed in obtaining much of the information that makes up our daily intellectual fare. We shall first show how this apparatus is firmly rooted in human experience before explaining its usefulness in our intellectual life.

The Apparatus of Scientific Knowledge

In the analysis of the events that precede another event, it is possible to single out some that are indispensable to the occurrence of the second event and some that have only a minimal connection with it. In the practical activity of building a house to be used as a human shelter against cold, rain, and wind, it makes a difference whether bricks or lumps of mud are used to form the walls; but it makes little difference whether the piles of materials to be used are three feet high or four feet high. The piles of materials must have some height, and if they were eight feet high this could be inconvenient for the builder, but with respect to the actual building of the house these heights are of little importance. The building of the house is the assembling of the various materials; if these materials are merely laid upon one another without using cement and nails, the house will not be what it was meant to be, namely, a durable shelter.

In this practical activity we can discern certain indispensable elements. The materials *must* have certain characteristics if they are to withstand the elements. Furthermore they *must* be put together in such a way as to form a durable structure if the house is to last for a number of years. Even though we state the necessities involved in this example in a hypothetical manner, the necessities *are factual, not hypothetical.* To be durable, according to man's experience to date, building materials must be of brick, stone, wood, metal, or glass. In short, among the many details involved in the erecting of a house some can be easily recognized as absolutely indispensable to the success of the venture *because of what a house is.*

THE NOTION OF CAUSE

Since many naturally occurring things are composed of parts that are not just stacked together but are bound to another (as the seeds, core, meat, and skin of an apple) so that they have a unity within themselves (evidenced by the fact that a certain combination of parts occurs constantly), it is legitimate to consider such parts as *essential* to the being of the whole. They may be said to be *causes* of the whole inasmuch as, that a thing be of a certain kind, is caused by the presence of certain constituents in it. The bricks and wood are the constituent elements of the house, and what we intend in building a house would not come into being if we moulded it out of soft mud which would crack and fall apart in the sun or simply flow away into a puddle in the rain. The indispensability of the proper kind of materials for the formation of a house is easily seen; this indispensability of a certain kind of material for the achievement of a certain kind of result is one of the meanings signified by the term *cause*. A *constituent cause* of something is an element of that thing upon which depends the kind of being that the thing is. Sodium is a constituent cause of table salt, and when some other metal combines with chlorine to form a compound, different properties result from the different constituent cause present.

A second notion of cause is that upon which the coming into being of something depends, not for the materials involved but for the activity by which the effect is brought into being. This notion of cause, as *an efficient agent* producing something that was not there before it acted, is easily derived from an analysis of human experience. Thus there are numerous examples of this kind of causality in our practical experience where we have complete control over the things involved. For example, the door to a room opens as a result of our pushing it and stays shut if it is not opened; food appears on the table when we put it there and will not be upon the table unless some physical motion brings food and table together. In general, our experience is that nothing that happens happens in total independence of all the things that exist prior to its happening.

Although the notion of an event's being quite dependent for its coming into being upon something else antecedent to it is well grounded in experience, it is not always an easy matter to apply this notion in realms where we do not exert any control. Thus in the matter of analyzing the weather in order to know what causes are at work, much progress has been made in determining how areas of high and low pressure and masses of cold and warm air affect the weather in a particular place at a particular time, but to get this information requires a great deal of effort by many persons and the use of ingenious instruments. Moreover, the analyses upon which predictions of future weather are based necessarily involve many factors whose essential characteristics are not sufficiently known as yet. We can see that theoretically, where both the antecedents of an event and the event itself are known, the possibility of knowing how the event evolved from its antecedents is there, but on the practical side the realizing of that possibility may involve more difficulties than we can overcome. The fact remains, however, that a characteristically human way of analyzing our experience is to sort out those factors that are indispensable to the occurrence of an event, and those resulting from them.

The use of the notion of efficient causality, *that the existence of one thing entails the existence of another*, and its limitations, is perhaps best illustrated in the analysis of past events where both factors are fixed. Consider, for example, how we might reason about what appears to be the site of a man-made, cave dwelling of prehistoric times. One might say that being man entails having the use of the ability to reason and to act rationally, so that where we find a work that is a work of reason we assume that a rational agent performed it; that is, if the work is one that comes within the range of man's domination over matter and bears other marks characteristic of a human agent, we tend to assign its production to a human agent. Possibilities being what they are, however, we can always be in error. Perhaps what we take to be a cave dwelling shaped and furnished by men was actually brought about by the forces of nature, and the human bones and artifacts found in the cave were perhaps transported there by natural forces or by animals. Of course, if drawings were found on the walls, drawings such as the famous "Animals of Lascaux," it would be rather difficult to doubt that a human agent had produced them, especially since in our experience no earthly creature other than man has ever actually produced drawings on its own initiative.[8] But to be absolutely safe we should restrict ourselves in the beginning to this judgment: *Whatever produced the drawings had the ability to produce the drawings*. Their present existence as something that not only has not occurred by natural nonhuman agents according to our best knowledge of them covers all possible criteria that we can apply to determining what the existence of the drawings in the present entails. As we have shown, the act of judging is one of testing one apprehension by another. We could conclude that, according to all of the criteria that we can apply to the fact that the drawings exist now, some human agent quite probably made them.

JUDGMENTS OF NECESSITY

What we do when we reason about the connections between antecedent events and consequent events is to attempt to form in our intellects a connectedness in thought that conforms to the actual connectedness in things. Now, the observed connectedness in things is one of essential union between the composite parts of an entity, or one of contiguity in time and place, or one of regular succession in time. The very term "essential," used to designate the union of parts that constitute a naturally occurring whole, indicates the following understanding: Certain parts constitute a certain kind of whole, such that if the parts are varied, the specific nature of the whole is necessarily other than it was. Examples of this have already been given in Chapter 2. The necessity involved here is the ineradicable necessity that *a thing is what it is.* This necessity is cognized by the intellect in reflecting upon the specificity of natures and activities.

The same sort of reflection is applied to regular successions of events when we attempt to determine whether they just happen to occur and might occur differently, or cease to occur. We may use as an example of temporal succession the sequence of risings and settings of the sun. In the discrimination of this sequence we can find no indication that the succession must continue for there was no necessity manifested in the constant repetition of the sun's rising and setting. As to the fact of the succession that we have observed in the past, however, there can be no doubt; so that a knowledge of what the succession is, the sun's appearance in the east and its disappearance in the west, is obtained with certitude.

In analyzing a succession of events the question of necessity is not so much the necessity that the fact be what it is, but rather involves the reason *why the antecedent acts and the consequent ensues.* If we can be sure that the antecedent must occur, that the sun must appear first in the east before it disappears in the west, we can speak of necessity in one part of the sequence.

Similarly if we can be sure that once the antecedent occurs the consequent must follow from it, then we can speak of necessity in the actual sequence itself. With respect to this latter entailment, however, we must distinguish between high probability and absolute inescapable necessity.

When we make a physical model of the apparent motion of the sun around the earth, the model indicates the necessity that the sequence occur regularly as long as the direction of the apparent motion does not change. When we change the model in accord with contemporary astronomy's notion of the revolution of the earth on its axis, the same necessity in the sequence of the appearances of the sun to a man on the earth is made evident. Thus if the earth continues to revolve on its axis, making its yearly journey around the sun in its usual orbit, and does not fly off into outer space; and if the sun continues to shine; and if nothing whatsoever interferes with these orderly activities; then the sun *must* continue daily to appear first in the east and set in the west. The forces at work in these activities must act according to their natures and cannot of themselves act otherwise, but they may suffer interference from other agents. This interference could upset the orderly recurrence of the sun's appearance in the east and disappearance in the west. Since we do not understand many aspects of the motion of the earth we must conclude, that although *it is highly probable that the sun will continue to appear as in the past*, it could be otherwise. With respect to the past, however, since there was no interference with the sun's shining and the earth's daily revolution and yearly orbit, *it was absolutely necessary that the sun appear in the east and disappear in the west.*

Necessity regarding Common Natures

In order for the intellect to possess the certitude that it seeks with respect to a knowledge of natures and of causal dependencies, it makes use of the properties that befall notions of what is common and enduring because they are possessed by the intellect. It was pointed out in the previous chapter that such notions are atemporal and are not restricted to any definite location in representing the enduring aspect of things. In other words, the natures so considered exist in the intellect in a completely immaterial manner because of the kind of power that the human intellect is. Consequently, in talking about these common notions we sometimes speak of them as we conceive them in the intellect and we sometimes refer to their basis in actual things. For example, we may say: All water is capable of dissolving salt, thus predicating the capability of dissolving salt of *all of that substance we call water* considered simply according to its nature as water. Or to indicate that we are talking of something that actually does exist now, we might say that this is water and therefore it can dissolve salt. The meaning of the two expressions is the same, but the first way of expressing that meaning has been a source of much controversy.

The universal manner of predicating can be interpreted as making claim to a knowledge that no mere human being can obtain. The statement, "All men are rational," applies the characteristic "rational" to all men, even though some of them have already passed away and some have not yet come into existence. How can we be so sure as to what was the case in the past and as to what man will be like in the future? No mere man can know the future with absolute accuracy because of the radical contingency of all material things.

Our concern here is not to enter into the historical controversy on universals, nor the contemporary controversy about their status in symbolic logic.[9] Rather we intend to explain to what extent universals are grounded in experience and how they come into being, so that the reader will understand why they, like causes, are a proper subject for the exercise of critical judgment when we are concerned with accepting them from others as well as when we are inclined to make them ourselves.

UNIVERSAL STATEMENTS ABOUT OUR ACTIVITIES

The easiest universal to understand is the one used to phrase a statement about mathematicals. For example, (1) "Every circle has a constant radius," and (2) "Every circle is bisected by a diameter," are *A* propositions that are necessarily true. The predicate of the first proposition is part of the definition of the subject and therefore is true of every figure of which the name "circle" is properly descriptive. The predicate of the second proposition is not part of the definition of the subject, but can be proved to be true because of what a circle is and what a diameter is.

As we have already pointed out in Chapter 5, the circle exists primarily in its definition as an intellectual thing; it has no existence materially, and its depiction in the imagination cannot correspond exactly to its definition. Lines drawn in matter are tridimensional and irregular; lines drawn in the imagination (figuratively speaking) can be looked upon from just two dimensions when we blot out the third one, but this is one more than a defined line has. Similarly perfect curvature can be defined easily in terms of constant radius, but it can only be approximated in reality and in imagination. The reason why the first statement can be made universally is that the question of whether and how circles exist under the stricture of being located in a definite place and in a definite time is quite irrelevant. A circle is what the definer of circle says it is, and no argument as to what exists in a material manner can possibly be alleged against this. What mathematics takes to be the subject of its inquiry is a matter of postulation. In short a circle is what it is because we make it to be such; its atemporality is due to its abstractness, which is due to its being a mental entity.

A universal statement about a kind of human activity is similar to one about mathematicals, because we are the authors of such activities and thus determine what they are. For example, "to speak" is to utter words and "to nourish oneself" is to assimilate food into one's own physical being. The meanings of the terms used are easily gathered from experience; once the meanings have been gathered, the definitions of "to speak" and "to nourish oneself" can be considered apart from any actual instance of them. They can be talked of as activities that can be thought of in themselves apart from any connection they may have with anything else. Thus to say that "All speaking is uttering words" and "All self-nourishing is the assimilation of food into one's own body" is simply to say what is evidently the case. When people uttered words in the past and took nourishment in the past, they were speaking and feeding. The same applies to the future. Thus it is certainly the case that knowing what a human activity is now is knowing what it was in the past and is knowing what it will be in the future, for the simple reason that *knowing what it is is knowing what it is.*

Granted that speech is uttering words, that speech should have occurred in the past or that it shall occur in the future is quite irrelevant to what speech is. In fact, it is also quite irrelevant for the understanding of what something is that it should exist in a material way at all. As we have clearly indicated, the question of the mode of existence possessed by some entity is settled by the intellect in its act of judging whether or not an object of thought possesses the characteristics seen to be indicative of the various modes of existence. In the majority of propositions that a person uses to express his thoughts, it is taken for granted that the hearer is well aware of what mode of existence is possessed by the things being talked about. Where such assurance does not exist, the only way to be absolutely sure of what is meant is to ask the speaker where he locates the things he is talking about. If his intention is to be unclear, or if, as sometimes happens, he is not sure himself as to whether he is talking of material reality or of something purely hypothetical, then the listener will have to make the distinction for himself as best he can. When this can not be done successfully, the statement can only be received politely as a vague opinion. Thus for many persons statements about what mathematicals are have the status of opinions, because they cannot follow the explanations of their origin and nature.

Universal statements as to what things are, concerning entities that are neither mathematicals nor human activities, involve special difficulties, for we usually cannot have the assurance that comes from producing such things, thus knowing exactly what material and formative causes are involved. The pieces of copper we examine in order to discover their common properties are not under our domination in the way that our customary physical activities are. As to our activities, we know their origin and mode of action, as well as what will result from them; but in the beginning of man's experience with copper he knew only the appearance common to all of the samples of copper that were experienced, plus the usefulness of the material having this appearance for making utensils. No more information about this metal was deemed to be necessary than what was required to bend it to man's uses.

The same attitude toward knowing what things are in terms of their potential uses has prevailed through the centuries and to a large extent still prevails in our attitude toward many items of our experience. Nevertheless the desire to pin down specific natures by definitions has been present in man's mind at least as long as he has been concerned with having proof that knowledge is correct. There is no overt evidence that men were greatly interested in the universal attribution of predicates to subjects before the time of the Greek philosophers—the desire for proof brought the notion of the universal statement to the fore.

The importance of the universal statement to our intellectual desire for true knowledge, for knowledge that is representative of the actuality of things and that is also aware of the mode of existence possessed by that of which the representation is a concept, must be kept in perspective. Although the universal statement is indispensable in demonstrating a property of a subject (especially in mathematics where the reason for the inherence of the property is most clearly seen), it is not at all necessary in the judgments whereby we say to ourselves that some attribute belongs to some nature. In such judgments we assert that to be such a nature is to be possessed of such an attribute. Thus whether the subject be atoms or angels, as long as the person who names the subject attributes to it what he really understands to be common to things so named he cannot be in error. He is making the statement be true, just as surely as the mathematician who coins a definition of a triangle by saying what he means by that name is making his statement conform to his thought. He could only make a mistake by being inattentive to what his experience actually reveals or by using a name contrary to its generally accepted meaning without realizing that he is doing so. But if he is mistaken in assigning the meaning to the name on one occasion, he could hardly fail to correct it when he discovered his mistake. When his senses and intellect are functioning normally it seems unlikely that his abstraction could go awry, since the intellect only apprehends what is actually present in the senses and it is not difficult to distinguish what is actually being sensed from what is being presented as something remembered.

When a person is being conscientious in expressing his thoughts exactly, and checks his statement with his thought, it is impossible that he should predicate falsely about those of his understandings that are firmly based on experience. Thus the man who apprehends triangles for the first time and apprehends only isosceles triangles may indeed equate the name triangle to the meaning "having two equal sides and two equal angles." But surely he has expressed truly what he understood; his error is in the use of a name that had been given a different meaning by someone else. Similarly when we say what "apple" is or what "copper" is, although our knowledge may be very elementary compared to that possessed by an expert botanist or chemist, it is knowledge obtained by determining what is common to the apples or the copper that we have experienced. It corresponds to things to the same degree that our experience corresponds to them. Consequently, to the extent that our experience is genuine our knowledge is representative of things as they are, and our judgments that this is so are true.

SOURCES OF ERROR

The variety of ways of being in error about something is considerable, but some of them are so widespread and persistent that they are standard. We shall consider them now briefly as the kind of human fallibilities which we ought constantly to guard against when we are seeking a true account of things. One of these fallibilities arises from our readiness to accept as a matter for understanding anything whatsoever that can be phrased in words whose meanings are not mutually exclusive nor greatly contrary to experience. The fact that *we tacitly assume statements to be true* that are not declared to be false and that do not obviously strain credulity is the source of the error here. Many intelligible statements and even complete explanations of phenomena are not in accord with the facts. For example, we can understand the statement, "The sun is a planet of the earth," which means that the sun orbits the earth. But the intelligibility of the statement and the apparent motion of the sun from the east to the west around the earth is no guarantee that the statement accords with the facts. Thus although there is some evidence upon which the statement of solar motion is based, a careful scrutiny of the presuppositions of the statement (especially the presupposition that the earth is not in motion) and of the appearances of the sun and the other heavenly bodies has led to the conclusion that the earth is a planet of the sun which orbits the sun once a year. It is evident from this one example that we can understand many things without thereby knowing whether our understanding corresponds to the way things are or not. In order to be sure that our knowledge conforms to the facts, when the facts are not perfectly evident to observation, we need to have proof of the conformity. Briefly, since there can be several diverse explanations of the same facts, when mere observation cannot settle which explanation is correct, one must resort to proof.

Another common source of error in our attempt to know things truly arises from what might be termed *mental laziness*. Many things are understood sufficiently to enable us to carry out successfully the activities we consider to be worth doing. A critical appraisal of the end of such actions, however, and of the suitability of the means directed to the attainment of that end, often reveals that the end is not something we really desire and also that the means being used to attain the end are not the most efficacious ones we could use. For example, a person might maintain a vegetable garden year after year because he had been trained to work in his parents' garden. The produce from his garden is fresh and easily available all summer, yet this person can use only a small portion of the produce and must either give the rest away or dig it under in order to dispose of it. He is carrying on an activity long after it has ceased to be of any measurable use to him, simply from habit. If he likes the outdoor work, he might direct his efforts to a flower garden, thus getting the outdoor activities he desires without producing food for which he has little use. Or he might find any one of several outdoor sports much more satisfying to his urge to be outside.

Mental laziness can be operative in other ways, such as when we accept something as proved on the word of someone else without determining whether the proof is valid; or when we accept a statement as being based on experience without verifying it; or when we accept a conclusion as being the only one that follows from the given premises, whereas other conclusions could be drawn with just as much probability of being true, or when we accept opinions about matters for which the truth can be ascertained, and so on.

The last typical human fallibility that we shall consider arises from our *confusing the mode of existence of an attribute in a subject with the mode of existence it has as an intellectual entity*. For example, in order to understand what it means to have an opinion we need to consider the human intellect as forming a statement about something concerning which there is some doubt and no easily applicable means of proof by which to dispel the doubt, for instance, that every molecule of water in the earth's oceans was in the earth's atmosphere at one time or another. From our extensive analysis of the nature of intellectual operations it is obvious that the intellect can form a composition that is quite intelligible, but which does not thereby attain the status of being a true statement. To hold to this statement as being probably conformable with the facts, is to have an opinion.

Now, to pass from considering the nature of intellectual activity in forming and holding an opinion to the act of attributing what it is to have an opinion to every intellectual composition and division is to attribute *that which was considered in itself absolutely as belonging to the subject of which it was considered absolutely*. We do this, for example, when we generalize from our experience of a few instances of being wet by a warm summer rain to holding that all summer rains are warm. Our mistake is in attributing what it is to be a warm summer rain to *all* summer rains. What is required in both of these examples in order to avoid error is a judgment as to whether the characteristics being attributed to composition and division, and to summer rains, respectively, belong to them contingently or necessarily. If we do not see any necessary entailment we should not generalize, simply because we have not considered those compositions that we know certainly accord with the facts (and therefore are true), or simply because we have not experienced a cold summer rain. On the other hand, where we discern an essential entailment we need not be timorous about expressing it in a universal statement when the occasion demands. In brief, we suffer from a tendency to generalize upon the basis of experience without having the assurance of knowing that the predicate of our statement has an essential connection with the subject.

SUMMARY

Because the discussion of the human intellect as a power to make judgments has been somewhat lengthy, we shall briefly describe its characteristic operations once again before proceeding to examine its daily use as a critical faculty. Since the primary aspect that the intellect cognizes about sensible things is their being present to a sense, under a formal aspect proper to that sense, in this it will not be mistaken. We may fail to discover anything more than the mere appearances of a thing, however, and consequently be limited to knowing it as a visual, tactile, or auditory phenomenon of some kind. In such an instance, only the being of the experience is known with certainty. For example, to see a pinkish light streak quickly across a small portion of a distant part of the night sky is to be left in doubt as to what was involved in the activity giving rise to such brief visual appearances. The experience may even have been illusory in character, resulting from rubbing the eyes, or it may be an afterimage consequent upon a concentration of sight upon some well-lit colored scene. While the experience is occurring, however, there is no doubt that it is occurring.[10]

There is also an unfailing apprehension of being when our intellect abstracts under auspicious circumstances. Unless there is some depiction of reality present our intellect has nothing to discern. But when there is some sensory representation of things our intellect cannot refuse to assent to the presence and the characteristics of that sensory representation any more than normal sight can discern without discerning what is actually present to it. No matter how strong an opinion we may have formed about something, the discovery of a fact contrary to it cannot be rooted out of our apprehension, for it is about that which our intellect directly cognizes that we are most certain. The expressions "I cannot understand it" and "I do not believe it," when uttered by a person grasping the facts of an event from the actual experience of it, are indications of the destruction of an opinion or a set of opinions, by the recognition of the certitude of facts that render the opinions about the subject in question no longer defensible. The term "infallibility" is not to be used lightly but it does seem appropriate when applied to the intellect's judgment that it has grasped the being of our sensory experience as it is presented by the senses. There is nothing prior in our intellectual cognition to its apprehensions of the aspects of things presented in the acts of the senses discerning what is. In discerning what is common to several things presented in sensation we do not depart from the realm of what things are but merely make a distinction within that realm between those characteristics that always exist in a definite combination and thus indicate a certain kind of thing, and those characteristics that are variable and contingent in the things possessing them.

A multiplicity of apprehensions about one kind of thing is accompanied by acts of composition and division as a concept is built up, so as to represent in thought the multiplicity of essential aspects possessed by the kind of thing being understood. The desire for a richer knowledge of a singular thing, or of a kind of thing, leads to an investigation of its antecedents, perhaps to an experimental investigation of its physical constituents, and even to a deduction as to what is likely to eventuate from it in the future. It is with respect to this richer knowledge that we especially feel the need for proof. In seeking this richer knowledge we depart from a consideration of what something is to seek out aspects of it that are hidden in time or in the being of its components whose specific characteristics are subsumed by the nature of the presently existing whole. In the ferreting out of this richer knowledge the corporate human intellect is still in the novice stage; our island universe has not been greatly expanded yet. Nevertheless, we have developed out of our experience some of the notions (necessity, contingency, causality, uniformity of nature, proof) that are very useful in analyzing our universe and its history. These notions and the sure knowledge that we have obtained by use of them are the fruit of the exercise of critical judgment.

Critical Judgment in Daily Affairs

As has been explained the term critical judgment is an expression that we have adopted to indicate our intellectual ability to discern various modes of existence and to discern whether compositions and divisions conform to the combinations of essential parts and accidental characteristics actually existing in the things being thought about. As that which has brought about great progress in man's practical domination of matter, it has been exercised and developed by the cooperative efforts of many individuals. The parallel line of growth in the development of the individual person's use of his intellect as that by which he is critical of his experiential and verbal apprehensions is quite familiar, but unless we reflect upon it a bit its importance to our personal development may not be fully appreciated.

We start out our conscious lives as a receptacle of impressions that aid slightly in the fulfilling of desires, such as the desire for nourishment, which arise as a result of our metabolic condition. For the most part, however, others have to do for us whatever is required to satisfy our natural needs. By the time we can walk and act on our own we have attained a fund of knowledge of an immediately practical kind, plus several beliefs in what will happen when we act in one way, and verbal assurances as to what we should believe will happen when we act in a way prohibited by authority. The authorities that impress us are numerous. There is the authority of each parent plus the authority of all the pleasant and harmful things in our environment. The latter authorities may induce beliefs more forcefully than our parents do, for the parents are inclined to use love and force in connection with verbalizing. But mere words are only signified reality rather than actual reality itself. Actual reality is the hard, the hot, the sharp, the unpleasant tasting, as well as the soft and cuddly, the cool and refreshing, the soft and comfortable, the taste-delighting, and so forth. These actual realities are powerful guides in the formation of our early beliefs as to what is worthwhile doing and what is worthwhile avoiding. The beliefs are gradually superseded as repeated experience gives rise to practical truths as the basis for confident action.[11]

As we grow in experience we establish the necessary basis for further advance in practical knowledge. Just as the Greek geometrician proved what could be constructed by constructing it, so we in our efforts to do things for ourselves gradually realize the possibility of fulfilling our desires by actually fulfilling them or come to the conclusion that their fulfillment is not possible to us yet. We thus set the pattern for our way of doing things, which will persist unless some different way of acting is forcefully impressed upon us or we use our own discriminative ability to devise better ways of attaining what we desire.

Verbal education is provided to us since we need to master the language and to supplement our limited experience by learning from others the many useful and informative facts based upon their experience and passed on as our intellectual heritage.[12] But the very act of substituting words for things in order to communicate knowledge, experience, and beliefs has certain disadvantages that are not easily overcome; this substitution can be the source of serious consequences for whoever does not guard against them.

LIMITATIONS OF VERBAL APPREHENSION

By verbal apprehension we mean the obtaining of information about something solely through the understanding of the meaning imparted by words.[13] Of course, there must be some personal experience involved in the relating of the words being used to the things they describe, but the fact that these words do have a basis in our experience is no guarantee that what we apprehend through verbal communication is correct. Consequently we should not let eagerness to learn move us to pass judgments of truth upon statements that do not contradict our experience, and judgments of falsity upon statements that say something contrary to what we have experienced, because the same kind of experience can be understood correctly from contrasting viewpoints. In other words the same attitude of wanting to be sure should accompany our verbal apprehension as well as our experiential apprehension. We have already mentioned this matter in the latter portion of the preceding chapter. But now we have elaborated some of the standard means of testing a combination of words to see if they state the truth or not.

The necessity of being critical of statements purporting to represent the truth is easily illustrated. If a child takes as literally true the statement that "What is written in books is of no account, for experience is the only teacher," he will not only have great difficulty with those members of society dedicated to his education but he will also deliberately cut himself off from a vast fund of practical and speculative information that could be of great use to him and could give him joy in its mere possession. It is true that no one can give understanding to another, because understanding is something that the intellect achieves by its own effort of relating new information to that which it has already understood. But it is obvious that to cut off arbitrarily the greatest source of information is to diminish greatly the materials upon which the intellect can exercise its ability to understand. In our times, when an individual person's life is affected by so many events both close to home and far away, of which he can have knowledge only by verbal communication, failure to take advantage of such communication is to abandon his role as an informed participant in the affairs of the society that nourishes him as a social and dependent being.

Much of what we receive through verbal apprehension should be entertained as mere opinion because it is expressed as mere opinion, although in our desire to obtain information we may fail to note this fact. And much that is expressed as being universally the case should be accepted as mere opinion, also, whenever the bond of necessity that substantiates universal truths is not given. This is especially true of universal statements based upon statistical samplings of human activities that are matters of choice, for the basis of universal truths about specific natures is the *predetermined* mode of being and activity which indicates the kind of nature in question. *Matters of choice are based upon predetermined activities but have an element of* contingency *about them that* escapes *the* predictability *possible for nonvoluntary activities.*

Verbal apprehensions about practical matters can often be put to a practical test by actually attempting to act according to their directions. When this is not possible it is usually the case that the practical information in question has no relevance for us. But when it has relevance and we cannot test it because of the undesirable consequences that will probably result from its use, we should apply the same tests to it as are required for validating speculative conclusions. That is, we should check our knowledge of the kinds of things involved to be sure that it is knowledge of what is essential and necessary, and check our conclusions as to what will happen to see that they follow validly from the prior knowledge of the natures of the things involved.

The case is similar for beliefs that greatly affect our future; they may appear to be quite innocent and in accord with common sense until we spell out for ourselves their ultimate implications. In reverse order to this we may find ourselves seriously pursuing a line of activities because it seems to be the thing to do in keeping oneself occupied, but the activities may be directed to attaining a goal that a little rational effort will disclose as being unattainable or not really desirable. For example, a boy might engage in various athletic contests as a pastime and find himself gradually spending increased effort and concentration on high-jumping, because he is competing successfully in this sport against keen rivals. But he is neglecting his school work in order to keep up his performance as a high jumper, although he started high jumping only for the fun and exercise of it and knows that he has no ability to enter into serious competition with really good high jumpers. When he realizes that he does not really want to spend his time at high jumping except as a friendly contest to provide exercise and relaxation, he stops devoting to it the time that he needs to concentrate on attaining goals he really does desire to achieve.

TRUTH FOR ITS OWN SAKE

Equally important along with our awareness of the need to scrutinize and to seek confirmation for much that is told to us by others, and with the necessity of foreseeing the ultimate implications of a belief, is the cultivation of our personal intellectual life. For just as seeing is a joy to sight and hearing is a joy to the sense of hearing, so the act of understanding that accompanies sensory apprehension and the act of understanding that sometimes terminates acts of reasoning are a joy to the human intellect. The kind of understanding most suited to the human intellect is that in which we not only understand what and how things are, but also see that our understanding is true. Our apprehension whereby we merely understand, that is, merely know the meanings of words and apprehend some combination of them as possibly corresponding to the complexity of some being, is incomplete both regarding what is possible to our intellect and as regards what we desire. We are not only capable of knowing on many occasions that our understanding is true but we also desire the truth in preference to mere opinion.

We need to distinguish between the human intellect questing for truth and the human intellect knowing the truth. In questing for truth our initial state may be one of knowing truly or of holding an opinion. When matters of vital importance to us are concerned we are seldom in doubt about our state of mind, but at other times, even when very important matters are concerned, we may overlook the distinction between truth and opinion because we do not feel that we need to be vitally interested at the moment. We cannot be *knowing the truth as the truth* without adverting to the distinction between true and nontrue. For example, we can easily verify the statement that the road is wet by feeling the moisture upon it or by seeing water upon it. We need not assure ourselves that the judgment is true in order to be sure that the road is wet. We perceive both the fact and the conformity of the statement to the fact simultaneously. But if a few days after experiencing the wet road someone wanted to be sure of what we had experienced, we should have no difficulty in asserting the truth of our statement—we need only recall the visual or tactile experience in question to see that our statement accords with it. We did not explicitly advert to the distinction between true and nontrue of the time of making the judgment because the truth of our judgment was tacitly evident, and recognized. Thus we need not constantly pass formal judgments of truth upon our apprehensions and compositions and divisions in order to be sure that they are true. We perceive the contents of sensation as the senses present them and we are simultaneously aware of the proper functioning of the senses (provided we are being properly attentive to the matter at hand) and of the sureness (or lack of it) of the intellect's understanding of what has been imparted to the senses as information by the things in the environment or by verbal communication.

It is easier to illustrate our discovery that falsity is involved because this is the exceptional thing and impresses us as such. Thus when we have said that the door was shut and someone proves the contrary by pointing out that there was a piece of wood between the door and the jamb, we realize that from our position we could only see that the edge of the door was visually in line with the jamb. We could not see whether the door was actually shut or not, since our distance from the door and our angle of vision did not permit close enough scrutiny. In this way we come to see both our error and the falsity of the judgment based upon it, as well as the reason for the error.

The important fact is not that we can make errors and be unaware of them at the time; it is that in our normal state of observing and understanding our intellect perceives what is regular in the appearance of things and in the operations of the senses; thus we can distinguish the apparent from the actual, especially

Judgment and Truth

after profiting by some mistakes. We do not have to make false judgments in order to be fully aware of the nature and value of truth. But we do make them, because there are so many things of interest to the human mind that distraction from what we ought to be concentrating upon is inescapable. The man who wishes to progress as an intellectual being profits by his mistakes so as to be able to recognize the circumstances under which they are likely to occur and to be on guard against them.

THE GROWTH OF INTELLECT

We have described a nature as an intrinsic source of activity that belongs to that which possesses it essentially rather than accidentally. In the examples given to illustrate the various kinds of natures, those that were living natures were seen to be constantly active in various types of self-perfective activities. Thus their natural activities were seen as processes of constant change within fixed limits, which prevent the changes from becoming a dissolution of the living thing's very substance. For example, the living thing takes in nourishment and maintains its own chemical activity by reacting with it, so that the nourishment is transformed but the chemical activity of the living body does not proceed so far as to transform all of the body into lifeless chemicals. Rather the chemical activity proceeds within the limits imposed by the requirements for physical self-maintenance and growth.

The human intellect is a power of the soul which has operations that are specific to it and by which it grows toward a state of maturity. The intellect is nourished by information which it transforms into true knowledge or opinion. When the information is obtained from experience it undergoes the refinement and transformation involved in abstraction, and when it is apprehended verbally some modification of the expressions used by others is usually required to accommodate them to the terms that one customarily associates with his own understanding.

In the intellect's desire for true knowledge, the primary concern is to determine the meaning of things; but words play a large part in the acquisition of this understanding and in the formulation of judgments. Nevertheless, words are only signs of understanding and are not capable of being substituted for actual understanding, even though we may often delude ourselves in this matter by holding to groupings of words as meaningful without resolving them in such a way as to know whether they really make sense or not. In holding to such verbal groupings as though they were meaningful expressions we are engaging in pseudointellectual acts that are a burden to our verbal memory and detract from true intellectual growth by being a source of confusion in the attempt to really understand.

The true growth of the intellect toward maturity involves the possession of an indubitable knowledge upon which further understanding can be built and worthwhile opinions based. Growth in the possession of true knowledge is obtained by adding true judgments to the knowledge of things already understood and by forming true judgments about things being apprehended for the first time. By building up our knowledge in this way, rather than by accepting all kinds of unverified and even implausible opinions, we have a double-check on the verity of our understanding. The correspondence between the actuality of a being and the judgment we make as to its actuality, one check, must itself be in conformity with that part of our already ascertained knowledge to which it is related. That is, the absence of self-contradiction, which is characteristic of actual being, must also be found in comprehended being.

That which we have already understood also plays a role in our acquisition of new knowledge by influencing our choice of interests, for every person is aware that there are many areas of knowledge that he will never attempt to master because he cannot develop any interest in them. Also, some of the areas of knowledge in which he is now interested were opened to him by the circumstances of his home life and education; he probably would not have become interested in them otherwise.

The very profusion of information about the wide range of subjects that men have investigated is a challenge to the person who wishes to advance in knowledge, because the expansion of one's island universe of knowledge to encompass all that has been learned by man is an impossible task. But we do not need to master all of the details of a subject in order to know it in a general way. One can understand what kind of knowledge geography is, for instance, without being an expert in it. It is possible, then, for a person to increase his general knowledge about the universe in which he lives and also to specialize in some one area of human investigation. The two pitfalls to be avoided here are to take the specialized knowledge one may come to possess to be the most important knowledge there is, or the only possible way of looking at a subject, and mistaking the competence in discussing a subject that arises from a general knowledge of it with the competence arising from being truly an expert on the basis of having a vast experience with it.

A man can live an intellectual life separate from the immediate practical affairs of daily life, inasmuch as the practical affairs do not add to, or detract from, the pursuit of knowledge for its own sake. They merely procure the maintenance of the peaceful life that is a prerequisite to continual speculative learning. In this intellectual activity knowledge is in a way self-augmenting, for not only does what we already understand enable us to assimilate information we could not assimilate otherwise, but it also provides a rich ground for contemplation in which we can enjoy the truth that we already possess, and come to possess in an explicit manner some of what is implied in the knowledge already possessed. Thus a person may have acquired extensive experience and understanding of the geographical features of our planet and of how they resulted from natural forces such as erosion by water and displacement of land masses by earthquakes. His present knowledge of the forces at work in this matter contains many implications about the past history of the earth and its future, which he can work out by carefully scrutinizing, and reasoning about, that which he already knows.

Our comparison of the human intellect with a living nature fails in one point. The living natures that we can observe objectively are physical entities whose degree of development is strictly limited and whose direction of development is predetermined by the kinds of things they are. Intellectual development in man has no intrinsic limit—it is limited by the brevity of man's temporal life and his necessary preoccupation with practical matters. Nor is the growth of the human intellect predetermined in any other way than in its dependence upon something already understood for understanding something new, and in its dependence upon the senses for fresh information about the material aspects of the universe. Thus the human intellect has an unbounded scope for acquiring knowledge and a perpetual capacity for enjoying the possession of it, which is one of the imperishable delights open to man.

CHAPTER 7

*Motivation on the
Animal Level* ~ In general, the an-
swer to the question "Why does a person do anything that he
does?" is simply "Because he wants to." Within this reply are encompassed all the motives that underlie the multiplicity of actions
that a human person posits in the course of his life. The expression
"to want to" signifies that various needs are impressed upon our
conscious selves, and it also signifies the justification for many, but
not all, of our actions. Some of our actions are posited to satisfy
simple desires, but some of them result from an interplay of wanting what is pleasant and a decision as to what is really best for us.
Thus a person may eat what he wants or drink whatever beverage
pleases him and walk when he wants to, and so on. Sometimes,
however, he does what he does not find any pleasure in doing, because although the action is undesirable in itself it is judged to be
an indispensable means to something desirable. For instance a person suffering from some malady will take unpleasant medicine or
undergo painful treatment *without feeling that he wants to do so,*
since it is the only means of realizing his hope that his state of
health will be restored. In this instance one desire is temporarily

suppressed for the sake of satisfying a more important need. The reason for taking the medicine, nevertheless, is to procure something that he wants.

Terms Relevant to Motivation

The expression "a want" is somewhat ambiguous in ordinary discourse, because it can signify a mere absence of something suitable and also a positive state of being attracted to something that is not possessed. Since these two significations are not the same, we shall use the term "a need" to signify the nonpossession of something suitable, the term "to desire" to signify the state of being attracted by something not yet possessed, and "to delight in" or "to enjoy" in order to signify the satisfaction that can accompany the possession of some object of desire. Thus the hungry person, because he has a need of food, desires to have food and delights in the consuming of it to the extent that it overcomes the feeling of hunger and is pleasant to the sense of taste.

A person may further desire to possess the enjoyment of food in the future, but then the desire and the enjoyment refer to different moments. The desire exists in the present, whereas the need to which it is directed and the enjoyment of its fulfillment are yet to come. Thus it is inconsistent to say that we simultaneously desire and enjoy the same satisfaction in the same way (we may want more of it, or the prolongation of it), for the very enjoyment of what was desired fulfills that specific desire and thus eliminates it as a desire for that specific thing. For example, a person actually drinking cool water to slake his thirst can wish that it were colder water, that there were more of it, or that it were some other liquid; but he cannot desire the goal of having the water actually coursing down his throat because its very presence fulfills, and thus eliminates, the desire for it. Desire, then, is the being drawn to union with a goal the attainment of which extinguishes the desire in proportion as the attainment measures up to what is desired. The satisfaction of desires for what is pleasant, however, is usually a temporary thing so that we desire the same kind of satisfaction, tasty food for example, over and over again.

Kinds of Desire

Conflicts among the various desires of a single person may occur. The desire to play and relax competes with the desire to be busy in making a success of a career that requires unstinting effort. The desire to admonish a friend who has done us an injury, so that he may not do it again, conflicts with the desire not to admonish him for fear that he will be offended sufficiently to withdraw his friendship. The desire to continue playing an enjoyable game or to continue any pleasant pursuit that can be enjoyed only in one place at one time conflicts with the growing pangs of hunger that demand that we go where food may be obtained.

These examples illustrate not merely a variety of conflicts, but also a variety of *kinds* of desire. There is a distinct difference between merely *recognizing* the lack of something that would be to our advantage to have and a *positive physical feeling* of being drawn to the having or the doing of something whether we recognize a real need for it or not. Thus a forest dweller may look to the immediate future and recognize that he will need to obtain firewood in order to stave off the cold of the impending winter, but nevertheless may find himself totally lacking in any feeling of wanting to go and chop wood now. His conflict is in the same category as the conflict between the desire to relax and the knowledge that success in a career is jeopardized by relaxing now. The difference in the two instances is that in one case there is a *felt desire* opposing *the judgment of what ought to be done*, and in the other case, there is an absence of a felt desire in favor of or against the judgment of what ought to be done. The similarity in the two instances is that a *judgment of need* and a consequent *wish to fulfill it* exists, in spite of a felt desire to the contrary and in spite of an absence of any felt desire.

It should be clear then that the independence of the two kinds of desire and the difference in their characteristics demand a distinction within man of abilities to desire, similar to the distinction of abilities to know. It is easier here to resist the temptation to reify powers of desiring (consider them as being things in themselves) than it was with powers of sensing, because there are no *external* organs obviously dedicated to their use. Some of the felt desires can be located in a general way (as we shall explain a little further on), but not so as to locate an organ whose function is solely to desire, as the sole function of the retina is to be sensitive to light. Consequently it is by distinctions in the objects of desire that we shall distinguish kinds of desiring, and where necessary, powers of desiring, which we will call appetites.

The first distinction is made between a desire that arises as a result of the making of a judgment and those desires that arise in other ways and may be in accord with the desire resulting from judgment or opposed to it. Because the first mentioned kind of desire arises through the intellect's act of judging that something is good for us, and we then proceed to direct means to the attaining of this good according to the aspect of it that the intellect has judged upon, we shall call it the *intellectual appetite*. The act of this appetite is commonly expressed in saying that *we will do something* or *we will not do something*. Consequently we shall call it *the intellectual appetite* or the *will* indifferently. Since that about which its desires are concerned includes the objects of desire of the other kinds of appetite, and more, we shall treat of its nature and activity after they have been analyzed. Thus the will and the human act of free choice are the subject matter of Chapter 8, whereas the present chapter is devoted to the *animal appetites* that man has in common with other animals. They should not be called the sensory appetites even though the objects towards which they are attracted are presented in the acts of awareness of the senses, for each external sense has a natural tendency to behold its proper sensible. *Sensory appetite* should be used to distinguish these tendencies.

Animal Appetite

The term "animal appetite" is indicative of an ability shared by man and the higher animals to instigate actions with respect to things in the environment. Inasmuch as animal appetite desires things that are known, it depends for its activity upon sensory apprehension, and in animals possessed of memory, upon the subsequent remembering of things. Since man remembers many things that do not give rise to any desire to possess them, we must look for some particular formality to explain why these desires occur on some occasions and not on others. Before we proceed to discuss the origination of desire and the formality proper to animal appetite, however, we must note how appetite and desire differ from the physical action posited to satisfy desire. In this way we shall have as precise a notion as possible of the activities under discussion.

APPETITE AND ACTION

Appetite is the name given to the actual tending toward union with something that will be beneficial to that which tends toward it. Animal appetite is the ability to desire something; its *desire* is the positive tending to unite with some object that is suitable for possession. Thus appetite is found whenever there is tendency but animal appetite is not found apart from awareness, for the desire of something is a conscious tending that presupposes consciousness of something as desirable. The initial and predominant motivation of man's animal appetite is directed to the possession of what is suitable for the physical well-being (the health, shelter, and so on, necessary to pleasant living) of the individual person. But that well-being may be threatened by enemies and other unsuitable environmental factors, such as flood waters which may inundate a dwelling place. Consequently the desire to preserve physical well-being may involve the turning away from, and consequent avoidance of, what is unsuitable to and even destructive of that well-being. This turning away tendency is called *aversion*. There are other kinds of action on the part of the animal appetites beside desire and aversion, which we have cited here as examples because they are so easy to identify in every person's experience. We shall treat them in detail further on.

Desire and aversion are the *activities* of an appetitive power just as discriminating colors is an activity of sight. They are feelings of liking and disliking which arise within us; if the occasion for their arising persists and impresses us, they remain within us and may move us to do something about that which produced them. The termination of these feelings in the success of the actions which they caused, or by their simply being crowded out of our consciousness by more important considerations, also is within us. The physical action instigated by these feelings, however, goes out from one part of the body to another, as when we desire to walk and our muscles move our bones; or to some external object according as knowledge directs it thereto, as when we turn aside when walking to avoid a puddle in our path. It is through our feelings that we respond to physical states produced within us by our environment. Thus the heat of a summer day causes us to perspire and lose water from our body. As a consequence thirst is felt within the body and can only be satisfied within the body, but the action to satisfy thirst is executed by the hands which give motion to a container of water so that the water spills into the mouth. Thus desire supplies the reason for acting, and action can be effective in satisfying desire.

The moving to satisfy desire is the act of being moved by something not yet possessed and perhaps not yet in existence (a structure to be built, a tasty food to be prepared). But this does not mean that there is no aim directing such actions to the attainment of what is desired. The reason for the actions is something that is present now in our memory. It is the desired thing, present intentionally, considered as something that can actually be present to us materially in the near or distant future as a direct result of activities our bodies will perform. When we act to obtain some physical benefit we act because we have a real or an imaginary need, and therefore the instigation to act is on the part of our sense appetites; but we cannot actually direct our desires or our activities to an end until the end is made evident to us in a conscious manner. Otherwise how would we know the strength of our desire and the direction our activities should take to satisfy it? Actions directed consciously to a goal are said to be *teleological*, that is, actions directed toward an end. Inasmuch as the end to be attained by such activity does not yet exist as attained, teleological activities are directed to ends that preexist in our awareness. By preexisting there they serve as guides in estimating how much effort the attainment of a given end requires and the direction to be given to the means to be used for that end. Such activities in man are activities with a *purpose*. Thus to have a purpose in acting is to have an end in view toward the attainment of which we direct our actions.

Origination of Needs

If a well-fed and thirst-requited man slumbered content-
edly in his bed in a state of suspended animation so that very
tiny amounts of energy were used up in his metabolism, he could
stay there for a whole year and never experience a need that had
to be satisfied to prevent him from perishing. The same well-
refreshed person, however, in a state of normal animation, would
pass less than twenty-four hours before he would be strongly
impressed by his hunger and thirst. This fact illustrates that the
biological needs toward which much of our desire is directed
originate within us spontaneously. In a normal state of physical existence man experiences the constant recurrence of biological needs,
and the existence of these needs is made to register upon some of
the senses. Thus the need to rest because one is "bone weary," or
the need to move around "to stretch the muscles a bit," is made
known to us through kinesthesis; and pain and pressure in the
various organs of the body are made known through the pain
sense and through interoceptive awareness other than that of taste
and smell. The deficit of water in the body is signaled by a feeling
that we call thirst and the deficit of food in the body is signaled by
our feeling of hunger. The deficits occur as metabolism uses up the
available supply of food and water, and the feelings come into our
consciousness and grow more persistent as the deficits increase. We
do not know exactly how the deficits produce the feelings of hunger and thirst, although these commonly experienced feelings are
localized in the stomach and duodenum and in the pharynx, respectively.[1] The satisfaction of these felt needs benefits the whole
body; the failure to satisfy them results in the failure of metabolism and the consequent death of the whole body.

Although no knowledge is required to arouse the tendency to eat, and to drink, and to rest, knowledge is required in
order that these tendencies be successfully carried out. The pangs
of hunger cannot be diminished in man by the swallowing of
sawdust or stones, for he has no ability to draw nourishment from
these although some animals are nourished by wood. Thus he
must select from all of the objects of his environment those that
will successfully fill the need of which hunger is a sign. It is the
same with the use of liquids to supply the water deficit in the

body. Some are suitable for human needs in ways that are characteristically human. In short, what suits man does not suit every kind of animal so that we can distinguish the objects of his desires from the rest of the environment by designating them as "suitable for man." The ability of the members of a society to adapt the things in man's environment to serve their desires in the most suitable fashion is a sure sign of the human ability to profit from experience and to exercise critical judgment on the relative merits of various means for the attainment of what is suitable for man.

Since man acts to obtain what he deems to be suitable to him, and different things may be suitable in satisfying the same basic needs at different times, there must be some power by which a variety of objects can be apprehended as satisfying the same basic need. In a previous chapter the recognition of apple as a subsisting locus of sensible qualities was used as an example of the intellect's attaining an understanding of apple. Included in its intelligibility in that discussion was the notion of its edibility. Now that notion is based upon sensory apprehension of the suitability of the apple in relieving hunger without producing any concomitant ill effects. Thus the value aspect of the consuming of apples for the satisfaction of food deficit was apprehended on the *sensory level*, although its incorporation into the meaning of apple was seen to be an intellectual act. Therefore it is on the sensory level of cognition that we need to look in order to discover the kind of activity that enables one to use the experiences upon which estimations of value are based. We shall look then into the activity of the external senses, very briefly, in order to see if there is some aspect of their activity that explains how we are led to experiences in which we detect that what is suitable to our well-being is different from what is unsuitable to it.

Sensory Appetites and Experience

Each of the exteroceptive senses attains its proper sensible when it acts, for the proper sensible moves the sense to action and specifies the content of its awareness. The tendency of each of these senses, then, if we can judge by what they attain to, is to be aware of the sensible proper to it. Thus the act of seeing, considered by itself, is pleasant and desirable rather than the opposite. For instance, note that when we are well rested and conscious we seldom close our eyes deliberately as though it were unpleasant to be seeing whatever is available to our gaze. Of course the tendency to look at things serves other ends than the pleasure of merely seeing color patterns, for we recognize many things by their visual appearances and thus know them intellectually at the same time. We may also look over familiar scenes as an aid to recalling pleasantries of our past experience. Nevertheless, seeing is an activity that can be performed simply for the sake of enjoying the beholding of its proper sensible. The same conclusion applies to the use of hearing, for we often enjoy hearing pleasant sounds for the sake of their pleasantness, although very many combinations of sounds have a meaning for us that we detect even while enjoying the sounds as a listening pleasure. Thus a person can take delight in the beauty of a symphony without passing judgment as to how well it is played or as to the "meaning" that it may be meant to express. Similarly one can enjoy the beauty of a fine voice even while being unfavorably impressed by the message that it is expressing. Because smell and taste subserve somewhat different purposes than do sight and hearing, their activities for the sake of enjoying odors and flavors are more obvious upon casual consideration, for we very often use these senses solely for the pleasure of using them, whereas in using sight and hearing we are seldom free from the act of acquiring knowledge. The sense of touch also can be exercised just for pleasure, as when we enjoy the smoothness of velvet and the warmth of a spring breeze. We can find pleasure of a kinesthetic sort, too, as in the exercise of walking.

Inasmuch as the exterior senses detect only signs of what the things in our environment are, we can say that the tendency in each one of them is to enjoy the pleasure of each one's proper activity. But they are never moved to the sensing of something as though they were attracted to a knowledge of the *nature* of that thing or to a knowledge of its usefulness to us as a whole, for such knowledge is not within the scope of proper sensibles. Nevertheless, the act of satisfying the sense of taste and of eliminating the feeling of dryness in the mouth and throat with a pleasant liquid unites us with what is suitable for overcoming the food deficit and the water deficit. Similarly the act of relaxing tired muscles according to the tendency of kinesthesis gives the body the rest that it needs; when we do not respond to this felt need by follow-

ing the tendency of this sense, the body just relaxes because un-
consciousness in the form of sleep makes us incapable of exerting
effort. Also the relief experienced by ridding the body of waste
products whose accumulation causes discomfort and muscle tension, with the consequent tendency in certain muscles to act so as
to cause elimination of these waste products, is sufficient motivation to prompt these activities. Thus the arisal in consciousness
of felt needs tends naturally to prompt the actions that will meet
them.[2] Everything that pleases taste will not prove to be equally
beneficial as food nor are all tasty liquids capable of satisfying
thirst satisfactorily. Some discretion must be exercised in the assimilation of nourishment and in the positing of other activities
to take care of basic needs. But the senses we have just been
considering do not discriminate between what is apparently beneficial and what is really beneficial for our bodily maintenance.
Therefore some power that can profit by experience must be
recognized here as exercising discretion in singling out the most
suitable from among all of the objects that can possibly satisfy
our basic needs.

A further factor should be noted in the positing of actions to satisfy felt needs. Conflicting desires do not arbitrate
among themselves. A longing for one type of food or drink does
not consult a longing for a different type of food or drink to discover which has precedence. Since arbitration of these demands
involves knowledge, the power in man by which the desires that
arise spontaneously within him are followed out, or turned aside,
must be a cognitive one. This power is the estimative power
which profits by our experience with the results of actions
posited to satisfy desires (see Chapter 4). By the use of this sense
power, which we call the *estimative sense* or the *cogitative sense*,
we seek out and recognize by their sensory appearances many
kinds of things for the use to which we can put them, and in doing so we make estimations as to which needs are more pressing
and which can be postponed.

The close similarity of this power of discriminating the
suitable from the unsuitable to the intellect's act of discriminating the true from the false (which includes the truly valuable
from the falsely, or only apparently, valuable) makes it the most
important sense power for the achieving of the integration of actions with the needs of the body and with the aims of the intel-

lect in man. The role of the estimative sense as integrator of the needs of the body with the possibility of successful actions is not carried out in separation from the influence of our intellectual powers. For the sake of clarity, we shall consider it in this role now and leave the integration of the animal appetites with the intellect and the will to a later chapter.

Estimation and Animal Appetite

Although the biological needs that are accompanied by felt desires can be satisfied by the plainest and least tasty food and by plain water, and although protection from the elements can be provided by unadorned and simple structures, or by naturally occurring shelters, nevertheless man is prone to try to satisfy these needs in ways that are conducive to his physical comfort. Thus the same cogitative sense exercised to relieve the unpleasantness of naturally occurring physical conditions is also directed to finding the most pleasant way possible to satisfy these physical needs. There is a parallel here between the individual's gradual acquisition of experience of what gives pleasure and the increase in the desire for the varieties of pleasant experiences, and the gradual development by mankind of varieties of foods, drinks, and artifacts that aid in giving bodily comfort. Throughout this growth of the capacity for pleasure in the individual, and of inventiveness in mankind in general, the basic biological needs have remained the same and can be met by the simplest kinds of food, drink and shelter. This increase in the recognition of what is pleasantly suitable is due to our profiting from experience and our ability as rational creatures to fix upon *enjoyment* not only as an inducement to do what is necessary for self-preservation and preservation of the race, but also as something to be possessed in increasing degree for its own sake.

The activity of the cogitative sense, however, is not the only activity involved in the quest for the pleasant. We must distinguish a distinct type of appetite in this quest for the agreeable. We have already described it in contrast to the intellectual appetite, but have not shown the need to posit it as a distinct kind of power. In pointing out at the beginning of this section on animal appetite that some of the objects met with in experience do not give rise to any desire or aversion, we mentioned that there must be some formality they lack but which is present in the objects that do give rise to desire and aversion. This task has been partially accomplished in pointing out that each external sense has a proper object to which it naturally tends, and in doing so it tends to unite with what is useful for our physical maintenance; and that other biological needs that make themselves felt as painful muscle tension are productive of tendencies to that which satisfies them. That which the satisfactions of these various tendencies have in common is the aspect of *pleasantness*, of *physical enjoyment*. Therefore since all of these satisfactions are sought under this one formality, we shall assign this formality as the one governing those estimations of our cogitative sense that decide that these benefits should be sought for. It is the quite distinct difference between possessing the knowledge that something is desirable and the actual fixing of desire upon that something as that which is being attained by physical activity, or can be so attained, which leads to the positing of a distinct kind of appetite. As a sure sign of the correctness of this distinction, note that the act of knowing the availability of an object that will satisfy a biological need is terminated as an act of knowing, for our cogitative sense is not fulfilled in any physical way by the actual physical possession of the desired object. The whole body is benefited in a physical way. Our cogitative sense is also benefited by our appraisal of the degree of suitability of the object to the satisfaction of desire. But this is a byproduct of the physical activity, and when the action that is used to achieve a physical end is posited according to a habitual way of acting, we add little to our experience by its success. We must, then, distinguish an appetitive power which is moved to desire union with what is pleasant.

THE CONCUPISCIBLE APPETITE

For many centuries the term "sensual" has been used to indicate acts that are performed for the attainment of pleasure for its own sake. The term "concupiscence" has also been used to indicate the craving for what is delightful to the senses. These terms, however, which refer to the desires and acts of a certain appetite, have come to be used in everyday parlance to denote something unsuitable to man because of excesses in seeking what is pleasant; in many contexts they are meant to signify sexual lust.

The gradual change in the meaning of these terms causes a difficulty in assigning a fitting name to the animal appetite that we have been discussing. It is customarily called the *concupiscible appetite* to indicate its being drawn to union with that which is pleasant to have and not difficult to obtain.

Since no suitable name devoid of pejorative connotations has been generally agreed upon as a replacement for "concupiscible," we shall have to continue to use it to designate *that distinct power that is prompted to act by the biological needs which arise within us, and also by the things in our environment that we evaluate as being pleasant to unite with or as unpleasant to unite with.* Although by this appetite we are moved to desire something according to the formality of the *pleasantly suitable* (and consequently to aversion, by what is unpleasant), it is impossible for any physical action to be directed to a common nature or to a formality common to several things. Actions are necessarily quite determinate since they are concerned with singular things while common natures exist as common only in thought, although one and the same formal aspect is found in a multiplicity of things. Therefore this appetite by which we are drawn to all things and activities that are recognized as pleasantly suitable needs to be specified, so that we fix our desire on something determinate and cause a definite line of activity to be followed for its own sake (skating) or to obtain or to avoid union with something. Consequently to the definition just given of the concupiscible we should add that *the actual suitable that the concupiscible desires and the actual activity that it instigates is usually specified by the estimative sense.* The exception to this qualification occurs when some object attracts one of the external senses to it without the intermediation of any estimation by the cogitative sense. In such an instance the concupiscible enjoys that which pleases the sense.

The biological needs that instigate activities to satisfy these needs can be conveniently grouped according to the ends that their fulfillment attains. Thus the partaking of nourishment serves to supply the body's needs for rebuilding tissues and replenishing the supply of energy that is constantly being used up. The use of the bodily organs having a sex function tends to maintain the continuity of the human race by supplying ever new members. Thus if we look at man's activities solely as animal activities, he differs little from other animals in his motivation. The presently existing members of other animal species exist now only because they were generated as offspring by their parents. The parents acted in such a way as to maintain their individual lives by feeding and by besting or avoiding enemies, and in general by following their natural inclinations. These biological needs which make themselves felt, and the continually present tendencies of our sense powers to enjoy the sensible available to them, supply all of the motivation that underlies our physical activities in perfecting our animal natures. Thus swimming, running, building a house, storing food, racing in a boat, traveling in an airplane, even the use of language to some extent, are activities enjoyed for the sake of the pleasure they accord to some sense, or for the physical good of our bodies as a whole, or for the physical good of the human race as a whole.

Individual persons vary rather widely in their susceptibility to the pleasantly suitable according to their circumstances and physical temperament. Thus some delight in food and drink to the extent of building a daily ritual around their consumption, while others find the physical activity of locomotion in playing games or in manual labor greatly to their liking; others who are engaged in absorbing intellectual activities sometimes consider the satisfying of basic needs to be a mere ritual for the maintenance of life. Also, the activities considered suitable at one period of a person's physical life may be deemed quite unsuitable at another period. In short the exercise of the concupiscible appetite in human activities is a matter of personal preference based upon needs, opportunities, and physical temperament, as well as custom.

THE IRASCIBLE APPETITE

There is another set of activities required for the perpetuation of each individual person's existence. These activities are directed to the overcoming of obstacles that hinder the obtaining of some object of desire of the concupiscible appetite. In discussing the concupiscible appetite's activities in the previous paragraphs we concentrated on just one aspect of it, the attraction to what is pleasant, and merely mentioned the activity of aversion in indicating the scope of action of this appetite. Just as the tendency to what is pleasingly beneficial is governed by the discretion of our cogitative sense, so the tendency to turn away from what is unpleasant, although it arises spontaneously upon the recognition of the unpleasant, is subject to the decision of our cogitative as to what is best. Thus the spontaneous aversion to some food that has offended our taste every time we have had to eat it tends to make us turn away at the mere sight of it, but the necessity of satisfying the increasing pangs of hunger wins out in our estimation of what is best at the moment and we swallow the unpalatable food.

For the same reason that we posited a distinct ability to desire the pleasantly beneficial according as the cogitative placed such a value upon an object, we must now posit the existence of a different power, which is moved to act not by the formality of something pleasant but by quite the opposite formality of something difficult that must be overcome. Since the most obvious of the several signs of the activity of this appetite is the appearance we associate with a person's being angry, we name this appetite from this sign and call it the *irascible* (from *ira*, Latin for anger) appetite. To illustrate its occurrence consider how a person feels when he is about to enjoy a tasty morsel of food that cost him considerable effort to obtain and he accidentally drops it into the dishwater. His feelings can range from rage, a very intense anger, to deep sorrow over the loss of his treasure. This rage will not do him any good on this occasion, but rage might help him to overcome the obstacle to his obtaining what he wants on another occasion by impelling him to beat down the obstacle or put it to rout. In any case rage is not a feeling that we associate with the fairly easy attainment of a pleasant benefit.

It is apparent that the irascible appetite is moved by the awareness that dawns on us that something is amiss or will be amiss with our personal well-being. We may occasionally identify our benefit with that of a close friend so that what angers him angers us because it angers him, just as we may desire his obtaining a benefit for himself because we love him. This identification of what is good for another as our own good is much more characteristic of the act of the will than it is of the act of the sense appetites. Consequently we shall define the activity of our irascible appetite only in so far as its acts concern us personally. *The irascible appetite is a power which is prompted to act by the estimation that something which is difficult to obtain should be ob-*

tained or by the estimation that something which threatens the possession of what is desirable or threatens the activities directed to obtaining what is desirable should be fought off. The understanding of the variety of acts attributed to the animal appetites presupposes their distinction as different appetites which are directed to the attaining of what is suitable but in quite different ways. Now that the distinction has been made we shall examine the acts of each appetite in detail.

The Passions

The felt needs, which we have discussed as being the originators of various actions to relieve them, are called *felt* needs in contradistinction to *reasoned* needs because the felt needs manifest themselves physically to various bodily senses. They arise within us and move us to act in many instances with respect to external objects, but before we can act successfully we have to apprehend their existence as sensibles and evaluate their appearances so as to decide whether union with them or avoidance of them will be beneficial. This evaluation process does not have to be repeated endlessly, however, for on many occasions as soon as we recognize the appearances of a thing being apprehended, in terms of our past experience of pleasure or dissatisfaction with it, we are attracted to it or repelled by it. In these instances its appearance evokes a love or hate for it because the remembered appearances are automatically associated with a remembered evaluation of the thing. It is in this activity that the memory of the estimative power plays a paramount role in enabling us to locate previous actual experiences and recall the evaluation of them in terms of pleasantness or its opposite, and the other aspects of the suitable. *It should be noted, however, that no moral evaluations are made by the sense powers.* Thus the person who likes to smoke or drink coffee may occasionally debate with himself whether he *ought* to indulge in these pleasant activities, and thus consider them from a moral point of view explicitly; but the appreciation of their pleasurableness is a sensory activity. Consequently, the desire for these pleasures recurs as regularly, as often, and as insistently as do the demands for activities directed to purely biological needs, according as the feeling of a need for these pleasures registers on our cogitative sense. The dispositions to smoke and to drink coffee, however, are not innate but are acquired as a result of the estimation made of their pleasurable or otherwise suitable benefit to the individual involved.

Two aspects of our environment move the concupiscible appetite to its proper activity. What sounds pleasant or tastes pleasant is enjoyable immediately upon our feeling the pleasantness involved; no estimation is required to determine that this is pleasant. Rather, the pleasantness determines how the experience is evaluated. Similarly what grates upon the sense of hearing causes us to wince or shudder and to take action to stop the sound or to block it off. In general, what affects the senses in a pleasing or displeasing way *immediately* arouses the concupiscible appetite to love or to hate. That which appears attractive or offensive to us, *not immediately* but through the evaluation afforded by the use of past experience, moves this appetite in the same way.

Obviously many things that register upon our sensory awareness will evoke no appetitive response because they are not exciting to us and do not make sufficient impression to distract our attention from whatever it is engaged in doing at the moment. But many things do disrupt our train of intended activity, drawing our attention to them. When this drawing of our attention occurs it can be accompanied by a strong feeling, as in the instance of a noise that grates upon our hearing, or it may be accompanied only by an interest in knowing something about the item that has caught our attention. The feeling that sometimes accompanies these apprehensions is designated by the terms "emotion" and "passion." The terms are used synonymously here and designate *the act of one of the animal appetites accompanied by an organic change*. The act is one that arises within the appetite; it differs from the mere sensing of something by sight or by kinesthesis in that the act of the sense makes the sensed thing present in our awareness but the act of the appetite is a tendency arising in us and going from us to the thing desired. This activity of the appetite is accompanied by organic changes so that the body is looked upon as being passive to changes produced by the activity of the appetite. Thus the term "passion" is used to describe this overt effect. When a person feels scared or feels happy, when he hates something or sorrows over something, when he feels hopeful or dejected, he is experiencing a passion.

The number of words that can be used to describe how we feel is very large indeed. In using such words we do not usually bother to distinguish between feelings that arise from the functioning or malfunctioning of our body, feelings that arise from our act of sensory apprehension of what is external to us, and feelings that arise upon our receiving of pleasant or unpleasant information. All of these feelings, however, are distinguishable from the sensations that accompany them. Thus "feeling poorly" is often used to describe our emotional reaction to a persistent awareness of a painful muscle, bone, or organ; and "feeling down" is often used to describe our emotional reaction to sad news or to an actual apprehension of an impending unpleasantness. Thus our emotions are aroused in various ways, but all of these feelings have this in common: they are organic, and when they are strong, signs of these feelings are revealed organically. For example, a person who is "feeling blue" has an appearance that we associate with sorrow or hoplessness, and one who is "feeling on top of the world" has a look about him that we associate with happiness. These signs, however, are not usually easily recognized in strangers but they can be detected in those with whose appearance we are familiar. They are not always reliable as signs of a particular emotion, because tears can be a sign of both joy and grief. Our point in mentioning them is that since all of us have experienced emotions of joy and sorrow we can distinguish between our *awareness* of the pleasant and the unpleasant and the effects of this *awareness* which are revealed in our countenance and in other parts of our body.

CONCUPISCIBLE PASSIONS
REGARDING THE SUITABLE

In order to give a clear account of the arising, succession, and termination of feelings involved in the use of the concupiscible appetite, we shall use a well-established set of terms to describe the experience that they name. The name "concupiscible" has been given to the appetite whose activities are signaled overtly by actions to attain or to avoid something; these actions have been explained as motivated by *desire* or *aversion*. But desire and aversion are not the initial acts of the concupiscible appetite, for *love* is prior to desire and *hate* is prior to aversion. We can distinguish these various emotions from one another because love can occur without desire and hate can occur without aversion. By *love* we mean only *our attraction to something as being desirable* without a distinct desire on our part for it. Thus when a person who has no present inclination toward food says that he just loves sea food, he is merely expressing his sentiments that sea food is a delectable treat. He is assenting to the implied statement that if he were hungry and in good health, enjoying his normal appetite, he would desire to have sea food and would enjoy the eating of it.

The fact that *desire* and *enjoyment* are not identical is easily seen by anyone who recalls the countless times that an eager desire was disappointed by the most meager satisfaction, and the many times that an eager desire was frustrated completely and no enjoyment at all occurred. It would be strange if joy and desire were one feeling with two different intensities, or if, being one feeling, it were both present and absent at the same time. Joy and desire are different feelings, as we have argued in the first part of this chapter, but this difference does not mean that they come into existence independently of one another. Nothing is truly desired for its own sake unless it is loved; since desire is the actual tending to unite with the object loved, its termination is union with what is desired or the failure of this. One of the terminating passions, joy, puts an end to desire fulfilling it, but joy can also come into being without being preceded by a distinct desire when it suddenly is aroused by union with something pleasurable and quite unexpected. For example, a person working in a hot room steps outside to give a message to someone and enjoys the sudden relief from the heat imparted by the contact with cooler air. Of course, he could not enjoy the cool air unless it were a relief and it could not be a relief unless it were needed. So we may say that the desire is there potentially, inasmuch as if the person thought about the cooler air outside his room he would probably desire to be cooled by it.

Love as used here designates only the feeling of attraction to the suitableness of some object or activity by the one noticing it. The word as it is often used in conversation is applied to the act of desiring; this is the act that is most noticeable inasmuch as it usually involves physical activity to obtain something not yet possessed, whereas love (in our sense) precedes the physical activity and enjoyment follows the possession that results from the physical activity. There are of course physical activities that are enjoyed for their own sake. Love and enjoyment can exist simultaneously—one does not cease to assent to the pleasantness of what he has attained by his actions just because he ceases to desire it. In fact the enjoyment of what has been acquired, provided it is enjoyed in moderation, tends to increase the love for it. The enjoyment of anything that suits us as animals is a fulfillment of our love for such things and therefore is something that is sought after for its own sake. Sometimes, however, we settle for the love of something that attracts us without actually acquiring union with it; in this way we enjoy it in imagined possession rather than in really possessing it. Daydreaming is an example of this kind of thing, for in daydreams we often recall pleasant events of the past and dwell upon them, enjoying them in an imaginary way. Similarly we can project ourselves, in our imagination, into possession of something delightful that we never did actually possess but which we deem would be very suitable to us if we could possess it.

Concupiscible Passions
regarding the Unsuitable

Whatever offends a sense, or is detected by some sense as an immediate threat to the body, evokes a feeling of *dislike* for it because of the unpleasantness involved. Dislike may also arise, when there is nothing ostensibly offensive present, from the estimation of what is likely to happen in the near future according to our experience of a similar situation in the past. Thus a brilliant light falling upon the retina will disrupt normal vision; having foreseen our probable contact with such a light, we move so as to evade its shining upon our eyes. Similarly a feeling of faintness or suffocation prompts us to lie down or to seek air to prevent the impending consequences of which these feelings are a sign; the indication which we have in the morning that an intensely hot day is beginning can prompt us to plan our activities for that day so as to be always where it is cool. Estimations of this kind, that something is or will be unpleasant, concern not only what offends the senses and what will be unsuitable for the body, but also verbal criticisms that will make us feel bad. Uncomplimentary remarks upon our appearance or physical abilities also hurt us, but not so much physically (although they may make us droop with dismay or burn with anger) as in our feeling toward ourself as a distinct *physical* individual. Thus we tend to avoid the persons who make such personal remarks. Our evaluation of ourself is slighted and we feel hurt in such an instance.

This self-evaluation arises necessarily in each person's exercise of his cogitative sense, for each person necessarily forms estimations as to what is suitable or unsuitable to him. This estimation, in order that it may relate the possible use of an activity or an object to the kind of physical entity that the person is, must presume some characteristics in the self in order to estimate what will be suitable to such characteristics. Obviously, what is exactly suitable to one person is not exactly suitable to all, and the estimative sense is concerned with details. Thus, basically, most of our activities regarding the suitable are directed to the notion that we have of our physical self, as the term of benefit of such activities. There are a multiplicity of aspects, however, according to which this self is apprehended. For example, it is regarded as a hungry self or as a thirsty self, as a pain-fearing self or work-hating self, as a physically strong or physically dexterous self, as a handsome or unhandsome figure, as a handsome or pretty visage, and so on. We can love any part of us and any aspect of any part of us as the concupiscible appetite moves to obtain what is beneficial in any physical way. Thus at the root of any one of our estimations is a "picture" of our physical self that serves as the image to which we refer in judging what is beneficial for us and what is not. We might express this fact more succinctly in saying that our experience reveals all of those aspects of our own physical self according to which we estimate that some thing or activity is suitable or unsuitable for our possession. When we consider this "revelation" of experience by itself, we are beholding our "picture" of ourself.

Of course large areas in the scope of our physical desires are common to all human beings, since all of us are impelled by metabolism to desire food and drink and rest and recreation. Consequently some aspects of the "picture" that each one has of himself will be similar to those of the estimations that other individuals have of themselves. Nevertheless, there are individual tastes which we acquire and picture ourselves as delighting in, individual skills, and differences in physical appearance, which serve as the inner term of the relationship, "suitable to." From the reactions that a person makes to praise of some aspect of this "picture," or criticism of it, an observer may gauge roughly what kind of estimation that person has of himself with respect to the aspect commented upon. Thus the reactions may reveal that he does not esteem his physical being, nor any physical ability that he excels in, to be of surpassing importance for he does not show any anger over the slighting of them. Or, on the contrary, they may reveal that he values some aspect of his appearance or some physical ability to an extent that even he was not fully conscious of until a passing remark brought forth an effusion of assent for him. In short, these "pictures" of his physical being are a part of each human personality; they are indicative of what is valued most and of what is valued least in a physical way.

Each person has an estimation of himself as a physical entity even though he may not consciously single it out to dwell upon very often, rather tacitly assuming it in each estimation that he makes about what is suitable or unsuitable to him. Moreover we may never have discerned in our individual "pictures" those aspects which others criticize, although criticism certainly draws them to the fore and makes us acutely conscious of them. Thus to be called ungainly, unkempt, sickly, or the like, will offend us if we have an estimation of ourself contrary to these descriptions, even though the descriptions may be correct. Similarly if someone verbally or tacitly (by their actions) misconstrues our goals, in our animal activities, we are offended and react accordingly. We react joyfully to the opposite kind of personal remarks when someone sincerely praises our physical appearance or activities. *The truth in these matters, however, requires the exercise of critical intellectual judgment in comparing our imagined physical self with our actual physical self dispassionately;* it is not an easy task to be completely objective about one's physical self when others say what we hate to hear or what we love to hear. This critical evaluation of our "physical image" will be considered in Chapter 8.

The characteristic reaction to the apprehension of the unsuitable is dislike, a reaction which may or may not be sufficient to prompt an activity. In some circumstances it may happen that the unsuitable that we apprehend is of such magnitude that it paralyzes us with fright and this state of being rendered motionless prevents any avertive action. But when this is not the case we act so as to steer clear of what is unsuitable to us. Thus *dislike* (hate) is followed by *aversion*, which when successful may be followed by relief. This relief is a kind of enjoyment, resulting from the continued possession of the well-being that was menaced. When the aversion is unsuccessful we feel the same passion that terminates unfulfilled desire, as we *sorrow* over the unsuitable event that has befallen us.

Passions of the Irascible Appetite

The passions of the concupiscible then are love, desire, enjoyment, or sorrow regarding an object or activity that is beneficial to us; and hate and aversion followed by joy or sorrow regarding an object or activity that is unsuitable to us. Another kind of activity on the sensory level, which is opposed to the natural avertive activities of the concupiscile, is manifested when we encounter difficulties in the *avoiding of union with something that we hate*. The basis of the hate is ultimately the love of one's own being and the desire to conserve it against the unsuitable results of union with the harmful object.

For example, a hunter who has used up his ammunition and has only a hunting knife to defend himself against a predatory cat desires to save himself from death; but being unable to avoid his attacker, for lack of speed and cover, he must live through the moments until he is attacked. *Dread* of the ordeal to come may so unnerve him that he simply waits supinely for his destruction. As he cowers in *terror* of the actual attack he sees a possibility of gaining an advantage over the cat who is attacking from the front instead of from behind. He hopes to take advantage of this openness to counterattack. Buoyed up by this *hope* he overcomes his terror for an instant and thrusts the knife upwards into the heart of the attacking cat and kills it. To accomplish this deed he needed to feel *daring* in the face of the terrifying aspect of his attacker; this daring arose from his desire to preserve his own life and the hope of preserving it through his own action.

Fortunately we do not have to undergo such ordeals as a

routine thing, in order to see clearly the kinds of emotion that fear and daring are. *Fear* is an emotion arising from the realization that there is a difficulty that we must overcome in order to *avoid a union with what is unsuitable*. It arises because in our estimation the chances of successful avoidance are slim and we approach the struggle fearfully rather than confidently. *Daring* concerns the same situation, but in sizing up the situation, we judge that although the difficulties are very great and the union to be avoided is decidedly unsuitable, action will be successful in destroying the unsuitable or in successfully eluding it.

By our irascible appetite also we are often the subject of two passions concerning that which we esteem to be both *suitable but difficult to obtain*. Thus when we *desire* to be united with some suitable object such as an apple high up on a tree; or desire to put forth, or to be the recipient of, some activity (as when we want to go swimming or to be warmed by the sun) and there is considerable but not insuperable difficulty to overcome in attaining these goals, we *hope* to overcome the difficulty and put forth efforts to obtain that end. We sometimes use the term "hope" in place of "desire," for instance, when we hope the sun will be shining when we get to the beach. The emotion of hope is a feeling regarding what we believe we can do something about, and of course it springs from desire (as our example in the previous paragraph illustrated); the two exist simultaneously as long as there is difficulty to be overcome. Thus one does not "hope" to drink the cup of hot coffee set before him unless he is so busy carrying out some physical activity that he cannot free his hands to drink the coffee before it cools off. If there is no such impediment to his drinking it, he simply follows his desire and drinks it.

When the object or activity to which we assign a value is a suitable one that we strongly desire to have, but we gradually lose hope of attaining it, the diminishing desire is accompanied by *despair* of attainment. Thus despair is an emotion that succeeds hope upon the realization that the suitable is unattainable. Desire gradually is replaced by sorrow when, out of despair, we give up all attempt to obtain the suitable. Thus, in our example of hoping to obtain an apple high up on the tree, we first attempt to scale the tree, then finding that this is impossible, with diminished hope we resort to shaking the tree and perhaps even to heaving stones at the desired apple. When these efforts fail we may get angry and execute violence upon the offending tree, but usually we simply give up hope of obtaining the apple; although our desire is unfulfilled we turn our attention elsewhere.

Our usual, typical reaction to something that we dislike is to avoid being united with it, but the effort is often unsuccessful. When *the unsuitable proves to be unavoidable* the passion accompanying the union with it may be sorrow at our misfortune or it may be anger. For example, a person holding a bulky object in both hands views the number of steps he has to descend in going down a stairway with some consternation, and determines to be careful so as not to misstep. When he does stumble, or receives a jolt by trying to take a further step when there are no more, even though he is not pained very much physically by the misadventure, he nevertheless may feel a surge of anger at the offending steps. If he negotiates the steps without mishap he feels a joyful sense of relief. The anger, which is an irascible passion, arose from the failure to avoid an unpleasantness that was disliked in advance but which overtook him nevertheless. Another person might pass off the incident with no emotion whatsoever or merely feel sorry at the slight discomfort to himself. The difference in these reactions to the mishap points out the salient feature of anger as distinct from sorrow. *Anger is directed to something else as offensive to us whereas sorrow is directed to oneself as the subject of misfortune.* Anger is comprised of a feeling of hurt because something we love has been treated shoddily, and we sorrow over this hurt. But it also involves a hope of gaining revenge upon that which has offended us, a wish to injure that which we hate.

Thus *anger* is not purely optimistic as are hope and daring, nor purely pessimistic like fear and despair. Rather it has a twofold aspect because it can give rise in us to actions by which we *destroy what is obnoxious;* in doing this we *vindicate ourself* against the slight that produced the anger. Thus we associate the feeling of anger with *revenge* directed toward the offending something. The revenge, when achieved, makes us feel better although the obtaining of it entailed the inflicting of a physical evil upon what offended us. The optimistic side of this passion is manifested in our expecting to salve the hurt and thus to feel better as a result of inflicting injury upon what angered us. The tripping upon the step is a reflection upon our physical prowess; we feel incompetent in the difficult action of treading the steps without the aid of vision. It may help a little to kick the offending steps on the basis that one contempt deserves another; it does help quite definitely in releasing the pent-up energy that accompanies anger. The pessimistic side of this passion has a resemblance to hate inasmuch as anger is an emotion that impels us to inflict injury upon what offended us. In neither of these passions do we ever feel urged to do good to the thing we hate and the one whose union with us evokes anger. We may, however, experience a different passion immediately following anger, upon recognition that what appeared to be a slight to our importance or prowess was quite accidental. In such a case it is our rational ability to distinguish the real intention from the apparent one that changed our estimation of the situation with the consequent replacement of anger by mere sorrow and perhaps even a judgment of forgiveness. The concupiscible and irascible appetites in their activities are thus complemented by rational control exercised upon our sensory ability to estimate the suitableness and unsuitableness of things and activities.

THE PASSIONS AND REASON

As we mentioned in the beginning of Chapter 4 it is quite difficult to separate the acts of the intellect from the acts of the senses when the several powers act simultaneously. This relative inseparability is present here in the discussion of the appetites because the "picture" that each individual has of himself has both physical and intellectual aspects. Thus a slighting remark evidencing contempt for a person's mental abilities, or for his capacity to act as a totally free agent contrary to powerful persuasion to act in some accustomed manner, will produce a similar feeling of anger with its physiological accompaniments to that produced by a physical injury. For example, to allege that someone is not very bright or that he could not give up smoking no matter how much he wanted to is to provoke a revengeful retort that impugns mental and voluntary deficiencies to the accuser. The insults are only verbal, but the "picture" one has of himself is none the less hurt for that. Nor are the physiological accompaniments of anger any less vehement because it is the mind and the will that are offended. This close interplay of the reason with the estimative sense and the animal appetites is a striking sign of the unity that obtains in the exercising of the various powers of the soul, for they act in concert with one another. It also signifies the unity in being of the one who feels and the one who understands, because these are activities of one and the same individual man.

The interplay of the various cognitive powers and the animal appetites will be considered at length in the next chapter when the exercise of right reason with respect to the passions will be considered. But here it is useful to consider an effect that the passions have upon our use of reason and upon our expression of what we think about things. The effect upon our rational power of apprehension is easily seen when we compare how the same things are interpreted by us when we are angry and when we are calm. A person seething with anger for which he has no outlet tends to see perfectly inoffensive acts as being contemptuous of him. An accidental jostling on the street, the borrowing of some possession of slight value can appear as overt aggression and as contempt for his ownership to a person in such a state, whereas he views such acts in their true light when he is calm. Also, to a sad person the outcome of some frolicsome venture appears bound to bring sorrow, whereas to one in a happy mood an impending ordeal does not look so bad. This effect of the passions upon rational consideration (and upon sensory estimations also, for the two powers act in concert when physical activity is involved) is to give different appearances to things, as far as evaluating them is concerned, than they actually should be given according to a dispassionate appraisal. It is not a misapprehension on the part of the direct senses but a faulty estimation of the values of things and of activities produced by the presence of the passion.

It is a matter of common experience also that our expression can betray our feelings by the inaccuracy that passion tends to produce in it. Thus a person who is being questioned about the competence of someone who is competing with him for a promotion may be carried away by a feeling of unfriendly opposition to his competitor and malign him, even though at the time he is doing it he knows that he is not speaking the truth. But hate is not the only passion that modifies the accuracy of our expression—a burning desire to obtain something of another person may induce us to slant a statement of our merit of the desired thing or our promise of what we will do in exchange for getting it, so that the statement does not coincide with factual reality.

No one has such control over the events of his life that he will never be taken unawares and find himself possessed by a great hate or anger or love that will seriously interfere with the accuracy of his apprehension of a situation and the accuracy of his expression about it. Nevertheless, it is possible for anyone to realize the effect that strong passions have in upsetting his rational activities and not only to discount the impassioned statements made by others but to be critical of his own judgments and estimations according as they are influenced by how he feels.

Customs and Basic Needs

We have described the passions only briefly, sufficiently to show the reader that they are directed to activities and to things according as they attract us or repel us, either immediately or through the mediation of judgments based upon experience. In doing this they tend to serve the fundamental needs required for propagation of the human species and to provide enjoyment for human beings in their daily life. In man, who can find pleasure in all kinds of things and who can make many objects in his environment serve as useful to him, the range of the animal appetites is very wide indeed, stretching to all of those things over which he exercises dominion. Thus he reacts to many different kinds of information about his surroundings: it is pleasant to view, to hear, to smell, to consume; it has objects that will be useful for building, for heating, for mending, for coloring, for clothing, for transportation, and so on.

As an individual person enlarges his experience he enlarges the scope of his likes and dislikes. That there is nothing automatic nor predetermined about this growth in man's appetitive activities should be obvious when we consider how great are the differences in likes and dislikes among various individual human beings having similar backgrounds, training, and opportunities. The range of human desires for material benefits is a distinctive characteristic when human activities are compared to those of other animals. Also, the wide range of preferences for material benefits among people of the same occupation and background is a sign of the nonpredetermined affinity in man for that which suits his comfort and gives him enjoyment.

Yet, for all the variety of tastes and all the varying intensities with which their satisfaction is pursued, men in satisfying their basic physical needs for food, drink, shelter, and physical activity act in much the same way. Consequently what man's basic activities to satisfy these needs will be can be fairly well predicted in a given set of circumstances. As a sign of this throughout man's history each grouping of men into a social unit has been accompanied by the agreement among them upon a set of *mores*. These are customary ways of acting with respect to satisfying man's physical needs so that the means of satisfying them would be available in one way or another to all of the members of the group. Thus the customs of a group that lived by hunting their food differed somewhat from the mores of those who survived by raising crops and by domesticating animals. Similarly the mores of our present highly industrialized society include the acknowledgment of many rights and duties that were not dreamed of in earlier societies. This is so because of the different kinds of actions that are deemed to be in accord with right reason in our society and because the scope of human activities ranges to so many more activities and objects now than it did in previous civilizations. Nevertheless, the basic requirements for the preservation of the race remain much the same as they were in previous centuries; customary ways of acting still acknowledge the rights of individual persons to live, to use property, and to marry.

That mores developed was inevitable and that they exist today as the basis for distinction between permissible overt actions and actions detrimental to the rights of others testifies to the fact that an individual man acting according as his passions move him runs into conflict with other men acting according to the motivation supplied by their own animal appetites. Thus, if there is an insufficiency of food and drink for a group of people, the desire of each individual person to have what he needs despite the needs of others may be strikingly illustrated in quarrels. But even under normal circumstances, by the very fact that each individual person possesses something that is his and someone else is naturally moved to desire it and strive to obtain it, strife among individuals is bound to arise unless there is a code of rights and obligations to regulate the acts of men. Since the animal appetites have very little altruistic tendency, certainly not sufficient to acknowledge the rights of strangers to that which is desired for oneself or for a loved one, it is obvious that it is human reason that has established the various sets of mores that have obtained in various groups of men.

INNER CONFLICTS

Conflict is not restricted to the overt activities of men striving for the same goods. There are many conflicts within each one of us that do not manifest themselves in any external way, although they are quite real. Thus the necessity of enduring the continued existence of something we hate and would love to destroy conflicts with the desire to destroy it. The unceasing attraction we feel for something that we cannot obtain by any means available to us conflicts with our enforced acceptance of that which we can attain by our own efforts. If we learn to live with these frustrations and to subordinate them to a minor role in our conscious life, and if we learn to channel our activities along lines of endeavor that are acceptable to us (even if less desirable than others) and to society, this is a sign that we have reached emotional maturity. There is nothing automatic about reaching this stage of personal growth, and the pain of reconciling our desires to our abilities and to our fortunes in life is only slightly lessened by the realization that we are facing facts. No one can achieve any mastery over himself unless he does this. To be always in a ferment of frustration or to retire always to a dream world where everything is imagined to happen according to our desires is to be always unhappy or to be happy at the expense of being out of contact with reality. What is most desirable in this matter is a reconciliation of the desires and hates that have no possibility of being satisfied. Their reconciliation in man cannot be effected on the sensory level without the aid of the intellect and the will, because in many instances the abiding desires and hates directed toward physical things receive their abiding characteristic not from some unchanging suitableness or unsuitableness for our physical being, but from the fixing of the will upon them as a paramount good or evil. Consequently it is within the power of our rational appetite to change its tendency to love or hate something according as by the use of reason we change our evaluation of the things toward which our desires and hates are directed. These changes of evaluation and the consequent reconciliation between desires and possibilities will be discussed in the next chapter.

The hard facts with respect to the animal appetites are these: No sensual pleasure is so suitable to man that he will be completely satisfied with it, and his needs are never exhausted to the extent that he should not expect their recurrence in the future. We must take nourishment, rest, and exercise over and over again in order to maintain life and health. Thus we follow a routine similar to that of the other animals, a routine of being aware of needs, of satisfying them, and so on. Whether we like it or not, a fair amount of our time is spent in answering the call to action sent forth by feelings brought on by the endless process of metabolism of our bodies. In this we achieve the same purpose over and over again, namely, the daily prolongation of the vital processes within ourselves. The limit of man's love of life, however, is not set by the scope of his animal appetites; he is in possession of a limitless capacity for happiness—the human will.

CHAPTER 8

The Will and Freedom of Choice ~ IN THIS CHAPTER WE

continue the analysis of human motivation by going beyond the consideration of man's desires for what suits his animal nature to consider at length the ability of every rational person to strive for goals that come into his view only as a result of the judgment of reason. This ability is called the *will;* it is a distinct appetite that is moved to the desiring of something according as that something is deemed to be beneficial by the judgment of the intellect. Since will is a distinct power we shall argue to its existence and then discuss its formal object in the first part of this chapter. In the second part, we shall explain what is involved in man's freedom of choice and then analyze the role of the will as the prime agent in man's deliberate activities and the roles of the other powers that are affected by the will's agency.

The Existence of the Will

In the beginning of the previous chapter some examples were used to distinguish the various kinds of desire from one another. Those examples made clear the difference between motivations that arise primarily from felt needs and those that are based upon reasoned needs by showing these motivations in conflict with one another. It is true that our animal desires are often in conflict with what we will to do, but it is not in the nature of the powers having these desires to be always in conflict. In fact it is quite possible for the majority of our concupiscible and irascible tendencies to be in accord with what we deem to be really suitable for us. This is so because all of the activities that we deem to be desirable for concupiscible or irascible reasons come under the consideration of reason and many naturally conform with what reason sees to be correct, while some of the remainder can be extensively modified and even changed altogether by the use of reason. Let us consider some further examples of the interplay of the various kinds of motivations in order to show the role of our intellect in determining which motivations shall predominate in moving us to act. Since our will is moved to its acts by the judgment of our intellect which directs our deliberate actions to their goals through the mediation of the cogitative sense with its fund of practical knowledge about effective action, we shall first consider the way in which reason, in conjunction with the cogitative sense, can integrate all of the various motivations for the good of the whole individual and then proceed to analyze the interaction of reason and will.

RATIONAL CONTROL OF ANIMAL APPETITION

The control of animal appetition by reason through actions that are proper to reason as a cognitive power is effected by producing a change in the sensory estimation as to the actual suitableness of an activity. For example, consider the act of running for the fun of it or of eating olives for the sake of the delight in tasting them. Running as a pleasant exercise is a delight to the kinesthetic sense; as a bodily satisfaction it is a delight to the concupiscible appetite. Therefore the only innate restriction upon its enjoyment is that it not be prolonged until the unpleasantness of exhaustion sets in. And yet there are many rational considerations according to which one might suddenly curtail this enjoyable pastime while in the very act of enjoying it. Thus one might consider a weakness of the heart that could be aggravated as a result of running, or one might recall an obligation to impart some very useful information to another person and go off and take care of this commitment. These reasons for curtailment are not involved in the running activity itself and therefore do not affect the concupiscible appetite directly so as to produce aversion in it. The prompting reasons for curtailment of the running mentioned above are the acts of recollection that concern the possibility of a physical disability's occurring, and an obligation to a friend. The prevailing reasons are the effect that the possibility of physical disability has upon our judgment of the value of the exercise, and the effect which the awareness of obligation to a friend has upon that judgment, respectively.

Similarly, in the case of eating olives for the pleasure of their taste the consideration that eating the olives will probably severely mitigate the effects of a reducing diet directed to the recovery of a desirable body weight, or the maintenance of it, may be sufficient to cause us to judge that we should stop eating them. In neither of these examples do the considerations of reason affect the cogitative sense through what we have actually experienced, unless there has already been an experience of the discomfort of heart trouble or of severe overweight. But in the absence of any experience of these two, there is nothing in the sensory experience upon which our estimations of the desirability of running and of eating olives is based that can modify those estimations to the extent that the running and the eating of olives no longer appeal to us. In fact the cessation of running and of the eating of olives is quite contrary to the original desire for enjoyment.

Two distinct possibilities need to be considered in accounting for the cessation of the activities. In one case the sudden realization that the information required by our friend is of momentous importance to him could drive all other considerations from our attention except those essential to the act of imparting the information. This presupposes only the rational ability to discern and to be impressed by the tremendous importance to our friend of the information that we have for him.[1] In the other case the consideration of reason could be imparted to the estimation of the cogitative so that the estimation changes to the extent that what had appeared to be desirable no longer appears so. That this is not a mere hypothesis but a fact is obvious on those occasions when the estimations of the cogitative sense are changed, although there is no alteration of any kind in the appearance or circumstances of what has been deemed desirable nor in the physical state of the person involved. Thus, in the example of the person who enjoys running, his estimation that running is a pleasant activity for him could be changed to an estimation that running is dangerous to him upon the consideration that it definitely might provoke a physical disability whose occurrence would be hateful to him. His feeling of wanting to run is replaced by an aversion to running. The act of the reason involved in bringing about a change of this kind in the estimation formed by the cogitative sense is a comparing of that which it knows to be a factor in bringing about a heart malfunction with the proposed acts of running and seeing that the two coincide. The same act of comparison is found in weighing the pleasure of tasting the olives against the highly probable gain in weight that will follow the breach of dietary regulations.

The act of right reason is the human intellect holding to a judgment that its evaluation of an end that is possible of attainment is suitable or unsuitable for a human agent. The evaluation results from a consideration of the nature of man and of what is suitable to that nature. It may be arrived at by a snap judgment or by deliberate consideration or it may merely be accepted as a way of acting that is explicitly accepted in the mores of the group to which an individual belongs.[2] The criterion of right reason is used whenever we act fully deliberately (rather than from habituation) since deliberation involves the comparison of various means to a desired end and the evaluation of the end in question in terms of what we know to be best for human agents and best for us individually.

The act of comparing the desirable and the undesirable aspects of proposed activities is seldom made in the absence of a felt desire for the activities themselves so that a tendency toward the activities (or away from them, in other instances) already exists and exerts an influence upon our rational evaluation by making the proposed activities appear to be quite desirable even though we know excellent reasons why they should not be engaged in. No one can predict what the outcome of such a clash of motivations will be even in the case of a person who consistently disciplines his feelings to keep them in accord with what his rational judgment discerns as being truly best for him. He may follow his usual course of action or he may decide that in this instance the pleasure to be obtained from the running or the eating is the best thing for him and engage in these pursuits. If the person is very strongly impressed with the high probability of heart trouble by the advice of his doctor in this regard he has more motivation for refraining from the enjoyabe exercise than if he merely were guided by the general rule that overweight people past a certain age are more susceptible to heart trouble than others. But even so, there is no predicting with certitude whether or not he will change his estimation of the value of the exercise so as not to have any desire for it any longer.

Whenever we act contrary to the tendencies of the animal appetites we frustrate a felt tendency in order to achieve some goal that we consider to be of greater importance than the one toward which the present felt tendency pulls us. Thus we may restrain from indulging in an activity that we desire now in order to betake ourselves to another place where we can enjoy some different pleasure. In other words we arbitrate between desires according as we judge which of two available pleasant activities is most suitable to us now. This ability to evaluate suitabilities is attributed to the cogitative sense on the sensory level and to the intellect on the rational level as exercising its ability to compare goals and to evaluate them. These two cognitive powers are not so disparate as are sight and intellect, for example. For sight discriminates what is actually visible and present to it and no intellectual act can change the sensory impression. As we have seen in a previous chapter, though, the intellectual power works intimately with imagination in its creative activity and in mathematical abstraction. This power also works very closely with the cogitative power—it can modify and even reverse its estimations. Because our intellect can have such a direct influence over our cogitative sense, this sense power is likened to reason in the act of considering alternative ways of responding to apprehended sensibles. In a person whose conscious tendencies are not completely dominated by his animal desires, many estimations of the value of a proposed goal for action can be reversed easily by a rational evaluation of the same matter with which the cogitative is concerned. Thus not only can this sense power evaluate a present situation in terms of past experience with the elements that make up the present situation, and modify or completely change its evaluation in the face of a new appearance put upon the singulars with which the action is concerned, but it can also present to our conscious self on an instant's notice a "picture" of our physical self and of our physical abilities to serve as a basis for actions that are proposed as a result of rational considerations of what is the best thing to do.[3] In this way it serves to integrate the activities of the animal appetites with the reasoned desires of the will by modifying the estimations that move the animal appetites in accord with the conclusions of reason as to what is best.

INTEGRATED HUMAN ACTS

By integration we mean the resolution of conflicting motivations so that the human agent acts for the end that he intends in the best manner suited to attaining it. It involves the modifying of very strong passions, the fortifying of weak ones, and the overcoming of deficiencies in the estimations based upon accumulated sensory experience. This integrative action is seen especially in the instances when we give up an intended line of action that we know to be rash and unjustified because "common sense" prevails. Thus when we are angered by trivialities —someone's keeping us waiting beyond an appointed time, or jumping ahead of us in line, and the like—the first intention that arises in us alongside the passion of anger is to forsake the appointment and take revenge upon the latecomer by not being there when he arrives, or to complain loudly about the line crasher and even direct violence toward him. But the considerations that the latecomer may be justifiably late or that the line crasher may have excellent justification for his action can stave off our tendencies to act impetuously.[4] Another way in which the cogitative can serve as integrator of appetitive tendencies is by the modification of suddenly aroused passions through the consideration that such passions are physiological and temporal in character and therefore are to be used in accord with what is known to be the best way of acting at the moment rather than to allow them to run their course and provoke the unhappy consequences that often follow impetuous and unreasoned actions. Thus a parent angered by his children's disobedience can be as irrational as they by giving vent to his anger even though he realizes that children are forgetful and exuberant, or he can use reason and deliberately calm his anger, adopting an attitude of patience and tolerance in reprimanding those in his charge.

Restraint is not always the mode of influence of the reason upon the estimations made by the cogitative power—we feel the need to reinforce our desire to perform a difficult task or to eradicate an obdurate source of dislike. For example, hours of effort to dig a trench to provide drainage for a piece of property may well be accompanied by feelings of sorrow at the difficulty of the work and the amount remaining to be done; nevertheless our efforts can be bolstered by the consideration that the digging cannot go on forever and that there will be a substantial benefit to the property to be drained when the job is finished. Similarly the effort to unmask the wily deceit of some other person whose ability to be charming tends to put us off from our task can be reinforced by the consideration of the intrinsic evilness of his lies.

Each individual human being has his personal strengths and weaknesses, which represent the accumulation of experience that makes up the content of his memory. In order to profit from such experiential information one needs to be objective about the strengths and weaknesses so as to capitalize upon the strengths and avoid the exploitation of the weaknesses. To be objective about them is to evaluate them from a critical point of view, which is proper to reason. The cogitative itself is not too trustworthy in such matters because its concern with events is to record the details of our personal experiences and to aid in projecting future actions in terms of their recognized suitability in the past. This aspect of suitability, however, is a physical one, limited to our physical and emotional life as animals. Consequently it does not include of its own accord the criteria of right reason and therefore cannot evaluate our activities according to the best standard of success, which is the one derived by a reasoned comparison of how our actions turn out with how they ought to turn out. For example, as far as sensory estimation is concerned an enemy that is destroyed is just as successfully removed as one that is merely frightened away; whereas these two acts are not the same thing at all according to reason when the enemy is a human being. It is obvious that the proper evaluation of the success of human actions and of their failures according to right reason is the task of an intellectual power that can be aware of the norms suitable to man as an animal, as well as those that are suitable to him as an intelligent member of human society. Thus it belongs to the intellect to make up for deficiencies in the estimations made by the cogitative sense and to detect strengths and weaknesses that are revealed only when a knowledge of what is best in human activity is used as a basis for comparison. One important result of such critical evaluation is a person's ability to make a better choice of his life's work by explicitly enumerating to himself his special talents and his persistent weaknesses and then using this knowledge to guide him in his choice, as far as circumstances permit. In this way he can capitalize upon his strong points and safeguard himself against being victimized by his weaknesses.

The superior ability of human reason to recognize the value of goals for human action and the variety of ways of attaining them can exert other influences upon the animal powers of man for his benefit. From the few that have been analyzed, however, it becomes clear that reason can have a profound effect upon our animal sensibilities and can dominate them to the extent that a person can act always, or almost always, in a truly rational manner. But control of the animal appetites by reason does not arise spontaneously. Rather in the early years of our life the animal desires arise spontaneously from within, and with the widening of our experience and the consequent extension of the range of our desires, are elicited spontaneously by the things presented in our experience. Not only do we come into full possession of reason after our senses have been functioning excellently for some years, but we also come to realize *the difference between the apparently suitable and the truly suitable* only after we have been desiring the apparently suitable for a number of years. Thus each person has to work at integrating his various motivations; success depends more upon conviction than it does upon sheer will power, because enforced integration tends to be disrupted when the enforcing principle is relaxed. Thus the child who is moved by threats or by physical punishment unaccompanied by reasoned argument to obey commands to act that are contrary to his inclinations and convictions can be expected to revert to his unacceptable ways of doing things, since his convictions on the matter have not been changed. The reason why convictions on practical matters are not easily changed is because we tend to think that what works out to our satisfaction is right and the conviction of successful action is not easily displaced by mere words. Actions do speak louder than words, not only in signifying that our intention is actually what we say it is but also in convincing others that one way of achieving the stilling of desire (by satisfying it or by altering it) is superior to another. In these matters it is the actual experience we have had that we base our estimations upon; vicarious experience through what others relate to us is not really experience for us at all.

CONVICTION

The assurance that a way of acting and the end to which it aspires is eminently suitable, is not sufficient to guarantee that an action and its end are in accord with right reason. Thus a person who has formed the habit of talking volubly and loudly so as to command the attention of those near him may be blindly following his desire to be considered a person of some importance by others. If he reflects upon the actual effect that his conduct has upon others—drowning their voices out and boring them—or if he surreptitiously overhears himself described as a "noisy windbag," he may come to realize that his conviction about his image in the eyes of others is entirely mistaken. His new conviction that he is not superbly delightful company for other people has the advantage over his previous one because there are some reasons to support it. The criterion of finding reasons to support our convictions distinguishes convictions based on the apparent success of our activities from *reasoned convictions* arrived at by reflecting upon our goals and the actual efficacy of the means we use to attain them. The ability of man to sit in judgment upon his own actions is both a privilege and a burden, for by the use of it man can develop a critical judgment and escape being victimized by his own spontaneously acquired convictions. But it is a burden, too, for the exercise of reason in this way is not an easy task, not only because free advice is plentiful and conflicting, but especially because it is hard to be objective about the goals we most cherish and which dominate much of our conscious attention. Nevertheless a person can act (without coercion) only according as his convictions make actions appear suitable to him. *To fail to acquire reasoned convictions is to fail to achieve fully the rationality that every normal human being is capable of and this is to fail to fulfill the prerequisite for exercising free choice.*

THE WILL AGAINST THE PASSIONS

Let us consider the first examples that were used to illustrate the effect of rational judgments upon the estimations of the cogitative sense once again, for there is another factor involved besides the effect of the rational assessment of the value of the proposed activities upon the sensory estimation of their pleasantness. This factor is clearly manifested in the act of refraining from acting even when the estimation of the cogitative sense has not been changed and the impression remains that the running and the eating are absolutely desirable for the sake of the pleasure they will give. This is not a case of the obliteration of one consideration by another, which was exemplified previously. Rather it is the entertaining of two desires simultaneously, the desire for pleasure and the desire for health, without any suppression or diminishing of either desire, but with the suppression of the action that would frustrate the desire for health while fulfilling the desire for pleasurable activity now. Since the concupiscible appetite cannot be motivated by a value such as the health of the body, because no sense power can discriminate such a thing (except when the discomfort of a loss of health has been experienced and then discrimination is limited to such an experience), we cannot account for the repression of the tendency to run or the tendency to eat in terms of what the animal appetites do.

We must recognize here the existence of another appetite which is acting against the tendency of the animal appetite to engage in the pleasurable activities. Thus *our will* follows the decision of our reason that the pleasurable good is not the paramount one in this instance and is not to be pursued. The activity of the will in this example is manifested as an instrument of reason in effecting control of concupiscible desires which are seen to be perfectly legitimate in themselves but not suitable on this occasion. This kind of control does not depend upon persuasion but rather upon the subservience of the voluntary muscles of the body to the will. Thus we follow our animal inclinations if and when we will to do so, or contrariwise, we can ignore their clamoring. This autonomy exercised by the will, however, is dependent upon its being specified in its act by our intellect. We are moved to acts of preventing actions instigated by our passions by reasoning that something is wrong. We use the term "wrong" to indicate the characteristic of an action that is contrary to what we judge to be truly suitable for us. The term "right" is applied to actions that we judge to be truly, and not merely apparently, suitable for us. Thus to engage in running is *wrong* for the person with a heart ailment and to eat fattening foods simply for the pleasure of the taste is *wrong* for the person on a strict diet. The ability to prevent these wrong actions even though we strongly desire to engage in them is an ability prompted not so much by the projected actions as by the intellectual estimation of the irrationality of such actions. There is no other way for the aspect of an action that is contrary to the inclinations of the animal appetites to appear suitable to us except to give it the aspect of suitability by a judgment of reason. Thus it is by will power that we act contrary to what we consider suitable by deficient and defective estimations of the cogitative sense. These estimations are deficient when they do not include value factors that bear on the situation and are defective when they are unduly influenced by passion or other impediments to correct cogitation.

Examples of the estimative power being in error in its decision as to what is desirable are legion, such as desiring a refreshing swim in a treacherous current, desiring one more intoxicating drink on top of one too many, and so on. Our estimative power tends to produce action contrary to what we know to be right, not because the intellect is wavering in its judgment but because the actual presence of the powerful emotion of desire makes things appear so differently to us than when this powerful passion is not present. This fact is accurately expressed in the saying *"As a man is, so does the suitable appear to him"* because the animal passions when they are strong tend to dominate the whole of our awareness, intellectual as well as sensory, and to color everything we experience which has any possible recognized connection with the activity or thing that aroused the passion. Right reason about what is to be done is intellectual understanding and therefore remains unchanged. Therein lies our difficulty. If we could tremendously intensify our conviction of what is the truly best thing to do so that it superseded the intensity of the passion which it is pitted against, then right reason might prevail upon the movement of concupiscence or irascibility and thus supplant the aspect of desirability that initiated such movement. But mere knowledge is not variable in that way. But the act of the will is capable of variations in intensity; by this power we can adhere to the judgment of right reason with more vehemence than a fierce passion can work against it. As we saw in the last chapter the urging to action is a necessary function of the passions because we need to be emotionally and thus physically impelled to many suitable actions. Otherwise we would not be moved to do many of the things necessary to prolonging our personal life and also the life of the human race. Of course, as we develop our rational and voluntary abilities by which we can discern what is necessary for continued life and select the best way for us of directing means to that end, the activities prompted by the passions are not needed as directives to action because the reasoned need for acting is perfectly clear.

OTHER MANIFESTATIONS OF WILL

It is time to focus our attention wholeheartedly on the will in order to explore its nature as thoroughly as we can because it is evident by now that it is a most important factor in human activity. We shall examine its gradual assertions in the conduct of child life first and then define its formal object.

Out of experience we build estimations as to ways of acting that benefit us precisely as animals in obtaining both the facile and the arduous suitable, and in avoiding or overcoming the unsuitable. With increase in age from childhood to the "age of reason" we learn to understand, both through experience and by instruction. Consequently many actions that formerly simply *had to be done* because we felt like having pleasure and wreaking vengeance (strong feelings having the force of commands in the absence of any countering rational considerations), and because we were pressed to do them by those with authority over us, come to be done because we understand to some extent the relation between goals to be attained, the means for attaining them, and their actual attainment. This gradual achievement of rationality in childhood is accompanied by the gradual development of the ability to decide for oneself among the various possible short-range goals which ones are most suitable to our personal inclinations at any given moment and which are not. At the same time we develop the ability to apprehend less tangible benefits, such as the approbation and praise which nourish our personal image and the satisfaction that comes from doing things our own way. Recognition of this latter development is humorously (and resignedly) expressed in "He has a will of his own" and "He has a way of his own." Such independence in thinking and acting is not a sign of an aberration from normal growth in the process of learning from others the best way to do things; it is the normal assertion of the individual person's independence in discovering other ways to do things than those imparted by instruction and the exercise of the act of choice upon these discoveries.

Thus from the earliest stages of understanding that practical activities are aimed at goals that can be considered in themselves and therefore considered as the term of a variety of means, the ability to choose one way of acting over another is present. It may not be exercised very wisely since the child does not have sufficient experience or understanding to make him a Solomon in practical affairs, but the ability to confer upon lesser goods as well as upon superior goods the aspect of *the best obtainable* at the moment is surely present. There is another sign of the presence of the intellectual appetite in the child in his concern with long-range intangibles. Even naughty children can be appealed to on the basis that they do not want to grow up to be objects of public disgrace, and the majority of children can appreciate the undesirableness of failure to attain some modicum of happiness in the process of growing toward adulthood.

On the affirmative side the ability of children to believe equally strongly in the most unlikely and in the most unavoidable events of the future attests to a power of belief that goes further than understanding can follow. It is not uncommon, for instance, to find belief in ghosts (whose definition as sensorily evident, pure spirits is self-contradictory) firmly ensconced in the same child-ish mind that has a flawless love of truth, beauty, and goodness, which have been experienced in concrete instances but are loved as though they existed in themselves.

It is this power of belief that carries each of us from child-hood through difficulties to the attainment of long-range goals, because it is not enough merely to fix attention upon a futurable good to bring about its realization. We need to fasten upon that future good as an object of desire in order to sustain a continuous motivation over a period of years toward a goal that may be quite abstract even when it has been obtained. Thus the human activities of acquiring understanding and engendering understanding in others, of acquiring mastery over the passions, and the like, would be impossible to maintain if these activities depended upon attach-ment to an end by the concupiscible appetite. They regularly oc-cur because the appetite involved is not restricted to short-range and concrete goals and is not easily subject to alteration by the pleasures and difficulties of daily life. It is the intellectual appetite that we exercise in striving to attain goals that come into our awareness as goals through the judgment of reason.

The Good as Object of the Will

What is the scope, then, of this appetite that is moved by a variety of goals? Since it has such a variety of ways of acting, what can be its formal object? Aristotle expressed his under-standing of *the good* as *that which all desire*, and the object of the will according to Aristotle is the good. Now "good" is not the exclusive name of any proper or common sensible, nor is it the exclusive name of any sensible estimated to be suitable for us by our cogitative sense. Rather it is the name imposed by man upon anything whatsoever that he judges by a rational judgment to be desirable. It is in this sense that Aristotle intended his statement that *the good is that which all desire*, namely, whatever is de-sirable by any one for any reason can be named good. The *for-mality*, then, which can exert an influence upon the human will is the *rationally desirable* aspect in things. The good, however, does not move the will with the compelling necessity that the casually encountered pleasurable thing exercises over the concupiscible appetite. Rather the human will is somewhat indifferent to all sensual goods and differs radically from animal appetite by its ability to love the good of another for the sake of that other. To make the scope of the intellectual appetite more manifest we shall enumerate the various kinds of good toward which it can tend.

The Good of Others

To begin, we can distinguish between what is seen to be good because it is suitable for ourselves and what is called good because it is the object of tendency in other animals and in vegetative things. That which is suitable to ourselves does not necessarily have to be actually united to us, although this is often the case, but may be a perfection in something else which manifests some skill exercised by us in bringing that perfection into being. A green lawn or a healthy tree may manifest our care and skill, thus allowing their goodness to redound in a way to us. With respect to that which is good for other living things considered in themselves we do not detect the aspect of things, according to which they are suitable for nonhuman agents, by our estimative sense but rather by the use of reason—comparing the before and after stages of things, and noting the condition of such agents when their actions terminate. Thus in nonhuman things we can easily recognize states of greater perfection and the tendency of those activities leading to them. For example, in higher animals the state of being physically fit and capable of carrying out reproductive activities is largely a result of feeding, exercise, and growth. We can make any aspect of the living process of nonhuman things a good that will be suitable to us as something we can appreciate intellectually or aesthetically, or as something we can use. Thus the understanding of any part of the living process is a good for the intellect, both from the point of view of the partial satisfaction of our desire to know and also from the point of view of the pleasure in beholding a thing of artistic ingenuity. To cultivate an oyster bed or to help a grain crop grow to a bountiful harvest is to effect a good that befits the nature of something other than ourselves. This good is a goal for our personal desire inasmuch as the perfection of the other is useful to us in a practical way. It is evident, then, that the reasoned good includes

The Will and Freedom of Choice

whatever suits the intellect as a knowing power considered by itself, whatever suits the desires of the senses and of our animal appetites, and also the means whereby that which is suitable is brought into being.

The concern for what is suitable to some other person is manifested when one person assumes responsibility for the welfare of another. Thus the parent seeking to obtain what is best for his child or the volunteer worker giving his time to raise money for worthy causes are examples of agents whose voluntary actions are directed to the good of other human beings. The parent does not actually need what is beneficial to his child nor does the volunteer worker need the services he gives freely to others. Of course some satisfaction does accrue because these persons do not act without motivation and they do identify their personal good with the good of the child and the good of the cause, respectively. Nevertheless their motives cannot be concupiscible in nature but are rather indicative of the nature of the human will, which does not always desire physical union with the object loved as concupiscence does. This difference between the two kinds of appetition is especially manifested in the will's intention to conserve and to further the good of another person who is loved, whereas the satisfying of concupiscence is usually done at the expense of the thing loved, for it is made to serve the concupiscible desire in a physical way and is often consumed in this activity.

Merely Possible Goods

As our brief analysis has indicated the range of activity of our intellectual appetitive power is limited only by the limits of the human intellect in apprehending "being." The limitation of our intellect to the island universe of human experience and deduction, and its unlimited capacity that is due to its nature as a spiritual power, have already been mentioned in Chapter 6. Man's desire for knowledge matches this limited domain of our experience and also goes far beyond it in drawing our efforts at discovery to every intelligible aspect of being, no matter how faint our grasp of being may be. We need not understand something in order to desire it—something may merely be recognized as a being of some kind whose further investigation seems desirable. In this respect also the will differs markedly from the animal appetites, which are moved by the appearances of an actual or an imagined thing. The will of a man who seeks to discover the solution of a problem in mathematics or to reduce the number of hypothetical elements involved in an attempted explanation of a physical phenomenon is fixed upon a mere possibility. Nevertheless he holds his intellectual attention to the attempt to produce a being of reason whose characteristics are only vaguely shadowed by the elements of the problem, and which may never come into existence as an actual verified solution to the mathematical or the physical problem.

In many areas of scientific and practical endeavor our will leads the way for the intellect by seizing upon goals that may or may not be actualizable. Thus by believing in the possibility of their attainment, we hold to the task of actually effecting these goals or of discovering their impossibility. A justly famed genius of the twentieth century, Albert Einstein, bent his energies for many years to the discovery of a means of connecting the properties of the gravitational field with those of the electromagnetic field in order to discover a unified field theory (or explanation) that would reduce the multiplicity of causal factors in physical motion to one kind of energy or force. In doing this he applied all the power of his giant intellect to a problem whose solution he was never able to achieve.

Kinds of Belief

It is thus evident that the good capable of attracting the human will is coterminous with the being that can be apprised by reason in any way whatever. The good also extends far beyond the things we understand in those cases in which we believe in the existence of realms of being that our deductions show must exist even though we have never actually experienced them. The ultramicroscopic and the extra-galactic realms of matter are realms no man has ever seen or touched. Nevertheless, because we can form some kind of intellectual notion of them we can hold to their existence as a matter of reasoned belief; that is, by assenting to their existence not as a mere possibility but as an actuality we have not yet experienced. We use the term *reasoned belief* advisedly to distinguish the act of committing both the intellect and the will to something that experience has never detected from *mere superstition* and *blind credulity*. In the latter two instances of belief, the signs that lead to an intellectual acceptance of the existence of what is believed are not sufficient to warrant such acceptance.

Reasoned belief is the acceptance of the existence and characteristics of something by the intellect on the basis of rationally evaluated evidence without the proof of experience. It differs from the act of vision on the part of intellect, when we understand what something is and when we see that certain conclusions follow necessarily from understood principles, in that belief is the assent to something on the basis of an incomplete apprehension. This occurs when we know something through signs that point to the existence of that something without revealing much about its nature. Thus to believe that the moon influences the tides of large bodies of water upon the earth is to assent to the existence of such an influence on the basis of the regular correspondence of high and low tides with the same positions of the moon.[5] But until the exact manner in which this influence produces the variations in the tide is discovered or proved from evidence that has already been ascertained, an individual person does not *know* that the influence exists, he only *knows* that such an influence appears to exist. Since our intellect is especially tenacious only in that which produces a genuine understanding of what something is, the will has a role in belief; it holds to the belief in a thing as an object of intellectual assent, even though our intellect does not find itself compelled to assent but only sees the indications of the evidence. Thus we will to give an intellectual assent to something for the sake of the benefit that derives to us from such belief, whether that benefit be something in knowledge or something of a practical nature.

BELIEF—A PRACTICAL NECESSITY

Belief is important in our practical activities because the futurable events toward which we direct practical actions often do not yet exist in fact, and we do not know with certitude that they will exist. But if we did not act upon our belief that they actually will come into being as a result of our efforts, they certainly will not come into being by our efforts. Recall the lengthy analysis of practical knowledge given in Chapter 6. In both the attaining of practical knowledge and the using of that knowledge belief plays a large role, for we do not act in a merely automatically responsive manner when we perform by habit the daily activities to which we have become accustomed. Rather we use our habitual ways of acting to attain many goals that we hope to attain only because we believe that they are attainable by such ways of acting. Hence most of our actions are directed to ends that have not yet been achieved and belief in their attainability is what prompts us to the actions directed toward attaining them. Especially in those actions that are deliberately being done for the first time is belief an indispensable ingredient, because the assurance we have of their probable success is not buttressed by any accomplished activity, as is the case in habitual actions. For example, we may want worm-free apples to grow on the trees in our orchard because they are more suitable for eating. In achieving worm-freeness, however, we need to understand the various stages in the growth of the apple and the susceptibility of the apple in these various stages to infestation. Our belief in the possibility of worm-freeness carries us through various acts of understanding and reasoning, as well as through the various physical acts necessary to prevent the eggs from being deposited in the blossom or to prevent the larvae from growing into worms inside our apples.

Our Will Is Not Compelled

From the various examples given of the kinds of thing that our will desires, it is becoming evident that our will desires as good that which immediately befits either the body as a whole or some other power than the will itself. We desire knowledge as the good of the intellect; food, rest, and recreation for the prolongation of life; and the exercise of our senses for the sake of the delight that this brings. The enjoyment on the part of the will is concomitant with the attainment of what is desired for the sake of some other power and for our whole well-being. This tendency to procure that which befits the body as a whole, or some specific sensory power, is also found in the animal appetites but with a radical difference. Many concupiscible goods attract the concupiscible appetite so powerfully that of itself it is absolutely compelled to desire it; contrariwise, some things are so odious to our sensibilities that we are compelled to detest them.

No such compulsion necessitates our will to act, however, for that which suits it is not the good of any one power, as we have just seen; rather, all things that have an aspect of good from any rational point of view can be attractive to it. Thus we can exercise rational and voluntary control over the animal passions or suppress them altogether. There is also the possibility that we may even deliberately choose to act in a manner that we know full well to be contrary to right reason. Thus in the examples used previously to illustrate rational control we can also cite the instance of the person's enjoying the running and the eating of olives because he wants to enjoy them now. These are rather mild illustrations of deliberately wrong actions. Many irrational acts are so patently wrong that they have commonly accepted names held in disrepute: theft, murder, arson, wantonness, and the like. Consequently we tend to forget that the criterion by which they are distinguished from other acts is not their irrationality, for there are lots of acts that incidentally turn out to be irrational because we did not sufficiently foresee their consequences (jumping in a swimming hole and coming up muddy, for example), nor is it their contrary-to-right characteristic derived from the fact that they violate clearly established rights, which can also happen accidentally. Rather it is the fact that they are done in a *perfectly willingly contrary-to-right-reason manner* that makes them legally wrong.

With respect to the human will there is nothing that any of us has ever experienced that we absolutely *had* to desire, so that we could not will to do otherwise. Thus, although following the lines of action judged by reason to be best is what we consciously desire to do, nevertheless we sometimes act contrary to this by following some whim of fancy. The persuasion of a present passion is not the only factor that can lead us to act contrary to right reason, for a man may lose faith in the value of following right reason and deliberately decide to pursue some enticing goal regardless of the consequences to himself or to others.

We do not intend to enter into a discussion of moral matters and rights here, but rather to indicate that any good which moves the will to desire it is only partly specifying the will's desire for the good. This incompleteness of everything that we have experienced and understood, from the point of view of their being attractive to the will, is manifested in the fact that the happiness we seek is not identifiable with anything that anyone has ever attained. For no man can profess to be completely happy for more than a little while without appearing foolish. Even the phrase "completely happy" manifests the ideal nature of this goal; to be complete our happiness must be such that it lacks nothing, and cannot pass away. But this completeness, considered quantitatively, would have to fulfill all the tendencies of the senses, of concupiscence, and of the intellect. That this is impossible now is easily evident upon consideration of the incomplete subjugation of nature to our animal needs, and upon consideration of the primitive condition of our human understanding of all that there is to be understood. Thus the act of the human will is somewhat paradoxical, for we constantly strive to attain goods that we cherish even though the attainment of many of them is a purely temporary thing and the attainment of others is incomplete. The paradox lies in this—the will desires a happiness that cannot be achieved by any of the actions possible to us.

The Loves of the Will

The act of the will that is most often debated by those who do not understand the operations of this power is the free choice of means to an end. Since choice is only one of the customary actions on the part of the will, however, we shall treat it in its proper place in the sequence of acts that are proper to the will, in order to give a complete and orderly account of this appetitive power. Any appetitive power tends to that which has the appearance of being suitable to someone or something. The suitable as far as the tendencies of the senses and the animal appetites are concerned is something that benefits us personally and arouses passion by the appearance which the sensible has as it occurs in nature. But the suitable and unsuitable, which move our will to love and to hate, respectively, move it according to the apprehension of our intellect which knows things as the senses know them—through the mediation of the senses—and also knows the common natures of things.

Because our intellect knows the common natures of things and their common attributes such as unity and being, we can love and hate *kinds* of things, and also attributes that are common to *all kinds* of things, as well as *singular* things. Thus the actual damage that a person has experienced in the unjust seizure of what was pleasurable or merely useful to him can be depicted concretely and hated on the sensory level as *a disagreeable loss* and also all such instances of damage that are roughly similar. The general sense impression is the means of recognizing the instances of loss that are similar in this way. But intellectually, through our understanding of what human rights are, we can understand every kind of violation of them, and thus every kind of injustice. Consequently our will can *love every kind of justice* and *hate every kind of injustice*. Furthermore, since evil of any kind can be understood as a deficiency in what is owing to a thing or to an activity, according as they are of a certain kind, our will can hate every kind of evil. Since good can also be understood as that which is desirable to anyone for any reason, the will can love every kind of good.

LOVE AS ASSENT

Sufficient signs of the universality of the scope of the will have already been given in this chapter, so that we can now examine the acts of the will that are directed to universal goods and also to singular goods. The act of the will directed to a universal good, such as every kind of true knowledge and every kind of virtuous deed, is a love of things of which we possess only a small portion. Our knowledge is limited; deeds are proper to the doer and cannot be shared in the way that knowledge is. This means that in loving knowledge and virtue we are loving what benefits others than ourselves, for the knowledge possessed by another person is a good for him and although the virtue that he possesses may benefit us in a roundabout way (inasmuch as it moves him to act so as to benefit us) it is absolutely a good for him. When the act of the will in this instance is one of loving knowledge and virtue in their own right regardless of who possesses them, it is called *the love of assent*. In fact we are assenting to them as being desirable whether we actually desire to possess them for ourselves or not. It is incidental to our assenting to their goodness that they be possessed by this or that person or only by God. We assent to them according as we recognize their desirability for every rational being, and no other consideration is relevant to this love.

It is obvious that we have a stronger love for many things than that of mere assent to the good whenever it is encountered. This stronger love exercised by our will can transform altruistic love to love of a *benevolent* kind whereby we actively will good to another, that the other may possess its perfection and possibly increase it; it can also be a *love of desire* whereby we will good to ourselves. In benevolent love the will is attracted to the goodness of that which we love benevolently, so that we are drawn to loving it without any special regard for our own self. In the love of desire we have already assented to the goodness of the thing in question; since we now want to be united with it, it is to this union that the desire is directed.

ALTRUISTIC OR BENEVOLENT LOVE

When we not only assent to the goodness of some subsistent being, but also desire that the good it possesses continue to belong to it or increase in magnitude, we are loving what is good for another person as being good for him.[6] To love thus is *to love altruistically*. We love altruistically when we champion the beleaguered hero of a novel and when we approve of the victory of a virtuous man over the attacks of his enemies. The altruistic character of our love is not diminished by the feeling of elation that we experience over the outcome in these two instances, for the good of another is in no way diminished whether we rejoice in it or merely will that it continue or increase.

It has been contended on many occasions by many men that there is no altruistic love, that is, that there is no benevolent love that is anything else than a love of desire which only apparently assents to the good of another. Thus the love of another person's justice would be interpreted on this basis as a love of justice because its presence in the other person is beneficial to me, for it disposes him to respect my rights. A similar interpretation could be given for love of knowledge inasmuch as its possession by another person not only enables him to use it for his own benefit but also keeps him at peace with the world and others.

The basic presupposition to such arguments is that all love is similar to animal love, which is essentially self-centered, and is altruistic only in that we can identify our physical good with a mate or with such things as pets, property, and wealth which are means to the preservation of our animal being and the enjoyment of it. This presupposition overlooks two indisputable facts: the sacrifice of personal goods for the good of another who is a stranger, and the impossibility of possessing or benefiting personally from the speculative truth possessed by another. Thus the teacher who strives far beyond the degree of effort needed to vindicate his receiving a salary so that his charges may be benefited by a fuller understanding of a subject that they may never have occasion to use, in order to perfect their knowledge for its own sake, is manifesting a true love of what is good for his students. To the extent that he must devote more time and more energy to this task than justice demands of him, he is sacrificing his personal good for their benefit.

Because some inner rejoicing accrues to the agent who actively promotes the good of another, it is always possible to cast doubt upon the sincerity of altruistic love. The main reason for this doubt may be found in the opposition of some minds to the conclusion that flows ineluctably from the recognition that benevolent love exists and is directed to the goodness of whatever possesses being. If the magnitude of our love is proportionate to the perfection of the good that we become aware of, then God, whose existence is provable by facts acquired from human experience (and is also a matter of reasonable belief), as the supreme good, is supremely lovable to the extent to which we realize His perfection. Consequently, greater homage should be paid to Him than to fellow human beings, such as pioneers in science, sports heroes, and space travellers. Of course, we do not know God as we know human persons worthy of praise, because we have no physical experience of Him through natural effects other than as our reason deduces His existence and some of His characteristics from effects of this kind. Nevertheless, considered in the abstract, the most lovable being is the Supreme Good which contains all the goods of all creatures in His creative and conserving power.

Therefore, since all things are lovable with the love of as-

Man's Physical and Spiritual Nature

sent and all spiritual beings are especially lovable with the love of benevolence, for only spiritual beings are capable of increasing their perfection significantly through an increase in knowledge and an increase in power over themselves through the exercise of free choice, then God is most lovable as the supremely perfect spirit. Our love of God, however, cannot be directed to any increase in his perfection but rather to the recognition and approbation of his existence and a desire for its continuance. Thus our benevolent love of God cannot be effective in the way it is for someone to whom we can impart some good. This limitation of the effects of our love can also be noted on those many occasions when it does not lie within our power to confer any benefit on what we see to be good because it is a past event; we can only praise the athlete who hit a home run or made a touchdown, we cannot add anything to the accomplished deed but praise. Although approbation is a benefit it is not a physical one, nor is it to be identified with knowledge or virtue; it is rather a unique kind of good especially suited to the will, as we shall show in the next section.

Love as Desire of One's Own Good

Since the range of the things upon which we can confer approbation equals the range of our knowledge and of our belief, we can say that the object of the will is a universal good. This is not to be understood in the sense that the will is restricted to desiring a knowledge of common (universal) natures, but rather in the sense that the will can assent to the goodness of every being and can desire whatever it has assented to as a good for the person whose will it is. Of course, we can desire *effectively* only what is in some way attainable to man.[7] Thus, in the universal good for man we certainly include all the knowledge of which the human intellect can have an inkling, which is far greater in scope than the knowledge any man has attained to date. We also include all facile internal and external control over our own being, so that we may freely act according as our right reason may decide, and as much experience and pleasure as is consistent with this freedom to act for what is best. In short a fitting goal for human activity is everything that befits human nature.

We usually denote that toward which our activities are freely directed as *happiness*, as when we acknowledge that what we want most of all is to be happy.

By our will we will happiness for ourselves. This fact is not in opposition to the preceding analysis of the will as a power that is attracted to goods in proportion as reason apprises their goodness, for the will whereby a man is attracted to what is good is his personal intellectual appetite and thus an essential part of his individual nature. As such the will shares the desires proper to that individual nature as proper to itself; it is in no way actually separate from the other powers of the soul to the point of having an existence of its own, even though in loving some great good intensely we can speak of our will as being carried out of itself and being totally concentrated upon that good to the exclusion of everything else. But even such moments of rapture are delights for our own personal human nature; the good involved may be the good of another, as the superb playing of a difficult violin concerto by a flawless artist, but the delight in it is a delight for the hearer who is enraptured by the playing.

An individual person's desire for what will make him happy is as natural to him as the tendency of one chemical to act with another and as natural as the growth of a living thing to physical maturity. In fact, it is by the exercise of the will in accord with right reason that a person grows to emotional and intellectual maturity so that he is master of his actions to the extent that circumstances permit. By contrast those who direct their will-acts to an unflagging pursuit of the pleasurable passions, failing to exercise reason to distinguish the proper function of the passions, fall short of reaching emotional maturity, and often fail to appreciate the value of knowledge as a good in itself and as a means of understanding human life. Whatever the individual case may be with regard to being enslaved by the passions or being their master so as to use them and enjoy them intelligently, the fact remains that man constantly acts in the expectation of being better off personally for acting than for not doing so.

We can distinguish two aims in the natural love by which a person wills good to himself: (1) the natural desire for happiness, which is a desire to possess all that is suitable to him so as to be able to enjoy it without loss, and (2) the desire directed to acquiring those things that constitute such a total good, or to the selection and the use of means leading to the procurement of such things. This is the familiar distinction between *the end*, to the attainment of which our desire tends, and the *means* which we use to attain the end.

INDIFFERENCE OF THE WILL TO AVAILABLE GOODS

It has been pointed out already that the end, in the sense of the total good that will make man happy, is not attainable in full by any set of human actions. Our knowledge of being is incomplete and the necessities for physical life are such that we must avail ourselves of them over and over again. Therefore no good is actually given in our experience that can fulfill our desire for happiness so that we must desire it. This can be said with different emphasis. The human will is *relatively indifferent* to anything whatsoever that is given in experience. We are talking, of course, of the will in the abstract and not of the will in any individual person. In each person the motivations of the sense appetites predominate until the age of understanding is reached; and even when we are able to discern reasons for things, there are many goods that appear to be absolutely desirable and worth any price that may be exacted for their attainment. Thus the individual person's attitude toward what is good for him is already strongly formed before he realizes fully what a variety of goods there are to be had by striving for them. Also, each person lives under circumstances that affect his opportunity for choosing among the various goods attainable by human action. Nevertheless, *nothing* is given in our experience as intellectual and physical beings *that can unfailingly and universally command our desire.*

Two common signs of this indetermination of the will with respect to goods that can possibly be attained are the temporariness of the satisfaction that any man has with any good he possesses and the difficulty we have in actually committing ourselves to the pursuing of some chosen good in the face of the attractions exerted by other attainable goods. Who has enough knowledge so that he cannot be moved by a desire for more? Knowledge is one of the few permanent goods that man can possess; another is achievement, for which we may receive praise from others or accord it to ourselves. Who has achieved so many praiseworthy goals that he cannot find others he would like to accomplish or see room for improvement in what he has already achieved? Moreover, who can deny the anxiety that accompanies the commitment of one's time, energy, and thought to the attainment of a goal that we believe will prove fruitful and more conductive to our happiness than other goals we might select? A further sign of the absence of predetermination in the act of the will when considering possible courses of action is the confusion on many occasions as to what to do with oneself; even when this has been decided one may still be confused as to which way to carry out what has been decided upon.

PRAISE AS A GOOD OF THE WILL

Praise most especially suits the will in itself in our present life, because if we do anything that is truly praiseworthy (and not an achievement executed by luck), it is because we have set our will to it and labored single-mindedly to attain an end whose achievement is obviously laudable. Whether the praise be self-administered, in the *approval* that we accord to ourself when we have accomplished something difficult, or administered by those who recognize the value of our achievement, it is the spiritual food of the will. It is the unique sign of love of the good that we have achieved. The expression of praise was mentioned previously as the kind of overt act by which man could signify his appreciation of the goodness of God and of an already finished human achievement. In those instances only praise of what already existed was proper; but praise is also most useful in spurring on another person to achieve a praiseworthy goal. Thus praise can be recognition not only of a good already achieved but also of the direction of activities currently being undertaken as tending toward a praiseworthy end. We even praise activities projected for the future according to the end toward which they will be directed, even though they have not yet begun.

Of all the goods available to man, knowledge and praiseworthy achievement are especially suitable to the intellect and to the will, respectively—and they are enduring. Achievements may be surpassed by others or nullified by events that destroy what has been accomplished, but the fact of the accomplishment is as ineradicable as is any event that is now a matter of past

history. The exultation that arose along with the achievement
of a laudable goal lives on as a delightful appetitive accompaniment of the cherished memory of the achievement. Men will
often exert themselves to do something, because of the praise
they can accord themselves or elicit from others, that they would
never do otherwise. For example, an athlete may endure great
and prolonged pain to achieve the honor of being victor or even
runner-up, or even to vindicate his reputation by lasting the
course. It would take a very satisfying goal to make him endure
such discomfort and so to strain his resources otherwise. Whether
we call the fruition proper to the will in man's temporal state, self-
approbation (the approbation of others is a vindication of this) or
self-confidence, or praise, it is evident that a known confirmation
of the goodness of one's aims and actions is a good which we
delight in.

THE DESIRE TO BE LOVED

A slightly different viewpoint in our approach can make
the subject of the preceding paragraphs appear more familiar.
Every act of willing what is good is directed *to something* and
for something. Thus in benevolent love we wish well to someone;
in love of desire we wish some good to accrue to ourselves.
Among those goods is approbation of others. That is, we love
to be loved by another being who is capable of manifesting approval of us in some overt way. Among those having this capability, animals and societal groups rank below individual persons in the ability to know us as being praiseworthy, for animals
cannot appreciate our spiritual goodness and groups cannot
share our conscious life intimately so as to appreciate what we
are really like and thus determine that there is a solid basis
for admiration and praise. But the overt signs that an individual
shares the same attitude and purpose of the other members of a
group are sufficient to win him the approval of the group. For
example, a man may be rather indistinguishable in other ways but
be a very good and dedicated ball-player. This one accomplishment can be sufficient to elicit the admiration and friendliness
of the other members of the team, even though on all other
counts they are not attracted to him.

There must be some basis for admiration from others, because our will's spontaneous desire can be necessitated only by a total good and all commitments to one among many possible goods are based on the apprehension of its having some superiority over other goods. The basis for our being chosen as lovable varies considerably according to the motive of the one who loves us. A love based upon our ability to be of service to someone else, to supply some need for them, can be quite strong and can involve some affection but there is no strong reason for it to endure once the usefulness ceases.[8] A love based upon our ability to engage with another in some activity that is mutually pleasing is likely to involve more affection between the parties involved than one based on mere utility, but it also has no strong basis for endurance when the activity loses its appeal. A love based upon a conscious awareness of what is truly laudable in us for its own sake, a dedication to doing what is right, a continually exercised tendency to pursue knowledge, a genuine devotion to the common good, or a genuine charity (concern for the welfare of others) has a basis for lasting that is as firm as the laudable quality itself. An enduring love must have an enduring foundation and must not be easily susceptible to change. The basis for an enduring love of friendship, for instance, must be some real good in us, because a merely apparent good can lose its aspect of goodness at any time.

FRIENDSHIP.   Our desire to be loved arises out of the need of the will for approbation of the acts that it wills and of the ends that give to those acts their character of being laudable. To put it another way, we long for approval of those good qualities we possess by nature and of those we have attained by our own effort. The possession of friends who approve of us not only because we are of service to them or engage with them in mutual pleasure, but also because they see something in us that is admirable for its own sake, helps to show us that our own approval of that good quality existing in ourselves is justified. Since admiration can be extended, however, to an apparent good as well as to what is critically analyzed and judged to be good by right reason, the more lasting kind of friendship can exist between knaves as well as virtuous men. It is not possible for it to exist between a knave and a virtuous man because there is no mutual basis for friendship.[9]

The lesser kinds of friendship can be found among every

Man's Physical and Spiritual Nature

kind of person for they do not presuppose any abiding intrinsic goodness but only a physical disposition to perform acts. The *ideal instance* of the abiding type of friendship is that in which we have only truly good habits and the facile use of them, and a friend of the same qualification who reciprocates our appreciation of such good habits and deeds. The *usual instance* of the abiding type of friendship is that in which we have a partial basis for eliciting admiration and have a reciprocal admiration for the same goodness in our friend. Thus friendship may be greater or lesser in intensity according to the degree of appreciation between friends and they may be restricted to two persons or shared by a small group.[10] Also, one person may have various friendships with different persons because he possesses a variety of good qualities that are variously appreciated by others. The common element in all friendships is a reciprocal interest of persons in one another because of some purpose that they share in their activities.

From our analysis of friendship it becomes obvious that both *obtaining a friend whose love is enduring and fulfilling the prerequisites for being truly lovable are matters involving considerable effort.* No one can coerce the love of another; love can only be elicited by presenting to another that which appeals to that other person. Friendships are easily begun, though, because there are so many points of similarity in desire between individual persons, as is manifest in similarities of taste. The maintaining and augmentation of a friendship, however, requires something more enduring than a superficial similarity of tastes.

That which is most befitting to human nature is the basis for commendable self-love (as distinct from the love of gratification of disordered desires), and also for friendship. Thus love of another person is not inimical to the natural love that each of us has for himself. Rather, it is an extension of one's personal appreciation of what is truly best in human nature; for to be a friend is to appreciate and to share the good qualities possessed by another person, thus increasing the scope of one's enjoyment of those qualities. The expression "alter ego," (another I) is indicative of the closeness between two real friends. It indicates that the reciprocal admiration of friendship is based upon the same kind of qualities in each friend and an intimate awareness of this principle of identity between them.

The Will and Freedom of Choice

A person who appreciates the potentialities of his own human nature and develops them to the point of achieving the degree of perfection possible for him in the various areas of human endeavor that interest him acquires both the qualities that others will find laudable in him and an awareness of these qualities as they are mirrored in others. Thus by perfecting his own nature as a rational and voluntary being, and by developing those abilities for which he has an innate disposition so that they become commendable talents, a person makes himself fit for enduring friendship and disposed to become a true friend of others whose good qualities he can appreciate.[11] One who has very little in the way of developed good qualities in himself will have a poor ability to appreciate true worth in others and will have little to attract the love of others to himself.

It is not necessary that each person have a good friend, but a good friend is a source of enjoyment to which nothing else can be compared, because no other relationship than being approved of by one we admire can satisfy the need of the human will for true appreciation.

Choice as an Unpredetermined Activity

Whether or not one chooses to seek to form enduring friendships is a matter each person must decide for himself; whether he chooses to bring to a state of perfection tendencies of which he is aware in his physical and rational self is also something that depends upon his own effective decision. In fact, making decisions is a constant occupation for man because the predetermination characteristic of his chemical and physiological processes is not to be found in activities that he performs according to reason. In his rational activities man directs himself, whereas in his physiological processes there is a necessary dependence of presently occurring activities upon preceding ones and the consequences of the presently occurring activities are predetermined so that they vary but little as they occur over and over again. In his rational activities man must determine which activity of moving or desiring or thinking will follow the present one and he must gauge the probability of the success of these actions in attaining something he wants. Consequently acts of decision are man's constant concern—sometimes a bane and sometimes a delight according as he sees himself compelled to continue an action he cares little about or faced with a host of delightful possibilities among which he may choose.

The human will not only delights in that which is suitable to man according to his various powers, but also forms the determination that one or other of the powers subject to the will (a power capable of being used or left inactive) shall be exercised now or later to attain something suitable to it. It is our will continually committing us to some specific activity that provides the continuity of our life as beings who are striving to attain beckoning ends. In committing ourselves to a continuous succession of acts we are constantly acting for what is best; what is best for us at any moment is something that reason is constantly deciding. This joint activity of reason and will is *choice*.

The Twofold Basis of Freedom of Choice

From the discussion presented so far in this chapter it is obvious that man has two powers by which he decides when to act, how to act, and whether to continue acting or not. Our intellect is that power whereby we consider the possible ends attainable to us at any one time and also determine by rational consideration or by habituation which one is best for us. The will is that power whereby we adopt our decision that such and such an action is the one most suitable to us at the moment and set about doing it, or we reject that decision and do something quite different because it has more appeal at the moment.

In many instances when we do not act habitually, but thoughtfully consider what we ought to do next, there may be no opposition between right reason and what we find attractive at the moment. Nevertheless it is always in a person's power to consider whether he will act for what he sees by right reason to be best, or act differently for another reason, or simply deliberately switch his attention to something else. Thus the basis for doing some act according as it pleases us is *rational*, in considering the possibilities, and *appetitive* in selecting one or none of those considered. In short our will is not altogether bound by the decision of our reason as to what is best but has its own tendencies whereby it can will not to will what rational consideration

The Will and Freedom of Choice 293

has shown to be best. For example, a person may form a perfectly clear resolution not to engage in idle gossip or not to take any more than a stated amount of intoxicating drink, and mean it as that which he surely intends. Nevertheless, when in the company of gossiping companions he may calmly enter into conversation with them without a thought of his good resolution to the contrary. If he thinks of it, he may calmly ignore its intent and follow the habituation to which he has long become accustomed. Similarly in the tavern, or in the comfort of his own sanctuary, he drinks for the joy of exhilaration and then for the total peace of oblivion without paying any attention to his excellent resolution to be moderate.

In both of the examples just discussed, however, it is quite possible for this person to reverse his accustomed ignoring of his well-intended resolutions, strike out on a new path of conduct, and hold to it resolutely. The basis of that tremendous ability is the relative indifference of the human will to all of the goods that it encounters. No matter how strong the habituation to a certain good (or vice) may be, the possibility of supplanting it exists as long as the will is capable of being drawn to something else equally compelling or exceeding it in desirability; that is, as long as the relation of the will to that good is only one of *temporary commitment* overcoming the relative indifference which may reassert itself again. That relative indifference is overcome, when it is overcome, by the act of choosing to act one way rather than another. Thus choice is an all-important act in the life of man.

TERMS DESCRIPTIVE OF WILLING AND CHOOSING

A fairly well-established terminology exists with regard to the interplay of will and intellect in proposing, choosing, and acting for the attainment of that which is deemed to be good.[12] We shall now consider in detail the activities to which the terms correspond and their implications for the kind of life that is good for man.

INTENTION. Since both wishing and desiring have already been explained in sufficient detail we shall first discuss intention, the act by which we tend toward something that is desired. The term intention is a synonym for *effective desiring* and points to the will's fixing upon an end as obtained through the use of some means. As we mentioned in the preceding section it is our will that provides the continuity of our conscious life by desiring and carrying out the execution of the succession of activities that make up our conscious life.[13] Thus we listen to some sounds that obtrude upon our awareness because we will to listen to them and we focus our attention on some other sensible when we will to do so. We may also make a comparison between the sound and a similar one heard previously, or we may decide to stop the sound and consider the means available to carry out this decision. We are constantly deciding which of several possible lines of activity we shall engage in, which of several sensory receptivities to pay attention to, whether to cease activities of a motor and perceptory nature in order to reflect upon some object of memory or of thought, or simply whether to rest in sleep.

The acceptance of the decision and the fixing of desire upon what has been decided as the thing to do can be called *commitment;* the tendency of the will to make the desire effective is *intention. Intention* is not mere wishing but a definite motion of our will to the procuring of a desired end. Ordinarily we have several intentions simultaneously. The overriding one is the intention to obtain happiness for ourselves, and in line with this aim we intend a variety of long-range and short-range goals. It is evident, then, that to have an intention does not mean that we are continuously conscious of the goal to which it is directed. Rather we are conscious of it when the occasions for exercising the acts that carry out the intention arise, if we are not so distracted by other intentions that we cannot concentrate on the goal. Thus many intentions to attain short-range goals will be ordered to the attaining of some long-range goal that is ordered to the intention to procure the ultimate goal of happiness which everyone naturally desires.

The intention of the will is a motion toward the desired goal. This motion is not physical, although physical motion is caused by the will's intending the achievement of some good. For example, we may intend to have supper at a café in half an hour's time. This intention moves us to take a taxi to the café while the workers in the café, who have been instructed of our arrival by telephone, are moved to the physical action of preparing food by our desire to have some choice viands. In this way our intention is the direct instigation of physical activities in ourselves and in others who subject themselves to our intention.

The kind of causality involved when intention on the part of our will instigates physical activity at the opportune time (which is decided by reason) is completely mysterious in terms of the physiological explanation of muscular activity. There is a moment when no motion-causing impulses are flowing along the motor nerves, and another moment immediately following when impulses are flowing along the final common paths of many nerves to excite many muscle fibers to activity. This activity is motion of our limbs and sometimes motion of our body in place. The impulses travel when we decide to move and cease when we decide to stop. In this way the predetermined activities of the chemical agents involved in our moving and stopping are perfectly subjected to our intention. Of course, such agents in the body have their limits and can be exhausted so that no intensity of desiring will move an exhausted muscle, but intensity of desire can indeed move us to exert ourselves with far greater strength and endurance at one time than at another.

DELIBERATION. In order to keep the various aspects of the will's activities clearly under our scrutiny, we need to isolate as well as we can the role played by the intellect. In line with our previous analysis of the nature of the will, some act of apprehending a good is the occasion for our desiring to be united with it. This apprehension is said to specify the act of the will to the degree that it provides a specific thing to be considered as an object of desire. It does not specify the will's act in any coercive sense, for we can easily will to consider something else. Nevertheless there are occasions when the desirability of what is presented does "entrance" us, arousing an overwhelming wish to be united with it. But this wishing is not effective desiring, because effective desiring is based on the knowledge that the desired thing can be attained.

Thus the intellectual acts that precede intention consist in apprehending something as a good (maybe only apparent, or real) and as possible of attainment. If this good is apprehended as something quite fitting for us when we shall have obtained it, with no reference to our future state after we have possessed it, the good is desired as an end in itself whose possession will yield us some happiness. Our intention to have it leads us to consider which means (if there is more than one) to apply to the obtaining of the good. If, however, it is desired as a useful good, then the act of desiring as an end to be used as a means to something else requires the prior consideration of its suitability as a means to something else. Thus each distinct act of the will, whether it be wishing or effective desiring, is directed to a good that has been apprehended as such by the intellect.

When the end desired is not immediately obtainable but requires some activity to make it present, it is tended to by the will and a choice of means must be made.[14] On the part of the will this choosing is an act of electing to adopt and put to use the means proposed to it by the intellect. There is an intellectual act which precedes this, however; it is a consideration of which means are available and an evaluation of the suitability of each means to the end in view. This act of consideration is called *deliberation*, that is, the weighing of (assessing the suitability of) the various possible means to the end in view. Deliberation may be contrasted with habitual choice, which does not rely upon a present evaluation of the means but upon those made in a similar type of situation in the past, and with spontaneous and random action which is the case when we attempt to use any apparent means to become united with the end. *Deliberation is the consideration of an end as obtainable by several definite means*, as a preliminary to selecting one definite means and using it to obtain union with the end. If there is only one means available for attaining the end, then deliberation is not concerned with weighing several means but with deciding how suitable the only means available is to the actual and complete attainment of the end.

CHOICE. This act of our will is the preference of one thing over another. It depends upon the indication by our intellectual consideration as to what is preferable. This indication will specify the act of preference, if we commit ourselves to it. Quite often, however, we reject a decision of the intellect, both as to the possibility of the means attaining the end and also as to the desirability of the end in view over other possible ends. It is happiness that is sought by the will, and the end in view may

The Will and Freedom of Choice

augur less than we feel inclined to exert ourselves for at the moment. Or, the means we see to be the most suited to the attaining of the end may not be good enough to suit us, so that we abandon the whole project for the time being and turn to other matters. Thus choice is an act of our will regarding an action proposed by our intellect—we accept what is proposed by our intellect or reject it as not good enough.

We have to learn to discriminate what is good enough from what is not by experience. The recorder of experience is the memory power and the intellect (of understood experience). The will, however, has an act of its own in this matter, whereby it not only intends the end, selects the best available means, and uses it to attain the end, but also has dominion over the abilities to remember whereby it can reject the present decisions of the reason as to what is to be done and can desire that considerations regarding another matter be taken up. It does not seem reasonable, though, to grant to the will the ability to discern being as a cognitive power does. The way in which we as human beings are forced by our limitations as knowers to consider complex matters in their simple aspects presents a barrier to understanding precisely how our will directs the intellect to halt considerations presently being made and to turn to some other specific matter. The fact is, however, that we do this continually, not only in rejecting a decision as to what is best but also whenever we will to turn to a new topic which had not been under consideration. We do not just cease to think about x whereupon y pops into our thoughts; rather we go from thinking of x to thinking of y, even though y has no recognizable relationship to x.

If we analyze the action of our intellect upon our will, we meet the same difficulty in understanding how they can cooperate. The intellect is a cognitive power which not only understands something of the identity of things but also exercises a critical judgment as to whether individual acts and beings are really desirable. Such evaluation of the suitability of an end is that which induces the will to exercise its act of assenting to that end as good or as desirable personally.[15] That the will's act of desiring is elicited is sometimes beyond doubt; but how can it be drawn to a recognized good if it is not a cognitive power? It must be that the intellect and the will are such a unity that one can be said to exist in the other. On the sensory level we can distinguish

Man's Physical and Spiritual Nature

organs of sensation (to some extent) from the appetitive feelings which pervade certain organs and surface parts of the body, on the basis of the specificity of the organ and the variability in the intensity of the passion. On the intellectual level the will's intensity in loving and hating varies without any variation in the intensity of the act of knowing. On both levels, of course, there is opposition between knowing what is so and desiring something contrary to the evaluation of the cognitive power. Yet for all the evidence as to the nonidentity of cognitive power and appetitive power, the fact remains that such powers unite in unity of action that is little short of identity. Especially is this so for the intellect and the will whose atemporal and aspatial natures preclude their distinction through distinct organs. We can look upon the will as ever tending toward the possession of a good that will satisfy it and upon the intellect as directing the will's attention (so to speak) to various things the intellect judges to be good as productive of some happiness or useful in the obtaining of such a good.[16]

Our will has the ability to exercise its act of selecting a good from those made known to it, or of not committing itself to any of them. We can even will that which amounts to suspending the act of the will—for instance, we give up our conscious voluntary control of ourselves when we go to sleep. This ability of the will we call its *freedom of exercise*, for what shall be desired and what shall not be desired depends ultimately upon whether we exercise our ability to desire or not.

USE. The application of something to an operation, such as the application of soap in cleaning one's hands, is the use of that something in that operation. We use the intellect's ability to make a critical appraisal of some matter, and we use the memory of the experiences we have had to guide us in successful action in the present. In the latter case we also use our muscles and external matter to get us around in place and to transmit our intention through instruments into the production of some effect. Our intention to apply a means to the attainment of an end produces *use;* consequently use stems ultimately from the will's acting according to the directions of reason. It is carried into external matter according to the guidance of the senses by which we discern the various things in our environment and by the activities of the muscles that respond to the will's desire.

ENJOYMENT AND DISAPPOINTMENT. The result of an activity is either the attainment of the end in view, something less than this, or something beyond it. In each case there is a reason for bringing the action to a term. If the end is attained and fulfills our expectation, then we delight in (enjoy) this end. If the end surpasses our expectations, then there is more reason for rejoicing. But if it falls short our enjoyment may become proportionately lessened or turned into disappointment. In any case there is as much reason in the will for terminating an activity as there was for beginning it. Thus we may start to read a book in order to be informed by it or amused by it, and cease reading when this end has been attained or when we become aware that it will not be attained. We may stop reading because we have reached the end of the book or because some pressing need or obligation is brought to our attention. Even in these instances, however, we realize some enjoyment or disappointment in proportion to our attainment or frustration.

Our will is the agent whereby we move ourselves to use our senses, our speech, and our locomotive abilities. Consequently it is also the power that shares the success or failure of all of the other conscious powers we have. Thus the love of concupiscence and the hate of anger, as well as the rest of the animal passions, are shared by our will, controlled by our will, and used by our will; the outcome is delighted in or sorrowed over by our will. We have stressed the role of our will here since it is the agent involved in effecting use, but our intellect is involved in every act of our will as well as in the acts of our senses. Our intellect extends its act of cognition to every aspect of our physical being and every facet of the universe around us that can be detected in any conscious way; our will is moved to be interested in or indifferent to, to accept as desirable or reject as undesirable, everything upon which our intellect can form a judgment of suitability and attainability.[17]

Freedom of Choice and the Will as Prime Agent

Since choice is the act by which a person prefers one means to another as a step to the attaining of a goal, choice is the proper name for the act of preferring one good over another in our effort to attain that which will best fulfill the will's tendency toward a total good.[18] Any end that is altogether good in itself has a stronger attraction for us than one that is only partly good. Thus we prefer to have truth rather than probable opinion and will often reject the latter, preferring to be free of the encumbrance it will place upon our inquiry by prejudicing our assessment of the evidence. Nevertheless, we often need to select among a host of possible goals, each of which has a beckoning aspect that tends to draw the will's desire in several directions at once. Whether these goals be considered as ends in themselves or as means to something else, *the act of choice is equally necessary* in order that one goal may be selected and the activity directed to attaining the goal may proceed.

Role of Experience in Assessing Goods

It is a fact of experience that there are few enjoyments that do not pall after a while; also, what strikes us as odious or disappointing moves us to turn away and direct our attention and our activities to what is pleasant or useful instead. These experiences are concrete evidence of the inability of any joy to delight us perpetually, and of the control that we have over our own lives, at least in many matters, whereby we can at will change from one activity to a more satisfying one. The insufficiency of the goods available to us not only makes the desiring of something else possible, but also provokes us to seek after new goods in our attempt to increase enjoyment up to the capacity of our will. There can be no predetermination of our choice as far as the various goods sought after are concerned, because they cannot be desired unless we are first made aware of them and the cognitive powers are exercised according as we desire to use them. These powers cannot be forced to exercise their act except when we are subjected to overpoweringly intense assault upon them (loud noises, fierce tactile stimulus, and so forth). The thing cognized determines what they shall cognize; we determine whether we shall use our senses or not.

A determination of a kind that does prevent the deliberate exercise of choice, however, can be found at work when there is insufficient experience upon which to base a proper assessment of

The Will and Freedom of Choice

apparent goods. The attraction of some good can draw an inexperienced person irresistibly to it so that he has no will for anything else. As long as he cannot be aware of the relative aspects of this good he has no basis for preferring anything else. In a similar fashion an inexperienced person may pursue as many pleasures as time and energy allow him in an attempt to fill up the capacity of his will by the sheer multiplicity of goods. Such persons are bound by their ignorance of the true nature of a reasoned good. They need to learn that the capacity for human happiness cannot be fulfilled and that the more one puts his love in passing fancies the greater the sorrow when they pass. Concentration upon temporalities prevents the attainment of more durable goals. Experience and its assessment is indispensable to understanding the distinction between passing enjoyment and enduring satisfaction and to the intelligent use of choice with respect to both.

Closely allied to the correct interpretation of experience is the ability to distinguish successfully goods that are merely means, which cannot be satisfactory ends, from goods that are ends in themselves and whose use is to satisfy to some extent the will's desire for a total good. For something to be an end it must be enjoyable either to the one who procures it or to someone for whom he procures it. The end may also be capable of being used as a means to something else. For example, the teacher who helps a singer to develop his voice is aiding in the perfection of a capability within the singer that can be enjoyed for its own sake or used to bring pleasure to others. But some ends are purely means. Distasteful tasks, unpleasant medicines, money, are examples, because they can be considered as goods only in virtue of what they procure. To desire them as ends in themselves is to invite frustration, for they cannot of themselves satisfy any worthwhile ambition or perfect any capability within us. It is not uncommon that our urge to be active leads us to engage in activities that satisfy the urge to be active but do not bring us anything else we can enjoy. In this case we may be misdirecting our energies through a failure to distinguish the best way to make our activities serve our desires.

The Knowledge of Means

Another factor involved in the good use of the act of choice is a knowledge of means precisely as means. To apprehend something as desirable is easy enough to do, to determine whether or not it is available by our own effort or by any effort that we may command very often requires thought. There are two aspects to the problem of weighing the means to an end according as the end in view is seen to be: (1) an *ultimate* one in which total happiness will be obtained or (2) a *limited* one well worth attaining for its own sake since it is a reasoned good (enjoyable in itself and useful for progress to an ultimate good, or at least not a hindrance to such progress), but which may be sacrificed if necessary for the attainment of an ultimate end. If the end in view is our complete happiness, then it is imperative that we single out means that will unfailingly produce happiness and apply them. But if we are striving for a lesser good that holds only an equal rank with other partial goods, we may direct our means toward both goods, determining which one is preferable during the course of action toward them.

There is a further consideration regarding the means which can give us a better ability to choose, since it reveals the degree of probability with which the means may be successfully applied to attaining the end. This consideration regards the actual details of the various possible means that could attain the end, for we often foolishly simplify the difficulty involved in attaining a goal by overlooking the actual multiplicity of the means involved and by failing to foresee realistically the amount of effort and perseverance their successful use would involve. For example, a man with energy and natural ability fixes his intention upon having a certain size and style of house and determines to build it himself in his spare time. He is certain that he can build a house because millions of houses have been built by men and some have been built by untrained workers following an architect's plans and the advice of others. But in starting the job without further inquiry into what the completing of a house involves he is engaging upon a series of activities that will take him much more time to complete than they would a skilled worker, because of his inexperience. Quite often the result of

The Will and Freedom of Choice 303

such house-building experiments is that the would-be builder eventually calls in the experts to do the task properly. If he cannot afford to do this, he must settle for a jerry-built house or spend months beyond his original estimate of the time required in order to build the house well.

The failure to discern accurately what is actually involved in attaining an end can very often defeat one's intention to gain it. On the other hand, the careful discernment of the factors involved in attaining a goal that others claim is difficult to achieve can give the assurance needed to attempt it in spite of discouragement.

FREEDOM OF CHOICE

A knowledge of the various factors regarding the nature of end and the interrelation of means and end is necessary for any good use of the ability to make a deliberate choice. The lack of consideration of these various factors can seriously affect our pursuit of happiness, but such a lack does not deprive our choice of its unpredetermined character. Freedom in our act of choice is evident because there is no predetermination prior to rational consideration that makes the use of one means binding to the exclusion of other means. It is up to us to consider as many of the factors as may bear upon a matter proposed for choice in order to have a proper basis for making a choice. When we fail to do this, we fail to exercise our intelligence for our own betterment. The result of such failure may make our choice a poor one, but it does not make the choice any less determined by our own thinking on the matter. If we be somewhat mistaken in our intentions, as when we are influenced by a suppressed desire and are not conscious of this influence, we nevertheless base our choice upon the recognized intention. How could we base our choice upon the unrecognized factor, since the will is directed by our knowledge of what is desirable and attainable? If our choice is influenced by a habit so strong that it binds us to a set pattern of means to an end, we do not exercise our choice upon the means but we do exercise it upon the decision to pursue that end now rather than later.

It is evident by now that the basis of freedom of choice is to be found in the intellect's ability to weigh the suitability of various means to an end and in the relative indifference of the will to any good that is not apprehended as a total good.[19] Nothing that limits our choice—ignorance, the reduction of the means to only one, the application of threat or force—can remove the character of freedom from our deliberation. The act of the intellect is free because no physical cause can act upon it, and all of the other factors that can affect our choice can be considered as precisely that: factors to be considered in deciding what is the best thing to do. When a man says that he cannot make a choice because he is under threat, does not know what is involved, or can see only one path open to him, and then makes his decision, he is exercising choice because he thinks it better to do so than not. In short, he decides, and he acts upon his decision. He has dominion over the act of deciding and over the act of implementing the decision. He is free to the extent that he can choose—he possesses his freedom more perfectly to the extent that he can be aware of the multiplicity of internal and external factors that affect his choice and can subject them to his intentions. He has some freedom by nature; he can achieve greater freedom by succeeding in the effort to subject his passions to reason and to be prudent in his deliberations.

PERFECTION OF CHOICE

While many of our choices can have consequences of great importance to our future, inasmuch as a slip or miscalculation can end our lives or the lives of others, or can expose our material goods to destruction, we look upon most of our choices as being important in a routine way. Thus we regard some choices as momentous and most of the remainder as part of the sequences involved in daily living. The momentous choices decide our overriding beliefs and goals (for those who deliberately choose their beliefs and goals rather than just grow into them) and the acts that will direct the path of our future life. The lesser decisions are directed to activities we need to repeat over and over again. It is not possible to repeat truly momentous decisions over and over again, because unless such decisions are followed out, they are not momentous. Thus if a man decides once and for all to forsake a certain way of life and does not, his decision was not very important after all. The same applies to a man who decides to become a skillful surgeon and then does not even enter medical school. It is the activities we repeat constantly that give us the opportunity to improve upon bad choices and to develop a prudent use of our ability to choose. Our natural love of what is best for us engenders a tendency to improve upon the choices that fail and to repeat those that we judge to have been successful. This natural inclination to do what is best for us, when deliberately cultivated, becomes a habitual way of seeking out the best means to the various ends we desire.

Our ability to improve upon our choices depends upon the same power as does choice itself. Because we have dominion over what we shall do and how well we shall do it, we can improve upon our actions. It is the will, our desirous self, that has the operations of all of the voluntary powers at its command. Consequently, since free choice is the source of our deliberate acts, and since we are not determined in advance to favor moral good or evil, it is the will that executes our chosen patterns of activity according to what our personal right reason sees to be best, or contrary to this. In this matter a kind of necessity operates; for if we do not improve our actions, then by repetition a tendency to do them constantly in the same unimproved way is necessarily formed. Our attention is drawn to that which most interests us, and consequently in matters of little interest we follow what worked in the past rather than seek a better way of acting. For example, a person dedicated to succeeding in a line of endeavor that will absorb as much of his time as he can devote to it, of necessity must neglect a great number of things that he ought to do in order to keep himself healthy, well informed, and in favor with his family and other friends. In these latter matters, whenever the necessity of considering them is forced upon him, he does what he can to get by. The alternative to acting this way is to subordinate his success in business to a place of equal importance with the other ends mentioned by valuing success in business less and health and spiritual growth more. Thus either the choices must be improved and a norm as to what is best arrived at by reason or our actions must occur in line with our predominating desire without too much concern as to their efficacy, as long as the ends that have to be attained are reached in some way.

The improvement of an activity can proceed only so far,

since there are a limited number of variables that can be ordered to the best attainment of the end in view. Our desire to bring perfection into our constantly repeated voluntary actions will either achieve the greatest possible efficacy or stop somewhere short of that; then we will perform such actions with whatever ease of accomplishment and success of attainment we have ordered into them. When we have so ordered actions in this fashion that we have to exercise only the minimum of attention in carrying out these actions, *we have formed a habitual way of doing them*. It is quite possible to repeat the actions that make up some aspect of our daily activity in a rather indifferent fashion and thus form a habitual way of doing them with ease, but inefficiently. In this way we distinguish a bad habit from a good habit.

The will is the supreme motive power in man. It is in our competence to be critical of our use of this power by exercising reason to distinguish activities and goals that can truly perfect the capabilities with which nature has endowed us. It is also possible to bring order, efficiency, and facility of accomplishment into our daily activities by the exercise of prudence (the wise choice of action) in examining and reexamining our experience to discern the lines along which improvement of our activities and the formation of good habits should develop. In order to appreciate more fully the ends towards which our self-perfective activities may be aimed, we turn in the next chapter to a consideration of the natural immortality of man's soul and its implications in his present life.

CHAPTER 9

Man's Spiritual Nature ~

ALTHOUGH we have been considering man's spiritual powers in Chapters 5, 6, and 8 in treating of man's cognition as atemporal and aspatial (in varying degrees) and of his attraction to all things that reason judged to be good, we shall now consider them as the powers of a spiritual soul. We shall consider the transcendence of man's spiritual soul over the limitations of his temporal, spatial, and corruptible body.

We have already considered in some detail the first three of the answers proposed to our opening question, "What is man?" We have seen that man is indeed a mass of protoplasm and a masterpiece of workmanship in bone, muscle, and nerve who surpasses all other animals in his ability to adapt his environment to his own desires. Indeed, he is capable of devoting his life to a headlong pursuit of food and drink and sex and other pleasures that suit his fancy, but if he does devote his life to such pursuits he does so only by his own personal commitment, ignoring the future and the insubstantiality of such temporal goods. Every human being is endowed with a natural propensity for pleasure, is born a hedonist as our analysis of appetite in Chapter 7 made clear, but each person is also normally endowed with reason whereby he can integrate his various passions with actions directed to goals made evident by a critical assessment of what is truly suitable to the nature of man and perfective of individual capabilities.

We now turn our attention to the fourth of the proposed answers: that man is not a lonely battler against cruel fate, but rather a member of a group of very special animals with common interests and capable of sharing one another's friendship. Man has abilities that so obviously transcend the limits of animal nature that he is an entirely different kind of being with a destiny that includes continued existence in separation from the body. That man has sufficient dominion over his acts to direct them where he wills, was made evident in the last chapter. We now consider what happiness man can hope actually to possess as a result of his deliberate activities, first attempting an accurate description of what kind of being man is in order to determine the kind of future he has as an individual.

A Mind-Body Problem

The necessity of considering man as a conscious being to the exclusion of his chemical and physiological aspects, because their analysis throws no light upon what it is to be conscious, has given rise to what we may call a *mind-body problem*.[1] This is the problem of discerning accurately how the conscious aspects of man are present to his body. Are they simply temporally and spatially located in the sense of depending upon the bodily organs to make contact with matter as the occasion for discerning the appearances and abiding characteristics of things? Or is the human body identical in kind with that of any fully formed higher vertebrate with the intellect and the will imposing their authority upon the body by making it do their bidding? If such were the case the intellectual soul would be related to the body after the fashion of a person riding a horse. That it is not so related we can show by considering what our analysis reveals of the various aspects of man as a whole being.

THE UNITY OF MAN

In Chapter 2 it was necessary to consider the various characteristics whereby living things differ from the nonliving and one kind of living thing differs from another, in order to concentrate upon the notion of the soul as the one all-pervading form of a living body and to account for different perfections in vital activities by different souls. Now it is necessary to consider this notion of form once again to bring our reasoning ability to bear upon the evidence of what kind of being man is.

The chemicals that enter into a living being exhibit properties as parts of a living system which they do not exhibit when they are analyzed apart from living matter. The explanation of this fact (Chapter 2) is that the chemicals are organized as to their position and function by the vital principle that is present when the living thing exchanges energy with its environment, and absent when the chemicals act according to their chemical natures as we know them when considered apart from living matter. The corpse gradually loses the quantitative form proper to it when life was present, because the chemicals of which it is composed act spontaneously according to their proper natures, which are predetermined to react with one another in set ways. In the living body these predetermined activities are subordinated to the living processes, such as self-maintenance, motion in place, and sensing and feeling. When this subordinating principle no longer dominates their reactions the chemicals no longer remain parts of tissue, for the tissues decay; they no longer retain the spatial arrangement whereby they served as the physical apparatus for vital actions since their spatial disposition is now controlled by gravitational and other nonliving forces rather than by the laws of cellular arrangement.[2] Whether the corpse be that of a human being or that of an amoeba, the cessation of vital activity is accompanied by the freeing of the chemical components from subordination to the soul of the living thing.

THE SENSE IN ACT

The preceding analysis concerns only one aspect of the activity of the soul. In things devoid of knowledge this aspect

Man's Physical and Spiritual Nature

may be the only manifestation of the presence of the soul, because growth and reproduction are basically biochemical activities. Conscious living things have a kind of activity that goes beyond anything that can be ascribed to a chemical nature—the act of being conscious of both self and nonself. This activity is performed through the bodily organs which are composed of various chemicals, but it is not merely the activity of any chemical.[3] Seeing is not an activity of visual purple, but there is no discrimination of faintly illumined objects unless visual purple is present in the rods of the retina. There is also no resynthesis of the visual purple in the rods where bleaching has occurred under strong light, unless the eye is the eye of a living animal.

We have here an opportunity to exercise critical judgment as to how dependent vital activities are on the presence of the soul. On the one hand, the reaction of the eye to the stimulus of light is a photochemical one and the self-propagating impulses in the optic nerve have no marked differences from the impulses in any other neural fibers. On the other hand, the tremendous complexity, biochemically and physically, of the sensory receptors is not duplicated anywhere in inanimate nature. Nor does it ever occur under natural conditions except as the growth of a living animal germ cell. Moreover *these receptors will not function as sensory organs unless conscious attention is directed to them,* even though they be healthily alive. To claim that the bodily organs are only the occasion for the exercise of conscious discrimination of sensibles is to overlook the fact that the organ is produced in the same process of growth which gradually completes the formation of the body as a sentient body and that it is only the diversity of the end organs so produced which enables us to discriminate the various kinds of sensibles. That the sense organ can be stimulated without evoking sensation because our attention is elsewhere shows only that there is a degree of independence exercised by the sense power so that it need not always be operative when stimuli are present to the organ.

Just as the triangular shape carved in the surface of a piece of wood makes that surface be actually triangular, and just as the combination of sodium and chlorine is productive of a molecule that is actually salt, so also the combination of the biochemical components of a muscle and their formation in a spindle which contracts and relaxes is actually a muscle. Similarly, the formation of photosensitive tissue into a retina which reacts to every variation in the hue of light that falls upon it is actually a sense organ. The actuality that is the wood is simultaneously triangular; the actuality that is sodium and chloride is simultaneously salt; and the actuality that is a spindle-shaped assemblage of biochemicals is simultaneously a muscle fiber working at one time so as actually to move the bones, at another time resting. The actuality that is an assemblage of biochemicals having a very specific sensitivity to stimuli is simultaneously a sensory organ moved to act by an impinging stimulus and by our intention that prompts us to listen or to see or to feel, and so on, whatever is present in a sensible way. The unity of the biochemicals of the organ and the act of sensing is as great as that of the muscle fiber and the act of flexing, and as that of the union of sodium and chloride and the state of being salty to the taste. All three are superior to the unity of the triangularity and the surface of the wood, because these two may exist separately and do not have the necessary interdependence that the other unities have.

The sense organs are not only the locations for the sensations; they also participate essentially in the sensations to the extent, that if their biochemistry is defective, the sensory impression is defective or totally lacking. Obviously then, the organ (receptor, nerve fibers, and brain) is just as essential to actual sensing as the muscle fiber is to the actual moving of the bones. They differ in that the passivity of the muscle is to a stimulus that usually originates within the animal, whereas the stimulus for the external senses, and through them, for the mediated senses, is originally from the environment.

This difference in origin of muscular and of sensory activity points to a further indication of the essential unity of body and soul, for in man the muscles are directed, in voluntary actions, according to the intention of the will and as reason directs our acts in terms of what the senses discern about the external environment. Thus will and reason cooperate to form an intention to be carried out by the muscular use of a physical means, whose use is impossible unless the senses present it to us as temporally and spatially located so that we can direct our body as a whole to it and our limbs to the laying hold of it. There is a unity of the environment with the sense also, so that the sense in the act of sensing is the sensible aspect of the thing sensed, for the stimulus is physically (and therefore chemically) present in the sense and is the agent in the biochemical reaction essential to sensation. There can be little doubt as to the unity of the animating principle and animated matter on the merely living and on the sentient level, but the unity of these factors with the higher conscious levels needs a little further discussion.

THE VOLUNTARY ASPECT OF SENSATION

The presence or absence of a sense power to the organ, whereby it becomes aware of the presence of an impression of a sensible thing, is to some extent under our control, since we can direct our conscious attention where we wish and can withdraw it when we wish to do so. Thus we see what we want to look at, for the most part (sometimes circumstances severely limit our choice) and can cease to exercise one sense in order to concentrate upon what is present to another sense when we wish. When we are asleep we are not attentive to our external senses and they are largely inoperative. But we cannot, under other circumstances, voluntarily withdraw our conscious attention from a sense organ so effectively that it cannot be impressed by a sufficiently strong stimulus, because the senses are actually formed by the soul and our ability to be impressed by a sensible is actually present as long as the soul is present to the organ.

Voluntary control over the internal senses, when we are fully conscious, is more extensive than over the external senses, for we cannot only imagine and remember what we wish, but we can also create by the use of imagination and can plan the actualities that will occur in the future, on the basis of our remembered experience. By the use of the internal senses we can settle the many details involved in carrying out our intention to attain some end, because we can picture to ourselves how the various details of projected activities can be ordered physically to the actual possession of the desired end. For example, in digging up a fair-sized tree or shrub, which is to be planted in another location, the use of imagination can indicate that if the shovelfuls of dirt are dumped two feet away from the base of the tree or shrub to be transplanted, then once the digging reaches a depth of a few feet it will be necessary to move the pile of shoveled dirt in order to enlarge the hole to have working room to go deeper. In matters of greater importance we can draw upon experience to picture all of the steps that must be taken to gain some goal and in our mind's eye foresee most of the difficulties to be overcome and the opportunities to be pursued. In brief, the estimative sense and its memory are indispensable in the development of the voluntary habit of prudence.

The unity of the will and reason with the sense powers that unite the environment to us intentionally and with the muscle motions that unite us physically with what we desire is the unity of one agent carrying out one intention with a multiplicity of means. The senses and the voluntary muscles are entirely at the disposal of the will and the reason in a healthy person. There are other examples of unity of this kind, the unity of command in an army or in a civil government, but the control we exercise is absolute and brooks no rebellion, so much so that conflicts of motivation are sometimes suppressed rather than resolved in our desire to end a dilemma by taking forthright action. Thus it happens that a person who unexpectedly is placed in a position where he alone must make a choice of one from several apparent goods relieves the anxiety of having to make the decision by fixing his choice upon one without really seeing anything preferable in it, only to discover shortly thereafter that his choice frustrated his desire in the matter. But many choices are irrevocable under ordinary circumstances, and the same unity of purpose that attempts to attain what is truly best for us may in fact be taking us further and further into unhappiness.

There is both power and fearfulness in man's ability to make a deliberate choice and to carry it out with such thoroughness that his whole being is subordinated to the fulfilling of an intention. By the exercise of choice he can change his occupation, his attitudes and opinions, and his physical habituations. He can direct the whole course of his life along new lines so that in effect he is starting a new life. In every act of the will the visualization of physical goals and use of the means for attaining both physical and spiritual goals can be carried out successfully because of the dominance over the senses exercised by the intellect and the will. That man is one substance is manifested by this unity in his actions.

Man's Physical and Spiritual Nature

The Transcendence of Soul over Matter

Having considered the unity of soma and psyche in man, we shall now explain how the human psyche not only quickens the body, but has operations quite independent of the body. For those who hold that man is a dual entity, a soul using a body, the problem here is to understand what enables a spiritual entity to contact a physical entity, and to understand what limits a soul to the location of the body of which it is the soul. For our understanding of man as essentially one being, the problem is to explain how a form whose very function as form is to quicken the body so that it is both body and living can also have activities that transcend all material activity, so much so that we are constrained to say that man is distinguished from all other animals by his spiritual soul. Let us approach the problem by examining the transcendence of the human soul as sentient and as intellectual (we have already discussed the transcendence of the soul as vital principle of the living body over the limitations of purely material forms, in Chapter 2).

In sensation the impressions of the sensible are received physically by the sense organ and intentionally by the sense power. Only one sensible impression is involved, but its reception is twofold because the receiver is twofold. We recall it here merely as an example of the transcendence (surpassing the intrinsic limitations of an inferior agent) of the sentient organ over merely material receptivity and activity. The transcendence of the soul over matter is defined as the ability of a soul to do by itself, or in conjunction with the body, things that nonliving matter simply cannot do. Of course in all organic activities it is man as a whole who acts, and not the soul by itself.[4] But in activities such as the exercising of critical judgment upon understandings to see what is implicit in them, and activities such as desiring happiness or desiring understanding as a means to happiness, no sensory or animal appetitive power is involved. Consequently, such acts are acts of the soul alone. This fact needs to be more clearly manifested because it is the key notion in establishing the absolute transcendence of the human soul over matter. It will be sufficient to establish the complete immateriality of the intellect, since its manner of moving the will to act—by judging that something is good and to be desired—presupposes that the will is a kind of power that can be moved by the kind of nonorganic activity proper to the intellect.

A cognitive power is an ability to receive the being of something else in a representational way; in so doing it makes events present to us more fully than they ever can be physically. Our sensory experience gradually becomes very rich so that it encompasses a large number of the practical aspects of single things and of the environment and its contents as a whole. Our intellectual comprehension is also capable of being quite extensive and has an advantage over mere experience in that it often encompasses the "why" as well as the "how" of the interconnectedness of events. In both kinds of cognition the thing known is present to us in a representational way. By contrast no matter how we manage to possess a thing physically, by consuming it and thus destroying it, or by possessing it for use or aesthetic appreciation, and so on, it can never enter into our very being so as to become part of us as it does by being known.

Physical being is obdurately spatial; our physical being is just as exclusive of the presence of other physical beings (except through metabolic assimilation, or a similar absorption process in which matter becomes living substance or occupies interstices of the body as foreign matter) as they are of one another. It is a property of matter, that because it is spatially extended one quantum of matter excludes another from its place. Thus one stone excludes another, one molecule excludes a second, one subatomic particle excludes another.[5] The actual material being of anything is proper to it and cannot remain proper to it and be physically communicated to another material being at the same time. For example, to become living matter this piece of food must surrender its identity as food to take on the nature of living substance. Only by ceasing to be what it is can one physical thing be truly made one with another.

By contrast a knower assimilates thousands of impressions transmitted to him by the sensibles around him in any given waking period and neither he, as conscious receiver of impressions, nor the sensible things, considered as to their substantial natures, are modified substantially.[6] Thus the endless process of sensing sensibles is one of constant assimilation of sensory impressions into a boundless capacity for knowing. On the intellectual level there is the same capacity to receive without any modification of the nature of the power. No alteration of a sensory organ accompanies the intellect's act of cognition, however, for no sensory organ is involved as the complete aspatiality and atemporality of intellectual understanding indicate. Such independence of the properties of matter as that which is possessed by our act of understanding is the principal indication of the complete immateriality of the intellect and of the natural incorruptibility of the human soul.

IMMATERIALITY OF THE HUMAN INTELLECT

In understanding things the human intellect forms for itself representations that are neither visual, nor auditory, nor in any other way determinate. They are totally unrestricted as to time and place. Consequently, such representations are not only as immaterial as our visual and otherwise sensory representations that depict things in a spatial way without being equal in spatial extent to what is depicted, but they are totally immaterial inasmuch as they represent what it is to be spatial, apart from any given instance of spatial extension. Similarly these representations indicate what it is to be motion apart from any given instance of motion, and so on, for the other *kinds* of things understood by man. Thus our understanding of an eternal motion in place requires only some understanding of movement as something successively in different places, plus the understanding of perpetuity. We can visualize some such motion as that of Mercury around the Sun. But if our experience of motion has been extensive, we do not need to visualize any example of a path that could be traveled endlessly. The words "motion" and "eternal" are sufficient to move us to think about motion, endlessness of path and time, and to see nothing contradictory in the combination of the three.

The perfect freedom on the part of the intellect from the limiting factors of sensory apprehension, namely, from apprehending only concrete instances of things, is beyond doubt. One can think of "circular" as "having constant curvature," and of "motion" as "the successive passing through of positions," but when we visualize "circular" it is always of a very definite radius and when we visualize "motion" it is of some singular thing or things in a definite spatial frame of reference. Thus we can attain an understanding of being extended, of being circular, and of being in motion from any few instances of extension, circularity (approximate, of course), and motion in the concrete. But that understanding transcends the spatial and temporal conditions of existence of those few instances.[7] Once attained it no longer needs to be referred to them, for it applies to all instances both actual and possible of extension, circularity, and motion. No actual moving thing can be representative of all motion, because its motion is full of thousands of incidentals that do not occur in other motions, and other motions have numberless incidental details that do not occur in the one under examination. Similarly, no sensory image can actually depict the details of the many instances in which an apple has been seen—the details of each instance are determinate and the sensory depiction of an apple is determinate in the same way. But things that are quite determinate exclude one another from the same place. Consequently the determinateness of the details in our sense impression of apples excludes all of the variations in such details occurring in actual apples.

This radical difference in the act of the intellect understanding and the act of the sense sensing is not explainable in terms of any "appleness" or circularity existing itself apart from things, or of any motion existing in itself apart from actually moving things.[8] In fact, it is over the attempted explanations of the origin of understanding in the human intellect that many philosophers and philosophies differ most profoundly. On the presupposition that no merely material agent can act upon an immaterial power (the human intellect), the explanations have sought another universe as the referant for intellectual cognition, or have given the intellect the ability to generate in itself and to impose upon matter the basic formalities (categories) of its understanding, or have devised a second intellect to produce a suitable means for informing that intellect by which we are actually aware of things.

We find none of these *explanations* in accord with actual experience and consequently prefer to make no hypotheses on this matter. We accept the manner of the presence of the intellect to the senses as a mystery of the same kind as the intentionality of the sensory impressions. They are both mysteries about the kind of thing that a cognitive power is. Neither power in its act of

being the other as other is physically locatable, for neither awareness has a physical description.

We shall continue with the analysis of the immateriality
of the intellect by using the notions that have (in our estimation)
a solid basis in the acts of sensory and intellectual awareness that
are experienced by every rational animal.

The radical difference between intellectual and sensory
awareness points to a radical difference in the power to which the
thing being known is present. It is not correct, however, to consider the intellect as a receiver even though its awareness extends
to every impression made by any sensible that registers in our sensory consciousness.[9] There is only one kind of action of the stimulus in the organ. In its reception the chemical natures of the
organ's chemical constituents are operative, as is the sensory power
that they serve.But both of these receptions are absolutely determinate and in no way possess the indeterminateness characteristic
of intellectual understanding. The intellect does not receive any
impression from the sensible directly. Does it suffer action from
the sense power? If it did, the reception would probably manifest
the determinateness of the agent in question. Rather the sense
power that discriminates the sensible in its act of sensing is an act
of the same soul that possesses an intellectual power. Thus it is more
correct to say that man sees and man understands, because of the
unity of the various kinds of activity in the nature of man. It is
one man who understands what he sees; these two acts are simultaneous, so that both intellect and sense are present to the object
but the intellect is present to it through the sense.[10] It is the sense
whose act of discrimination is specified by the impression made
upon it by the sensible; it is the intellect whose act of understanding discerns both what the sense discerns and the conformity or
disconformity of the sense (as explained in Chapter 6) with the
sensible, and much more.

The relation of the sense to the intellect is of that which
is contained to that which contains, just as the relation of the sensible thing to the sense is of that which is contained by a semblance of itself to that which contains it by a semblance of it.
Now just as the sense can contain the sensible by a semblance of
it without thereby being identical in physical actuality with the
thing, so also can the intellect contain the act of the sensory

power within it without thereby being identical in actuality with that which the sensory power depicts nor with the sensory power's depiction. The powers are also related in this way whenever we direct imagination to form an image to represent some idea in the concrete (to imagine a triangle), or the sight to pursue a series of apprehensions that are of interest only to the intellect (to decipher a scrawled message).

In this somewhat mysterious realm of investigation of the manner of the intellect's presence to the senses and to things, we can be aided in our attempt to understand by using our knowledge of the will's presence to the animal appetites through intention. The animal appetites are elicited by the attractiveness or repulsiveness of what is discriminated by the senses. The intention of our will to attain something as an end or as a means to an end makes use of the love or hate of the concupiscible appetite to bring the end or means closer within reach without ever identifying the happiness that it naturally loves with them. We can desire the object of concupiscence with full recognition of its nature as a temporal and finite good without diminishing in any way our intention of attaining long-range goals. Thus the intention of attaining some long-range goal or happiness in the life beyond this terrestrial one can include within it thousands of lesser ends that are useful as means to the long-range ends, without in any way reducing those long-range ends to the status of the lesser ones. A vestige of the long-range end is found in each lesser end, which identifies the direction of the lesser end as tending to the long-range end. But in no way whatsoever does the presence of an intention to obtain something in the distant future change the actuality of the purely temporary and present good. Rather the intention to a distant goal contains the present good within it in the way that a means to an end is encompassed by the intention to that end.

In the same way the ability of the intellect to understand contains within it the understanding of singulars as they are cognized by the senses and the understanding of what characteristics in singulars identify them as being of a certain kind. There is but one reception of the sensible into the soul. There are two conscious receivers, only in the sense that the intellect is an ability to discern what the sense has discriminated without being reduced to the kind of discriminatory act that is proper to the sense. Our intellect is informed through the medium of the senses, which specify what it shall apprehend while leaving its mode of apprehension unrestricted in any way. The fact that by verbal apprehension, which is intellectual, we can assimilate a great deal of information which can be represented in the imagination and the cognitative by visual, auditory, and tactile impressions manifests an intimacy between intellectual apprehension and sensory depiction of what has been apprehended which is indicative of the unity of two kinds of power in one soul. This unity, however, would be impossible if both powers were present in the same mode of being; if both were present as sense powers, then a sense organ would be actuated in two diverse ways simultaneously, which means that the chemical constituents of the organ would be acting in two diverse ways which is manifestly impossible. The only conceivable possibility is that one power is present as the act of the organ and the other is present in a completely immaterial way, that is, not as the act of any organ.

Summation on Immateriality

The concepts of the intellect, that is, the acts of understanding the essential characteristics that distinguish things as being of one kind and not another, are utterly devoid of any actual sensory characteristics. Our understanding of what it is to be a sensible includes the notions of being audible, tangible, located, and the other essential aspects of sensibles; nevertheless the act of understanding has no sensible characteristics whatsoever. It is invisible, inaudible, intangible. The one concrete manifestation of our understanding of the sensible environment, besides our ordering of that environment according to our wishes, is the existence of words. Words are excellent substitutes for things, not only in our expression of what we sense or feel or understand but also as a means of apprehending what others think and feel and sense. Through this communication from others we can apprehend a great deal about our universe without having to abstract it from experience. Words have the ability to signify, because they are primarily signs of what has been understood; their very abstractness is an indication of the immateriality of our conceptual representation of things.

The nonphysical and nonsensory characteristics of our

intellectual knowledge are the indications by which we apprehend that it is a nonphysical thing and a nonsensory power. Its immateriality then consists of this: It is not material as a stone is material, nor is its immateriality that of a sense power whose act of being aware has no physical description, for its mode of possessing things in a known way has none of the determinateness in details that is characteristic of a sensory knowing. Consequently, since it is not material in its being, nor restricted in its knowing to the singular aspects of things but rather knows things absolutely, it is altogether immaterial.

Subsistence of the Human Soul

For something to subsist is for it to exist by itself without any dependence for its duration as an existing thing upon its being a part of something else. For example, an apple depends upon its parent tree for coming into existence, but once the apple has grown and fallen from the tree, it carries on life within itself independently of that which it shared with the tree. During the period that the apple exists independently of its source of origin, as an organic unit, it is said to subsist.

If the seeds that exist within the apple burst their shells and branch out with a life of their own, they will give rise to a sapling which will grow as an organic unit depending upon its environment for its sustenance. But even though it depends absolutely upon its environment for its supply of life-sustaining materials, its act of living is self-contained. The sapling does not live with the life of the parent tree; it lives by itself. Thus it has a set of operations that are proper to it, which originate and terminate in the sapling. It subsists, because it is a complete being possessing all that belongs to its nature as an apple tree. A branch cut from this tree would also subsist in the sense that it would be a quantitative whole existing by itself. If the branch dies, it no longer has the nature proper to it as a living thing and therefore does not subsist as living. But it does continue as an accidental unity of the molecules making up its woodiness. In this case, however, the molecules each subsist in their own right as individuals, even though they are held together by cohesive forces in an accidental unity of place.

That the apple tree subsisted as a living being is evidenced by the way in which it carried on living activities within itself. For only that which subsists can have an operation in itself. If something has an operation only as part of something else, although the whole thing of which it is a part may subsist, the part cannot be said to subsist or to have a subsistent operation. Thus the branch of the tree, as part of the tree, does not exist of itself but shares in the life of the whole tree. Once cut off from the tree and planted in soil so that it takes root and flourishes, the branch has subsistence as being complete in its nature and operations as tree.

A man, as a whole, is obviously a subsisting being, since he is not a substantial part of anything else. His hand exists only as a part of him; should the hand be removed from his arm it would then exist separately but only as an accidental unity of the molecules constituting it. If it could carry on its vital activities in the body, without depending upon the human soul for being the kind of organ that it is, then, upon separation, it could go right on subsisting apart from the body. That this is not the case for any part of the body is evident, because when death occurs none of the functions carried on by the various parts of the body continues unless the part is made subject to another soul by being a replacement for an organ in another living body (or kept alive artificially as a cellular entity).

The same condition that obtains for the hand as part of the body also obtains for the sensory powers, which are essentially dependent upon the bodily organs for their operation. Just as the hand is nothing living apart from the body of which it is a part, so no sense is capable of functioning except as the act of a sense organ.

The case for the intellect is different. Although our intellect depends for its information upon our senses and upon verbal communication through our senses, it does not otherwise depend upon the body for its operation. Its operation is entirely within itself, because it apprehends what is common and enduring in things not as the act of any organ but as forming within itself a notion that we discover in the sensory awareness of things. Our intellect's further acts of judging and reasoning occur entirely within itself. In the efferent direction its decisions are implemented by the will and guided in details by the various senses that discern the directions in which motion to a desired end ought to go. But even here the act of deciding is complete within the intellect and its act of command is conferred upon the senses and upon our voluntary acts. In short, our intellect is an immaterial power which has its proper operations of apprehending, judging, and reasoning entirely within itself, although it depends upon the body for obtaining something to think about and for actually implementing its practical decisions. This means that it exists by its own act of existence and does not depend upon the body as a whole or upon any part of the body for its existence. That is, the intellect subsists.

Or, more briefly, the intellect in its acts of apprehending and judging is actually independent of the body. It has an operation in itself. But only what subsists can have an operation in itself. Therefore, the human intellect subsists.

The Soul's Shared Subsistence

Is not the human soul the form that causes the human body to exist as a human body and to have sensory, locomotive, appetitive, and biochemical activities? How can this be if the intellect, which is an ability of the soul, subsists? It can only be the case if the soul of which the intellect is a power subsists, for then it could communicate its subsistent being to the matter that it informs. In this way the being of the whole composite is the being of the soul. To make clear how this is accomplished, we must digress a little to discuss how one kind of soul compares to another.

We call the human soul an intellectual soul, just as we call the soul of a monkey an animal soul in order to indicate what is distinctive and principal in the life of such beings. For both monkey and man have approximately the same metabolic processes, which are similar in principle (an exchange with environment for the materials and energy of living activities) to those of plants. Since the absolute unity of substance of living things, in spite of the heterogeneity of their various parts, indicates only one soul as the formative principle, it is necessary to indicate the different grades of living by terms that manifest not what is common to various forms of life but what is distinctive of them. Consequently in saying that man has an intellectual soul, or in saying that he is a rational type of animal, we indicate what is proper to man according to his superiority over other kinds of animals. But there is something more involved here than simply the correct designation of differences. The ability to be sentient, as we human beings understand it, presupposes the ability to carry on respiration; the ability to be cognizant of the natures of things presupposes the ability to receive and to retain sensory impressions; and the ability to desire happiness as a total good presupposes the ability to grasp the finitude of all concrete goods. Thus the soul which is designated as being superior has all of the abilities of the inferior soul plus those by which it is esteemed to be greater than them. Consequently to talk of the human intellect as subsisting, or more correctly to talk of the human intellectual soul as subsisting, is to talk about the form that not only forms every last minute part, as well as the gross parts of the body, but also overlaps the body (so to speak) so that some part (power) of it is not the form of the body.

As we have mentioned in previous chapters, nothing that is complex will differ from anything else according to its ultimate basic constituents (subatomic particles or energy, for instance). The difference of one kind of thing from another in appearances and in nature stems from the arrangement of the ultimate particles in various ways and from the various arrangements of such arrangements. However, arrangements are not produced by mere chance, but according to certain set formulas, as the multiplicity of individuals of one specific nature indicates. Moreover, these arrangements have a relative stability, for they exhibit the same natural properties and the same kind of physical components as long as the arrangement endures. The principle by which such arrangements exist is what we call the substantial form; it is not only the principle of arrangement, but also that which accounts for the *existence* of the parts as parts of this substantial unit. In other words, it is because of this formative principle that the ultimate constituents exist at this moment as part of this composite of constituents and that the whole composite has the properties that it has as a whole.

In living things the soul is the principle of arrangement of the parts and contains all the parts as an organic unit so that the parts are what they are and function in the life of the whole. In short, the soul accounts for all of the actuality of the living thing as living, that is, it gives to the materials out of which the body is formed their existence as parts of this living substantial unit now.

The Incorruptibility of the Human Soul

The only way in which anything can be corrupted is for its parts to be separated so that its existence as a whole is sundered. In those things whose parts cannot exist by themselves the sundering of the whole also signals the disappearance of the part as a part of that whole. Thus the death of a tree signals the death of its buds and limbs which might have had a life of their own under other circumstances. The reason for this is found in the kind of thing that a substantial form is. A substantial form not only gives order to the composite of things that it forms into a substantial unity; it also gives to the parts their very being as parts. Consequently if the physical components that are indispensable to the life of the whole are physically corrupted, then the life of the whole is corrupted. This means that the organizing principle that made the complex of parts to be living parts of a living whole ceases to exist.

The only exception to this kind of dissolution is that in which the soul has an operation of its own apart from the physical parts of the living whole. In such a case the act of existence belongs to the soul and the body shares in it. Thus when one of the indispensable parts of the body is corrupted so that it no longer plays a vital role, the whole body is unable to function as a living thing and the soul can no longer vivify it because there are absolutely indispensable conditions for the existence of the soul as the form of a living body—integrity of certain physical parts (the heart, for example) is one of them. Corruption of the body then leaves the soul incapable of acting as the form of the body. But since the soul exists of itself, its separation from the body is not accompanied by dissolution. *The soul continues to exist as an immaterial entity.*

We cannot visualize the incorruptibility of the human soul, because our discussion is in the realm of the immaterial which cannot be visualized. Nevertheless we can consider an analogue of a subsistent principle which continues on when the physical parts that it formed into a whole are no longer present to it. For instance, a man who understands how to develop a group of helpers and form them into an organization both makes use of their native abilities and gives to them positions and functions they can only have as part of the organization. Without them his organization would not be, and yet when it has served its purpose then each helper goes his own way with the leader remaining substantially intact and his knowledge in no way corrupted or diminished by its having been put to use and shared by others. This analogy is based upon a merely accidental unity of overseer and those who execute his directions; to that extent it falls short of depicting the kind of subsistence possessed by the human soul.

Our conclusion as to the incorruptibility of the human soul rests solely upon our understanding of the role of form in the composite of which it is a coprinciple. We know of no other subsistent principle of being and operation that is not joined in a merely accidental unity to what it forms and activates. Therefore, no exact analogy of the human soul as subsistent substantial form is possible.

Each individual human being possesses a rational nature. To such beings we give the name "person" to indicate their distinction from other kinds of animal beings and from inanimate things. The term "personality" is used to signify some aspect of human nature that is proper to an individual human being. It may signify some characteristic present in him from birth—shyness, irascibility, and the like—or some trait acquired by his own effort. In any case the trait is his and is a means of distinguishing him from other persons.

In a mature person the personality is an indication of his perceptiveness and his use of free choice. Thus the person who has inherited traits that he considers to be undesirable, or that men in general consider to be undesirable, will feel the urge to change them if they can be changed or to overlay them with more desirable traits. What the person does in this matter depends upon his perception of the traits as being undesirable, upon his perception of what is desirable, and upon the strength of his intention to change the trait or to acquire another. How his personality develops, therefore, depends upon the person himself as the possessor of the ability to think, to foresee, and to make prudent choices, as well as upon his genes and the influence of both his physical and cultural environment. Moreover, each person is something of all that he has experienced, inasmuch as his experience forms a background for the growth of values and for the exercise of reason by seeking to be prudent in choosing and carrying out actions that are best for him. Through experience, also, an emotional life is made possible not only in the opportunity for the exercise of the passions, but also in the profiting from experience by discerning the end results of emotional activities and forming habits of action that direct them with ease and assurance to desirable ends.

How a person's nature as an emotional, rational, and voluntary creature develops depends upon the end he has in view of the exercise of his emotions and freedom of choice. The number of possible realistic ends that he can know and appreciate as ends depends upon his environment, which constitutes his universe of actual experience, and upon his education which constitutes a second universe of acquaintanceship. For the apprehension of values in both of these realms, he needs to exercise critical judgment in distinguishing means from ends and in evaluating the desirability and possibility of attaining the various goods that are truly perfective of a human person.

Of great importance in this critical evaluation is the person's knowledge that his being as an intellectual entity is naturally indestructible and will endure after the dissolution of his body. Since this separation from the body will leave him incomplete as to the nature he originally possessed, the likelihood of being made complete as a person again should be seriously entertained. Each of us is aware that we have no power to give ourselves human life, to restore it, or to change its nature at all. Life is given to us, continues in us, and is taken from us without our having much to say about it. We can only cooperate in bringing life into being for others and in trying to make the best of our possession of it, according as our individual efforts and the circumstances of our environment permit. But our completeness as a person depends upon our possession of a body, and an eternity as an incomplete person does not seem entirely reasonable. In any case, the knowledge that man is brought into being without his assent, that by his own efforts he can improve himself and the lot of his fellow man, and that as an intellectual being he is a subsisting soul destined to live beyond the term of union with a body should be a weighty consideration in each person's formation of rational judgments about what is worthwhile and about essential goals for his life activities.

Notes ~

CHAPTER 1

1. We all realize that a large proportion of the statements that make up the intellectual deposit of information of any widely read person is based solely on authority. Even in fields of scientific investigation where *mere opinion* is abhorred, much that is accepted as true is not verified by those who accept it. This is because the verification often is not easy to make and few deem it desirable because that which is accepted is vouched for by reliable mechanical and human witnesses. Thus, that a standardized mercury thermometer measures the actual temperature of the medium surrounding it is seldom questioned, unless it belies the testimony afforded by the body itself or by another instrument for measuring heat.

This trust in the evidence of instruments and human reporters is based on two premises. The first is that *material natures act uniformly*—mercury expands at the same rate per increase of temperature in all mercury thermometers. The second is that *men naturally tell the truth* as they know it, unless some other motivation than sharing the good of the intellect tempts them to prevaricate. These two premises can be established by an individual who engages in the testing of the expansion of mercury under heat and who checks the statements of others against the facts. It would not take long for such a person to become convinced that the activities of mercury are predetermined by its nature and that they can be measured to degrees of approximation appropriate to man's desires. Similarly, he would soon become convinced that the general run of men in our present-day society speak the truth on topics to which they are emotionally neutral. He will be especially convinced of this upon perceiving that his own tendency is to communicate correctly when he is engaged in serious discourse and is fully conscious that it is the truth that is desired.

2. The notion of common consent or agreement as to what introspection yields is based upon the presupposition underlying all science *that natures act uniformly*. Human experience over the centuries of recorded history assures us that sodium is the kind of element that our chemistry texts describe, and so are the other elements. Therefore those men who have questioned the method of gaining knowledge called *introspection* have been challenging not just this method, but the very basis of all scientific knowledge. Our personal acquaintance with the scorners of introspection has revealed that their notion of this method is either somewhat distorted or very much clouded by the positivistic notion that if a thing cannot be heard, seen, touched, and so forth, it does not exist.

3. Synonyms for each of these terms are:
>existence—being
>substance—thing, mass (used substantively)
>quality—trait, characteristic, property
>quantity—mass, extension, amount
>action—movement, activity, locomotion

Each material substance has a size and shape that are the appearances of its quantity, and also a set of qualities and activities that distinguish it from things of a different kind. By these qualities and activities, as well as by shapes and sizes, we first distinguish objects and impose different class names upon them, as dog, tree, stone, and so on. But the knowledge by which we recognize gross differences and very obvious similarities is insufficient when we wish to study the nature of "dog" or "tree" in detail. For such a study one must consider the various aspects of things as a whole and also of their parts, whether they are living or chemical or mechanical. Aspects of the subject that were not explicitly involved in the knowledge of recognition are now upon closer study seen to be common to all the members of a group and to be therefore capable of being understood as something essential to that group —to all human hearts, for example. In general, what is incidental to one viewpoint can be essential to another, but it will not be essential to that other viewpoint until it is distinctly seen by some human intellect as essential. Thus the viewpoint that classifies human noses according to their shapes is considering an aspect that has no known connection with the vital processes of the body. But the manner in which the peripheral cells on terminating parts of the body such as the nose terminate the multiplication of constitutive cells (giving the size and shape to organs to some extent) is a vital aspect to researchers seeking to understand and to prevent cancer.

4. There are various historical sciences concerned with man's early history and his progress since the dawn of civilization. These analyses, like the analyses of man into his constituent parts carried on by the experimental sciences, are a continuing source of information to the philosophic account in that they clear up problems about the development of man's institutions and his culture and explain more and more about his physical make-up. But it is no more necessary to know this history and this physical analysis of man in order to know his characteristically human nature through introspection than it is to know the origin and physical constitution of hydrogen in order to understand its nature considered by itself.

5. Some scientists object that physical and chemical methods of analysis do not reveal anything more than physical or chemical operations in the activity of man, and this is quite true. But to then infer that therefore there are no living activities that are not of a physical or chemical nature is an obvious error in logic. A method of analysis solves only what it is designed to solve and nothing else.

6. By physical analogy we mean the comparison of the human living system to a nonliving but active physical system that we understand. For example, to compare the flow of blood in the body to the flow of water in a city water supply system is to use a physical analogy to explain a human activity. Every such analogy has its limitations, which must not be overlooked.

CHAPTER 2

1. The gravitational attraction of things for one another is proportional to their masses and inversely proportional to the square of their distance from one another. Thus it is because of the mass that each thing has as a result of the kind of thing that it is, that each thing naturally attracts, and is attracted by, other objects. To be attracted to a center of gravitation is to be passive to the agency of something else. Thus there is a passive aspect to nature as well as an active one, but it is the active one that is useful for our purpose in this discussion.

2. Certain types of activities are possible to a tree and many other types of activities are not possible. To say that a tree is *generally predetermined* is to say that since it is a tree it must do only what trees can do because of the kind of thing a tree is. Even man when he acts is limited to acting in accord with the kind of thing he is, so that when he executes his intention to act his manner of acting and the result can be predicted in a general way. Thus, if he acts to communicate his thoughts, he must use meaningful symbols or physical signs of some kind; he cannot ordinarily transmit his thoughts directly to another person.

3. A chemical substance like table sugar reacts in different ways with different reagents, and sometimes in different ways with the same reagents. Thus sugar dissolves in water and carmelizes with gentle heat. With intense heat it burns to a further state of oxidation. We do not have to test, however, to see if the sugar is ready to dissolve or to carmelize or to burn. It is always ready to react and always reacts with water and with mild and severe heating in the same ways. These ways are characteristic of the specific kind of thing that sugar is. Thus this is specific predetermination.

Notes

4. A few plants are carnivorous—they feed on animal substance. The Venus's-flytrap is an example. Bacteria and molds are plants and consume protein. Our generalization therefore is true of green plants, with some exceptions.

5. The fats and carbohydrates are principally used as fuel to supply the energy required for living activity, while proteins are the chief chemical constituents of protoplasm. The term *metabolism* signifies generally all of the chemical changes occurring in the protoplasm. Thus it includes the breaking down of food and the building up of living substance, as well as the maintaining of the supply of body fluids such as blood and cerebrospinal fluid. Most animals cannot make organic compounds from inorganic substances and therefore must eat some protein and fats to get the necessary food. The exceptions are certain chlorophyll-bearing protozoa. Green plants, however, by *photosynthesis*, can combine water and the carbon dioxide in the air to form glucose. (See Appendix 2a.)

6. The issues involved in our understanding of what living is when a part of the body is removed from its natural place in the body and kept alive under artificial conditions, and when artificial organs are inserted into the body and participate in its vital activities, is considered in Footnote 20 of Chapter 4.

7. There are analogues of living substance, considered from the point of view of a self-maintaining exchanger of energy for activity, which are quite inanimate. Thus an automobile engine exchanges the energy in hydrocarbons for useful activity of its parts, and "mechanical brains" exchange electrical energy for the manipulation of switches and reels of coded tape, and so on. These machines differ from living things in that they do not synthesize their own operating parts out of raw materials as living things do; they do not grow by themselves in size and complexity and capability but do so only by the ministrations of human agents. They also do not reproduce themselves. Thus the comparison of machines to living things as devices that exchange the energy of the environment (gasoline and electricity are the usable environment in our examples) for their own activities is corrct, but the analogy cannot go beyond that.

8. Of course we are all aware that chemical components of the human body exercise activities inimical to the body in the activity (or condition) called disease. Tissue that is diseased is not dead, although the diseased activity is often a process leading to the death and detachment from the body of the diseased part. We simply do not know what cellular disease is in relation to the coordinated activity of the whole body. Therefore for the present we must accept the fact that chemical activities and biological activities that are ordinarily subservient to the normal goals of self-maintenance, growth, and so forth, do become discoordinated and can even prove inimical to the life of the body. Cancer is an instance of this activity, in which (as far as we know to date) the activity of certain cells becomes greatly increased with ensuing multiplication of cancerous growth at the expense of noncancerous tissue.

9. Actually it is more correct to speak, for instance, of the sodium ion Na^+ and the chlorine ion Cl^- as the things that unite. Since the reaction usually involves large groups of these substances, it does not appear that any particular positive ion is predetermined to unite with one prechosen negative ion. What happens in ionic encounters is more easily visualized in solutions contained in beakers where free negative ions and free positive ions, as well as actual combinations of the two in molecules of NaCl, can be imagined. The motions of these particles in water (used as a dissolving medium for salt) do not give the impression that they are predetermined in their path. Their motions appear to be helter-skelter. Yet, until we understand why their paths in the solution are as they are, we cannot judge decisively that their motions are purely random. Our meaning, with respect to being predetermined, is that under the conditions obtaining in a solution of this kind some of the negative and positive ions must unite.

10. See the discussion of the gradual development of man's critical attitude toward explanations in Chapter 6.

11. Chemical analysis will find only chemical activity because that is all that it is looking for. In our example, digestion is a chemical process; the notion of directed activity here cannot be handled by such a method. Similarly, if an

animal falls off a cliff and is severely frightened, all that chemical analysis will reveal is the altered activity of certain chemical processes in the body; it cannot possibly reveal fright or the gravitational force that produced the fall. The fright in the animal and the gravitational attraction to the center of the earth are nonetheless real, although they are not capable of being analyzed on chemical principles.

12. The theoretical explanation of the chemical properties of the elements in terms of their outer orbital electrons is an example of giving a further explanation of the already known fact that the principle of their activities is something underlying their mere appearances. This, as later chapters will show, is characteristic of man's approach to things in his environment, for he is not content merely to recognize them, he must learn as much as he can about them. No other animal manifests this desire for knowledge.

13. St. Thomas faced the same problem in explaining how one substantial form specifies that a complex whole, such as a living thing, be of a certain kind even though the parts of the complex to some extent retain their specific identity. He felt constrained, as we do, to state the facts as observation and reason tell us to do, even though we do not understand very clearly how it is so. On the presence of the forms of the elements in a complex substantial unit, see *S.T.* I, 76, 5, ad 4, and on the presence of activities in the complex substantial unit different from those of its component parts, see *S.T.* I, 76, 1, toward the end of the article.

14. As the vitalizing principle the soul is everywhere that vital activity exists, even when the activities are heterogeneous. The activity ceases completely when some indispensable physical part malfunctions; it partially ceases when a physical part is removed from the whole and perishes. Parts other than embryonic ones, however, have been isolated from the whole and have continued to perform their special function as long as a supply of physical energy remained. This raises the question as to whether such separation results in a multiplying of souls to vitalize the separated parts. The alternative to admitting this is to hold that vital activities go on in organs that are not living.

This difficulty is also encountered in considering the ultimate living constituents of a complex organism, namely, the individual cells. Does each cell have its own soul? Each cell functions in maintaining itself at the expense of the energy contained in the chemicals that form its food. Each cell does have its own life, although this life is not separate from the living activities that can only be exercised by combinations of cells forming tissues and bones. Therefore it can function as a living unit when separated from other cells as long as it has a supply of food and as long as the other conditions necessary for its independent existence are met. In this condition the cell is not living by the soul of the substantial unit from which it was separated; it is living by its own soul. The organization of the cell's parts and their participation in living by interacting with one another are still present even though the agent conferring this organization and activity is no longer connected with it. On this matter, see Footnote 18, Chapter 4.

15. It may sound strange to one who holds the contemporary view of the universe that all activity is work requiring the expenditure of energy to read that there is activity that does not require the expenditure of energy. But the use of energy in causing activity is characteristic only of material activities in which the transition from potency to act involves the overcoming of the impediment offered by matter. In activities where no matter is involved, that is, in the immaterial activities of the intellect and will, the things known and the things desired are present to these powers in an immaterial manner; the actual exercise of these powers does not directly use any organ of the body. Consequently, the objects of thought and of volition (that is objects considered as good and not merely as suitable to us) partake of the spiritual actuality of the intellect and the will and do not have any physical actuality such as they possess when existing apart from our thought of them. The exchange of energy among the physical parts of existing things cannot be used, therefore, as an analogue of the activities of man's spiritual powers.

16. The cell is described in detail in Appendix 3a. It suffices for our explanation of protein synthesis to say that the body of an animal is made up of billions of little spots of living jelly, each of which is contained by a thin membrane and each of which contains a central part or nucleus.

17. In cell reproduction a part of the bulk of one cell becomes enclosed in its own membrane as it divides off from the remaining bulk. The two parts then live separate singular lives, although both of them are well controlled as to their place and function in the organism of which they are a part. In one-celled creatures, cell division results in their being two such creatures, each with its own cell body and nucleus.

18. The chromosome is so named because it stains deeply when injected with dye and thus becomes easily distinguishable from other parts of the cell. Experiments in the transmission of hereditary traits have led to the use of the term *gene* to stand for a factor in the chromosome that is involved in the determination of such characteristics in progeny as size and color. These factors have been isolated in the sense that the parts of the chromosome containing the hereditary factors have been isolated. The factors themselves have not been completely isolated.

19. DNA is Deoxyribonucleic acid, the name indicating that it is of the same constitution as ribonucleic acid, but with two less oxygen atoms. At first it was called simply nucleic acid, but with the discovery of ribonucleic acid another name became necessary. DNA has occupied researchers more than RNA because of its position inside the nucleus, which puts it at the physical center of trait transmission to progeny. The RNA is found mostly in the cytoplasm, but some also occurs in the nucleus.

20. St. Thomas Aquinas, following a laudable Greek and Christian tradition on the nature of man, distinguishes between the immortal soul of man and the temporal soul of non-human organisms. The souls of living creatures lesser than man are not subsistent, according to St. Thomas (*S.T.* I, 75, 3), and therefore are generated from the potentiality of matter (*S.T.* I, 118, 1). Thus the souls of brutes are corrupted when their bodies are corrupted (*S.T.* I, 75, 6).

CHAPTER 3

1. Much is known of the chemical activity that occurs in nerve-impulse transmission. To explain as much of this as the experts believe to be certain would presuppose that the reader have a highly developed knowledge of chemical

ions and ionic transfer in solutions, and of the storing and transfer of electric charges. It will suffice in explaining the physical basis of sensation to give a description of any level that is reasonably clear, for what is necessary here is a realization of how various physical activities in the parts of the body are ordered to conscious acts of sensation.

2. Many of the synaptic connections in man's nervous system, those involved in breathing and swallowing, for example, are formed before birth and follow a hereditary pattern that is pretty much the same in each person. Nevertheless, as the axons grow out from the neurons to make their contact with muscles and sense receptors they follow the easiest terrain to traverse. Hence they do not travel identical paths in every individual person, for there are many variations in the details of physical structure from one human body to another.

3. When the neuronal chain is stimulated electrically, all of the neurons in a given area are caused to discharge simultaneously, which is not how they act in natural neural processes. The application of strychnine to neurons in the brain causes them to discharge repetitively and thus give an indication of their function, but such discharging is not the same as the natural processes. The method of ablation (cutting fibers selectively, the spinal cord at its juncture with the brain, for example) reveals to some extent what the parts remaining intact after ablation can do; we can only conjecture what the severed part did.

4. For example, if an electrode is stuck through the membrane of a single nerve fiber and another placed on its surface, and the two electrodes are joined through a very sensitive galvanometer, a minute current flow can be measured. If the electrodes are connected to a very sensitive voltmeter, a measurable voltage difference can be recorded. The electrode in the interior of the cell gives a reading indicating a constant negative polarity of approximately 50 millivolts.

When another set of electrodes is set on the surface of the fiber and a current is passed between the electrodes, this current apparently travels along the fiber and reverses the polarity of the interior so that it registers positive. Once the conducted charge has passed by, the steady negative potential returns. The reversing polarity may be measured in the case of nonelectrical stimuli by attaching one microelectrode to the fiber or cell and grounding the other on the body elsewhere. The actual reversing of polarity produces a reading on a very sensitive instrument of the potential difference caused. This reading is called the *spike potential*.

There are other measurable potential differences accompanying the spike potential. No matter which method is used, the reader experienced in the theory of experiment will realize that the measurement could be of an artifact rather than of a natural phenomenon. The artifact could be caused by the interference of the measuring instrument with the natural processes.

5. The "sodium pump" theory holds that some mechanism constantly pumps sodium ions outward through the fiber membrane (making the outside of the membrane positive), until a nerve *impulse* reverses this flow. As a result of this action a concentration of positively charged sodium ions is built up momentarily inside the fiber, producing the positive polarity inside. As the *impulse* travels along the fiber, a reversal of the polarity accompanies it. The original polarity is restored at any point as soon as the charge passes that point.

The "sodium pump" explanation reconciles the two theories that the impulse is electrochemical in nature, but that the impulse travels very slowly by comparison with electromagnetic conduction (186,300 miles per second). Thus the impulse can be electrical without having to travel longitudinally through the fiber with the velocity of purely electrical impulses, for time is consumed in the chemical-ion interchange. Hence the rate of conduction of the impulse is also dependent upon this interchange, not merely upon the speed of electromagnetic radiation.

6. The entire refractory period is of about 80 milliseconds duration. The absolute refractory period is followed by a period of low susceptibility of 3 milliseconds duration when extra strong stimulation is required to trigger an impulse. This period in turn is followed by a brief period of high susceptibility to stimulus and then a brief period of low susceptibility to stimulus, respectively.

7. When more than two neurons are involved, one typical position of the third neuron is between the receptor and effector neuron. It is, in a way, an extension of the effector

neuron, but since it is located in the spinal cord, this neuron also serves as a connector with nerves running in other directions, such as to the brain or to the sympathetic ganglia.

8. A well-tested example of this activity occurs when the spinal cord of a dog has been severed just below the neck. If the dog's back is scratched gently, the flexor muscles of his hind leg contract rhythmically; if the paw of the hind limb is stimulated painfully, the flexor muscles contract vigorously to hold the paw away from the noxious stimulus. When both stimuli are applied simultaneously, the withdrawing reflex dominates the rhythmical flexing reflex, so that the noxious stimulus is avoided.

9. Nevertheless, this attempt has been made by some behaviorist psychologists who simply ignore the abundant evidence of the existence of uncoerced choice in man. In accepting only overt evidence they ignore the evidence that very many human actions are responses to needs detected by reasoning rather than responses to physical stimuli (storing food against a time of drought, for example). Furthermore, many of our needs, such as the need for knowledge, social acceptance, and moral conviction are not physical or chemical or physiological in nature. See Chapter 8 for a discussion of the true nature of habit.

10. The heart is the one exception to this classification, for cardiac muscle is like striated muscle, but the muscle fibers are cross connected so that contractions are disseminated through it in all directions rather than in just one direction.

11. The contractions would be jerky if all of the muscle fibers in a muscle contracted simultaneously. The reason why normal muscular activity is smooth even though each individual fiber twitches is that the twitches are not simultaneous in all fibers of one muscle, but are to some extent successive, and also because the rapidity of the successive twitchings enables later contractions to join with earlier ones that have not yet completely lapsed into relaxation, thus producing an even muscular motion.

All striated and smooth muscles cannot be classified as voluntary or not voluntary, respectively. Some muscles cannot be affected by the act of the will, while some can. The latter muscles, in carrying out intentions, are called voluntary—they are usually skeletal muscles. But the execution of a voluntary action entails a whole host of reflex actions. For example, to willingly take a step involves not only the deliberate lifting of one foot and setting it down, but also the simultaneous involvement of a whole series of reflex contractions and relaxations of the muscles necessary to shift the whole weight of the body to the foot not in motion.

12. Sir Charles Sherrington, a great pioneer in neural analysis, in his characteristically concise, vividly descriptive, and yet beautifully informative way of discoursing, has described the various receptors of stimuli in a way that highlights the significance of the various terms for the receptors:

> The *central* nervous system, though divisible into separate mechanisms, is yet one single harmoniously acting although complex whole. To analyse its action we turn to the receptor-organs, for to them is traceable the initiation of the reactions of the centres. . . . Multicellular animals regarded broadly throughout a vast range of animal types are cellular masses presenting to the environment a surface sheet of cells. . . . Bedded in the surface sheet are a number of *receptor* cells constituted in adaptation to the stimuli delivered by environmental agencies. The *underlying* tissues devoid of these receptors are not devoid of *all* receptor organs; they have other kinds apparently specific to them. . . . The most important of these deep adequate agents seems to be mass acting in the mode of weight and mechanical inertia involving mechanical stresses and mechanical strain. Moreover, the organism, like the world surrounding it, is a field of ceaseless change, where internal energy is continually being liberated, whence chemical, thermal, mechanical, and electrical effects appear. It is a microcosm in which forces are at work as in the macrocosm around. In its depths lie receptor-organs adapted consonantly with the changes going on in the microcosm itself, particularly in its muscles and their accessory apparatus (tendons, joints, walls of blood-vessels, and the like). There exist, therefore, two primary distributions of the receptor-organs, and each constitutes a field in certain respects fundamentally different from the other. The deep field we have called the *proprioceptive* field, because its stimuli are, properly speaking, events in the microcosm itself, and because that circumstance has important bearing upon the service of its receptors to the organism. . . . The surface receptive field is again subdivisible. It presents two divisions. Of these one lies freely open to the numberless vicissitudes and agencies of the environment.

That is to say, it is co-extensive with the so-called external surface of the animal. This subdivision may be termed the *extero-ceptive* field.

But the animal has another surface, its so-called *internal*, usually alimentary in function. This, though in contact with the environment, lies however less freely open to it. It is partly screened by the organism itself. For purposes of retaining food, digesting and absorbing it, an arrangement of common occurrence in animal forms is that a part of the free surface is deeply recessed. In this recess a fraction of the environment is more or less surrounded by the organism itself. . . . This surface of the animal may be termed the *intero-ceptive*. At its ingress several species of receptors are met with whose 'adequate' stimuli are chemical (e.g., taste organs). Lining this digestive chamber, this kitchen, the intero-ceptive surface is adapted to chemical agencies to a degree such as it exhibits nowhere else. C. S. Sherrington, *The Integrative Action of the Human Nervous System*, pages 316-317. New Haven: Yale University Press, 1952.

13. In the first stage of its development the sensory neuron had two processes extending from opposite ends of it. As the neuron developed, its surface changed so that these two processes came together and fused into one. Then this one process, extending a little way from the cell body divided into two separate processes, one of which extended to the spinal column while the other grew out to the skin. Thus the process extending to the skin originated in the same way as the axon and is to all appearances an axon. Because it regularly conducts to the cell body, it is called a dendrite.

14. A portion of the palm of the hand mapped for cold and warm spots would show areas responding only to warmth and never to cold, and vice versa. If the stimuli are made very intense, however, they cause pain; this masks the sensations of warmth or cold. Therefore, since warmth and cold are relative to the body's normal temperature, the limits within which heat and cold will produce sensations is approximately 50°C for warmth and approximately 18°C for cold. Experiment has indicated that the nerve fibers involved in our sensations of cold are quite distinct from those involved in our sensation of warmth, even though they may lie alongside of one another. But the application of heat may stimulate the cold receptors inadequately, and vice versa, giving rise to sensations of

cold and warmth when heat and cold, respectively, are being applied to the skin.

15. The cause of sound vibrations in the atmosphere is usually semirigid (the voice-causing apparatus in man) or almost rigid (musical instruments, colliding solids), but the air that transmits the vibrations to the human ear is fluid so that the strength of the vibrations is attenuated by the medium of transmission. The relatively soft vibrations of the air that are produced by speech and music making could not vibrate the fluid in the cochlea so as to set it in motion unless the bones in the inner ear strengthened them. This strengthening of the vibration occurs because the surface area of the stapes contacting the oval window is only one-twentieth of the area of the eardrum. This lessening of the area results in a twentyfold increase in the pressure per unit area. On the other hand, the hammer and anvil, which transmit the force of vibration of the eardrum, dissipate about half of it, so that the net intensification is ten times that at the eardrum.

When very loud sounds tend to damage the ear, however, the hammer, the anvil, and the stirrup bones act in a different manner than they do for ordinary sounds in order to lessen the intensity transmitted from the eardrum and thus decrease the pressure on the oval window.

16. To be aware of this blind spot, put two black marks about three inches apart on a white card and close one eye. Hold the card six inches away from the open eye with one spot straight in the line of vision ahead and the other to the left for the left eye, to the right for the right eye. Slowly move the card toward the eye, keeping the gaze fixed on the spot straight in the line of vision. As the movement proceeds the other spot will suddenly disappear, because its reflected image is striking the eye's blind spot.

17. To illustrate the relative inferiority of nonfocal vision, look fixedly at an object about three feet ahead. Note that objects to the far right and the far left can be seen but are quite difficult to describe accurately.

18. To illustrate rod vision in the absence of cone vision, have a colored object in a position to be seen but in a room devoid of illumination. The sensation accompanying the complete absence of retinal stimulation is a kind of black-

ness that by contrast with an illuminated black surface is rather dark gray. As the object is gradually illumined its features are detected but are seen as gray or light black against a black background. The illumination is now sufficient to stimulate the rods that do not detect color, but not the cones. As the illumination is intensified the cones become sensitive and the color and finer details of the object become evident.

19. From objects beyond 20 feet away, the light rays are practically parallel and do not need to be refracted through as large an angle as do the rays from objects quite close at hand. Hence, for far vision, the lens is stretched and its convexity is at its least; but, for near vision, the ligaments that hold the lens are relatively relaxed and the front face of the lens bulges out to its greatest convexity. The farthest object that we can see is determined by the size of the illumined area and the clearness of the medium between the viewed and the viewer.

20. A striking indication of this bleaching activity is given in the retina of a rabbit's eye that has been excised in a darkroom, exposed to some light, and then dissected in dim light so that the retina can be examined directly. This retina will reproduce as faithfully as a photograph a brightly illumined scene to which it is exposed. Thus, if the eye is exposed to the sunlight coming through a window, the area of the glass is etched upon its retina as a result of the bleaching of visual purple by the sun. This is crisscrossed by the unetched lines corresponding to the bars of the window.

21. Some older texts ridicule the notion of voluntary activity while more recent ones talk of the voluntary and autonomic nerve systems, explaining the latter but ignoring the former in its characteristic of responding to our desires. (For example, see D. Krech and R. Crutchfield, *Elements of Psychology*, Chapter 12. New York: Alfred A. Knopf, 1961.) These authors follow the general trend in attributing the initiation of human acts to some mysterious activity of the cerebrospinal system and putting off indefinitely the discussion of how physical and chemical activities of nerves can, or more precisely cannot, account for consciousness or consciously directed activity.

22. The dye usually kills the protoplasm, but reveals features of

internal composition and structure that we cannot easily observe otherwise. The electron microscope in its present stage of development quickly dehydrates and kills most living cells that are put into its highly evacuated observation chamber. Thus many of our observations are made upon dead cells. Some information as to the different substances within the cell can be obtained from a phase contrast microscope, which makes use of optical properties arising from the varying densities of the cell's components. Where direct and indirect observation reach their limits, we can still learn something of cellular composition by chemical analysis of the constituents of the dead cell.

CHAPTER 4

1. If there were but one man and his senses were defective in any way (by deafness or blindness), his knowledge of the universe would be restricted in the same manner as our knowledge is restricted by being limited to what our normally functioning senses can reveal. This man would err only if he attempted to go beyond what the normal senses revealed to him with certainty. Thus if he denied the existence of sound (he being deaf) by affirming that there are no determinate activities of things other than those that he senses, he would be in the same position as a person who denies that there are any determinate activities of things over and above those sensed by a person having full use of all his senses. One who alleges that there are no radio waves because he cannot sense them would be an example. Man has discovered other determinate activities of matter than those he senses, such as the electrical phenomena accompanying all sensation.

2. The three primary colors are red, green, and blue. Cases of color blindness in which *no* color can be seen are very rare. Persons suffering from this achromatism see colored objects as black and white and gray. Persons suffering from dichromatic vision are blind to red or green. But most cases of defective color vision do not involve total blindness to a color but rather subnormal detection of red or green. Since there is no universally accepted theory of color vision at present, there can be no universally accepted explanation of the causes of color blindness.

3. What new terms might be introduced is hard to imagine. Their use would cause difficulties because electromagnetic radiations and the other physical stimuli, which are mysterious emanations produced by the excitation of invisible particles, are essentially less well known to us than are the apprehensions of the senses that we customarily call color, and so on.

4. "A sensation can never be described in physical terms; such a statement is meaningless." M. A. Wenger, F. N. Jones, and M. H. Jones, *Physiological Psychology*, page 69. New York: Holt, Rinehart and Winston, 1956.

5. The physical nature of the stimulus can be made clear by the explanations given by physics. The psychological attributes of sensation, or "dimensions of sensation," according to Wenger, Jones, and Jones, are chiefly quality and intensity: "The first and most obvious dimension is quality. This is the unique characteristic which differentiates psychologically among different senses, as sound from color or warmth; and among different aspects of a single sense, as salt from sweet or red from blue. It cannot be defined verbally; it can only be pointed to.

   The second dimension represents the "moreness" or "lessness" of a particular quality—a faint sound or a loud sound of the same pitch, a light red or a dark red of the same hue, a slight warmth or a great warmth. Intensity may thus vary independently of quality." Wenger, Jones, and Jones, *op. cit.*, page 72.

6. Other stimuli, such as rubbing the eyes with the hands, and sustaining a blow on the head, agitate the parts of the receptor. This is often accompanied by visual sensations, such as seeing patches of color and "seeing stars." These stimuli, however, are not adequate to produce recognition of the stimulus as an object of sensation. The stimulus in question is recognized through touch. The images aroused in this way have no profitable import for the person in whom they arise, because no distinct object of perception is attained; nor is the cause of these visual phenomena detected through them by the intellect, as is the case for fully conscious intentional apprehension.

7. Size, shape, and the like, which are called *common sensibles*, are midway between *accidental sensibles* and *proper sensibles*, which are the objects of the senses. For the proper

sensibles first, and of their very nature, affect the senses, since they are the qualities that cause alteration. But the common sensibles are reducible to quantity. As to size and number, it is clear that they are species of quantity. Shape is a quality about quantity, since the nature of shape consists in fixing the bounds of magnitude. Movement and rest are sensed according as the subject is affected in one or more ways in the magnitude of the subject or of its local distance, as in the movement of growth or locomotion, or again, as it is affected in some sensible qualities, as in the movement of alteration; and thus, to sense movement and rest is, in a way, to sense one thing and many. Now quantity is the proximate subject of the qualities that cause alteration, as surface is of color. Therefore the common sensibles do not move the senses first and of their own nature, but by reason of the sensible quality—as the surface by reason of color. Yet they are not accidental sensibles, for they produce a certain diversity in the immutation of the senses. For sense is immuted differently by a large and a small surface, since whiteness itself is said to be great or small, and therefore is divided according to its proper subject. *S.T.* I, 78, 3, ad 2.

8. For a full treatment of the nature, attributes, and sciences of quantity, see F. J. Collingwood, *The Philosophy of Nature.* Englewood Cliffs: Prentice Hall, 1960.

9. If some marvelous surgeon could transplant the nerve endings from the optic nerve to some other part of the brain than where it naturally terminates, we should confidently expect (if functioning of the eye were not impaired) that the stimulation of the eye by color would still evoke the sensation of color. The only other conceivable possibility is that the central nervous system portion of the organ would be mutilated so that it could only report contact, that is, give an awareness of touch. (The contact produced by light striking the retina would be very slight.) How could it possibly be accompanied by sensations of hearing if the afferent nerve ends were transplanted to the area of the brain where the auditory nerves normally terminates, since the receptor is not adapted to receiving sounds?

As further evidence for maintaining the position that the brain alone is the location of sensed qualities, some physiologists allege that because the stimulation of an afferent sensory nerve in between the end organ and the central nervous system produces in the subject an awareness like that produced when the end organ is being stimulated naturally, it is evident that the CNS is the organ for differentiating between the various sensations. This argument would be conclusive only if the artificial stimulus evoked sensations of color in a person who was totally blind from birth, or of sound in a person who was totally deaf from birth. But this line of argument is futile, because it is already well known that defects in the receptor organs of sight and of hearing greatly modify the sensation. Thus longsightedness and shortsightedness are known to be due to abnormalities in the size of the eyeball. These abnormalities do not affect the nerve impulse to the central nervous system. Therefore, although the nerve impulse is the same as in that of a person having normal sight the vision is defective. This would not be so if the function of the stimulus receptor were not all important to the kind of sensation aroused. The facts of color blindness and of deafness lead to the same conclusion.

10. The brain is believed to be the center of sensory activities such as remembering and imagining, because afferent fibers from the sense receptors terminate there. There is no possibility, however, of a person's discerning one or another part of his own brain as an organ for sense memory or for some other internal sense. Thus spatial distinctness cannot be used here as a criterion for distinguishing various senses, as it can be for distinguishing external senses. Physiology, however, has long been concerned with the localizing of sensory and motor functions in the brain. Nevertheless, physiologists cannot claim to have been successful in locating *one* area used exclusively for *one* sense although the malfunction of a certain part of the cortex, through the presence of a tumor, for example, can very definitely be accompanied by loss of the use of a sense.

11. M. A. Wenger, F. N. Jones, and M. H. Jones, *Physiological Psychology*, page 6. New York: Holt, Rinehart and Winston, 1956.

12. To treat the will here would be to add one more to an already

large number of distinctions. The will and its acts will be discussed in detail from Chapter 7 onward.

13. Occasionally there are afterimages in vision, which do not last very long and usually require some kind of concentration to be attained. Thus, if a person experiences a very intense light, the immediate afterimage is a changing *sequence of colors:* purples, blues, yellows, greens, and so on. A glance directly at the high sun will produce this phenomenon, but care must be exercised because the eye is easily damaged by direct sunlight. *Positive aftersensations* may occur following a brief glance at a fairly intensely lighted scene. They fade quickly and are not easy to produce. In *negative after-sensations*, produced after long stimulation of the retina, the hues of the visual scene are reversed. Thus a red book will appear fleetingly as a green one when the gaze is turned to a blank white or light gray surface. In negative after-sensations the objects seen appear in their complementary color. Red and green, orange and light blue, yellow and indigo, are complementary colors. All of these afterimages seem to be accounted for by the refractory period of the cones sensitive to diverse colors (negative afterimages) and the chemical reaction in the cones that outlast the duration of the direct stimulus (positive afterimages and sequence of colors).

14. "Now, although the first immutation (production of an impression) of the imagination is through the agency of the sensible, since *the phantasm is a movement produced in accordance with sensation*, nevertheless, it may be said that there is in man an operation which by division and composition forms images of various things, even of things not perceived by the senses." *S.T.* I, 84, 6, ad 2.

15. Values are neither proper nor common sensibles. An account of their occurrence and role in sensory life will be given later in this chapter.

16. Obviously the imagination *is* concerned with what is actually present when it is receiving an impression, but our attention is directed to what we are actually sensing. Or we may compare it with what we have sensed. The imagination cannot imagine what we are actually sensing, because the retention of what we are sensing occurs automatically. We may, however, attend to the present sensible with

great care so as to assimilate the details very exactly and thus have a better retained impression than we would have had otherwise. Thus when we attend to our imagination it is to something that depicts what we are not directly sensing now.

17. For example, the color of the stairs he walked upon, the sound made by passing automobiles, the warmth of his office as he entered from the chilly outdoors, are the sensible factors that registered upon him but attracted his attention so slightly that he could not recall them.

18. Examples of this truth range the whole gamut of human experience. A colored light is reflected by a mirror but absorbed by an opaque surface and the retina of an eye; a person with a good memory and an interest in a subject can retain all of the technical data required to master it, while another person with a poor memory or no interest in the topic can attend the same course and remember very few of the details; a mathematician can appreciate a proof that another person cannot begin to fathom. Even in the realm of belief and opinion we can see that one who knows the fallibility of human authority will not be moved by the opinion of so-called experts, whereas a credulous person will give ready assent to almost any statement that is proposed by a "name." In every case the nature and condition of the receiver is the important factor.

19. We are begging the question here to the extent that we have already asserted the existence of the common power of sense as the one that identifies the common object of sense and touch. But he who accepts the objectivity of neuronal and cortical analyses that fail to turn up images must be just as realistic in realizing that the act of sensing very, very seldom apprehends images.

20. The question may well be raised here as to how far the influence of soul is to extend in explaining the minute details of living activity. As a general principle we can say that any activities of the chemical components that are not the same as they are outside of a living body must have this difference because the soul has subordinated them to its purpose. This means that the living activity of the most insignificant cell, inasmuch as that cell was produced in and through the living activity of the whole

body, is living by the vital activity of the soul. If the cell is an expendable one whose being as a cell is destroyed in some vital activity, the remains are nonliving. The same is true for whole organs. As long as they function as an integral part of the living body, they are alive by the activity of the soul.

Is the very form of the organ due to the formative activity of the soul? This much is sure—the shape and function of an individual organ is due to the quantity and kind of cells of which it is composed. Since all of these cells developed from one embryo, they were formed and moved to their respective function as this organ by the same vital principle that initiated the first division of cells at the beginning of growth of the embryo. It is therefore evident that the soul dominates all of the chemicals that enter into the body, but in varying degrees. The cells forming the parts of the vital organs have their specific forms and functions from the activity of soul—some body fluids, such as cellular protoplasm, are alive; and some cells and fluids, such as the contents of the bladder, are not alive. The latter are dominated only as to their whereabouts, whereas the living fluids and living solid parts of the body are not only situated where they are but also are what they are primarily by the activity of soul. Even so, they retain to some degree the chemical nature of their constituents. This is where our understanding is balked.

How can a chemical compound, a protein molecule for example, manifest both chemical and living activities simultaneously? Is "living" at one level simply chemical activity somewhat like the self-replicating activity of the DNA molecule, and at another level conscious awareness, and at the rational level deliberate thought? The unity of being and of activity in a healthy person seems to demand this diversity of activity on the part of one soul, rather than the positing of various life principles. The malignancies of a diseased body (cancerous tissue, for example), which grow contrary to the normal activity of body cells, seem to indicate the activity of a source of energy not dominated by soul, for no agent acts in one way and in a contrary way simultaneously. Perhaps the basic chemical activity is directed in accord with the spontaneous activities because of the natures of the chemicals involved, but not so dominated by soul that interference with those chemical activities cannot bring about reactions contrary to health.

21. The muscle of a frog's leg will continue to exhibit nerve impulsing under electrical stimulation even after the muscle has been removed from the frog. The frog will not be conscious of it, however, and the muscle will deteriorate after a while. The continued impulsing is carried on by the chemical energy of the parts of the muscle and its innervation. This continued impulsing does not prove, as some persons have maintained, that the body is a machine whose parts are wholes by themselves; so that although the machine cannot make use of the separated part, the part retains its integrity. What the facts do prove is that the chemical constituents of muscle and nerve fibers, and the cells that are the living parts of these fibers, are so organized by the soul that they carry on their reflex activities in a purely electrochemical fashion, as long as the deteriorating chemical compounds of the excised tissue have not yet destroyed the physical basis for such conduction.

Theoretically the same organ could be used by the soul or some other nonsoul-organizing form to carry on purely physical and chemical activity. But no organ could have awareness apart from the activity of the soul. Corneal transplanting from the eye of one person to another indicates the indifference of the power of sight to the numerical identity of the organ that it uses. When the skill of the surgeon becomes adequate, other parts of organs, and even some whole organs, will be transplanted from one human body to another. There is no expectation at present, however, that man will succeed in making an artificial organ with such fidelity to the original that it could replace the original in its compactness and in every one of its functions. There are mechanical hearts, lungs, and kidneys that perform much the same work as the natural organs, but they are rather cumbersome and cannot be carried around as personal equipment.

As far as theory goes, man knows of no reason now that would prevent the devising of artificial organs that could function as well as the originals. None of these substitutions for the original equipment of the body would have any implications for the personal self-identity of the individual, although they could greatly improve the health or activities of an individual and consequently alter his outlook and some of his habits. As we have indicated in Chapter 2, and shall explain in more detail in the later chapters of this book, the basic unalterable seat of selfhood for an individual person is his conscious power that transcends the limitations of the body as material.

22. The famous neurosurgeon Wilder Penfield, in collaboration with Lamar Roberts, a neurosurgeon and expert on speech defects, produced a very readable book on *Speech and Brain-Mechanisms*, Princeton University Press, 1959, in which they reported the effects of cortical stimulation (among other subjects). If the reader perseveres through the technical language of physiology to read the results of studies of stimulation and their interpretation, he will realize how close is the accord between our account of the actions of the sensory powers and their reality, and the contemporary account of what goes on in man's consciousness to the accompaniment of the physiological activity of the brain. A few brief excerpts follow (Penfield and Roberts, pages 45-46; 54):

> When electrical stimulation recalls the past, the patient has what some of them have called a "flash-back." He seems to re-live some previous period of time and is aware of those things of which he was conscious in that previous period. It is as though the stream of consciousness were flowing again as it did once in the past. Heraclitus said, "We never descend twice into the same stream." But the patient seems to do it. The stream is partially the same but he is aware of something more. He has a double consciousness. He enters the stream of the past and it is the same as it was in the past, but when he looks at the banks of the stream he is aware of the present as well.

> We interpret this as functioning of memory and general sensory consciousness. A little further on, an instance is cited of the effect on a patient's consciousness of stimulation by an electrode inserted into a specific part of the temporal lobe of the brain.

> "Oh, a familiar memory—in an office somewhere. I could see the desks. I was there and someone was calling to me —a man leaning on a desk with a pencil in his hand." All

the details of those things to which she had paid attention in some previous period of time were still there. Perhaps the pencil in his hand had seemed important, but other images that must have reached her retina during the original experience are now lost, probably because they were ignored originally.

Every individual forms a neuronal record of his own stream of consciousness. Since artificial reactivation of the record, later in life, seems to recreate all those things formerly included within the focus of his attention, one must assume that the re-activated recording and the original neuronal activity are identical. . . . One might suppose that originally, like a strip of film, its meaning was projected on the screen of man's awareness, and somehow it was held in place there for a brief time of consideration before it was replaced by subsequent experience and subsequent neuronal patternings.

Consciousness, "forever flowing" past us, makes no record of itself, and yet the recording of its counterpart within the brain is astonishingly complete. This counterpart, made up of the passing of potentials through the ever-changing circuits of final integration, is recorded in temporal succession between the experience that went before and that which follows.

CHAPTER 5

1. To indicate explicitly which internal sense is involved in the various steps preceding abstraction would seriously complicate the explanation. Therefore by "experience" we mean the accumulated information possessed by the cogitative power and its memory, by "memory" we mean imagination as a storehouse of appearances and also the memory for the cogitative power. We hope that the context will make clear which power is involved in each instance of the use of this term.

2. Of course there is more to know about the apple. A whole new field of knowledge is opened up when we begin analyzing the organic compounds out of which it is composed. These compounds when isolated, however, are no longer "apple."

3. The notion of substantiality as self-existing is not given at all by the senses. It seems inevitable, however, that one who first learns the philosophical definition of substance will identify it with the solidity of that which is the source of the sensibles that impinge upon our senses and thus initiate our knowing activities.

Notes

4. We recognize that the term "complex" as applied to composites of chemical elements in contrasting them with single elements is not quite accurate, because each atom of each element is known to be a complex of parts.

5. The subject of natures, their regularity and their transformations, is treated extensively in F. J. Collingwood, *The Philosophy of Nature*. Englewood Cliffs, N. J.: Prentice Hall, 1960.

6. Note the opinion of St. Thomas on this subject: "Therefore we must say in accordance with the Philosopher, that the forms of the elements remain in the mixed body, not actually, but virtually. For the proper qualities of the elements remain, though modified; and in these qualities is the power of the elementary forms." See *S.T.* I, 76, 4, ad 4.

7. In St. Thomas's discussion of cogitative power and memory, the preparation of the phantasm is a work ascribed to these two powers and to imagination. It is very difficult to say what a phantasm is if we ascribe its possession to only one power. The imagination is often mentioned as being the power presenting the phantasm for abstraction. But if this were so, nothing about time or concrete value considerations could be presented for intellectual consideration. Therefore St. Thomas's discussion of the acts of the cogitative power and its memory must be construed to indicate that the phantasm is presented by these powers, as well as by the imagination. For an interesting discussion of the role of cogitative and memory according to St. Thomas, confer two articles by Julien Peghaire on the cogitative sense in Volume 20 of *The Modern Schoolman*.

8. Some sciences are purely mathematical, since they have no concern with material being whatever. Some are mathematico-physical, for they use a predominantly mathematical method of analysis. Others also use mathematics in the investigation of their subject but less extensively, as an auxiliary aid to their main aim of studying the *nature* and properties of the subject. According to this distinction, physics is a mathematico-physical science, while physiology is a physical science.

9. For a succinct statement on varieties of abstraction, confer *S.T.* I, 85, 1, ad 2.

10. Although man indicates the differences in spoken words by the manipulation of his various voice-producing organs and thus uses naturally occurring sounds, he far surpasses any other creature in the variations that he can achieve by combining the different sounds that he can produce. He thus translates his understandings into voice modulations which by common agreement take on meaning. Some other creatures may communicate by sound modulations, but their range of communication is quite limited and is of quite practical import if their activities are a reliable sign. Only man uses artificial symbols formed from letters over and over again to impart an endless fund of information.

Man makes use of natural signs to a very large extent but not as a means of communication with other men. Rather natural signs, such as those specific to various kinds of chemical elements, are the means by which man ferrets out the various aspects of the intelligibility of material being.

11. Consider how the young child, who connects sounds with meanings, has to work hard at learning letters and words and their correlation with the familiar sounds that denote recognition, and to some extent, meaning. This is a sure indication of the nonspontaneity of the imagination's act of learning spelling and reading.

12. Belief and reasonable convictions depend upon the will; consequently they are considered in Chapter 8.

CHAPTER 6

1. Although instruments have far outstripped the individual human senses in the discriminating of very fine (submicroscopic) and very large (extramicroscopic) sensibles such as electrons and galaxies, nevertheless the instruments must be such that ultimately they can be read accurately by the unaided human senses and that their information can be cognized as apprehensions of proper and common sensibles.

2. As a sign of the key role played by the notions of *being* and *having* consider the facility in understanding a foreign tongue that is acquired by a person who mastered a knowledge of the verbs "to be" and "to have," and who proceeds to acquire the proper and common names of

things by merely pointing to them questioningly in the presence of one who knows the language.

3. Theoretically we would not need to define anything by the use of negations if the human intellect had progressed further in discerning the natures of things. Thus just any random characterization of something by a negation will not illustrate our point, for a positive way of designating this may be found after a little effort. However, we are safe in the example that we have given, for no one has satisfactorily defined "the straight" and its characterization as the noncurved is still acceptable.

4. By general power of sense we do not discriminate real from imaginary existence, but we do distinguish the actual sensing of something from the act of imagining something. This is the basis upon which we can then distinguish actual existence as a sensible from merely imaginary existence.

In the explanation of the interplay of senses and intellect in the act of judging about singulars, we did not include the role of the general power of sense for the sake of keeping the discussion from becoming too complicated. However, in its function as common root of all the other senses its act accompanies any act of theirs and consequently any intellectual act concerned with singulars.

5. Western civilization with its roots in Greek and Roman culture, has been selected for illustration because it is the one with which most readers will have had some acquaintance.

One of the great benefits brought about by man's use of his critical judgment is the present tremendous expansion of practical knowledge beyond that developed by the Greeks. In Archimedes' day there were practical arts concerned with the adapting of matter to serve man's immediate needs, as we have construction trades and food-supplying trades today. The Greek attitude toward the elements in man's environment that could not be put to immediate use of was one of wonder. Although earlier philosophers had left a legacy to the Greeks of Archimedes' era, and consequently to succeeding eras that inherited Greek culture, whereby they insisted upon the mutability of matter and recognized the practical sciences that order matter to man's benefit, nevertheless only over a period of many centuries did the obvious implications of this teaching come to be fully realized by Western society. For surely, if all material things are mutable, then man who dominates some material objects with ease need only seek out the ways in which all of the objects in his environment can be brought under his control. It involves man's utilization of the mutability of matter in order to learn how events in our experience come about. Other factors, of course, were involved in the gradual development of the notion that man should control matter for his own uses, but that such an attitude prevails in science today and that it has resulted from man's questioning of his relationship to nonhuman things is clear.

6. Where the phenomenon being investigated is primarily a matter of locomotion, a mechanical model of the path of the motion can often reveal the salient essential factors involved. For example, a man knowing the spherical shape of the earth and examining a model of the apparent motion of the sun around the earth can see that the sun necessarily causes six months of daylight at the North Pole when north of the equator and six months of darkness by its absence when it is south of the equator.

7. In the time of Pythagoras men thought of the sun as a ball of flaming fire. They probably reasoned this way: Fire produces light with heat, whereas luminiscents like fireflies produce light without heat; therefore, since light with heat is fire, the sun which radiates light and heat must be fire. Of course, this reasoning from terrestrial sources of heat and light to the nature of the sun was only tentative, because the dependence of the existence of light and heat upon flaming fire was not known to be absolutely necessary; in our contemporary knowledge of energy transfer we can produce light and heat without any accompanying flames. If one considers the primitive state of reasoned knowledge about natural events in Pythagoras' time, it seems impossible for those who talked and wrote about such matters to avoid the error of identifying the source of light and heat, the sun, with flames. Nevertheless, the fundamental principle that the sun must be understood to be the kind of thing that produced the effects on earth it *did* produce was firmly respected. The error arose be-

cause of the invincible ignorance of the men of the time as to the various chemical processes that emit heat and light.

8. Near the town of Montignac in Southwestern France is the famous Lascaux cave in which are drawings believed to be approximately 20,000 years old. The drawings were made on a white background on the sides and ceilings of the cave, which consists of chambers and connecting passages. The markings were made with charcoal and natural earths combined with animal fat. The figures for the most part are skillfully portrayed bulls and horses.

9. The universal attribution of some predicate to a subject was a source of controversy among some of the early commentators on the logical works of Aristotle, in which the necessity of universal statements to prove something to be necessarily so is first set down. The controversy may be found today in various textbooks of symbolic logic in which the authors accept from Aristotle the notions of what a valid sequence is and what logical proof is, but differ from Aristotle in their attitude that it is incorrect to hold that *A* propositions can say that something exists. Our analysis of the composition and division aspects of judgments shows that *A* propositions do not differ from any other propositions in this respect that they represent a combination or separation of aspects of that which is being thought about. They do not have the ability to indicate existence unambiguously, for the use of the verb "to be" without qualification as to the mode of existence that is being discussed signifies only a grouping of words. It is true to say that the expression, "If *x* is a man, then *x* is rational," does not indicate whether or not men exist as material beings or as imaginary constructs. However, the expressions, "There are some *x*'s who are men" and "There are some men," do not indicate whether men exist as material beings or as mere imaginary constructs, either. The verb copula of a proposition cannot indicate a mode of existence unless it is qualified by words that do this.

10. Anyone can easily duplicate another example. On a moonless but starry night a person with dark-adapted vision observing a bright star may detect a little twinkle of light near the right or left limit of his range of vision.

When he directs his gaze to this spot he does not see the light; therefore he can only judge that he had a visual impression but cannot understand what caused it. If he begins to experiment and succeeds in getting the view of the twinkle again, only to have it vanish when he gazes directly at it, he will be sure of what his vision is detecting but will be nonplussed as to what is producing the twinkle of light detected by his peripheral vision. A physiologist can explain that the rods of the retina, which are much more sensitive to light than the cones, are much more numerous on the outer edges of the retina and can detect sources of light that are too faint to stimulate the cones. The cones, which predominate in the fovea centralis, are the center of focus of the lens when a person gazes directly at something. If the person lacks this explanation, he will simply fail to penetrate beyond the notion of the twinkle's being a visual phenomenon. The case is the same here as with the senses which act because a stimulus is present to move them to act. If the intellect acts so as to abstract from experience, then the being of the experience at least is attained to.

11. The process of assimilating verbal teaching is not guaranteed to be smooth and likable. The facts of experience are irresistible, but the facts as reported can seem highly irrelevant and unimportant and therefore a chore to learn. The fact is that the growth of desires to do and to have many things that are not really essential for our daily existence often outpaces our intellectual love of knowledge for its practical utility and for its own sake. Now, judgment is drawn to pronounce upon objects of desire as upon that which is vitally important. It is impossible to realize that our insistent desires are in conflict with verbalized codes of conduct without exercising a critical judgment in order to decide which is better to follow. The code of conduct enforced by respect for what is hard, hot, and otherwise unpleasant also has its pleasurable side, inasmuch as we are naturally attracted to what appears pleasant to us whether it is really good for us or not. Thus conflict between what we want and what we have been told is right is inevitable and with it the *necessity* of deciding which authority to obey. As a consequence critical judgment in practical matters is apt to arise early

as the system of beliefs that served as initial guides to action gradually gives way to practical certitude about how to gain desired ends.

12. Although the old adage reads "Seeing is believing" and stresses the convincing power of a confrontation of the actual experiencing upon which a statement is based, "Reading and hearing are believing" better describes what actually does take place in the assimilation of information by contemporary man.

13. The fact of verbal apprehension is a witness to the tremendous capabilities of man as a knower. The ability to store data and to recall the tremendous number of verbal signs involved in language attests to the abilities of our memory, and the versatility of the intellect as a power of apprehension is clearly illustrated when a person reads any paragraph of writing that he easily understands. He immediately translates the symbols on the page into meanings, without the intermediation of any visual or otherwise sensory rememberings, and locates immediately and exactly the place (for want of a better term) in his thoughts where the new knowledge is to go to be incorporated with what he already understands. Thus, in the duration of one minute he assimilates dozens of concepts and relations between things, between concepts, and between concepts and things. Moreover, one word can symbolize and produce an understanding of countless things that have in common their being material or substantial, and so forth.

CHAPTER 7

1. The part of the brain called the hypothalamus has been experimented upon slightly in nonhuman animals. A lesion produced in one area of this organ is followed by an increase in consumption of a food; a lesion produced in a different area is followed by a decrease in food consumption. Spasms of pain, which we call hunger pangs, occur in the stomach; the parching sensation often called thirst is located in the pharynx, the organ that forces the food we have finished chewing into the esophagus (the canal leading to the stomach). The secretion of saliva is produced by putting food into the mouth and is therefore

an *unconditioned reflex* activity, whereas the mouth watering evoked by seeing or smelling food (or imagining its appearance, smell, or taste) is a reflex activity dependent upon prior experience and is therefore a *conditioned reflex* activity. See C. H. Best and N. B. Taylor, *The Living Body*, 4th ed., pages 348-49. New York: Holt, Rinehart and Winston, Inc., 1958.

2. We could construct a hypothetical case of a human child in a primitive society being left to fend for himself. Then his muscle and limb movements would probably be directed to touching the distressed areas of throat and mouth. He could thereby discover that moisture from his hands felt moist to his tongue and be moved to apply other moisture that is not salty to the relief of thirst. Similar actions with solids could relieve hunger; then the child could profit from the experience of the effectiveness of these activities. This hypothesis is given only to illustrate the logical conclusion of our line of analysis, namely, that nothing in the appearances of things indicates their suitability as nourishment until experience has discerned this suitability, and some actions must occur, no matter how tentative or unsuccessful, before any estimation of their usefulness can be made. Our example is hypothetical, of course, because no infant abandoned to its own resources could survive. Some experienced guardian would have to fend for it.

CHAPTER 8

1. If he is a very dear friend we will be much more impressed with what is beneficial to him than if he were merely an acquaintance, for we tend to consider that which is beneficial to those whom we love as though in benefiting them it benefits us. Prior to the consideration, however, there is the decision to pay attention to the importance of what we remember, which is essentially allowing ourselves to be distracted from the pastime that we are enjoying. It is easily seen from this example that there are many prior acts of the intellect and will that have a bearing upon any one act singled out to illustrate a point. In the present instance they do not need to be considered, but it must be kept in mind that often a presently occur-

ring act has entailments that go far into the past and consequences that may last far into the future.

2. Many factors are involved in the development of right reason in each person. Certainly the experience that a person has had as a doer is a powerful influence upon what he considers to be suitable to a human agent. Experience with successful actions that brought about rewarding attainments tends to confirm the original guess that such actions would be beneficial. On the other hand, experience with unsuccessful actions and with only apparently desirable ends establishes an attitude that such activities and ends are unsuitable personally, and perhaps for every man. For the unreflective person *what is right* will be determined largely in this manner and by the mores of the various social groups to which he belongs. The person who reflects upon the character of his deliberate actions, however, will establish in his way of thinking degrees of suitableness of various ends for human activity, as well as an understanding of why the mores of a particular group of people are adopted. In short, by reflection upon the possible goals of human action in terms of man's potentialities and certain inevitable facts of life and death, a set of judgments that we call right reason becomes evident to all who so reflect.

The set of judgments as to what is truly suitable to man may differ from one individual to another according to the number of indispensable necessities for life he takes into consideration and especially according to his judgment as to what comprises happiness for man. Thus a person who considers only food and drink and the avoidance or suppression of enemies to be indispensable necessities for the prolongation of life may have a cavalier attitude toward the rules of society concerning overt acts inimical to the common good or he may simply have no respect for them at all, obeying them because it is customary to do so. Such a person may adopt any one of many possible criteria as to what is truly best for him which could be shown to be false inasmuch as they do not include the individual rights of all members of society or the good of society as a unit. He may set out to victimize other human beings and society for his own gain by acting as a thief (robber, counterfeiter, confidence man, blackmailer, and so forth) or a lecher, thus attempting to obtain in ways that other people know to be wrong the two goods (physical sustenance and sex) that are indispensable necessities in the prolongation of the life of the human race. When degenerate men abandon spiritual values for fleshly pursuits they turn their attention to the goods that money can buy, or to money itself as representing those goods, and to the intense pleasures associated with sex. They thus indicate what things rank highest in importance to their animal nature, namely, the gratification of hunger for food and sexual activity. On the other hand, the person who is instructed on the basis of rights and duties and receives the instruction favorably is capable of discriminating the falseness of the various erroneous criteria that may be used by others and of opposing his will to theirs in the preservation of those ways of acting that are suitable to the rights of individual persons and to the preservation and enhancement of the societal groups of which they are members.

Despite the variety of ways in which the set of judgments that is right reason exists in various individuals, it is possible for anyone who reflects upon man's make-up and upon the indispensable requirements of those who live as members of a society to see the goals of human action that are absolutely desirable and to distinguish the best way of attaining these goals from inferior ways of attaining them according to the circumstances of the times in which a person lives. (See *S.T.* I, II, 94, 2 for a concise summary of the human inclinations upon which right reason must be exercised.)

The exercise of right reason in an individual person's daily life is not restricted to the consideration of actions directed to the physical maintenance of life and societal obligations; rather it is involved in all of our doings, for we always intend to act for what we judge to be the best under the circumstances. From this point of view right reason is the ability of reason to discern the true value of things as distinct from their merely apparent attractiveness or repulsiveness. In many cases it involves corporate activities, for example, in classifying drugs as harmful in some instances and beneficial in others. And in general the whole human effort to subject the environment to human usefulness involves the use of right reason to distinguish true benefits from merely apparent ones.

3. Far from being a contradiction to our previously stated principles governing the distinction of powers, the ability of the cogitative to be influenced by rational considerations attests to the unity of man through his various powers. Thus in looking for a two-leaf clover we know what we want although we have not seen it yet, since all of the ones we have scrutinized in the last half hour have had three leaves. We can have what we are looking for by pulling one leaf off a three-leaf clover, and then we have no difficulty in recognizing what we are looking for. What we recognized in a sensory way was a multi-segmented green solid having a characteristic shape which we identify by the word "clover." In an intellectual way we recognized in the sensory cognition the elements contained in the meaning of which "clover" is a verbal sign and among those elements a multiplicity corresponding to two.

When our intellectual consideration modifies an estimation of our cogitative sense it modifies not the content of the sensory apprehension of singulars (this cannot be altered although the impression retained in the imagination can be altered at will), but rather the aspect of desirability that depends on the "image" of ourself, the basis for determining which of the contents of sensation is suitable. That image is used in acts of evaluation which give to the contents of sensation (apart from those that evoke desires spontaneously) an aspect of desirability, or the opposite, in terms of what is suitable to the image. In some respects the image can easily be modified by imagining an unwelcome scene, such as the writhing and grimacing that are signs of pain, and associating a pictured disaster with the personal image. In other instances in which spiritual values are involved the personal image cannot be modified so as to include them. Thus the act of slaking thirst by consuming an orange has a pleasurable aspect which is not altered by the consideration that it is someone else's orange obtained by theft. The sense power can be habituated to following rational counsel, however, so that it does not continue to consider the object of desire even though it still exists as desirable.

4. Other examples of this come easily to mind, for instance, a consideration of a general kind by the intellect *that every kind of injustice is morally evil* can cause a feeling

of hateful vengeance which we had directed to wreaking some serious loss on another person to fade away before it is effective; and the knowledge that "All temporal things pass away" can mitigate the passion of sorrow considerably. In general the larger viewpoint entertained by reason can lessen the force of passion or contrariwise in its realization of the true enormity of an injury or affront or threat it can strengthen the passion. (Confer St. Thomas *S.T.* I, 81, 3.)

5. There are many other examples that illustrate how the concomitance of phenomena serves as a ground for our belief in their connectedness even though we do not have the assurance of knowing what the connectedness consists of. All gravitational phenomena are such examples.

6. Since knowledge and virtue are not subsistent beings but are rather qualities that inhere in subsistent beings, we do not will good to them as though they could acquire more perfection, for they cannot do so. Any love of knowledge and virtue other than that of assent to their goodness is either a love of desire by which we want to be united with them and begin the activities appropriate to producing them in ourselves, or the benevolent love by which we will them as goods to be possessed by someone else and set about showing him how to acquire them, and then help him to attain them. It is in the tendency toward such intangible goods as knowledge and virtue that the distinction between mere assent and actual desire are most easily noted introspectively, since the actual work of acquiring these goods is difficult and no amount of merely assenting to them as good will move us one bit closer to their possession than before we so assented.

7. We often entertain a powerful desire for a good that is attainable by man but not at the present. For example, a youth can desire now to be the best high jumper or president of his country even though he does not know whether he will have the means of attaining these goals when the time arrives. His belief that he can accomplish them, however, is sufficient warranty for his desire to be the best athlete or president, until the issue is actually decided.

We can wish to have been a friend of some great person who is now dead but we cannot desire it in such a way that the desire can bring the friendship about. We can desire effectively only those things that are possible. Ineffective wishing may be a very strong affection of the will, equal in intensity to effective desiring; nevertheless, the wishing is ineffective as long as the means of attainment are impossible.

8. There are many kinds of utility that can serve as a bond of friendship. One common utility is that which satisfies the need of human beings to share their woes and joys with someone who is understanding and sympathetic. Another is that which answers to the necessity for cooperation between various individuals striving physically for a common goal. Without reasonably generous cooperation and mutual tolerance of individual differences (that is, friendliness) between such coworkers, the end in view will be difficult or impossible to achieve. The belief in the value of the end is the basis for amiability here.

9. Appearances can be deceiving, for a person may appear to act laudably with admirable intentions and yet be merely "keeping up a front." The adage, "You can tell what kind of person a man is by the friends he keeps" has some validity because without reciprocal admiration there is no bond. The presence of a bond of friendship indicates an admiration for some qualities in the friend and a ready tolerance of the remaining qualities.

10. Friendship involves communication between friends and the sharing of interests and activities. These sharings are time-consuming and by that very fact self-limiting. Because of this, it is not usually possible to cultivate an affectionate friendship over distances of space and time, which keep would-be friends from communicating with one another. Many an apparently unbreakable friendship dissolves quickly when distance barriers make its continuance difficult. Such friendships are quite tenuous because they are based upon such frail connections as having a common dwelling or working place.

11. There is no one in whom there is an utter absence of good qualities. Thus it is possible to cultivate the good in anyone by *the proper use of praise and criticism* and direction (where necessary). Enduring friendship is not possible among those who are too young to appreciate what is really worthwhile in human nature, and it is not easy to cultivate in extremely self-centered persons, in those

who have not developed affability toward others, or in those who have neglected to develop any really laudable traits in themselves.

12. St. Thomas has an explicit analysis of all the elements of choice in *S.T.* I, II, questions 9 to 17 inclusive.

13. That there is what we may call "a stream of consciousness," which brings various notions into our present awareness on both the intellectual and sensory levels, can easily be ascertained by determining to stop thinking and then observing what happens in spite of one's attempts to carry out this determination. The various agents that transmit sensible aspects of the environment to the sense organs will act whether we wish them to do so or not, and our attention will be drawn to these actions so that we may decide what kind of sensible is engaging our attention, the characteristics of the sensible, or what meaning the sensible displays as a sign of something's occurring, and so forth. Even if all receptivity to external stimulus is cut off, the absence of the sensation engages our attention; there is also the activity of the imagination and the memory of past experiences, which normally are under precise control by the intellect, but which can in a more or less spontaneous and random manner bring up from their storehouses (figuratively speaking) various items for consideration. Even if we could suspend the operations of the intellect altogether, the spontaneously arising appetitive desires of the animal part of us and the suppressed but not extinguished desires of those appetites, because of the close interplay of sensory cognition and sensuality, would probably evoke some sequences of sensory rememberings. Also, if the senses could be totally suppressed, the possibility exists that the constant tendency of the will to enjoy what is possible for it to enjoy would move the intellect to the act of recalling something of what was understood for present consideration. Our intellect often does act in this way when we consider a subject that interests us and spurs us on to related research. Whether such a process could begin without some sensory consideration of a sensible or of a word is a matter requiring more acute discernment by introspection than we can muster. St. Thomas thinks that some sensory activity is indispensable to the initiation of

intellectual activity. (See *S.T.* I, 84, 7.) In any case, a stream of topics can invade our consciousness when we cease directed conscious activities, and even sometimes in the middle of other activities when random thoughts, impressions, or remembered experiences occur to us.

14. All ends are future goods in the sense that desire precedes fulfillment. But the desire to reminisce can immediately be satisfied by the act of reminiscing. The case is similar for any act of any cognitive power with respect to what is immediately present to it (the environment is immediately available to the external senses; many memories are immediately available to memory powers; retained understandings and the use of reason upon received information are immediately available to the intellect) and for the act of any voluntary muscle. Other goods are attainable only over a period of time and usually with intervening physical activity—means are needed to attain them.

15. Freedom of exercise does not extend to the will's recognition of that which the intellect deems to be good. There is no act of *desire* necessarily connected with this. But "the exercise of the will" refers to actively loving or hating something.

16. Cf. *S.T.* I, II, 13, 1.

17. Cf. *S.T.* I, II, 9, 1.

18. It has been the fashion in some recent popular literature and in many textbooks to view the possession of free choice by man as a matter of debate. Such a position is tantamount to debating whether the sun is shining while one is reading from a page whose visibility is produced by the sun's light. For what hereditary factors and what environmental factors necessitated the writers who are of the opinion that man has no freedom of choice to express it? If they could not but express this opinion, then it has no more value as an expression of inner tensions (or whatever name may be given to inner activities that produce overt behavior and expressions) than does a yawn or a cough, both of which signify physiological conditions. If they express this opinion, however, because they wish to point out a mistaken belief held by someone else, then they intend an end and a choice of means to that end which manifest both will and choice. In short, just as

Man's Physical and Spiritual Nature

there is no reading by sunlight unless there is a sunlight to read by, so there is no arguing about the freedom of choice in man unless one *chooses* to argue about it.

19. Cf. *S.T.* I, II, 10, 2.

CHAPTER 9

1. The exact relationship of man's intellectual and voluntary part to his body has been discussed through the centuries, at least since the time of Pythagoras who taught that the soul of a man who had died would enter into another body and continue its life there. Socrates is reported in the *Phaedo* to have believed that upon the death of his body he would enter into the company of better men; Plato in the *Timaeus* relates that the souls of men were placed in their bodies which had already been formed. Aristotle and his Christian followers insist that man is absolutely one, having a diversity of operations by the powers of one soul and the organs of one body. The Platonic tradition has persisted to the present because no attempt to explain consciousness, sensing, or thinking and willing in terms of the known biochemical properties of animal tissue has been successful in disproving it.

2. Chemical natures may by their predetermined activities form a respiring entity (as the Appendix to Chapter 2 indicates), but they do not have the ability to arrange themselves to form the bones, muscles, and organs of a living thing. The quantitative forms of living things require some other explanatory principle than the ability of the parts of a molecule to attach themselves to a central atom or chain of atoms. Molecules, even in their greatest spontaneous complexity, do not have the ability to orientate themselves as parts of a bone, muscle, or organ. From our analysis of consciousness it is obvious that conscious activity can never result from the spontaneous activity of mere chemical complexes.

3. For those who can master the archaic physics of the 4 elements and the 4 qualities, St. Thomas has a most succinct and penetrating summary of the transcendence of the various kinds of living things over the activities of inanimate chemical agents. For the discussion of this transcendance, see *S.T.* I, 78, 1 (beginning of the article).

4. It is easy in analyzing living things according to their constituent principles to fall unwittingly into the error of attributing all actuality to the soul because the very livingness of the composite is from the soul. But without the matter that it organizes and quickens, the soul could not exist, for in all other living things but man the soul is *only a coprinciple of being* that cannot exist, or be a principle, without its complementary matter.

5. That fields of force apparently pervade solids is a finding of contemporary physics as well as a long-standing theory about gravitational attraction. The modes of existence and operation possessed by fields of force appear to differ from those possessed by stones or molecules or subatomic particles considered as wholes. Our analysis in this matter cannot go any further than can that of contemporary science, from which it is taken.

6. In the transmission of light a photochemical change often occurs in the surface atoms of the thing which absorbs some part of white light and reflects the remainder, and there is a definite chemical alteration in the photosensitive components of the retina. But surface changes in most macroscopic things, although they may affect the molecules involved in a chemical way, as when bleaching occurs, do not affect the nature of the macroscopic entity so as to change it to a different kind of thing. Although the alteration produced in the sense organ does use up some of the molecular energy of the tissue that is sensorily stimulated, energy is constantly being supplied to the tissue and the alteration that is sensing (physiologically) is reversed constantly, so that the tissue may be altered again by successive stimuli.

7. In some accounts of the intellect's act of understanding, the expression, "dematerialization of the sensory impression," is used in expressing the completely abstract and nonsensory kind of thing that our understanding of something is. This expression cannot mean the removal of matter or the removal of the incidental aspects characteristic of the things that actually exist materially—this is manifestly an impossibility. Rather it must be understood to mean that our act of understanding discerns in the sensory awareness of things certain common and endur-

ing traits which it uses to recognize the singular things that actually exist as being of a certain kind.

8. Of all the arguments alleged against the Platonic notion that man learns by discerning ideas directly rather than by forming them himself on the basis of his experience, the Aristotelian axiom, "He who lacks a sense lacks an understanding of its proper sensible," seems to be particularly telling. For one version of Plato's teaching on the Ideas, consult F. J. Collingwood, *Philosophy of Nature*, Chapter 2. Englewood Cliffs, N. J.: Prentice Hall, 1960.

9. Some readers of St. Thomas may be inclined to interpret his adoption of the Aristotelian dictum, "The human intellect does not know singulars," to mean that the intellect has no knowledge of singulars, rather than to mean that the immateriality of the intellect precludes the existence in it of the singular in its mode of existence as determinately material. Such a misinterpretation makes an unfathomable mystery of the act of understanding. How can we ever explain the correspondence between what we sense and what we understand, which is so clearly manifest in our practical knowledge? Also, in view of such a misinterpretation how could one explain our ability to recognize the intelligible content of words, for there is in them no sensible content that admits of abstraction? Their intelligible signification can be recognized immediately upon their visual or auditory apprehension.

10. St. Thomas on several occasions mentions the transcendence of intellect over sense, but looks at it in diverse ways. For example, in *S.T.* I, II, 17, 7, he mentions that the act of apprehension on the part of imagination is regulated by the apprehension of reason as an example of a particular apprehension being regulated by a universal one. If this notion is combined with his teaching in Article 4 of the same question, "when one power is the mover of the other, *then their acts are, in a way, one*," it would seem to follow that there is but one act of two powers and that act is concerned with determinate sensibles. But this could not be the case unless the intellect were present to the sense in the manner in which we have described it.

On the other hand, St. Thomas in *S.T.* I, 79, 3, sets forth the notion of a second intellectual power which he calls the agent intellect, a teaching based on a very controversial and cryptic text in Aristotle's *De Anima* (III, 5, 430 a, 14-20). This second intellectual power is posited to explain how the regular (possible) intellect can receive information, since the sense power cannot act upon it. According to this account the agent intellect makes things actually intelligible by abstracting a representation of them from the material conditions under which the senses apprehend them, and then specifies the regular intellect's act of knowing by presenting this abstracted representation to it.

In our opinion, however, this account of the operation of the intellect overlooks the dynamic character of the act of sensing, for there are no static images of any kind involved in sensation. Sensing is an activity; when we are not actually sensing, there is no representation of sensibles actually present in our consciousness. Whatever may be the manner of operation of the imagination and the memory of the cogitative power, it is perfectly clear that there are no images stored in a static way in man's neural apparatus. Consequently, for some power to immaterialize the sensory representation means that the very activity of the sense is somehow transformed, so that its awareness of a sensible that is determinate as to details becomes indeterminate. This seems to us to do violence to the power of sense. But there is no alternative according to St. Thomas' account. It means that the agent intellect is intimately present to the sense power in order to dematerialize its representation or that the act of the agent intellect is not specified, that is, is not informing.

If, to use St. Thomas' expression, the intellect turns to phantasms (sensory impressions, either direct or remembered) in order to know, whenever we wish to consider some item of interest we need to explain how the senses can present the relevant phantasms, unless they are directed by the intellect to select among the items present to observation or to select among a great multitude of memories. But if the intellect's knowledge extends to the act of the senses, to the extent of directing them to ignore some sensibles and to consider others, then it must be able to discern what the senses discern in order to judge whether its direction has been successfully carried out or not.

That the intellect has the power to direct and command the act of the senses is stated categorically by St. Thomas in *S.T.* I, 75, 5 (Pegis translation). "The intellectual powers are prior (in the order of nature) to the sensitive powers; wherefore they direct them and command them." Our position, that there is only one cognitive intellectual power in man which is intimately present to every act of the senses, seems more in accord with everyday experience. This view also reduces the mysterious element in intellectual activity to the problem of understanding the mode of the intellect's presence to the sense, so that it cognizes what the sense cognizes but in its own mode of immateriality.

That St. Thomas sometimes considered the representation of things in the senses as though they were material images in the sense organs may be seen in *S.T.* I, 89, 1.

Index ~

Abstraction, from changing to enduring, 154-160
  erroneous notion of, 148, 149
  and experience, 153, 154
  kinds of, 165, 356
  and mathematicals, 160-165
  as means of understanding, 143-146
  not effortless, 152-154
  productive of categories, 184-187
  selectivity in, 182
  from singular to common, 144-154
  as subtraction, 161
Action, and conviction, 269, 270
  facility in, 306, 307
  failure of, 304
  integration of, 266-269
  of intellect with will, 299
  ionic, 335
  necessary, 272, 273
  and practical knowledge, 189-193
  predetermined, 29
  prompted by needs, 234, 235, 239
  and reaction, 26
  successful, 189-192
  termination of, 300
  unity of, 313, 314
  wrong and right, 271, 280
Activity, appetitive, 245-254, 262, 293-300
  habitual, 305-307
  immanent, 32, 33
  induced, 26
  location of sensory, 349
  natural, 22, 23
  predetermined, 27-30, 223, 310
  random, 335
  self-directed, 292, 293
  self-initiated, 31-34

  spiritual, 315, 337
  spontaneous, 21, 134, 369
  subordinated by soul, 310-313
Alteration, in sensing, 130-133
Altruism, 283-285
Amoeba, 86-89
Anger, 244, 254-256
Appearances, 134-136, 148, 149, 277, 278
  deceiving, 368
  modified by passion, 256, 257
  as practical signs, 117
  quantitative, 160-164
Appetite, animal (sensual), 233-265
  and action, 234, 235
  concupiscible, 241-244; not cognitive, 263; two-fold aspect of, 246
  formal aspect of, 241
  intellectual (see Will)
  irascible, 244, 245
Apple, abstraction concerning, 145, 146
Apprehension, failure in, 196, 219
  inseparable from judgment, 226
  modified by passion, 256, 257
  not physically isolable, 102
  of suitability, 237
  verbal, 222-224, 320, 321, 362
Approval, desire of, 285, 286
  role in friendship, 290, 291
Aristotle, 82, 83, 137-139, 371-374
  on categories, 186, 187
  on common sensibles, 109
  on the good, 274
  on intellect as a blank, 173
  on nature, 21
  on sense in act, 82, 83, 137-139

Estimation (*cont.*)
role of, in skill, 126-128
of suitability, 236, 237
of unsuitability, 249-251
Euclid, elements, proof in, 203
Evaluation, 264-268
of motives, 245
of self, 249-251, 327, 328
Existence, discerned by intellect, 177
intentional, 134
irrelevance to understanding, 214
judgment of, 196-199
modes of, 196-198, 213
perpetuation of, 241-243
shared by body, 324-326
Experience and abstraction, 144-146, 153
of causality, 208, 209
in choice, 298, 301, 302
criterion of belief, 222
criterion of hearsay, 174, 175
expressed as meaning, 166
as ground of universals, 212, 213
as guide to action, 299
limitations of, 171, 172
need of, 126, 127
refinement of, 226
in self-actualization, 35-38
and sensory appetites, 237-246
as source of mathematicals, 163
as source of personal traits, 267
universe of, 276, 277
as validating ideas, 140
wider than understanding, 152, 153
Explanation, 40-46 (*see also* Understanding; Scientific knowledge)
by causal dependence, 39
false, 216, 217
by form, 42
by invisible factors, 41-46
partial, 40, 41, 56

Faculty, 112, 113
Falsity, 225, 226
Fear, 252, 253
Feelings (*see* Passions)

Form, as determining, 311-313, 325, 326 (*see also* Soul)
inseparability of, 43
mathematical, 163-165
not nature, 46
as organizing principle, 41-43, 315, 352
quantitative, 163-165, 371
soul as, 41-43, 310, 315, 352
Free choice, 299, 304, 305 (*see also* Choice)
disputed, 370, 371
and personality, 327, 328
Friendship, 290-292, 368

Genes, 338
Goals, attainable through belief, 299
choice of, 301
critical evaluation of, 223, 224, 303
determinative of action, 328
immaterial, 288, 289
long-range, 295, 320, 328, 329
sensorily depicted, 313, 314
God, as supremely lovable, 284, 285
Good, available, 301, 368
as befitting man, 279, 280
cannot command desire, 287
coterminous with being, 277
definition of, 274
as end in itself, 297
incompleteness of, 281
intangible, 367
of the intellect, 275, 276
as means, 297, 302
object of the will, 274-280
permanent, 287, 288
useful, 297
Gravity, 333
Growth, emotional, 259, 260
intellectual, 227
as living process, 33-38
plan of, 35
predetermination in, 34, 35

Habit, motor, 126, 127
as so-called faculties, 113
Habitual actions, and reflex acts, 66
Happiness, available to man, 309

Happiness (*cont.*)
desire for, 38, 286, 287, 325
as goal of intention, 295
incompleteness of, 281
unattainable now, 301, 302
Hate, 251
Hearing, 75-77, 107, 133, 134
Hearsay, 143, 167-175
Hedonism, natural to man, 308, 309

Ideas, physical interpretation of, 129, 130
Images, discrimination of, 132
never truly general, 146-148
physical, not in sensation, 134-136
Imagination, 70, 115-119, 350
act of, 350, 351
composition in, 183, 184
conventional signs in, 168, 169
creative, 117, 118
escapes time, 157
Immateriality, intellectual, 317, 322
sensory, 135, 136
Impressions, in sense, 202 (*see also* Sense; Images)
sense, 115, 116, 135, 136, 219, 220
general, 143, 146-148, 282, 318
informative to intellect, 219, 220
nonmateriality of, 145, 146
retention of, 115, 116, 118
Incorruptibility (*see* Soul)
Information, 173, 174, 178 (*see also* Knowledge)
Intangibles, desired by the will, 273, 276, 277
Integration, of needs and actions, 239-241, 266
Intellect, 97, 143, 147, 148, 172-178
in act of belief, 277-279
atemporality of, 299
as critical power, 177, 198, 199
as form in man, 325
as generalizing power, 158
immanent acts of, 324
immateriality of, 317-322
infallibility of, 219
one power, 373-375
openness of, 173, 226-229

subsistence of, 322-325
transcendent of sense, 150, 317-321, 373-375
unity with sense, 149, 150, 319-321
unity with will, 298
Intelligibility, potential, 187, 188
requires judgment, 178
Intention, 294-296, 311-313
Intentionality, 130-140, 316
not fully understood, 318, 319
Introspection, 7-11
presuppositions in, 331

Joy, 248, 249, 279, 280
Judgment, as composition, 178-184
critical, 173-178, 220-222; in choosing goals, 328; in daily life, 220-222; on hearsay, 173, 174; on personal acts, 269, 270; of self, 251; in will-act, 307
false, correction of, 225, 226
negative, 182-184
objective, 120
practical, analysis of, 189-193
of singulars, 319-321
of suitability, 119, 240

Kinesthesis, 108
Knowledge, abstract, and experience, 152 (*see also* Judgment)
acquired by composition, 178-181
basically speculative, 205, 206
characteristics of, 156-160, 170-172
check on veracity of, 227
critical, 198, 199
fallibility of, 215-218
as a good, 285
intellectual, conformity in, 195, 196; atemporality of, 156-160; transcendence of, 158
love of, 282, 283
necessary to free choice, 304
not subsistent, 367
of recognition, 332
pitfalls in, 228
practical, 189-193; certitude in, 192, 193; in infancy, 221; mathematical, 164; test for, 190-192; use of, 279

Index   381

Sensation (*cont.*)
voluntary aspect of, 313, 314
Sense, absence of, 373; act of, 139, 310-314
in act, 82-83
defects in, 124, 196, 346
distinction of, 130
diverse organs of, 110, 111
errors regarding, 56, 57
external and internal, 69, 70, 114, 356
formalities of, 195, 196
formed by sensible, 138, 139
general power of, 122-125, 351, 358
knowledge of existents, 146, 196-198
mutually corroborating, 98
nonreflective, 176
primary function of, 103, 104
receptors, 70-80
rectitude in, 138
table of, 107-109
tendency in, 237, 238
unity with intellect, 195, 196, 319-321, 373-375
Sensibilities, affected by reason, 268
Sensible, accidental, 105, 106
Aristotle on, 82, 83
common, 104-106, 346, 347
contrasted with intelligible, 96, 97
correlative to sense, 100
in imagination, 116
intellectual grasp of, 319-321
not organ, 135
objectivity of, 99-102
retention of, 115-120
in the sense, 134-136
synthesis of, 125
Sequence, basis of proof, 204
Shapes, mathematical, 161
Sight (*see* Vision; Sense)
Sign, accidental sensible as, 105, 106
conventional, in imagination, 118;
in learning, 167-174
of feelings, 16, 17, 247
natural, 117
proof through, 205

in sensory inference, 121
used by intellect, 149, 150
Similarity, in sensibles, 142, 149
basis of categories, 186, 187
Singulars, judgment of, 194-196, 373
Size, relevance in abstraction, 144, 145 (*see also* Sensible, common)
Sorrow, 251, 254
Soul, corruptible in brute, 338
coprinciple of being, 372
incorruptibility of, 326-329
notion of, 43-46, 324, 336, 351
transcendence over matter, 315-322
Speech, role of imagination in, 118
a sign of rationality, 357
Statements, evident, 202, 203
on being, 214, 215
erroneous, 218
made true, 212-215
mathematical, 212, 213
on mathematics, 214
practical, 213
statistically based, 223
universal, 212-223, 360
Stimulus, 61, 62, 89, 347, 354
conscious reception of, 134, 137
physical reception of, 133, 134
and response, 58, 64, 66-70, 88, 89
role in sensation, 132-140
termination in receptor, 98, 99
Straight, model of, 161, 162
Subsistence, 321-324
Substance, 33, 42, 46, 154, 355
man as, 314
Subtraction, in abstraction, 161-163
Suitable, the, 236, 267ff., 271, 305, 363ff.
and difficult, 253
found in experience, 237
found in oneself, 25
maximum, 240
for others, 275, 276
personally variable, 243, 250, 251
pleasantly, 240-243, 288
and right reason, 364, 365
tendency to, 234, 238
to the will, 280, 288, 293

Will (*cont.*)
command of, over other powers, 300-307
development of, 272-274
enraptured, 286
existence of, 262-274
freedom in, 299, 370
indifference in, 287, 288, 294
loves of, 281-292
not cognitive, 298, 299
not compelled, 279-281
specified by reason, 270-272, 296
unlimited scope of, 276, 277

Will-act, antecedents to, 363, 364
paradox of, 281
parts of, 294-300
variable in intensity, 272, 299
Words, expressive of thoughts, 168, 169
inadequate to sensory details, 139
not matter for abstraction, 321
proper to man, 167
signification of, 168, 169
as signs of understanding, 226, 227
Writing, imagination in, 117, 118
Wrong, definition of, 271

The
Gift
of
Christmas

The Gift of Christmas

MYRA SCOVEL

DRAWINGS BY SUSAN PERL

HARPER & ROW, PUBLISHERS
New York · Evanston · San Francisco · London

The author gratefully acknowledges use of copyrighted material from the following publishers and publications:

Augsburg Publishing House for "Wise Men" by Myra Scovel from *Christmas,* Volume 26, edited by Randolph E. Haugan. Reprinted by permission of Augsburg Publishing House, Minneapolis, Minnesota, copyright owner.

The Democrat and Chronicle for "Roads Still Lead to Bethlehem," by Myra Scovel, first published in *The Democrat and Chronicle,* Rochester, New York.

The C. R. Gibson Company for "Christmas Wish" by Myra Scovel from *Follow Your Star* by Ruth H. Wagner, copyright © 1969, reprinted by permission of The C. R. Gibson Company.

Concern for "The Christmas Tree" (December, 1951) and "Christmas at Ming Sum School" (January, 1951) by Myra Scovel.

The Progressive Farmer for "The Christmas Gift" (originally entitled "Every Boy Should Have a Dog") by Myra Scovel, copyright The Progressive Farmer, October 1955.

The two quotations from Scripture appearing on page 1 are from *The New English Bible,* copyright © The Delegates of the Oxford University Press and The Syndics of the Cambridge University Press, 1961, 1970.

"How to make . . ." drawings on pages 100, 101, 157, 164, 165, 166, 167, are by Luba Litwak.

FIRST EDITION

STANDARD BOOK NUMBER: 06-067171-8

LIBRARY OF CONGRESS CATALOG CARD NUMBER: 72-78335

Designed by Yvette A. Vogel

For F.
What if it *had* been
chocolates!

Recipes

How to Make . . .

The
Gift
of
Christmas

The Gift of Christmas

Are you not content
to wear out men's patience?
Must you also wear out
the patience of . . . God?
Therefore the Lord himself
shall give you a sign:
A young woman is with child,
and she will bear a son,
and will call him Immanuel.
(That is, God is with us.)
                    Isaiah 7:13, 14

God was in Christ
reconciling the world
to himself.
                    2 Corinthians 5:19

ONE

Christmas at the home of the man with whom I had fallen in love was having its embarrassing moments. To begin with, the whole situation was iffy. Frederick Gilman Scovel, medical student, and I, Supervisor of Obstetrics in the Cortland County Hospital in his home town, certainly had something going between us. We talked about life as if we were facing it together. I had accepted the premise.

Fred was everything I'd hoped for and was afraid I'd never find: brown-haired, brown-eyed, six feet one and a half inches tall. Was he wondering how he would look with a wife a smidge over five feet high? I doubted it. How he looked never seemed to enter his head; yet he was aware of everything around him—chickadees in a lilac bush, fog coming in over the courthouse, a frond of fern. He was the kind of a man who might wake you up at dawn so you wouldn't miss the spectacular sunrise.

If he had any such ideas, so far he hadn't voiced them. True, there had been that night on the hill . . . But had he actually proposed? I couldn't be sure. The thought did not add to my comfort on this Christmas Eve of 1928.

Fred and I and his mother and father were skirting the edges of conversation, fumbling to know how to act toward one another. If I had been a stranger, I could have been taken into this home as a member of the family on Christmas Eve or on any other convenient or inconvenient time of year. But who knew? Would I become the daughter of this house or wouldn't I?

I dreaded the opening of presents next day, wondering whether or not the gift I had for him was too ostentatious for this stage in our relationship. I had had such fun buying "expensive" things, now that I had a job and my own money. The job had brought us together; Fred had spent a summer vacation working in the hospital laboratory. But that had been a year and a half ago. We had been separated from each other for long periods of time—he continuing at Cornell Medical College in New York City and I in a postgraduate course in pediatrics at Babies and Children's Hospital, Cleveland, Ohio. If Fred felt that I was just someone to pal around with when he was home on vacation, that silver-backed, hand-engraved brush and comb set was entirely out of place and it was too late to do anything about it.

I had worked myself up to a high pitch and there were still more of his relatives here for the Christmas holidays—Uncle Arthur, an inveterate tease, I'd been warned (teasing seemed to have been handed down to all the male members of this family); and Cousin Dwight, his suave, handsome, black-haired son.

Up to now, both of them had been very quiet. Aunt Katherine, wife and mother, had died and this was their first Christmas without her. How must they feel? I wondered, look-

4

ing at them across the table; lonelier than ever in this happy household where the Christmas celebration was going on as usual. What could I say to these strangers trying so bravely to enter into the festivities? Would they someday be my family?

The conversation flowed along, Fred's mother graciously explaining who people were as they were mentioned. His father kept urging me to eat more and more of the delectable food, and when I had to refuse third helpings in favor of breathing, he and Uncle Arthur made remarks to each other about how sad it was that I did not like Fred's mother's cooking.

Though I had known when I first entered this house that it was the kind of a home I'd always dreamed of having, and though I was enjoying every minute of the soft linen damask, the old silver, the Royal Crown Derby plates "used for very special guests," I suddenly wanted to escape this trying to cope. I wanted to be my own parents' child, small Myra Scott of Mechanicville, New York, with her own brothers and sisters on Christmas morning.

> I could feel the cold on my nose as I first peeked out from under the covers. Snow had drifted through the inch of open window. It was still dark, but surely it must be morning. Hark! Wasn't that a bird chirping? Or was it Daddy stirring in bed? Neither. There was no sound from the room of our parents— no sound from Bob's and Jim's room; no sound from our two little sisters. I'd have to wait; it might even be hours. Then the pat of quick footsteps coming off the porch next door, the squeak of snow getting louder as the sound passed our house. Mrs. Dalton was on her way to Mass! It must be six o'clock! *"Merry Christmas, everybody!"*
>
> "Oh, no, please. Not yet," from our Mother; then a sleepy yawn-of-a-"Merry-Christmas" from our father. We jumped out of bed and pounded down the hall to our parents' bedroom. We were not allowed to go downstairs until Daddy had found out whether or not Santa Claus had come (actually to light the candles on the tree). It took forever. Maybe Santa Claus *hadn't* come. We half-worried, half-knew that nothing that bad could

5

possibly happen on Christmas Day. At last we heard the longed-for assurance, "Well, it looks as if the Old Man has made it again this year."

An explosion of footsteps burst from the top landing, boomed down the stairs, and rumbled into the living room. What could be in all those packages? . . .

"All *I* want for Christmas is a pair of black pajamas."

It was Cousin Dwight and I was stunned back to the present by such an absurd idea. Nobody in our town had ever seen black underwear or black pajamas. We had heard of them, of course, but couldn't imagine "nice" people wearing them. I should say something to cover my lapse of attention.

"I can't imagine waking up at night and looking down on black pajamas" was what came out.

"Nobody's asking you to, my dear," said Cousin Dwight.

There was a spontaneous burst of laughter from the men. Even Fred's mother allowed herself one little run and a trill before composing her features into shocked silence, a silence which spread around the table in seconds. My face must have been the color of the poinsettias in the centerpiece. Fred squeezed my hand. His father burst into the breach with "Have another sliver of this steak, Arthur. How about you, Dwight? Louise, are there any more of your delicious rolls in the kitchen?"

Would I ever get through this Christmas Eve? To say nothing of Christmas morning and what used to be the exciting ritual of gift-giving!

The moment I had so dreaded arrived. Fred had opened my gift to him and everyone had ohed and ahed at the silver-backed brush and comb. "Much too good to use," Fred had said. "I'll keep it to look at, to remember this day." Now he chose a package from under the tree, walked across the room, gave it to me, and went back and sat down. Why this silence in the room, without even a swish of tissue paper? Why was every pair of eyes fixed on me?

"Open it," said Fred.

I took all the time I dared to untie the string and unfold the paper. At last, in my lap lay a one-pound box of Fannie Farmer's chocolates. I managed a weak smile and a more fervent (I hoped!) "Thank-you-you-know-I-love-Fannie-Farmer's."

"Why not open it now?" asked Fred.

"Yes, why not open it and pass it around?" added Cousin Dwight.

"Fannie Farmer's at this hour of the morning?" I hedged.

"There'll never be a better moment than this one," said Fred.

Well, if they wanted chocolates they could have them. I ripped off the cover and was about to thrust the whole thing into Fred's hands and disappear when I saw that the box was filled with tissue paper. In the center lay—Oh! a ring box edged with gold. I was going to cry, I knew it and looked up at Fred frantically. He crossed the room again, this time in one stride, picked up the candy box and took me by the hand.

"Come on, let's get out of here," he said.

Upstairs in his small study he slipped the glowing ring on the fourth finger of my left hand. It was a diamond, set in platinum—a ring more beautiful than any girl had ever worn. It was all the Christmases past and all the Christmases to come.

Mother Scovel served hot spiced orange juice to friends dropping in at the manse during the Christmas season. Here is her recipe:

HOT SPICED ORANGE JUICE

2 quarts orange juice
1 cup tea
1 teaspoon cinnamon ⎫
1 teaspoon cloves   ⎬ in a cloth bag
2 cups sugar   ⎭

Bring to a boil, then continue to boil for 20 minutes. Remove bag of spices. Serve with small squares of fruit cake. (We serve it in mugs, usually.)

The
Spirit
of
Christmas
Past

TWO

I had a lot to learn about the Birthday of the Christ Child and China was a good place to learn it. You don't usually celebrate with gusto the birthday of someone you know very little about. The better you know a person and the closer you are to him, the more fun it is to plan the little surprises and make the preparations for a birthday he will enjoy.

We sailed for China in 1930 with our three-month-old baby, James Kiehle Scovel. Following a year of language study in Peking, we spent five years working in a hospital in Tsining, a city in the interior of Shantung Province. There, two more children were born—Carl Robert, in 1932, and Anne Elizabeth, in 1933.

I came to believe that for me really to celebrate the Birthday of Christ, His birth had to mean as much to me as the birth of a child into our own family (which is never simply a matter of cake and candles and gifts once a year). We accept

11

the responsibilities the child's coming brings, rearrange our lives to devote ourselves more fully to him. We try to learn more and more about what his coming means, not only to our family, but to his world.

As the years go by, we find that not much of our life is what we planned it would be. But because of the child's coming, each day has been richer. There has been someone at hand when the going was rough, someone to laugh with at life's unexpected surprises. There have been difficulties we wish with all our hearts we could have avoided. There have been marvelous adventures we never could have dreamed would be ours. Above all, we know we are loved. Someone who believes in us, wants us and needs us. We can't help feeling we are very important people—at least to the child, and who else matters?

So each year we recall the mystery of his birth and the change his coming has made in us, in our world. We want to give him such a celebration as he has never seen before! We want to bring everyone we know into that circle of wonder, warmth, and love.

And since our Chinese friends shared with us *their* biggest festival, Chinese New Year, bringing us gifts and trays of specially prepared cakes and tiny meat dumplings to be steamed and later fried, so *we* entertained with our special traditions of Christmas and gave some small gift to each member of the hospital staff, to student nurses, and to other friends.

In China there were fewer distractions from the central theme of Christmas. They called it "The Day of the Holy Birth." In our city there were no department stores, no tinsel, no baubles, no neon-light Santa Clauses. No radios crashed continuous carols into the quiet streets where the sound of even one motor vehicle was a rarity.

But on that day Christians and other-than-Christians poured

into the lavishly decorated church to sing the familiar hymns and carols, to listen to the special music of the choir, to hear again the old story of Christmas told by their fine young pastor. Or just to see what the glad celebration was all about.

Since it was all in Chinese, we were pleased that we could now understand it.

(We didn't know anyone who spoke English except our family of missionaries—we Presbyterians in the South Suburb and the Southern Baptists in the city; Sister Toni, a Swiss nurse in the North Suburb, and the Wienekes, a German family not far from her. We conversed in Chinese with our German friends in the Roman Catholic monastery and convent at Tai Chia Chuang, six miles north of Tsining, since neither of us understood the other's language.)

We Americans would gather at one of the homes in either the Baptist or Presbyterian compound later on Christmas Day to feast on the traditionals (or "a reasonable facsimile" thereof) and to exchange gifts, lovingly wrapped in the same paper some one of us had used the year before, and the year before that and the year before that. New paper, appearing on the gifts of the family just back from furlough, was passed around for all to admire.

Even the gifts themselves sometimes reappeared. Never a Christmas came and went without our recalling the episode of the argyle socks which, not being all black or brown or blue or gray, were never worn, but passed from man to man, year after year, until the Christmas when they landed in the lap of Frank Connely, who had started them off in the first place. He opened the package with a hoot. "I've watched these go around year after year and knew I'd get them back someday. I'm going to wear them," he said. And he did!

Christmas preparations began in July when Fred took the children and me out to the coast to escape the heat. We did the bulk of our buying for the year at that time—grocery staples, household supplies, yarn for the winter knitting, and so forth. Over the years our Tsining stores gradually carried more imports such as coffee, spool thread, toothpaste, and the like. But Christmas shopping was still done in summer. When we could afford a special gift for each child from Montgomery Ward, the orders were sent at that time, too. There were, of course, no air flights to China, and the long sea journey, plus the usual delays from the disruptions of war, might hold up the packages for months.

Thanksgiving Day was my deadline for having all the presents bought, wrapped, and "hidden" in the Christmas trunk. Who knew who might come down with measles between then and Christmas? Besides, it left me free to plan the parties for the staff, the student nurses, the doctors and their families, and to enjoy the children's preparations for Christmas—making cookies, "helping" the cook do the fruit cake, making the floating candles for their mission "aunts" and "uncles," and walking into the city to find "something special for Daddy." A second trip with their father was required, which I, of course, knew nothing about.

Each year we all went by ricksha to the Catholic school and church in the city, then on to the monastery at Tai Chia Chuang to see the beautiful crèches with almost life-size figures. The children would stand in awe as they were allowed to touch the Christ Child. The figures in the crèche in the city church had been made in Germany by a brother of one of the nuns. We marveled at how they had ever made the journey to China without a tiny chip or crack.

It wasn't customary, then, for Protestants to have a crèche in their homes, but Fred and I wanted one. We thought it would help to remind us that the Manger, and not the Christmas tree, was the center of our celebration. We two will never forget the year Fred's mother gave us ours.

14

This is how we made the gifts the children gave to the mission "aunts" and "uncles":

HOW TO MAKE FLOATING CANDLES

Collect all candle stubs during the year
    or buy cakes of paraffin wax
Also needed are:
    1 box of colored crayons (We used very inexpensive wax
        ones found in the Chinese market.)
    Several tin jello molds (Ours were star-shaped.)
    A few empty cans
    An old chopstick, *wooden*, not plastic
    Two-to-three-inch lengths of rather thick, loosely woven
        cotton string to be used for wicks, or buy candle wicking

Melt the candles in separate cans over boiling water.
Add a small piece of crayon the color desired to each can.
Stir with the wooden chopstick till all the color has melted.
Add more color if needed. When the mixture is smooth and
the wax has entirely melted, pour into jello molds.

Watch rather carefully to see when the wax has set enough
to hold the wick; then insert it. Be sure the wax is liquid
underneath and has only a little scum on top. Be sure the wick
goes down to the very bottom of the mold.

When cold, turn out of mold and wrap for Christmas.

If you want to give a somewhat larger gift, set them in a
small porcelain bowl with instructions to add water, a few
floating leaves or blossoms, and use as a centerpiece for the
Christmas table.

15

ThRee

We left China in 1936 for a year of furlough and study in America. Before we were ready to return, the Sino-Japanese War was in its early stages but had not yet reached Shantung. We hoped that before that happened the war would be over. Now I, who had had qualms about going to China with one small baby in the first place, found myself praying that the way would open for us to return to our home in Tsining with three, aged three, five, and seven. We had also persuaded Fred's mother to make her home with us. Father Scovel, whom I loved so very much, had died the year Carl was born. Mother was alone and we wanted her with us.

The prayers for our return to China were answered, and we started out full of hope.

Who, on that happy Christmas Day of 1928, when Fred and I became engaged, could have pictured us in the port city of Tsingtao on December 22, 1937, preparing to drive cross-country on a 700-mile trip in a Ford truck-to-become-ambulance, straight into what might well turn out to be the line of battle?

"If this is the right thing to do, it will be right all the way," we had told our friends in America who had protested our leaving the United States. "We have to take the first step into the water before the Red Sea will part." It turned out to be somewhat more of a sea than I had envisaged.

We'd been stopped in Japan, Fred only being allowed to go on to China since he was needed in his hospital to care for the scores of wounded soldiers both Chinese and Japanese. Eventually, Mother and I and the children had been able to obtain passage from Japan to Tsingtao, on the coast of our own province. We had taken a house and had planned to remain there until we were sure it was safe to proceed to our home in Tsining. Fred would come out to the coast to be with us for Christmas if it were at all possible; but he would have to return to his work within two or three days.

On the night of his arrival in Tsingtao we were both awakened by a strong compulsion to get up, take the family and leave the city. We were all to go at once to Tsining. At first we were embarrassed even to speak of this inner urging, neither of us being accustomed to such experiences.

"It's just plain silly," I said when the compulsion became too strong to ignore. "You're worn out from your trip getting here. You certainly can't turn around and go back without some rest. And who in his right mind would even consider taking Mother and the children on such a journey?"

As we talked it over later, we both knew we had to do it. And Mother, courageous soul that she was, agreed, even though it meant she might have to stay in Tsingtao alone, unable, perhaps, even to hear from us. We were not happy about leaving her behind. The command, if such it could be called, had included "all of us," but we were not sure she could stand such a trip.

Miraculously, we learned of a special train leaving Tsingtao the next night, and we arranged to have her travel with two members of our mission family, Mary Stewart and Helen Christman, who had been trying in vain to get back to Tsining and hadn't heard about the train until we phoned. Fred then wired to Deane and Stella Walter, evangelists in our mission station, asking them to meet the party at Yenchowfu by car (one of the few cars in all the area). Our branch railway was not running. That special train, we learned later, was the last one to leave Tsingtao for many months.

The next morning the rest of the family piled into the truck with all our things, including an old-fashioned coal stove, which we could not buy in Tsining and which we needed badly. It was December 23. We might well have to spend Christmas along the way, but we were prepared for such an emergency by a suitcase containing a small Christmas tree and a gift for each child, wrapped and ready for any celebration we might be able to produce.

The storefronts of Tsingtao were still boarded up for the night as we started out. Vendors of steaming gruel and crisp crullers were catching the first straggle of customers. Outside the city, day was just beginning to break over the flat country-side where the world was only an inch of brown field against a horizon of vast sky. This was going to be fun.

Fun? Memories of that trip are snatches of a continuing nightmare. Some of the bridges had been destroyed so we had to go through a winding river eight times, never knowing for sure how deep the water was, or if there were any holes in the bottom. One bridge we crossed was only as wide as the inner rear wheels of our six-wheeled truck, so that we bumped over the piles which held it.

We spent the first night with Katherine Hand at Ichowfu,

18

another of our mission stations. She couldn't have been more surprised if Martians had driven up to her gate. Katherine hadn't seen another American for months. She begged us to stay and have Christmas with her and what a temptation it was! But we knew that Mother would be arriving in Tsining and that she and the others would be anxious about us since we could send no word.

We left early in the morning of the 24th for another series of nightmares. Snow had begun to fall. By dark we found ourselves driving behind a column of soldiers who we thought were Japanese. It seemed wise not to ask, since they paid no attention to us, probably thinking that our truck was a part of their unit, a little late in catching up. Eventually the marching file turned off. Some miles farther, our road ended in the middle of a small village where the truck slithered down into a deep water-buffalo wallow and stopped.

If Katherine Hand had been surprised to see us, what of these villagers who had never seen a white person before? They did not flee, perhaps thinking that people dumb enough to drive into a buffalo wallow wouldn't be capable of doing much harm. In typical village fashion, they gathered, a circle of friends curious to know all about us, enjoying especially the children. "So fat, they are; so white their faces!" "The little one's hair is like gold thread and it's all in circles."

The crowd increased and all but smothered us until a motherly soul elbowed the children and me through the crowd and into her small mudbrick house. At her insistence we took off our shoes and sat or lay on her welcome bed. There we waited and waited and waited. At last Fred came in, but only to tell us that the Japanese Army had commandeered all the animals, so there were no oxen to pull the truck out of the mud. There were no animals in any of the surrounding villages either.

"What are you going to do?" I asked him. His face looked

19

tired. Pale shadows flickered over it in the firelight from the cauldron where sweet potato soup was on to boil.

"I don't know," he said, "I just don't know." Then quickly, "But don't worry. We'll work out something. I'll be back soon."

As the door closed behind him, that steel rod of courage I'd been holding myself erect with suddenly slid out of my backbone. I collapsed on the bed, sobbing. The children, quiet since our arrival—numb, perhaps—were awestruck to see their mother crying. Small Jim became the man of the family in his father's absence. "Don't cry, Mother," he whispered, patting me awkwardly. "You know you said God would take care of us."

God, and a dear Chinese woman, I thought, in this strange little village that might have been Bethlehem, this room so like the room of His birth. "Thanks, dear," I said to Jim. "God *will* take care of us." I'd forgotten. I'd been thinking we'd have to do it all ourselves. I dried my eyes and got up; and this time I didn't need the cold, steel bar.

Outside we could hear the men singing their work song for the heaviest of jobs. What were they doing? The soup was ready now. "Here, this will help," said our hostess. "You're hungry, that's all. I'll feed the children."

I didn't realize how hungry until the thick soup with delicious soft chunks of sweet potato warmed us through and we began to come alive. "How can we thank you?" I asked.

"*Mei yu shen ma* (It's nothing)," she replied.

What was that? A triumphant shout from outside. We hurried to the door. The truck was on dry ground. The motor was running! Those angels in Chinese padded garments had tied ropes to the front and put their shoulders to the back of the huge vehicle and by sheer man power had pulled and pushed it out of the hole.

"You are about five hours from home," said one of the men.

"But too tired to travel," added the woman. "You must all spend the night here."

20

Five hours. If all went well, we could be home before day-break. We decided to press on; the children could sleep in the truck.

"But not before the doctor has had his soup," said the woman.

We did our best to express our gratitude, knowing that all our lives we could never repay the debt we owed them.

Aside from having to awaken the magistrate of Yenchowfu to obtain permission to pass through the city gates, the rest of the trip went smoothly. Before dawn on Christmas Day the truck rolled into the mission compound. We were *home* after more than a year away. And the empty, aching weeks of separation from husband and father were past. Whatever happened now would happen to us together, as a family.

It was a morning of miracles, and again the ministration of angels, which may be only another word for friends. The children's grandmother, hearing the truck, came over from her house to greet us. So did "Aunt" Stella Walter, who had opened our place, had it thoroughly cleaned, taken the dishes and linens from the storeroom, made the beds, and—

"Look, Mother! A Christmas tree!" said Carl as we walked into the living room.

Even a Christmas tree! I knelt to unpack the Christmas suitcase and prayed my overwhelming thanks to God as I laid the presents under the beautifully decorated tree—that over-and-above gift of love from a very understanding friend. We were home for Christmas and we could all sleep in our own beds.

Mother had us over for a very late breakfast. Then she gave us the present she had carried with her on her difficult journey on the crowded train. It was a German crèche! Each of the small, exquisitely colored figures was perfect, each face portraying emotion—the Mother, serene; the Shepherds, anxious in their haste; the Wise Men, solemn. Even the animals were expressive. The little donkey with head on one side seemed to be saying, "What?" The cow, serious, "Hmm. We'll have to look into this." And the Baby—"Look, He's laughing," said Anne. And He would bless our Christmases from this time forth.

Fred came back from the hospital a few days later to tell us he'd just heard the Chinese had begun to plow up the roads over which we had come. "They're planting them with winter wheat," he said, "so the Japanese won't be able to find where the roads were. If we hadn't come when we did, who knows *when* we would have. And I hear Tsingtao has been bombed."

Wise Men

"You must return by another road,"
 the Wise Men heard God say.
Another road? The old road
 was the known, the safest way.

But the Kings had been to Bethlehem,
 had knelt as humble men;
and nothing, after Bethlehem,
 could be the same again.

FOUR

Three weeks later our city fell to the Japanese. From then until 1943 we lived in the midst of a war that fluctuated in and out of Tsining. Two more children were added to the family during that time—Thomas Scott, in 1939, and Judith Louise, in 1941.

Those were difficult, hungry years, but always we managed to celebrate Christmas; and always with deeper gratitude that we were alive; that we were together; that so far we had been able to obtain enough food to keep us going. Poor as we were, a special halo encircled those Christmases. Fred looks back to the fun he had carving a horse's head from a block of wood, fitting it to a broomstick, gluing on a dashing black mane—a strip from the bottom of my fur coat. It was our gift to Tommy.

And I remember making bookends for Fred by covering two heavy bricks, first with burlap, then with pieces of gold brocade left over from a Chinese jacket, which I sewed around the burlap tightly. The card read, "Darling, I have never handed you a gold brick before. I hope you will forgive me for these."

Fortunately, there were often books which, when they first arrived, had been too old for the children. These had been stored away in the Christmas trunk. There might be a doll or a doll's bed for the girls. I had started the Christmas trunk early in our married life, after a few lavish Christmases when the children had received far more than they could use or enjoy. I would watch to see which presents they played with most. By the end of the first week, those seldom touched were quietly picked up and stored away. Then on a rainy day, months later, or when one of the children was sick in bed, a new puzzle or a book or a toy would be taken from the trunk and the giver of the present recalled.

But the trunk was not the miraculous pitcher of Baucis and Philemon. There came a time when the wine no longer poured out when it was needed. Orders from Montgomery Ward could not get through, nor could the gifts of friends and relatives in America. We had practically nothing for the children and no money to buy whatever might be found on our city streets. I warned the children that it would be a slim Christmas as far as presents were concerned.

"But what are we going to give to the Baby Jesus?" Anne asked. "It's His Birthday, not ours."

"How would you send it up to heaven, silly?" one of the others asked.

We talked about what might please the Christ Child: "being good"; "not quarreling"; "giving to people who needed things," the answers children give the world over. But I still knew that however happy our Lord would be over such gifts, the children would feel that it wouldn't be Christmas at all if they received no presents.

Well, there were enough scraps to make a rag doll for each

of the girls. An old sweater could be ripped up to make a new one for Tom, with some left over for socks or mittens for Jim and Carl.

And it cost nothing to fix up the cherished old toys, as we did every year so the children wouldn't feel that as soon as a new gift arrived, the old ones could be thrown away. Fred repaired and repainted carts, doll carriages, and toys; I mended, washed, and starched the old doll clothes, sewed on arms or legs, and patched the places where the stuffing had fallen out. The last thing we did on Christmas Eve was to put the old toys in a special place in the living room and line the dolls up along the back of the sofa.

As the years passed, the sofa became fuller and fuller, the dolls less and less recognizable (to any but their owners), but we had sown the wind and had to reap the whirlwind of never being able to throw anything away, even when it came time to pack. And nothing pleased the children more than to run downstairs early Christmas morning to see what was in their stockings, then to play with their renovated toys. Everything new had to wait until after breakfast.

"It won't take long to open the presents this year," I thought as I sewed button eyes on the rag dolls. But this was the Christmas when the Russian fur buyers, "Uncle" Motia and the others, arrived from Tientsin without the red suits but with packs on their backs.

Some years earlier Fred had been called to see "a foreigner" who, he was told, was dying in a warehouse across the Grand Canal. Fred thought there must be some mistake. To our knowledge the only foreigners in Tsining were those in the missions. He hurried to the warehouse and found a White Russian, desperately ill with pneumonia. In those days before antibiotics, nursing care was essential if the man were to live, so Fred brought him home and the children and I nursed him back to health.

26

From then on, the Russian fur buyers brightened our lives whenever they came to Tsining, not only with piano playing and rollicking songs in Russian (or very sad, beautiful ones), but with feasts of delicacies brought in from Tientsin—zakuska, Kiev cutlets, piroshkis, desserts, coffee, and, of all undreamed-of things, chocolate bonbons!

Never before had the men appeared in December. What a Christmas it turned out to be, especially for the boys, who received as gifts battleships and guns, the instruments of war their parents would never allow them to have! We *had* to succumb this time, seeing how delighted the Russian "uncles" were at the boys' enjoyment of their presents. After the Russian friends had left, I explained to the children that their father and I would never buy them guns nor allow *them* to buy such toys. Guns were used to kill; we were people who healed.

The year came when we meant it literally when we prayed, "Give us this day our daily bread." And as for sugar to make Christmas cookies, there was none of it in the house, none at all. The idea of our traditional fruit cake was so far out of the question it barely entered my head. But no cookies? No gingerbread men? No Santas, bells, or stars made clumsily with dirty cookie dough? We'd have to think of a lot of things to do if the children were to be diverted from making (and eating!) Christmas cookies. Even one cup of sugar, even half a cup, would do.

I had had that much sugar carefully hoarded, but late one cold afternoon, a Japanese officer had called, bringing with him a waif of a girl, one of the young Japanese who had come into the city to cheer the occupation forces. The girls had been in for months now. This one looked so sad and so thin and lonely that I brought out the sugar for their coffee. I measured a meager teaspoonful into each of their cups. As soon as I gave her hers, she ran across the room, took the sugar bowl in both hands and dumped its entire contents into her coffee which she gulped down ravenously.

"Forget the sugar cookies," I said to myself, knitting furiously one afternoon. It was only a few days before Christmas and I would have to hurry if the doll sweaters were to be finished on time. Chang Ta Ke, our gateman, came in to say that two of the Sisters from the Catholic school were here to wish us a Merry Christmas.

We always loved having the Sisters come. I hid my knitting as Jim, Carl, and Anne came in from their play. Tom and Judy, hearing our voices, asked to get up from their naps. Chao Ta Sao, their second mother (and mine!), had them dressed and downstairs in no time.

Sister Lucentia (whom Fred called Sister Licentious so he could watch her throw back her head and laugh her jubilant laugh) was holding a package on her ample lap. It appeared to be fragile. She waited until the children had gathered around her, then she slowly opened it. I gasped when I saw its contents—thin, crisp sugar cookies; not one or two or even one-apiece for the five of them, but a whole lapful of angels and stars and bells—enough to hang on a tree . . .

"Enough to eat a few while hanging them," said Sister Lucentia, holding the cookies in her skirt as she wriggled out of her chair. "Come, Sister, let's show the children how it's done."

The young Sister, recently arrived from Germany, was already halfway across the room.

After Christmas, when we all went in to see the pageant the girls 'school was producing, Mother Superior told me how she had been able to find the sugar and how she had bought it at an "exorbitant price."

"I vowed these Sisters, who have worked so hard and who have gone without so much, would have sugar for Christmas if it took every cent in our deflated treasury," she said. But the Sisters had insisted on using half of it to make the cookies

28

for our children. "We love them very much, you know," said
Mother Superior.

Their love which included sacrifice was the best gift any of
us would have that year.

Today, in a country so blessed that most of us take for granted having all the needed ingredients at hand for most anything we want to make, our youngest daughter uses this recipe:

VICKI'S SUGAR COOKIES

Cream together
  1 cup shortening
  2 cups sifted sugar
Stir in and mix well
  3 eggs
Sift together
  4 cups flour
  4 teaspoons baking powder
  1 teaspoon salt

Gradually add the dry ingredients to the first mixture, stirring well after each cupful. When three cups of the dry ingredients have been added, stir in
  2 teaspoons vanilla
then continue to add the dry ingredients, stirring well, until you have a very stiff batter. Try to use all the flour if possible.

Chill dough in refrigerator for at least 12 hours. Then roll out the cookies, between sheets of wax paper, until very thin.

Cut into trees, stars, angels, etc. with Christmas cookie cutters.

Bake in a 350° oven on *greased* tins for about 5 minutes.

Let cool for 2 minutes before removing from the pan carefully, with a spatula. (If you are going to hang the cookies on your Christmas tree, be sure to make a hole for the silk thread to go through before you bake them.)

FIVE

On March 19, 1943, Fred and I and the children were taken to a Japanese internment camp in Weihsien, Shantung Province. Mother Scovel had returned to America the year before to attend the golden wedding anniversary of her sister and was thus spared the concentration camp experience.

We wondered how many Christmases would pass before we saw her again. But it turned out that we were more fortunate than many others. We were among those chosen for repatriation on the Swedish liner *Gripsholm* on her last trip from the Orient. On December 1 we arrived in New York, after seventy-two days at sea, just in time (and only just!) to have our sixth child, a girl, born in Presbyterian Hospital, New York City. We named her Victoria. Three weeks later we were able to leave the hospital to spend Christmas with my family in Mechanicville.

It was a dream come true—a dream we hadn't dared to

31

dream, this being with Mother and Daddy and my sisters, Helen and Geneva. Brother Bob had brought his bride from Texas and we fell in love with Dorothy. Our youngest brother, Jim, was in the army on the west coast and couldn't be with us. But Mother Scovel, too, was on hand to celebrate the Holy Birthday with us and to see her new grandchild—"the best Christmas gift anyone could possibly have," she said, "the baby, and having you home."

Thinking of our friends left back in the internment camp, we couldn't help feeling how undeserved were our blessings to have been among the three hundred (out of fifteen hundred) to be repatriated. Our baby was *alive* and we were free! A live baby and freedom—could anyone in this beloved country of ours realize what gifts these were? Why, we could take her anywhere we wanted to without first having to get a travel permit! We could pack a suitcase and know it would not be ransacked or even searched! Our friends could drop in to see her without endangering themselves by calling on us! What a Christmas! It was glorious to be home, with all the dangers passed. We moved to Rochester, New York, where Fred joined the medical department of Eastman Kodak. We even found a furnished house there, when everyone knew we couldn't.

One of the first things we did in preparation for the Christmas of 1944 was to buy another copy of Charles Dickens' *A Christmas Carol*. We had lost everything in China but our clothes. There were things we needed more than books, but *this* book we knew we couldn't get through Christmas without. We bought a small 1940 edition (put out by the Monastery Hill Press for Holiday House, New York) with good print and delightful illustrations by Philip Reed.

Soon after we were married, we had begun to read aloud, each Christmas, the *Christmas Carol*, all five staves of it—one a night, the last stave on Christmas Eve. It was fun to watch the children grow with the story, to see their faces light up as they recognized a nuance for the first time; to hear them quoting lines in the context of their everyday lives:

"You're a 'squeezing, wrenching, grasping, scraping, clutching, covetous old sinner! Hard and sharp as flint, from which no steel has ever struck out generous fire . . .'"

"'Come in! And know me better, man!'"

How they loved the Fezziwigs' Ball, with the fiddler tuning "like fifty stomachs" and Mrs. Fezziwig, "one vast substantial smile," then old Fezziwig himself, dancing and cutting "so deftly that he appeared to wink with his legs. . . ."

We all delighted in the descriptions of the shops on Christmas Eve: the fruiterers with "great, round, pot-bellied baskets of chestnuts, shaped like the waistcoats of jolly old gentlemen, lolling at the doors, and tumbling out into the street in their apoplectic opulence . . ."; and the "ruddy, brown-faced, broadgirthed Spanish onions, shining in the fatness of their growth like Spanish Friars . . ."; and the fish, "gasping round and round their little world in passionless excitement"; "and the grocers! Oh the grocers!"; and Mrs. Cratchit, "brave in ribbons," cooking her Christmas dinner and supplying us with a line sure to be pronounced by some man in the family, whenever a roast is brought on, no matter what the meat: "There never was such a goose!"

I usually did the reading; that is, until we reached the scene where the Ghost of Christmas Yet to Come shows Scrooge what will certainly happen in the Cratchit family if things go on as they are. I could never get through the death of the Cratchits' Tiny Tim. Year after year I would try. By taking deep breaths, I could manage the arrival of Bob Cratchit, his tea ready for him on the hob, and their all trying "who should help him to it most," but before the moment came when the grieved father cried, "My little, little child! My little child!" one our our children would say, very softly, "Now, Daddy." And Fred would reach over for the book, to read on to the place where the

Spectre takes Scrooge to see what might become his own dismal future, and I would have stopped crying enough to go on reading.

By Christmas Eve I was always much too tired and had far too many things left to do to use the time it took to read the last stave. But if I didn't, that would spoil it all! The book had been written for this final chapter; every word had led us to this point. And who could resist its opening?

"Yes! And the bed post was his own. The bed was his own, the room was his own. Best and happiest of all, the Time before him was his own to make amends in! . . . Heaven, and the Christmas Time he praised for this! I say it on my knees, old Jacob; on my knees!"

Who would miss the fun Scrooge had in righting all his wrongs, his being so excited he made "a perfect Laocoön* of himself with his stockings"; or the "intelligent boy!" the "remarkable boy" who bought the prize turkey—"Not the little prize turkey; the big one" for Scrooge to send to the Cratchit family; or the morning after Christmas when Scrooge frightened Bob Cratchit almost to the point of calling for "help and a straitwaistcoat" because the old man said, "I am about to raise your salary!"

Scrooge "did it all, and infinitely more; and to Tiny Tim, who did *not* die, he was a second father . . . and it was always said of him, that he knew how to keep Christmas well, if any man alive possessed the knowledge. May that be truly said of us, and all of us!"

Thank you, Charles Dickens, wherever you are, for your gift of *A Christmas Carol.* Who of us could fail to keep Christmas better, having once known Scrooge!

* Fortunately, the Calvert Course, which I was teaching the children, had supplied us with a photograph of the magnificent Greek statue of Laocoön wrestling with the sea serpents. Making a perfect Laocoön of oneself became a frequent saying, as for instance, when I was caught trying to paper the bathroom with strips of contact paper.

Living as we did for so many years in places where we had no television and no movies, the books we received as Christmas gifts meant a great deal to us. We often said that a book was just about the nicest present anyone could give us.

Perhaps you would like to keep a list of the books you get for Christmas each year.

BOOKS FOR CHRISTMAS

Year	Title	Author	Given by

SIX

Fred was among the first of our missionaries to return to China after the Sino-Japanese War. He went out on a troopship which was not about to take aboard a woman with six small children. That Christmas in Rochester, without husband and father, is one we would choose to forget entirely were it not for our good neighbors next door, the Alexander Russells. Alex and Editha came over to open their gifts with us and stay to dinner; then they had us all over at their house for supper. They made our day and we will ever remember their loving thought of us. Still, my diary for December 25, 1945, reads, "Christmas in a world at peace, and the loneliest one of my life."

But I had a special gift from God that Christmas, a gift which has helped me through many Christmases since. It was another lean year; our meager salary had to cover the running of two households a world apart. Fred lived on practically nothing in Huai Yuan, Anhwei Province, where he was rehabilitating our mission hospital ravaged by war. I did the best I could to feed, clothe, and house the seven of us with my more than half of the salary, plus honoraria from speaking two or three times a week. Then came Christmas. How could I buy things for the children, for the family, and for friends who had done so very much for us?

One of the lessons in giving, and perhaps the hardest to learn, is acceptance. One might paraphrase a line of Scripture and say, "It *is* a happier thing to give than to receive." But it is also a loving thing to accept gifts graciously and thankfully. I had decided that this is what I would do for the coming Christmas. I had had the fun of giving all my life. This year I would gratefully accept.

Then I found my gift from God. I was reading the Moffatt translation of the Bible, the first new book I had held in my hands after the internment camp. Fred had given it to me in the hospital after Vicki was born. Popular translations of the Bible were not so common then as they are now. How I reveled in this new leather-bound book with all the freshness of meaning it brought!

At the moment, I was reading in the ninth chapter of Second Corinthians. I could almost feel the eighth verse being laid in my hands: "God is able to bless you with ample means, so that you may always have quite enough for any emergency of your own and ample besides for any kind act to others."

I believed it; I accepted this gift, though it wasn't what I had had in mind when I talked to myself about acceptance. But what a joy to be able to accept *and* to give! The promise was true; I had enough money to buy a present for each child, I don't know how. I suddenly remembered the star candles we'd made when the first three children were small. So I asked Central Presbyterian Church if we could have the candle stubs left over from Sunday services and were given a whole box of them. Everyone we could think of, relative or friend, received floating candles from the Scovels for Christmas.

The diary for December 25, 1946, has this entry: "What a strange way to spend Christmas—taking sulpha and looking at the canvas bottom of the bunk above me. *But* going to Fred!"

The six children, Mother Scovel, and I were aboard the *Marine Lynx*. Having been separated from Fred for a year and a month, our visas for China had finally come through. Mother Scovel was ill; so was I. Hourly, I thanked God for friends like Dorothy Wagner and Stella Walter, and the young bride, who took care of us and the children.

I don't remember how or when I actually wrote the entry in my diary. I don't see how I could have found it or the pen or the strength to write. Perhaps it was early on Christmas morning, when I tried to arrange the crèche for the children.

I do remember crawling out of the bunk while the children were at breakfast, and the endless time it took to arrange the figures on the flat of the suitcase with the ship rolling from one side to the other. I remember the effort it took to haul out the suitcase that held the presents. And I remember the relief of being in the bunk again after the preparations were finished. The rest of that day was for me merciful oblivion.

It was, as Carl once said, "a Christmas by which to judge all others." Years later he would write this memory of it:

CHRISTMAS AT SEA
by Carl Scovel

Christmas in 1946 was a gray day. The sky was gray, the sea was gray, the ship was gray, and even we were a little gray after two weeks of sailing across a choppy Pacific. We were

38

two hundred children and wives of missionaries returning to China on an old troop transport named the *Marine Lynx*.

Seven of the two hundred were Scovels. Our father had preceded us to China by a year. He had reopened a mission hospital closed by the war and was continuing his work as a missionary doctor. His letters to us in Rochester, New York, had been filled with reports of change and turbulence. It didn't sound like the old China we had left.

He would meet us when the ship arrived in Shanghai. Jim and I, the two oldest children, would remain there for boarding school; the younger four would stay with our parents three hundred miles away in the interior of China.

As I look back on this voyage two things impress me. First, I am impressed with the dismaying uncertainties toward which we sailed—a country and a history in upheaval, and for Jim and me the prospect of living apart from our family for the first time at a school which we knew nothing about. Second, I am impressed with how little we thought or felt about these uncertainties. I don't remember discussing them. I don't remember worrying about them. We accepted them without reflection.

You must understand these uncertainties if you are to understand the Christmas Day which we spent aboard the *Marine Lynx*. It was a day with a color—gray. The ship was pitching and I doubt if I ate any more than my usual few mouthfuls. The meals aboard the *Lynx* were so tasteless that to this day I have no specific recollection of eating during those seventeen days. Indeed I have only one clear memory of Christmas Day itself.

Six children, aged sixteen to four, stood around their mother's bunk, the lowest in a tier of three, in a great room in the ship's hold. Our mother was not only seasick; for five days she had been ill with lobar pneumonia. She had put the family crèche on top of the suitcase beside her bunk and arranged the gifts

39

in front of it. We opened the gifts, we thanked her, and then she went back to sleep and we went up on the deck to play. And that was Christmas.

Except for one thing more. Every night after dark the high school bunch gathered in an empty gun turret, snuggled up to one another, and there in the warmth of our peer group told stories, swapped jokes, and sang camp songs, folk songs, and hymns. On that Christmas night I am sure that we must have gathered in the gun turret and surely must have sung some Christmas carols.

As our rolling ship carried us through the night and over the tossing sea toward an uncertain future, the experience of singing with my peers was a little sign of graciousness in a very frightening world. To be sure, there was not grace enough to hold back the darkness, or revolution, but there was a sign at least. That much. And in this world we can be grateful for a sign.

King's Chapel
Boston, Massachusetts

SEVEN

The celebration of Christmas in our new station, Huai Yuan, brought a new joy—two teen-age boys, home from Shanghai American School! They couldn't believe their sister Anne had grown up enough to give a concert. From then on her father always asked her to sing "O Holy Night" for him on Christmas.

We lived in a huge, beautiful old house and brought in a tree from the garden so large it had to be sawed off at the top and even then, it completely filled one end of the living room. Our ornaments looked lost in it.

Mother Scovel, now in her wheel chair, enjoyed every minute of the festivities, and so did we all.

So did we all, not realizing that by next Christmas Mother would have gone to sleep after her long illness to awake in her Real World. We were in Hackett Medical Center, Canton,

41

when she died on December 2, 1948. We had moved ahead of the advancing Communist Army in order to be able to work as long as possible.

Canton fell on October 14, 1949. By then Jim and Carl were in America in college; Anne was in school in Hong Kong until the following year when she flew to the United States to take her last two years of high school at Northfield School for Girls. The youngest three were still with us.

We had made our decision to remain in China under the Communist regime, thinking that Fred, being a doctor, could carry on as usual since he, too, had the interests of the people at heart and was a "worker" not a "preacher." By December, 1950, we knew that our position was untenable. Fred was not allowed to continue his teaching at the Ling Nam Medical College, nor to practice his profession at Hackett Medical Center. On December 3 we registered our application with the police for permission to return to America. We would be with the older three for Christmas!

But in spite of frequent visits to the police station, no permit was issued. We found we couldn't remain in Communist China, nor could we leave it!

Again there were no gifts for the children, and again we had a miracle for Christmas. No wonder Anne once said, "Mother, it gets so I *expect* miracles to happen." Being all together as a family in America was not one of them. But we were grateful for the miracle of gifts—this time through the head post office in Canton!

We received word that a package of Christmas gifts had been there for about two years and no one had claimed them. We could have the package if we were willing to pay the duty —a nominal amount. When we had cleaned up the contents of the package (a can of tomato juice had exploded and dried over everything), we found the perfect gift for each child— a game for Tom, a baby doll apiece for Judy and Vicki. Tom and Fred went to work at once to make wooden cradles for the dolls, and we bought Ping Pong paddles and balls for Tom.

Judy would recall that Christmas in Canton in a Christmas letter:

Tehran, Iran
December 29

Dearest Dad and Mom,

Happy Holidays! Here's hoping your Christmas was as merry a one as ours! It arrived here, of course, before finally heaving itself around to you. Since we were only a part of a fraction of a percent celebrating the event, Tehran went on as usual. On the way to church that morning, we drove through streets seething with normal, daily traffic. But things looked different, just as they do when you go outside on your own birthday—the pale sunshine was a bit brighter, the streets a bit cleaner, and the snow-splendored mountains a bit more awe-inspiring. Our drab city was truly blessed by the torch of the Spirit of Christmas Present.

In church this was even more obvious. I played in the Service of Morning Prayer and the sanctuary was full of those willing to greet total strangers warmly. We met many people we'd never seen before, like the crew from the BOAC 747 who'd just touched down in Tehran and wanted to celebrate Christmas.

Elizabeth behaved very well for a three-week-old baby. Granted, she chose an opportune moment to break forth into a rafter-shaking yell (the Old Testament reader was just be-

43

coming eloquent in his rendition of "For unto us a Child is born"); and she *did* insist on making impolite digestive noises during the sermon; but nobody seemed to mind.

The beauty of the Episcopal service and the serenity of the pine-scented chapel sank into an inward feeling of calm as we arrived home and exploded into activity. It's always chaos before a big dinner, isn't it? But so much fun! I love having millions of little black, bubbling pots all over the stove, each gurgling and cooing ecstatically. And our goldening fifteen-pound turkey was already sizzling busily in the oven, working hard to permeate the whole house with its aroma before the guests arrived.

I, of course, had little time to notice, what with running around like a scalded cat trying to (a) find things (I'm sure there was a can of cranberry jelly carefully hoarded in the garage with the newspapers and the hiking boots), (b) make things (ever peel 47,000 shallots and roll pie crust simultaneously?), and (c) arrange things (why, on special occasions, do flowers always look seasick and hang biliously over the edge of a bowl?). Well, the Tornado Warnings were still up when the guests arrived.

In they came—the English couple whom John found in the international telephone office when he was phoning you about Elizabeth's birth (He remet them when he was serving at Midnight Communion on Christmas Eve. Their hitchhiking trip to India had to be given up because of the India-Pakistan War.); another English couple, both doctors, who were working in Quetta, Baluchistan, Pakistan, and were evacuated due to the same war; the exhausted, strep-throated Episcopal Vicar, followed by his equally drained wife and two sons—in they all came, as I have said, and were very kind in helping with the last-minute preparations.

In no time, well, it was actually 2:45, we were sitting down to a meal of

44

Toasted Sesame Seed Crackers
Roast Turkey with Celery Stuffing
Mashed Ginger Squash
Roast Potatoes
Mashed Potatoes
Gravy
Buttered Peas and Baby Onions
Tossed Green Salad
Warm Apple Pie and Cream
Christmas Pudding and Custard Sauce
Coffee   Tea
Pistachio Nuts

For the rest of the afternoon we sat around "doing our own thing": John and the male Quetta doctor played jazz on their guitar and clarinet; Elizabeth slept; the traveling couple went back to the international telephone office to call parents in England; the women talked babies and the Vicar clung to the kerosene heater like a ship to the Lorelei and smiled drowsily at the air in front of him as he listened to the music.

Later that evening, when quiet had settled on the debris like snow on autumn leaves, I got thinking of other beautiful Christmases—the funny one when you gave Vicki and me the "hippopotamus"; the miraculous one in Canton when we were under the Communists and that rotting package appeared from nowhere. In it was Betsy! How I loved that doll, even after the foam stuffing came out of her arm because the broken tomato juice tin had torn it! Little did I know then that many beautiful Christmases later I'd hold my own baby in my arms— Elizabeth, a "doll" who looks very much like the original Betsy!

And because of our baby I think this has been an even more miraculous Christmas, even more blessed, with a deeper feeling that God is with us. Isn't it absolutely amazing that the love

John and I have for each other is so strong it can create something tangible, a complete little human being?

And perhaps at last I realize what the First Christmas was all about.

May its joy be with you both throughout the coming year.

> Love,
>
> Judy (Scovel Robinson)

P.S. Herewith Elizabeth's footprint.

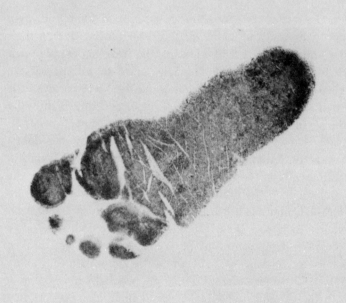

EIGhT

One Christmas gift I would never have chosen, but realize now the valuable experience it was to learn how it feels to be "the enemy." It was difficult to go through, *especially* at Christmas. True, there were many Chinese who reached out to us in efforts of kindness (like whoever it was at the Canton Post Office who remembered that our children might be without any gifts). Our Chinese friends and acquaintances never forsook us, and continued to put themselves in difficult positions to show their love and loyalty. Still the bulk of the Communist propaganda and the harassments were planned to make us feel that we were "despised and rejected" of *all* men.

The gardener was not allowed to bring in our usual potted evergreen, and he made it clear that we should not try to do it ourselves. Not having the tree was a small thing, but it hurt deeply that the children were the ones who were going to feel the deprivation most.

It seemed strange to be literally sitting around doing nothing the week before Christmas without the usual round of visits to the schools and to the homes of our Chinese friends. We couldn't do this without being an embarrassment to them, perhaps even a danger. We missed seeing the Christmas pageant at Ming Sum School for the Blind. It had been such a moving experience the year before that I'd come home and written a poem about it. I found my notebook and read it to Fred:

Christmas at Ming Sum School

Little blind angels in "heaven,"
little blind shepherds below,
singing of Bethlehem's Baby,
leading each other they go.

Little blind Mary, adoring,
Joseph with downcast mien,
crimson-robed Wise Men presenting
gifts that they never have seen;

satin-clad fairies of Christmas,
elves and the cherub who sings,
shifting the while on his shoulders
heavy, uncomfortable wings;

little blind flutist piping
softly, while blind angels hum,
O dear little blind beloveds,
the Light of the World has come!

"I wish you'd write more poetry," Fred said. "You have the time now."

48

"The time, but not the inspiration," I told him.

"Why not give it a try?" he urged.

I tried. I sat at my desk and went through the motions and only became more and more furious at myself because I could not rise above the cold, dank walls of the living room, the too-many sweaters binding my arms, the gray sky closing me into this prison of waiting—this *agony* of waiting. According to the date on the calendar, we were to have been with the children in America by this time.

"God, I can't bear it," I said to Him. "I just cannot bear it. It's this terrible weather, for one thing. This chill would be depressing even with a roaring fire and a glowing Christmas tree."

"It won't do," I said to myself. "It won't help any to rail at God. You'll have to get hold of yourself. Maybe you should try a concrete poem, something that would only take the mechanics of drawing a picture with words."

But what? Well, I could try a Christmas tree.

A

fir

stood

There was the peak of it! The "A" even looked something like a star! Hmm . . . not bad . . .

A

fir

stood

proudly

in the wood

I had no idea where this was taking me. A Christmas poem should have more in it than the description of a fir tree standing in a wood.

A
fir
stood
proudly
in the wood
outlined by sky.
A child cried, "Look!

Then it all came!

A
fir
stood
proudly
in the wood
outlined by sky.
A child cried, "Look!
The stars are all caught
in
it.
God has made us
a Christmas tree!"

And so He had! "Dear, dear God, You've done it again," I prayed. "This time I was sure even You couldn't manage it." I was elated over this small Christmas tree; so was Fred, and the children caught our enthusiasm.

"Let's find some wood somewhere, build a fire in the fireplace and pop that last can of popcorn," I suggested.

"Let's make some popcorn balls too," said Judy. "We can eat them even if we can't hang them on Mother's tree."

"And some fudge," said Tom.

"And let's set up the crèche now," said Fred. "Shall we put it on the mantel where we had it last year?"

Such a wonderful afternoon! We even read the first stave of

the *Christmas Carol.* And when we found that the nose of one of the little lambs was broken, Vicki discovered that if you cuddled its face in the hand of the Christ Child, it didn't show. With so very much for which to be thankful, I was ashamed of my reactions earlier in the day. We were together, we were well, we had a roof over our heads and enough to eat. Above all this, we could trust God for our future.

And before December 25 we even had a Christmas tree. A dear friend, the maintenance engineer at the hospital, had gone out to his family graveyard, cut down one of the evergreens (an unheard-of act), and braved he knew not what to bring the tree into the house of "imperialist Americans." "There," he said when the lovely tree was in its place. "These children are going to have their Christmas tree."

No words could express what his gift meant to us, and certainly not because we had our Christmas tree. We already had the one God had given us. But because amid all the unpleasantness of the weeks past, we knew we had a friend—a friend who was willing to give not only his gift, but himself.

A month later, on January 24, 1951, we crossed the border into Hong Kong. We were free, *free*, FREE! And no longer an embarrassment or a danger to the friends we had to leave behind.

NINE

Color and sun exploded upon us as we walked the streets of
Ludhiana, a Punjab city in northern India where Fred had
been assigned in 1953 as Professor of Medicine at the Christian
Medical College. India was so full of color it looked like
perpetual Christmas. In the hospital the women doctors and
medical students wore the usual long white coats, but from
underneath them, soft saris of red, brilliant blues, pale pinks
or yellows billowed to the floor in wavelets as they walked.
Outside, white coats off, the compound looked as if it were
filled with moving blossoms under the flowering trees—
laburnum, flame-of-the-forest, and the orchidlike camel's foot,
named for the shape of its leaves.

Up in the foothills of the Himalayas Tom, Judy, and Vicki,
aged fourteen, twelve, and ten, were attending Woodstock
School. But they would be home for their winter vacation in
early December, in plenty of time to help with Christmas

preparations. Their arrival on what was known at Woodstock as "Going-Down Day" was one of the most exciting days in the year, a fitting start for the Christmas season.

Their usual train was due in at 3:21 A.M. What a thrill to hear it thunder down the track, the old station platform shuddering as if in dread of its approach! But on the train would come, grumbling into silence as it drew to a stop to spill forth what might have been Disneyland on one if its busiest days. Children were running in all directions, sorting out parents, some of whom were still hurrying the length of the train to find their children, anxious expressions of "What-if-they-haven't-come?" on their faces.

"Mommy! Daddy!" We knew those squeals from all the rest! We hugged the dusty coats and kissed the sooty faces. Tom and Fred found the suitcases. We did our best to shorten the farewells to classmates going on to farther destinations, hurried the children into the rickshas waiting to take them home through the dark, quiet streets to cocoa, "*hot* toast—what a change!", baths, and bed.

The next two days would be spent unpacking, shampooing the dust-stiff hair and having it "cutted," according to Vicki; washing the woolens, sorting the piles of laundry for the *dhobi* to take; all the while talking and talking and talking, playing records, making fudge; this interspersed with Tom's urgings for the girls to drop everything and "come out and run the mile."

Fred and Tom took care of most of their own Christmas shopping, the girls and I did the rest. The bazaar in Ludhiana could produce almost anything we needed, if we used our imaginations a little—kite paper in strong, clear colors made excellent wrapping paper, gold and silver braid (sari trimming), or strands of yarn were the tyings.

It was fun to walk the rutted stone of the narrow streets to

53

look into the small shops, slowly edging their way to the middle of the road. Shopkeepers, measuring out yards and yards of silk or ribbon which piled up in their capacious laps, sat on carpeted platforms at eye level with the customers.

Suddenly one of us would disappear—Vicki, perhaps, to return to the bell shop to buy a pair of the anklets dancers wore for the Indian classical dances. (Both girls were taking lessons and both had made surreptitious suggestions that this would be a good present for the other.) Judy and I would stay at the ribbon shop till Vicki came back so she could find us, then pretend we hadn't noticed her absence. Judy would take her opportunity to disappear for the same purpose later.

"How do you say 'sequins' in Hindustani, Mother?" she now asked.

"Judy, what in the world do you want sequins for?"

"Do you really want to know? It's Christmas, remember?"

"Okay. Let's see, how can I describe a sequin . . ."

I turned to the shopkeeper and asked, "Sir, do you have any of those *tikas* women wear pasted between their eyebrows? Only these have two little holes so you can sew them on things."

"*Sequins mujhe de dou* (Give me the sequins)," he said to his helper. That troublesome word seemed to be the only English word he knew.

That Christmas I received a beautiful red table cloth made of woven cotton from Gandhi's Ashram, embroidered all around its wide border with green Christmas trees spangled with sequins. No wonder Judy had had her light on until 2:00 A.M. Christmas morning! I couldn't have been more thrilled with my gift if I had been Tom, Judy, and Vicki on their first Christmas in India, receiving *their* gift from our fellow missionary, Mildred Hoffmeister, principal of Ewing Christian School. She had come in with a handful of wiggling black cocker spaniel.

I had told the children firmly that they would not be able

54

to have any pets in India. Having to go away and leave a loved animal behind, no matter how trusted the friend or relative to whom it is bequeathed, is an occupational hazard of missionaries. We had had a dog while we were on furlough in America. I had not wanted us to have a dog then. With six children, I had enough muddy feet running in on freshly cleaned floors, and enough experience to know who had to remember to feed all household pets, whatever member of the family claimed ownership.

But I had relented. And who cried the hardest when we had to leave our cocker in Rochester, New York, with our adored Kiehle cousins? Me. And who was the pushover the moment she saw the litter of puppies Mildred's honey-colored cocker, Texas, had produced? The same.

"Would you let me give the children one for Christmas?" she had asked.

"Oh, Mildred, that would be just wonderful of you! How about the little black one? It looks just like the one they had to leave," I had replied.

The children named him Tuffy "because he has a white 'tuff' under his chin," said Vicki.

(Tuffy gave us six years of love, torment, and affection, and when we left India, Mildred took him back. Texas had died and it comforted her to have the son of Texas become the school's new mascot.)

The Christmas Gift

Every boy should have a dog.
I've had it drummed into my ears
continually for all these years.
Of course, a boy should have a dog.

I have succumbed to pleading eye,
to smudge of mud on quivering chin,
his hopeful father joining in
to ask again the reasons why.

And now I find this muff of joy
that chews his shoes, that licks his face,
has proved beyond the slightest trace
that every dog should have a boy.

In June, 1956, Tom left us to attend Wooster College in Ohio. That first Christmas away from home must have been difficult for him, as it was for us. His letters spoke of our celebrations, the parties, the carollers, and of the Christmas when we were given "his" dog, Tuffy.

Years later, in Thailand, he would write his thoughts of one lonely night in New Mexico, where he had gone to spend the holidays with a classmate:

ON TRUCHAS MOUNTAIN
by Tom Scovel

It was very cold, very clear, and very quiet on Truchas Mountain on the night of December 23, 1957. I had come to spend Christmas with a college friend in New Mexico, and, half by whim and half by predilection, had decided to climb this snowy peak just north of Santa Fe alone, quite alone.

There had been moments of embarrassment. It was difficult for me to explain to Jon and his parents why I should go trekking off by myself at Christmas time, up a mountain I had never even seen. We had just arrived in Albuquerque after a two-day drive from Wooster College in Ohio, and there was much to do: horseback riding along the Rio Grande, sightseeing among the nearby Indian tribes, and partying with Jon's former highschool buddies. But all that had to wait, although it was

57

difficult to explain just why. However, Jon and his family were understanding, and with gentle reluctance, saw me off on a Greyhound bus bound north to Santa Fe and to the mountain beyond.

It had also been embarrassing to set out from the bus, clad in an assortment of flannels, denims, and woolens, with a huge army duffel bag strapped on my back. To the passengers at the bus terminal and to the few people who passed me in cars, slowing to give me the curious glances that all Americans seem to give those who deign to walk when God gave us cars to drive, I must have looked like a coat rack that had just emerged from a nearby hunting lodge. But embarrassment evaporates with solitude, and as I trudged higher up the road away from cars, houses, and people, I lost my self-consciousness. How strange that you do not feel self-conscious when you have no one but yourself to be self-conscious of!

It was late afternoon by the time I reached the deserted ski area. My mountaineering instincts usually force me to attempt to reach the top, but this time I had no desire to do so. Plodding softly through the deep snow, I came to a ridge where I camped, the peak itself still glistening coldly several thousand feet above. It was evening and I turned to catch the sun going down in a classic Southwestern sunset.

Sitting alone on a cold, lonely mountain, I could remember things so vividly. It may have been the coldness of the snow, the clearness of the mountain air, or the quietness of the solitude. Perhaps it was the propinquity of time and space. Just as my gaze wandered from near to far—from the ridge itself to the slopes beneath, to the twinkling lights of Santa Fe, to the ever-darkening horizon—so my thoughts wandered in concert from events near at hand to memories far in the past.

The most recent memories were of the *Luminarios* at Albuquerque the night before. Jon and I had driven up the mountain west of the city after dark and had looked down at the thousands of homes lit with candles placed in sand at the bottom of paper bags—something as simple and as drab as sand and paper bags, but so lovely illuminated by candles and seen from afar.

We had had a candlelight carol sing at college before driving out, but the memory was dark despite the image it contained. This was the part of being alone that I was afraid of; no friends, no classes, no sports, no music, no plays, no distractions of any kind to delude me from the knowledge that my academic life had been dark and cold. Even now, I had a premonition it would be even darker and colder. And what good would it do to sit on Truchas Mountain and nurse the recent failures at school? Perhaps I saw them for the first time and recognized them for what they were, just as I could recognize the confines of Santa Fe much more clearly from the mountain than from the town itself. And just as I could see the town lights in the context of the whole panorama, I learned to see some of my failures within the vast sweep of time.

But there were happier memories—memories farther back in time and space. There were memories of mountains, many memories of many mountains far away: the Himalayas and the many climbs with Bill and Tom and Bren, climbs we would never take again; Bear Mountain in New York with rocks and forests (but, to the disappointment of a boy, without bears!); Lan Tau, the island mountain in Hong Kong harbor, always surrounded by mist. I smiled as I recalled the time when my sisters and I got lost in the mist on our way to breakfast in the dinning hall and ended up (and very nearly *in*) the rocky swimming pool. And of course there were memories of my very first mountain, East Mountain in Huai Yuan, where we went picnicking as a family during my childhood in China.

But it was Christmas, wasn't it? And didn't these memories

59

go even farther back in space—far, far back to some hills where Someone else had been alone, not once but many times? Back in time, too, to a time when men were guided by a star?

There were many stars, and as I looked up at them and at the starlit peak, I felt that somehow it was good to be alone. I lay down to sleep. The next day I would return to Albuquerque and to Christmas. It was very cold, very clear, and very quiet on Truchas Mountain.

Chiengmai University
Chiengmai, Thailand

60

TEN

The Ludhiana Staff Christmas party was an annual event we had started early in our stay at the Medical College when we found that the unmarried women of our college and hospital had little or no Christmas celebration for themselves. They spent all their time and energy on Christmas for the students, hospital patients, workers and their families. They lived in a dormitory, so we decided to give them a party in our home. In the end we invited the whole senior staff, married and single. We were Indians, Americans, Canadians, Scots, Australians, Germans, and Irishmen. We sent out sixty-two invitations that first year. By the time we left India six years later, there were nearer a hundred twenty-five. Not all could accept, of course; Christmas or not, the ill must be cared for, perhaps all the more lovingly at Christmas.

Our hundred-year-old mud-brick house was ideal for a party. The rooms were large, the ceilings high, some of them over twenty feet high; the floors were cement; double doors could be opened to allow for a flow of movement. And there was a fireplace in every room.

Chandru, the cook, and Balu, boy-of-all-trades, cleaned, pushed back the beds in corners against the wall to be arranged as couches, opened the dining table to its full capacity and moved it to the end of the dining room to provide a buffet. The married women of the college offered to bring the food— the specialties of their countries or families: thick, syrupy Indian sweets; the German cookies called pfeffernuesse; small mince pielets from England; Mexican tea cakes (brought by Rusty Rice, an American); fudge (chocolate and the white Indian kind, with cardamom seeds); cookies of all kinds, cakes, salted nuts, and so forth. The girls made popcorn balls. One year Chandru and I tried out Roma Chauhan's recipe for Christmas cake. (Roma was the wife of our Ludhiana Magistrate.) Tea, coffee, and Grandmother Scovel's hot spiced orange juice were also on hand.

We missed Tom's help that year, but at last everything was ready. We had only to cover the "couches" with Indian drapes and do the arrangements of evergreens, pine cones, candles, wax angels, whatever, on the dressers and mantels. Of course, the *big* mantel over the fireplace in the living room already held the crèche. Our Indian friends enjoyed picking up the figures to study the faces. Many of them had never seen a crèche before. But the Christmas tree was another thing. I kept wondering what they really thought of it, especially after my bout with our Hindu gardener. Did it really look all that silly? I certainly hoped not.

I like to think of the Christmas tree as a symbol of the joy and gaiety and lively fun of Christmas, a sign of the blessing of trees to this earth and to us, a sign of the abundance of life and living that Christ came to bring. Some of the Indian Christians outlined the roofs, windows, and verandas of their houses with little clay lamps filled with oil—a witness that Christ was the Light of the world. We might have followed this custom, but others of our Christian friends felt it was too reminiscent of the Hindu Divali Festival, from which the custom sprang. We thought it might be best to go on with our own traditions, since Christmas was universal. But the gardener had shaken my confidence.

"You mean you want this tree dug up?" he asked, incredulous. "It's doing very well here. Arborvitae trees don't like to be moved."

"I know, but you can do it carefully. You're good at transplanting," I told him. "Just put it in this box."

"You want it planted in a *box*?"

"Yes, Mali, so we can bring it into the living room."

"You want it in the *house*?"

"Yes. We're going to decorate it with strings of popcorn and . . ." The further I went trying to explain, the worse it became. I gave up. By sheer dogged determination I persuaded him to bring the tree into the living room. And here it stood, our lovely tree; there was nothing I could do about it three hours before the guests were to arrive. And what on earth would *they* say when they saw some of our new ornaments, purchased in the bazaar—brightly colored small round brushes used on ricksha wheels to whirl off the mud?

"I wouldn't worry about it if I were you," said Fred when he returned from his final rounds at the hospital.

"Yes you would worry about it if you were me," I told him. "You wouldn't worry about it only if you were you."

"Now, honey, don't let it spoil your whole evening. These people have seen Christmas trees before—the Germans, the English, all of them and most of the Indians. Probably everyone who comes will be glad there is a Christmas tree. And think how disappointed the kids would be if we didn't have one."

"It's just part of the family fun, decorating the Christmas tree," I admitted.

"To tell you the truth, I wouldn't want to miss it either."

" 'My husband is my youngest son,' " I quoted.

"Better be sure Tippy and her kittens are locked up to-night," he said, ignoring my remark. Tippy was our Siamese cat. Her kittens were sure the tree had been set up just for them. They scrambled up it and into it, batted at Christmas balls, knocking them to the floor, tangled themselves in the tinsel. Tuffy did his best to bark them down, which only resulted in their climbing so high they almost broke the top branches. While we were trying to catch one, another would break away and run for the tree again. At last we rounded them up and banished them to the back of the house.

"They'll be all right unless Chandru needs something from the storeroom and forgets they're in there," I said.

"Any hot water for a bath?" Fred asked.

"Yes, Balu has had the charcoal burning in the *hamam* for a long time. And I have your tuxedo laid out on the bed."

"My what? Don't tell me I have to—"

"But darling, you said you would."

"I know, but that was a long time ago. Well, okay, I suppose I'll have to."

"Daddy, you always look gorgeous in it and you know it and you really like it," said Judy, coming into the room and following her father to the foot of the stairs as he hurried off, chuckling.

The party was all we'd hoped it might be. The men were handsome in their evening attire, the Indian women resplendent in their beautiful saris; but then the Indian women always were. It was the foreign women who were completely transformed by their long satins, chiffons, or taffetas. We were so used to seeing one another in uniforms or cotton dresses or in suits and sweaters we'd been wearing forever.

There were quantities of the delicious and exotic cakes and pies and cookies; there were games and there were carols, including all the verses of "The Twelve Days of Christmas" sung at gratifying speed; there was Santa and an exchange of gifts—everyone had something from the old Saint; there was the usual request for Dr. Kundan Lall's solo, *"Those days were very, very, beautiful—ah . . ."*, and there were "adverbs" and there were charades.

I was used to the simple charades, worked out on the spot by dragging in an ironing board and getting Anne to press a pair of her father's pants as she sobbed and wiped away pretend tears—obviously, "Pressed-by-teary-Anne" denoting our denominational persuasion. But these charades, put on by the English members of our staff, were theatrical productions, with props and elaborate costuming. And they were not easy to guess, either.

When we had laughed till we were exhausted, and the props and costumes had been stuffed into suitcases again, our Indian pastor, Padri Amos Boyd, rose to say a parting prayer, raising his hand to invoke a Christmas blessing upon each of us, upon our work, and upon those we loved "wherever they may be."

The good-nights said, we came back into the living room for one more look at the candlelight flickering on the figures of the crèche. Occasionally, one of us would rise to rearrange an ornament on our shining Christmas tree, which, after all, *seemed* to have delighted our guests, reminding some of former Christmases, viewed by others as something new and beautiful. Even the wheel brushes had contributed their moments of amazement or amusement.

ROMA CHAUHAN'S CHRISTMAS CAKE

(her mother's recipe)

Note: 1 seer is equal to about two pounds
  1 seer butter
1¼ seer eggs (in shells)
  ¼ seer sugar
  ¼ seer mixed citrus peel
  ¼ seer crystallized ginger
1¼ seer raisins
  ½ seer manaka (large raisins)
1½ seer petha sweet (pumpkin preserve)
  1 seer almonds (in shells) or ¼ seer (shelled)
½ seer flour (or slightly more if needed)
  2 jaiphals (nutmegs)

Each of the following should be equal in weight to the 2 jaiphals:
  javathri (mace)
  small elechi (cardamom)
  stick cinnamon

Powder the above condiments and strain through muslin.

Cream butter and sugar well, add the beaten egg yolks, and cream a little more. Add the fruit, almonds, and spices. Last of all, add the flour and stiffly beaten egg whites. Add a little burnt sugar as desired, for coloring. Bake as for any fruit cake.

Makes five or six good-sized cakes.

Rusty Rices's recipe for

MEXICAN TEA CAKES

Mix together thoroughly
   1 cup margarine
   ½ cup sifted icing sugar
   1 teaspoon vanilla
Sift together and stir in
   2¼ cups sifted flour
   ¼ teaspoon salt
Mix in
   ¾ cup finely chopped nuts

Chill dough. Roll into one-inch balls. Place on ungreased cookie sheet. (Cookies won't spread.) Bake until set, not brown. While still warm, roll in confectioners' sugar. Cool. Roll in sugar again.

Temperature: 400°.

Time: Bake 10-12 minutes.

Amount: About 4 dozen one-and-a-half-inch cookies.

ELEVEN

Joy and sorrow battled each other in our emotions during Christmas of 1958, our last in India. Fred would be leaving us on Christmas night and would not be back until February. He had been asked to become Secretary of the Christian Medical Council for Overseas Work, with headquarters in New York City. In this capacity he would be concerned with the medical interests of over a hundred Protestant denominations. In order to familiarize himself with more of this vast field, he was to visit hospitals in Taiwan, Korea, Japan, the Philippines, Thailand, and Burma. We would all be leaving India after Judy's graduation from Woodstock in May.

And I had been asked to take a position in the Communications Department of our own United Presbyterian office and would be writing of our overseas work. The decisions had not been easy to make. We had planned on a lifetime of service

68

abroad. But Fred and I both felt that the call had come from God and that part of the reason for the call was for us to be in America with our children during these important years of their lives. Anne and Carl had both been married and we hadn't been with them. We wondered how we could have allowed ourselves to be separated from them for six very long years.

Now we would be together, all of us, for Christmas, 1959! I almost choked with joy at the thought of it. Meanwhile, there were all the wrenchings to be faced of a last Christmas in India. Not that the hilarity abated—1958 was the year I was given a pencil at the Annual Staff Party.

To be sure, it is not unusual for a writer to be given a pencil, but this one was three feet five inches high, twelve inches in circumference, and weighed a little under ten pounds, if our bathroom scales were to be trusted. It felt even heavier. The remark "Why not? It's a *lead* pencil" was greeted with groans. Its hexagonal length and symmetrical point had been perfectly constructed of teak—by the carpenters at the hospital, we gathered. The wood had been sandpapered to a satin smoothness, then stained and varnished to resemble a pencil so perfectly one knew that if the Jolly Green Giant ever gave up canning to become a writer, he would have just what he needed here. He couldn't run off with it, however, for along the side was printed, "M. SCOVEL—XXX H.B."

The perpetrator could only be Mr. R. W. Royston, out from England for two years as business manager, and living with us. It may have been in retaliation for our Christmas gift to him the year before. R. W. had an elaborate system of using razor blades to make them last longer, one every so many days, with a rest period of varying days in between—something about the molecular structure. To him it was all very simple; to the girls and me, unfathomable. We joked about it a lot and decided we would give him razor blades for Christmas.

Not just a package of razor blades, mind you, but a package every hour for eight hours. Each one was wrapped in something different. He might find his razor blades in a mug, or between the pages of a paperback, or inside one box after another, or in a bag of sweets, and so it went.

(In the end R.W. got the best of that joke. His razor blades have long since been used up. Or have they? I still have the pencil and he should know what it has done to complicate our lives when packing and moving! Each time we start to measure it against the length of a trunk, dreading the expense of ten pounds extra weight, my mind knows I should get rid of it. But my heart? Well, there it stands, my pencil, in the corner of the study as I write.)

The party became quieter than usual for Padri Amos Boyd's prayer that night, and I held back the tears when he blessed us and when the good-nights on the veranda, under the stars, held the feeling of good-by.

As the members of our household who called themselves our servants gathered in our living room that Christmas Eve, Fred told them, as he had each year, how grateful we were for all they did to help make possible our work at the hospital. He reminded them that, in God's eyes and in ours, their work was every bit as important as his. Even our Hindu gardener was present. Usually he would not remain for the meal we ate together later, but this time he said he'd stay and have some tea and perhaps some cakes we'd bought in the bazaar especially for him.

The table had been moved back and we sat on the floor, Indian style, a tablecloth spread before us. Chandru had cooked the food, unwilling to take a chance on what I might prepare. Judy and Vicki waited on table between bites. It wasn't quite so much fun without Tom. This was his third

Christmas away from home. In the past he and Chandru had kept up a running banter thoughout the meal:

Chandru: A little more service here, young man. I'm out of tea.
Tom (*quickly throwing a towel over his arm*): Tea coming up, sir. Any other service?

Now Chandru wanted to know how Tom was; what his last letter had said; was he doing well in school?
Umda, Chandru's wife, drew a long sigh.

Would ever a Christmas come without our thinking of our Indian friends dropping in on Christmas Eve to sing the carols in English, Punjabi, or Hindustani? We would recall the groups of villagers singing their syncopated *bhajans* to the rhythm of the *tubla* drums; teachers from Ewing Christian School, whose accompaniment was the beautiful sitar; the different groups from the hospital, and especially our students who every week met in our home with Dr. Lakshmi Rao, Dr. Mukerji, and other faculty members for Bible study or an occasional party.

They came in, that last Christmas Eve, and stood in a circle, light from candles shining up into their faces. I wanted to name each name, take each hand, look into each pair of eyes. "Children of ours, where will you be the next time we see you," we wondered.

More carolers and more— Suddenly we heard, in English, a strange song to be hearing in India:

> *Home, home on the range,*
> *where the deer and the antelope play. . . .*

Who in the world? . . . and a guitar accompaniment? It couldn't be! We rushed to the door as in trooped our neighbors, the whole Sardar Khan family—mother, father, children, and

71

grandchildren—all of them having a good laugh at the look on our faces.

"We thought we'd surprise you with a real American song," said Sham Shad, who played the guitar and had even found a cowboy hat.

"You certainly did," said Fred. "We were sure we weren't hearing what we thought we heard."

As they left, Padri Sardar Khan took our hands and wished us a blessed Christmas.

Still the carolers came, until we could stay awake no longer. The rest of the night we called from the upstairs porch, "Merry Christmas," or the Hindustani equivalent, "*Bara Din Mubarik Ho* (Blessings on you, this great day)," and caught what sleep we could between greetings.

That was the year we gave Judy and Vicki the hippopotamus for Christmas.

We were used to hearing the current popular songs sung when the children came home from Woodstock School, and always enjoyed being brought up to date on "the latest." But every time I tried to pin the girls down to what they wanted for Christmas, they came out with the same song, "I want a hippopotamus for Christmas, and nothing but a hippo will do." I couldn't get a thing out of them except that dratted song.

"Okay," I said to myself. "If that's what you want, that's what you're going to get." And Fred was more than ready to cooperate.

But hippopotami, alive or stuffed, are not easy to come by in India. We thought we might have to give up the project. Then one day when I was playing the piano for the Christmas songs at Ewing Christian School, I remembered *their* stuffed animals. One of the ways Mildred Hoffmeister had devised for teaching arithmetic was to have the children build life-size

72

animals to scale. She had on hand a baby elephant made of papier-mâché over a wooden frame and stuffed with straw. Yes, she would loan it to us.

After the girls had gone to bed on Christmas Eve, Fred, Chandru, and the men he had collected to help him, carried the huge animal on their shoulders, ever so carefully, and wedged it, head first, into the dressing room off Fred's study. Its hindquarters completely filled the double doors and sufficiently resembled that end of a hippopotamus to fulfill our purposes. On the tail we pinned an envelope for each of the girls, containing enough money to buy a sari and a few other things they might want from the bazaar to take home from India when they left.

"Now what?" asked Judy on Christmas morning, as we gave them a ball of yarn apiece, told them to start winding and follow wherever it led till they came to their presents. To see their faces and hear the laughter was more than enough to repay our efforts.

Myrtle and Raymond Cray, Ohio State representatives from the Government Agricultural College across the city, came in just in time to see the fun. Their usual ritual was to arrive on Christmas morning with a freshly baked stollen to eat with our coffee after all the gifts had been opened. They wouldn't stay. We were all going to be at their home for dinner that night. Ray would take Fred to the train afterward.

If I could manage to live without him until February, it would be our last family separation for a long time. The thought of our next Christmas at home, all of us, in America, would help to carry me through. But no matter how many joys there were to come, the words of Dr. Kundan Lall's solo would still be true:

Those days were very, very beautiful—ah. . . .

Here is a Christmas tree decoration I wish I'd known about when we were in India because our Indian friends would have enjoyed it (and besides, spices were not as expensive in India as they are in the United States!):

FRAGRANT SPICE BALLS
(not to be eaten!)

Take applesauce
Add ground spices
  clove
  allspice
  nutmeg
  cinnamon
until the mixture is the consistency of clay
Take up enough of the mixture to roll in the palms of your
  hands to make a ball the size of a large walnut
Tear 2-foot lengths of the smooth, paperlike ribbon (used
  to wrap presents) into ⅛-of-an-inch-wide strips
Thread two or more colors of these strips into a darning
  needle and pull the ribbon through the spice ball (far
  enough into the ball so the ends don't show) and out at
  the top
Close the bottom of the hole with one whole clove used as
  a plug, the "pin" end inside the ball
Tie the ribbons at the top in a fluffy bow, leaving a loop by
  which to hang your spice ball on the Christmas tree
(The balls will dry out and become hard, and can also be
  given as gifts for use as a small pomander)

74

The
Spirit
of
Christmas
Present

TWELVE

Before the next Christmas, 1959, we had found "River Bend," our dream house overlooking the Hudson River at Stony Point, New York. The children came whenever they could to scrub, tear down walls, replace windows, paint, and settle. And we were all together for Christmas.

We even had snow! With very few exceptions, all the Christmases of our married life had been spent without that commodity which New York Staters feel is essential to the true Spirit of Christmas. "It just isn't Christmas without snow," we say to one another, knowing that there was probably no snow in Bethlehem; that people of every climate celebrate the Birthday of Christ.

Our Indian friends, visiting us here, laughed at our one little plant of poinsettias, remembering the wide hedges of them in their country, growing six feet high and covered with huge, brilliant blossoms. To us, snow for Christmas meant home, in our own country where "Christmas looked as it ought to look"—as our Indian friends would say of the poinsettias when they returned to their homes.

Fred, Vicki, and I unpacked the crèche and the two small Indian angels of beautifully glazed ceramic. They brought back memories of those wonderful Christmases in both China and India. But we were also overwhelmed with gratitude that after thirty-four moves in thirty years, we were at last celebrating under our very own roof.

"We don't actually own much more than the front doorknob," Fred reminded me.

We decorated our own front doorknob (and the rest of the front door and the back one) so the children coming home would have a Christmas welcome by whichever door they entered.

Vicki suggested that we also set up the crèche. We tried it in different places, eventually deciding on the sill of the picture window. At night it stood against the darkness, the houses of our neighbors down the hill below becoming the village of Bethlehem, with the river and hills as background.

The tree, a fine spruce, had been purchased earlier so it would have at least a week to stand in a pail of water in the cold front hall to bring out the green. We had had so much fun choosing it from a large selection on the lawn of the Garnerville Methodist Church, whose parishioners had brought them in to help pay off the mortgage. I cringed at the thought of our gardener, back in India, and what he would say about *cutting them down.* It had been trauma enough that he had had to transplant our small one.

Can anything in God's world be more exciting than children coming home for Christmas? Such a banging of doors there was; the snow blowing in with the suitcases hurriedly dropped for huge hugs into overcoats, for soft kisses on young, cold cheeks. Then the cries of "Where's the coffee?" "Where am I going to sleep?" "Here are your gifts; where shall I put them?" "Here's some maple nut loaf I brought for us to eat after we open our presents." "When is Judy coming?" "Vicki! You've grown up!" "When is Tom coming?" "He'll be in tomorrow." "Jim, you aren't married *yet?*" "Can't find anyone to support me in the way I'd like to become accustomed."

When the last plane had been met and the last car had driven in, there was the telephone call we came to expect sometime between midnight and dawn. "Tom! Where are you?" we would ask.

"I got a ride with a friend. I'm at the gas station on the parkway." (Or, "across the Tappan Zee bridge. Got a pencil? I'll give you the directions.") I couldn't resist going with Fred to meet him, though I knew we both had to get up and be ready to leave for work by seven-thirty the next morning.

We came home at night to find the table already set with Judy's Christmas cloth and a delicious meal prepared by daughters and daughter-in-law. The men did the dishes, then it was time to decorate the tree. Squeals and exclamations of delight followed the finding of the ornaments the children had made when small, or the appearance of a special favorite.

When Fred had set the star in place at the top and Carl had turned on the lights, I brought out candy canes, some to hang on the tree, some to be eaten—a treat we hadn't had overseas. Then I brought in a bowl of oranges and explained how we as children used to suck the juice of our one orange found in the toe of our stocking: "First, cut a hole in the stem end of the orange. Then break off about three inches or more from the bottom of your candy cane and stick it deep into the orange, leaving enough to suck, as if it were a straw."

"The juice doesn't come up," said Carl's wife, Faith.

"Mom, is this one of your little jokes?" asked Jim.

"You have to draw on it for a few minutes," I told them.

"The juice will begin to come if you suck it a bit longer and a little harder."

"Yeah," said Jim.

"It works!" shouted Anne, almost choking on the juice.

"It actually does!" said her husband, John.

One of the biggest thrills of our first Christmas in America was having near us what the children called *"real* relatives" (in contrast to the "adopted" aunts and uncles of a mission station). We could phone the Wixteds (my sister, Geneva, and her family) in Clifton Park, New York. My brother, Bob, and his family lived only a few miles away. He and his wife, Dorothy, and their children, Bob, Jr., Betsy, and Jim, ran in often during the holidays and we went back and forth to their house. The young people in the Scott and Scovel households were so compatible, they became far more like brothers and sisters than like cousins.

It was a perfect Christmas, and we could look forward to many more like it.

DECORATION FOR A DOOR KNOB

Measure the diameter of your door knob

Allow another 2 inches or whatever it would take to cover
   the knob up to the rod holding it

Cut a circle that large out of lightweight red or green felt
   (Our door knob is medium sized and the circle of felt is
   4 inches in diameter.)

Cut a 3-inch length of ¼-inch white, gold, or silver elastic and
   sew it together to make a circle

Gather the circle of felt into the circle of elastic to make a
   "cap" for your door knob

The "face" of the cap covering the door knob may have on
it an embroidered Christmas tree, a plastic Santa's face
pasted on, your initials embroidered in gold or just the one
initial of your surname, or any design you choose. Ours also
has a few strands of gold braid with very small brass bells
hanging from underneath the lower edge.

And just to assure you that Jim finally found her, and was willing to become accustomed to *any* way of living so long as it was with Dixie Lee Clifford, hear this:

NEWS BREAK
by Jim Scovel

In his *Christmas Carol* Dickens writes of the men who work on Christmas. He mentions miners and sailors, but not newspapermen although he was one himself and although working on Christmas is as much an occupational hazard. It happened to me on a good many occasions, but the one I recall was in 1962, known affectionately thereafter as the Big Story of the Smallest Tree.

I had drawn the night shift on Christmas Eve at the small upstate New York paper where I had been working. Bachelors working on small papers can expect this, although it was to be my last Christmas in that category since I was to be married the next May. But on this leaden gray afternoon it was all very far off as I checked in on the job.

Christmas comes and goes, but any eight hours in a city room presents its own litany: the peck of typewriters and teletypes, the smell of ink and hot lead. It was Christmas Eve but Santa's biggest present so far had been next year's city budget. After it was in, I checked out. I went back to my second-floor apartment and a surprise.

82

In the corner of the living room, clashing violently with the pink wallpaper, was the smallest Christmas tree in the Southern Tier. It struggled at the same time to support one string of lights and three ornaments while trying to remain reasonably erect. Which it missed by about 25 degrees.

Feeble as it was, it had been hard enough to come by. Dixie, my fiancée, had spent most of the freezing night trying to find a tree. The one she found was the last in a dreary East End lot and she had to wake up the dealer, in his home next door, to make the sale. The lights and ornaments were a present from my mother-in-law, a transfer from a far, far better tree than this.

With the tree, dinner. Dixie had also brought two steaks and one electric skillet, since the apartment's resident gas stove, moody at the best of times, took holidays off. There was also a salad. We ate, watching the tree inside battle gravity and those outside fight a rising Christmas wind while snow flurries scratched at the windows.

I can remember more elegant Christmases before and after the one in 1962, but none that left a fresher recollection that possibly it only takes two steaks to make a Christmas, or one small tree. Or one person.

East Setauket, Long Island

Thirteen

Here I must go on record that Christmas was the one time of the year when a career was the last thing on earth I wanted; when I was far too tired to do more than somehow pull through; when the pressures of the office covered like a gray blanket the hours of preparation and celebration. And it was especially difficult in those years when Christmas did not come on a weekend and we had only the one day or a day and a half off.

Remembering how the whole country of China took eight days off for Chinese New Year without the Republic collapsing, I hereby launch a campaign for an eight-day Christmas holiday; either the week between Christmas and New Year, when nothing gets done anyway, or, preferably, four days before Christmas and four days after Christmas. I know that makes nine, but an extra day, *The* Day, will do no harm. The four days before are so that Father can have some of the fun of the Christmas preparation and so the whole family can rediscover Advent, which much of the Christian Church has lost in the deluge of *things* to be done before the holy Birthday.

We are being told continually that we must find ways to use our leisure. We have no leisure. Working people simply take another job. Executives schedule more and more meetings on weekends. I am shocked that church executives are using weekends to do what they should be doing during the work week. Even Sundays are not kept holy. Incredible. Work has become a great juggernaut crushing down upon all we hold dear, all that would keep us sane—family, home, play, fun, laughter.

Time does not control us; we, by right choices, control our own use of time. It isn't impossible to say, "Sorry, I take week-ends off." It isn't impossible to say, "Sorry, I need eight days for Christmas, and so, sir, does everyone else." Christmas, but first Advent, is the time to rethink our values; to prepare spiritually for the year ahead, for Advent *is* the beginning of the New Year in the Christian calendar.

Right on, friends! Right on, for a Blessed, *Merry* Christmas!

And I wish we could invent a magnetic ring to encircle the season so that no bad news could break through. Though the day is filled with scintillating magic, there are no charms to ward off sorrow. There was one black Christmas when we learned, on December 23, what we had been fearing for weeks. Fred's department, as such, would be merged into another function and he would be without a job. The position offered in its place, at a higher salary, he felt he could not accept.

The news came at a time when his plans for the future were just beginning to bear fruit; when he was able to see ahead to what he was quite sure would eventually be accomplished. Fred accepted the deepest disappointment of his career with no bitterness. This could not be said of his wife and children. We tried, because we knew our attitude was only cutting deeper into his wound. Judy and Vicki, the two children left at home, showed their love for him in every little act. The other children wrote long, encouraging letters or phoned. But we could feel his fear for our future and we could not hide our fear for his.

Into such a world was the Christ Child born. It was such experiences that He came to redeem. Though we knew we should trust Him for the future, it was not easy for us to let go of our bitterness—to accept the gift He gave. In the end we discovered that Christmas did not have to be happy to be blessed. We were very close to one another across the miles that year as we celebrated Christ's Mass.

Within days Fred was asked to take a new and better position as Associate Director of the overseas medical work of our denomination. Nothing could have pleased him more.

"If we'd only known about it on Christmas, what a happy day it would have been," we said to each other.

Then it occurred to us that perhaps we had received gifts through this experience that we knew nothing about. We thought of Carl's Christmas at sea, which had been for him a growing up; and Tom's night on Truchas Mountain when he found a new perspective.

Perhaps the experience of suffering through a hard Christmas with her father helped Vicki to meet her difficulties some years later, alone in New York City on Christmas Day:

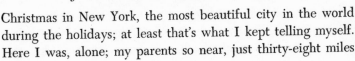

MY MOST MEMORABLE MISERABLE CHRISTMAS
by Victoria Scovel Harris

Christmas in New York, the most beautiful city in the world during the holidays; at least that's what I kept telling myself. Here I was, alone; my parents so near, just thirty-eight miles away in Stony Point, and yet so far, because I had to stay in the city to work. And speaking of being far away, Jim, my future husband, was in Florida.

And yet I couldn't ignore the bright lights sparkling from the skyscrapers, or the gorgeous shop windows on Fifth Avenue. The tree in Rockefeller Center had been exquisitely decorated and ceremoniously lit by the mayor. Even the salesladies were cooperating with Merry Christmas wishes to one and all as I emptied my checking account on gifts for my dear ones.

"What am I doing here anyway?" I kept asking myself. My realistic side replied that I had a good job as a reservation sales agent for the best airline in the country. Just because I had to work on Christmas Day was no reason to get overly upset. My inner self had a completely different answer to the question.

Christmas Eve came. I put up a little artificial tree in my window and decorated it with the usual lights and ornaments while listening to Christmas music on the radio. Then I phoned Jim in Florida to wish him a Merry Christmas. When I hung up I didn't feel any better.

Five-thirty A.M. is early any morning but on Christmas morning it seemed more like three. Before I got out of bed I gave myself a stern lecture. "Vicki, this is Christmas Day. Although you would like to be somewhere else right now, you have plenty to be thankful for. You have a family who loves you and is thinking of you, to say nothing of a wonderful fiancé with whom you'll be sharing many Christmases to come. You're in excellent physical and reasonably good mental health, so get yourself out of bed and face this day with the old Vicki spunk!" HA!

I got up and started off to work determined to maintain the Christmas spirit.

The subway station was deserted, except for a nurse in the

same situation that I was. I thought of going up to her to wish her the season's greetings, but one look at her face told me she could have competed with Scrooge for the annual "Humbug Christmas Award" and beat him. At last a subway screeched into the station. I stepped into a car and found four drunks passed out in various reclining positions. I chose a secluded seat and was just about to sit down when I saw that someone had been sick all over it. My Christmas spirit slumped considerably.

I was scheduled to work from 7:00 A.M. to 3:00 P.M. The day started out fairly light and we were instructed to answer each phone call as usual but to add a pleasant "Merry Christmas." Things were progressing smoothly until the weatherman decided to give New York a Christmas gift in the form of a blizzard. Slowly, air traffic came to a gripping halt. One by one, all three metropolitan airports had to close. Roads to and from them also closed. People were stranded and the airports were so packed with travelers that there wasn't even standing room. The restaurants began to run out of food. Our phone lines were jammed with irate calls. It wasn't long before I dropped the pleasant "Merry Christmas" because it was usually followed by a string of swear words accusing the airline of being completely responsible for the weather conditions.

As the hours struggled by, the situation only became worse. I was asked to work overtime and decided that I was better off there than in my room alone.

More snow . . . More calls . . . More swear words.

The supervisors came up with a wonderful idea. It was announced that we would be given a free Christmas turkey dinner. My stomach growled as I envisioned one end of the employees' lounge boasting a buffet table heaped with golden brown turkeys stuffed with delicious goodness and accompanied by fluffy whipped potatoes, steaming gravy, fresh vegetables, homemade rolls, and tantalizing desserts. I could hardly wait

88

for my break. When it came, I ran for the employees' lounge. As I entered the door, I was given a nickel and informed that if I stepped over to the automat dispenser, I could get my Christmas dinner. What was left of my Christmas spirit starved itself out of existence. I carried the cardboard dish of cold turkey over to the electronic oven to warm it up, and then joined my fellow workers for our Christmas feast.

After the sumptuous repast, it was back to the phone. By that time I was numb and didn't care what I was called. Priorities were determined and those who were sick or had small children were given first consideration. As evening came, things relaxed into a subdued hysteria.

At 10:00 P.M. I called it a day and stumbled back to the room I temporarily referred to as "home." I turned on the radio, collapsed on the bed, and thought about Christmas. The heavenly music of Handel's *Messiah* filled the room.

And suddenly it all occurred to me. Yes, my day could easily be considered a failure. I had not been able to hold that special happy feeling of Christmas. That had been stripped away and what remained was the simple revelation, *Christ was born*! . . . in spite of everything . . . because of everything!

I could choke over saying "Merry Christmas" but it was so easy to say "Welcome, Saviour!"

Kent, Ohio

FOURTEEN

As the children have married, it has become more and more Christmas-over-the-miles for all of us. And with fewer in the family, there is less and less to do at home in preparation. Too, I am no longer working in New York and can give myself my advocated eight-day holiday from free-lance writing. The celebration of the Holy Birthday becomes what it should have been all along—relaxed, worshipful, enjoyable.

Anne was the first of the children to entertain us all. She was living in an old manse in Goshen, New York, where John was pastor. The inlaid floors of the old house had withstood the feet of larger numbers than one mere family. Rooms opened into halls and halls into rooms, which seemed to have been waiting for just such a day as this. Our grandson, David, was three years old that Christmas, which gave his father the opportunity of buying a train for him. While David played with his cousins, Helen and small Chris, just arrived from Massachusetts with Uncle Carl and Aunt Faith, the men of the family had uninterrupted hours running the train.

Grandchildren for Christmas! Fred and I looked around and could hardly believe our eyes!

"It all happened so fast," said Fred.

"I know. And I can't help being glad that no one was talking about the population explosion when we were having ours," I said.

We have a variety of Christmases now—Christmas with our oldest son Jim and our daughter-in-law Dixie in their new, tastefully decorated home on Long Island, a fire on the hearth in the den; a turkey I haven't had to touch roasting in the oven, its delicious aroma spreading through the house. Fred and Jim discuss a recent article in *News Day*, the paper for which he is a reporter and editor. Seven-year-old Jessica and Beth, aged four, run in with their new books. "Read this one, Bachi, please?" (*Bachi* is Polish for grandmother, I am told. Jessica has a friend with a Polish grandmother and "she calls her grandmother Bachi, so do you mind if we call *you* that?" I love it.) Jessica shows me the essay she has written on "Feelings at Christmas."

Jessica S.

My sister and I
live in a coqntry
where there is a
war going on.
We are all a lone
In a tiny Hut.
It is Christmas
time. We chopped
our small ~~tree~~ tree
dowan this morning.
on the tree we

put berries. Under
the tree are two
presents. one of
the presents is
a carved necklace
My sister is too
little too give me
a present But I
understand.

Boston, where Carl and Faith are living, is a city which looks as a city should look at Christmas time. You pass a door with a huge brass knocker and look up, fully expecting to see a window flung wide and Scrooge leaning out, ready to shout, "What's today, my fine fellow?" One lovely old door does open —the wreathed door of the narrow five-storied house on Beacon Street. It opens with a bang and several shouts as Helen, Chris, and Rebecca run to meet us, followed by Faith and Carl and whoever else, in or out of the clan, happens to be spending Christmas with the Boston Scovels.

We love this house and the church, venerable King's Chapel,

restful in its simple and dignified white and mahogany, warm and welcoming with its red-cushioned pews. And the music—the recorders, flute, harpsichord, the trebles, and the bass viols, playing Bach; the organ and choir doing a new composition of the music director, Daniel Pinkham—how I have missed such church music! Then the traditional prayers of the church of my childhood, deeply moving, now, as they are read by the pastor of this church, our own son, Carl.

Back to the house to add more decorations to the tall tree standing in the bay window, the lights of the city and the Common visible behind it.

Helen has given me a handmade book of poems, the cover decorated with bright pink flowers and a tendril of soft green. Inside is this inscription:

> For Nai Nai
> To add to her collection
> of my poems. And I hope
> you have as much fun reading
> them as I did writing them.
> Love,
> Helen

(*Nai Nai* is Chinese for grandmother. It is what her father called his grandmother.) Helen is eleven years old. I am interested to see what she has written. I open the book and read the first poem:

Unexpressable

by Helen Scovel

Blazing fire
Bathrobe clad
Mug of cocoa
These I've had

Out the window
Snowflakes fall
In the house
Watched by all

Quiet murmurs
Suddenly break
By a noise
Only happiness makes

Warmth and comfort
Love does bring
Silence reigns
But hearts will sing.

Now that Anne and John and their three, David, Andy, and baby Lorraine are living in Saranac Lake, New York, we avoid the deep snow of the north country and make our visits to them when they are at their summer place on the lake, or in autumn when the color of the foliage is at its height (or, of course, when a new baby has just arrived, no matter what the weather!).

Our youngest, Vicki, and her husband, Jim Harris, make it seem like old times when they fly in from Kent State University where Jim is at work on his degree. During the week after Christmas, others of the family will be arriving to spend a day or two with them and with us.

We had Christmas early, in 1970. It began on December 11 when we arrived at Tom and Janene's apartment in Ann Arbor, Michigan. We'd hardly had time to remove our coats, much less stop to admire the beautiful things they had brought from Thailand (where they had spent a term as missionaries) when their four-year-old Derick pulled us into the living room to see the Christmas tree. It stood in the corner on a very low teakwood bed, and all the gifts were arranged on this "table" beside it. The presents had been exquisitely wrapped by Janene, each one a work of art.

But our very best gift came the next day as we watched Tom receive from the University of Michigan his Ph.D. in Linguistics. Only the fact that there seemed to be hundreds of other students going to the platform for the same purpose, kept us from *actually* bursting with pride. Now there were two Dr. Scovels.

Tom, Janene, and Derick are at present in Thailand, where Tom is teaching at the University of Chiengmai. Janene has written of another kind of a Christmas tree:

OUR CHRISTMAS TREE IN NORTHERN THAILAND

by Janene Nicodemus Scovel

The only fir trees where we live in Chiengmai, Thailand, grow in the Royal Forest Preserve on the nearby mountain. Instead of taking a picnic lunch up the mountain and coming back with a live, albeit illegal Christmas tree, we decided we'd do without one. However, it is difficult to make Christmas traditional for a five-year-old son without snow, grandparents, relatives, and all the decorations that somehow unite to make the season so warm, happy, and special for the little one. Derick asked how Santa would come from the North without snow, how he could come without a chimney, and wondered how presents could be left without a tree to put them under.

I knew we had to do something, so two weeks before Christmas I asked Tom if we could go out to the umbrella village and buy as many different sizes of umbrella frames as possible. I planned to arrange them on a stick and make them into our tree.

The umbrella village is about twelve miles outside Chiengmai, a good half-hour ride on our motorcycle through ripening

97

rice fields. The village consists of about thirty old, Thai-style teak houses built on stilts, lining either side of a long brown earthen road. Underneath the houses are the umbrella "factories." It is always a thrill to watch these skilled artists perform the many tasks necessary to transform simple bamboo and coarse brown paper into the beautiful handmade Thai parasols.

After passing the first few houses where the paper is made by smashing mulberry leaves, we found the house where a family was working together, cutting the bamboo frames. Only three different sizes were available; the tree would have to be small.

"Making a Christmas tree, huh?" one of the women asked as she wrapped up the bamboo frames. I was amazed that even way out in this little village they somehow sensed my need to have a tree.

When we got home, we excitedly assembled our tree. Derick found it so much fun, he made another one with his Tinkertoys and said we should have asked him to make our tree instead of going way out to the village.

We attached the umbrella handle to a small flat piece of wood to make a stand. All pieces were then spray-painted green and dried quickly in the hot afternoon sun. The largest frame was put on first and the smallest last. Each was fully opened to hold the strings of green, yellow, and red paper angels, bamboo stars, and other ornaments which we made from lightweight materials readily available at the local market.

The tree was just Derick's size to decorate and when it was all done, he clapped his hands with satisfaction over the colorful cheer that radiated from our Thai Christmas tree. To everyone who saw it, this tiny tree represented the great joy, beauty, and love of Christmas time.

Chiengmai, Thailand

DIRECTIONS FOR MAKING
A PAPER ANGEL

1. Make a pattern by using tracing paper and drawing off the angel-to-be from page 100.
2. Choose paper the color you desire your angel to be, the color on one side of the sheet, white on the back
3. Cut out pattern on solid lines
4. Put slot A under slot B and pull together (The wings will show white from the front)
5. Draw arms forward and down and slip tab C into slot D
6. Using a large needle, make a hole in the top of the angel's head, and with strands of colored silk thread, make a loop for hanging

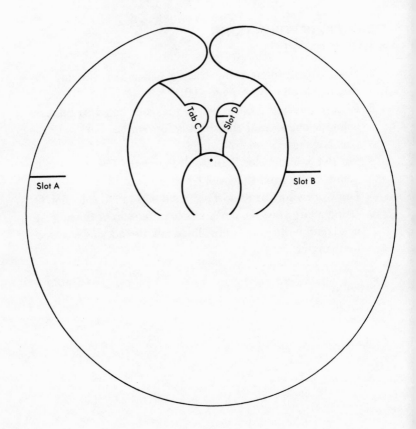

Janene's Grandmother Collier must be one of the best cooks in the world. Janene and her sister Diane, have collected Gran's recipes in a little booklet which we all use. Here are two of our beloved Gran's recipes which Janene uses for Christmas:

CRUNCHY CHOCOLATE SNOWBALLS

Cream
  1¼ cups butter
  ⅔ cup granulated sugar
Add
  2 cups flour ⎫
  ⅛ teaspoon salt ⎬ sifted together
  ½ cup cocoa ⎭
Add
  ½ cup nuts (finely chopped or rolled)

Form into balls the size of walnuts. Bake in a 350° oven for 15 to 20 minutes, according to size.

When cool, dip upper part of cookie into powdered sugar.

ALMOND CRESCENTS

  1 cup butter
  ¾ cup granulated sugar
  2½ cups sifted flour
  1 cup chopped almonds (unblanched) or pecans

102

Cream butter and flour until it is the consistency of putty (about 15 minutes). Add sugar and mix well. Add nuts.

Shape into small crescents. Bake on a lightly greased cookie sheet at 350° for 15 minutes.

Mix 1 teaspoon vanilla with 1 pound confectioners' sugar and roll cookies in this while hot. Makes about 4 dozen.

FIFTEEN

One glance through the preceding chapter and it is immediately obvious that the house described in *To Lay a Hearth* has outgrown a full family celebration. Taking into consideration the Scovel population explosion, it is evident that in our living room there isn't that much space left for a play pen, a doll's kitchen, a truck circuit, twenty-four people and fourteen cups of hot tea or coffee.

But lack of space is not the reason why Fred and I now feel that our children do not necessarily have to be with us on Christmas Day. We feel that home, each family's home, is the place to celebrate the Holy Birthday. The preparations beforehand have been tiring enough. This is not the time to travel all the day before (or all the morning of) December 25 to get to a place where no one will rest as well as in his or her own bed. Too, in our part of the country there is every chance that the travelers will have to battle with poor road conditions and that some member of the clan will catch a miserable cold.

When we returned to America, the marrieds spent alternate Christmases with parents and parents-in-law. We felt there would come a time, as the grandchildren grew older, when they would much prefer to stay at home. But having once set the pattern of alternate Christmases with parents, it would be most difficult to stop without the danger of hurting someone deeply. We decided that the move should come from our direction. We thought that perhaps the nicest gift we could give our children (and theirs) was to let them wake up on Christmas morning in their own homes; to have the day with one another; to begin *their* traditions which arise from their own surroundings, from their pasts and from the creativity of each member of the family.

And if there were parents who lived nearby, and if a family dinner would be enjoyed by all, including the one preparing the meal and doing the dishes (and the cook and dishwasher should be very honest about this), such plans could be made. My brother, Bob, always insists on taking his family out for Christmas dinner so Dorothy, too, can have a restful day.

Besides, Fred and I like to be alone. We thought we'd try it for Christmas once, much to the discomfiture of our children. We tried it, and we liked it.

We decided that our celebration alone was not to be a sad replay of past Christmases. We would dispense with the traditional evergreen tree, leaving ours to grow in the forest where it belonged. I didn't think I could face getting out the battered stars and rounds of cardboard with smudgy Santas pasted on them. The child-bearing, child-rearing period of our lives was over. Christmas alone together should have something new and somehow just our own.

That something is our Grail crèche, a gift from Judy and Vicki which has become the center of our Christmas every year. The simple figures have a soft terra-cotta finish, with no embellishments. No halos are necessary to show that this is the Holy Family; every line of the figure of Joseph portrays his awe at the miracle of birth and his concern for the Mother. The shepherd, wrapped in rough sheepskin, a lamb in his arm, has quickly dropped on one knee in adoration; and the Mother, looking down at the Baby in her lap, has such a calmness about her that Vicki once remarked, "All I have to do when I come into the room is to look at that figure of Mary and I relax; all my tension just drops off. She's so quiet and at peace."

There are two children in the scene, a girl and a boy. The little girl has clasped her hands in delight at seeing the Baby and is sitting back on her heels, watching everything He does. The small boy, kneeling straight and tall, has brought the Baby a dove, which rests on the curve of his arm. The Baby is truly *adore*-able. Our grandchildren, arriving during the week after Christmas, can never resist (nor can I) taking Him from His Mother's lap and letting Him lie on the straw mat for a few minutes. The bird can also be taken from the boy's arm and placed in a small basket "so the Baby can see it better when He's on the floor." And the lamb can be moved to lie at the Mother's feet.

Three Wise Men were added later, a gift from Judy and Vicki and their husbands, John Robinson and Jim Harris. They complete the crèche as they round out the circle of our world, for the Wise Men have evidently come from Asia, Africa, and the Arab countries.

Above the crèche hangs an arrangement of pine cones, nuts, and fruit—tree-shaped, to be sure. Small angels hang from it; a scarlet bird nests in its "branches." And at the top is a star from Sweden, made of straw. Sometimes we lay a branch of blue spruce behind the crèche; sometimes we set up a few large pine cones to look like trees covered with snow.

Ever since we'd had our Grail crèche I'd wondered about the person who had done the original sculpture. So one day recently I wrote to the Grail Shop in New York and asked where I might find the artist. To my delight Martha Orso, the manager, put me in touch with Trina Paulus, who offered to come into New York to see me. We arranged to meet at the shop within a few days, because it turned out that we both had to see publishers that morning.

I found the shop just off Fifth Avenue on 37th Street and took the elevator to the third floor. The door opened into what looked like spring. Where did all this light come from in mid-winter New York City? The white background, the lovely flower posters, bright cards, beautiful pottery and ceramics all helped; and certainly the cordial welcome from Martha did nothing to detract from the feeling of sun.

As I waited the few minutes for Trina Paulus, I wondered what she would be like—youngish, oldish? Shy? How would I begin? The questions were answered as she stepped into the room—not youngish, *young*! (She would always be.) A merry face above the smart brown cape, and she was not the least bit shy.

"Tell me, what do you want from me?" she asked. (In the workroom Martha had spread a table with a bright cloth, set paper plates and mugs when we decided on sandwiches and coffee here instead of going out.)

"I want to know how you felt when you were creating the crèche, how the ideas came, how your hands felt, everything, all about it. Where were you when you did it?" I asked.

"I was at Grailville," Trina began. "Martha and I both were. You would have to know something of the Grail, I think, in order to understand how I came to do it."

"Go ahead," I urged.

"Well, the Grail is an international movement of women, working in about twenty-two countries right now. As in the old legend of the search for the Holy Grail, which brought peace to whoever had it, the Grail, too, is a search for peace with justice and love for all people. It was for women because those who began it in Holland in 1921 felt that women had some very needed and significant things to contribute to this search for a new and better world. It was a movement because we would have to work together to be really effective.

"The Grail pioneered in a lot of things—in education, youth movements, the training and sending of lay people abroad, liturgy, art . . . It was probably movements like the Grail that helped prepare a climate in which Pope John and the Second Vatican Council could move. You see, although the founders were Catholic, it was ecumenically oriented from the beginning and now has members from many Christian churches as well as close relations with those from other religions. Men of the church have always been interested in our work, too. My father felt as if he belonged!"

"But you were not nuns?" I asked.

"We were never nuns," said Trina, "and many of us are married. Our spirit came from a sense of mission to the world which we felt should be common to all Christians."

"Now tell me about Grailville," I said, as Martha poured us fresh cups of coffee.

"It's a place; I guess you'd call it the physical rooting of The Grail in the United States," said Trina. "It's a four-hundred-acre farm near Cincinnati."

"The Grail came to this country in 1941," said Martha. "Grailville began in 1944."

"When Martha and I were there it was really like a kibbutz," Trina went on. "We had a community of about eighty, most of whom came for three months or a year before doing all sorts of other things, in and out of Grail structure. We were trying to make an integrated life-style. We shared all the work, were known for (and kidded about) organic farming and whole grain bread. There were cooperative canning, cooking, laundry, meditation, all centered around the liturgy—the great cycle of feasts and fasts of the church. When we see young people today go off to find community and a simpler life-style, we really understand—don't we, Martha?—for we have done it, too."

Martha nodded her assent.

"I guess I'm still looking and experimenting with life-styles that have both integrity and commitment to the larger community—the whole world," said Trina. "For instance, I'm very involved these years with a marketing project for the hand-weaving from the city in Egypt where I worked for a year.

"This building of a personal and communal life-style and caring about the whole world is in continuity with those Grailville years; but the forms, now, are different. Most of us are scattered and less definable as Grail groupings. Hopefully, we can continue to care and support one another's search, even if we are not physically together. It's a new era, a new search."

"And the crèche, how does it fit into the picture?" I asked.

"Don't you see? The whole idea of *living a life* and finding ways of *sharing that life* more widely was why we began the Art Production and Distribution program. Religious art for the home, especially in Catholic circles, was pretty awful! Plaster statues were synonymous with junk. It wasn't plaster's fault, either! It's a perfectly fine material if used well. We thought if we made good designs with the reproduction process in mind, and meditated on solid theology, we might produce something in quantity that was worth making and using. We believed it was okay to reproduce in quantity if we tried to care for quality—an admittedly hard job, since nobody wants to care for many things the way he can care for one thing. Maybe *more* technology would help here, freeing the worker from repetitive work for more personally creative work.

"This makes me think of another concern of mine. How can

110

people become more creative and believe in that wonderful gift we all have? I would hate to think that greater availability of art might stifle this essential personal expression."

"You needn't worry," I said. "You should see how creatively the grandchildren play with the crèche, moving the figures to bring more meaning to the arrangement, as they see it; and my daughter once spoke of how peaceful she feels when she comes into the room and sees the madonna. That's a very creative response. It makes me want to write a Christmas poem.

"But I still haven't heard how you made it," I prodded.

"It's not easy to tell; that's why I've been putting it off, I guess," said Trina. She waited a moment, then, "Well, all right. First of all, there was a need. Everyone concerned that year at Grailville, 1957, felt that the first thing we should produce for the home was something for Christmas, something everyone could identify with—Catholics, Protestants, the Eastern Church —a crib set or crèche for today would be great. But I just couldn't get the traditional crib set off my mind. I thought about it for a year; nothing worthwhile came. I made attempts; nothing happened that was worth producing or sharing.

"It got to be July, then August, and we wanted to get this crib out for Christmas marketing. That meant molds, color, finishing, catalogue, mailing—to share something that wasn't yet born! Finally there was just one week left in which to try. I went into the corncrib next to the art shop to hibernate and work, hoping that something would come. When you can't find the answer in your head, sometimes working with clay will begin to show you where to go. For three days I struggled, a few halfway adequate figures came, but after each one was done, I knew they were not brilliant and not the answer.

"I started again; finally a little girl came, then the boy, then the Mother and Joseph—I didn't stop to do the detail, I just let it flow. It was a marvelous thing, and a very rare experience. They were all right with each other and to scale, no

111

changes were needed! It had taken a year of doldrums, three days of anguish, but there they were! The first person to see them suggested a sheep. A sheep was made and the crib set was finished."

"And they really worked," said Martha.

"The next year," Trina continued, "everyone began to say, 'But we need the kings,' a thought which I found hard to accept. Kings! What do you think of when you think of kings?" she asked me.

"Crowns and gold," I replied.

"Exactly. And crowns and gold and finery just did not belong to this simple crèche. Kings felt all wrong. I just couldn't do them. But finally I became so convinced that we *needed* kings that I surrendered enough to work seriously at them. I began to meditate and pray about the meaning of this Visitation—this Epiphany. I forgot the word 'king.' 'Epiphany' means 'Manifestation,' the light of revelation to the Gentiles. It opened the whole world! They weren't kings (that concept was added much later); they were *wise men*, astrologers, astronomers. They were not Jesus' own people; they were strangers, foreigners. The liturgy makes it clear that their coming with gifts stands for the meeting of Jesus with the *whole world* and prefigures the whole world coming to Him. The Wise Men stand, even today, for all races, all peoples.

"I looked up the story of the choosing of the new Dalai Lama. How plausible it made the Christmas story of men from the East following a star! If such a search for a baby could happen in our own time, why not two thousand years ago? When the old Dalai Lama died, the wise men in Tibet searched for a sign in the heavens indicating where the new one would be born at the exact time of the old one's death. The Wise Men of Tibet brought him gifts, among which were things belonging to the old Dalai Lama. If the child chose these, it would be a sign he was the new one. He could be born of a poor family, but then he was to be taken to the monastery to be trained to be the spiritual and temporal ruler of his country.

"So I made the first wise man—an ascetic, a monk from the East which is so full of spiritual insights, meditation. I attributed to him the traditional gift of myrrh, standing for self-renunciation, suffering. The second figure is an Arab. He is, perhaps, white. The gift he brings is prayer—frankincense. The Arab world has such a spirit of prayer; the muezzin, calling people to worship so many times a day. The third is an African, black, kneeling on the ground which holds so many of earth's riches; bringing his gift, the celebration of the riches of *all* of life, which may be symbolized by the traditional gold.

"Then I felt that theologically we needed a different Child, more regal; no longer cuddled in Mary's arms, but the Son she gave to the world, who receives the world from His throne on His Mother's lap. What a thing to believe, God in a baby!"

Trina sat back in her white canvas chair. We were quiet for some moments, then she said, "No single work of art or life can contain fully any really important idea, but I hope this crèche shows forth something that is timeless coming from God in the flesh of man. This coming is *now*, too, as well as a great future coming. Christmas is all this—a great, many-layered event. I'm so glad the crèche has meant much to you. It's been wonderful to share this afternoon."

It wasn't easy to come back to Fifth Avenue and 37th Street.

With the arrival of the Grail crèche, we found we had to decide what we were going to do with our old German one, which, over the years, had come to mean so much to us all. Would we give it to one of the children? Which one? Well, then, should we divide it and give a few pieces to each family? Which pieces to which family? The more we fondled them, looking them over, trying to decide, the harder it became.

113

"We don't want to give them up, do we?" said Fred.

"No, we don't. But what will we do with the new one?"

"Can't we have two?"

I wasn't quite sure about having two Holy Families in one room; neither did we want to relegate this precious one to a study or bedroom. It evoked too many memories to cast it aside. So, across the room from the Grail crèche (which one sees when one enters the door), and in its usual place on the window ledge, sits the old German one, the angel's wing still to be mended each year, the little lamb with its broken nose still nuzzling the hand of the Christ Child.

Lest our children feel deprived, we have given each of the six families its own Grail crèche.*

* The crèche and other Grail art may be obtained from The Grail Shop, 6 West 37th Street (3rd Floor), New York, N.Y. 10018. Or from Abbey Press (which has now acquired the Grail art works), St. Meinrad, Indiana 47517.

SIXTEEN

The crèche, the tree, the hanging of stockings—three traditional elements of any Christmas celebration. Our children used whatever stocking happened to be longest—their own, or their father's (if he could find that many clean ones). We filled them with the usual fruits and nuts, small sacks of various hard candies (the ribbon candy of my childhood was not available in China or India; at least we were never able to find any). Small stocking gifts were tucked in, and at the top, *always* a new toothbrush. To this day it is very difficult for any of our children to buy a new toothbrush; they keep thinking they will get one for Christmas!

The fruit is not the treat it once was. Cousin Harriet remembers Hannah Dudley, when over ninety, saying that as a child she dreamed all year of the orange she'd find in her stocking.

Nothing in our family stocking tradition is very striking or original, but the mother of one of my favorite editors at Harper & Row added a new dimension to her child's pleasure in finding his stocking on Christmas morning. Each year she would sew to the long red felt stocking a symbol of something that had made the past year outstanding—his first bicycle, a book for his first year at school, a football for the year he went out for the team, and when he had his first steady girl-friend, a pair of rosy lips.

What a lovely way to pass on to his wife and children his whole life history! But if his family turns out to be anything like ours, I fear for him. I can hear his sons now:

"Come on, Dad, tell us more about those rosy lips."

But he will probably reply calmly, "They were your mother's only I didn't know it then."

Our first grandchild, Helen, has a Christmas stocking with a history. Helen is the sixth generation to use it. It was knit by her mother's father's great-great-grandmother, Hannah Bishop Payne, wife of the Reverend Solomon Payne, a Congregational minister in Canterbury, Connecticut, for their daughter, Mary Payne, who gave it to her oldest child, Hannah Bishop McLean. From her it went to Faith's grandfather, William Roger Greeley, to her father, the Reverend Dana McLean Greeley, to Faith, to Helen.

The stocking is three feet long, closely knit of very tough steel-blue worsted with a once-white-now-beige toe, a border of the same color at the top. It is still very sturdy and intact, and has the added advantage of being capacious.

Faith's mother has made similar stockings for the other children, beautifully knit in red and green wool. Faith writes, "When Helen gets ready to hang up her blue one that looks like a cross between tough wool trousers and an army blanket, she wears a quizzical smile as she smooths it in her lap. She's still not quite sure whether she's being gypped or honored by having this 'weird' stocking belong to her. I remember the feeling."

Hopefully, we have, as a nation, outgrown the sock full of coal for the naughty child. At least we can be thankful that it is all but impossible for a person to find coal. Surely this must be one of the cruellest and most harmful to the child of all practical jokes. And on the birthday of One who loved the unlovely, set a new path for the wayward, and forgave sinners!

But what about hanging stockings for two fairly sane adults? It seemed a bit silly. Judy, who always seems to get involved in Christmas sewing projects, solved the problem. She sent us two very gay socks of red felt, which she had made. Fred's is an argyle with green and gold diamond designs sewn on with gold rickrack to make the pattern. Mine is shaped like an old-fashioned high-topped boot with curlicue high heels. The buttons are gold and its flair top is edged with lace. Each year we hang them against a white door as decorations, though I am apt to find a box of Chanel No. 5 bulging from mine. And once, when there was hardly a bristle left in the old silver-backed brush, I put a new brush in his.

Christmas morning. The house is quiet. Too quiet. Imagine not having the far-too-short night shattered by whispers:
"Are they awake?"
"No. They don't move."
"What time is it?"
"I dont know, but you can see daylight coming."
"Is it safe to wake them up?"
"I guess so. Put on the Hallelujah Chorus, Vicki."
"Full volume."
I cannot honestly say I don't miss all this. But oh, it is luxury

to turn over and go back to sleep; to be wakened by a soft "Merry Christmas" muffled into my hair; to have a late, leisurely breakfast, go out to dinner, come home to sit by the fire and read the beginnings of five new books without one interruption.

And *then* to have the dividend of six joyous telephone calls from children and grandchildren and to know that some of them will be arriving during the week!

It's all very well to talk about Christmas alone when you mean two people alone together. What would I do if I were *really* alone? And for the first time? Supposing there were no children?

Many panaceas have been offered, such as "Stop thinking about yourself. Go out and find others lonelier than you are and do something for them." It's a good idea but it doesn't always work, as I well remember . . . When I was a student nurse at the Hospital of the Good Shepherd in Syracuse, New York, four women in the large ward were annoying the rest of the patients because they were so happy. They would call out to one another, shout with laughter, throw books across the beds—all of which troubled those who were very sick, and those who thought it improper to be happy in such a place.

At the other end of the ward was the saddest woman in the world—she knew it. And to prove it to all within earshot, she groaned aloud and cried a good share of the time. The problem looked easy to solve to a young student nurse. I put the hilarious women in wheelchairs, gave them a briefing on cheering the lonely, and wheeled them to the bedside of Mrs. Woebegone. All became quiet, and I went on with my work. After a reasonable length of time, I went back to find all five women weeping . . .

No, it might be depressing to look around my table and see five lonely people with smiles on their lips and tears in their hearts. To be invited to a happy family gathering might be even more painful. I doubt my ability to act out the role of Christmas-as-usual under these circumstances. All this would have to come later.

Christmas might be a good day to let the pain of loneliness take over—to accept the entire weight of it down into the very depths of being. It might be a day to remember that there was no joy at the beginning of the first Christmas; instead, a long, uncomfortable journey for a reason that must have seemed only bureaucracy, a crescendo of fear when no place could be found and the birth pains had already started. The time came when the pains took over and were stronger than the woman; when the man felt helpless, guilty to have taken her so far from those friends and relatives with whom she might have been during this experience, her first.

But see how the world was changed by that one troubled night! Years later, Mary may have sensed the import of it. Joseph probably never knew that the suffering on that trip to Bethlehem had any impact whatever, beyond the quiet joy of having Jesus in their family circle.

Thinking these thoughts might bring healing enough to do one thing, however small, to keep another from having such a lonely Christmas. If it were still impossible to face a person-to-person encounter, I might send a secret gift or order flowers and sign the card, "Guess Who?" What hopes *that* might revive in someone convinced that no one cared!

Or by now it might be possible to call on a friend in the hospital. Having been a nurse, I would *not* take a Christmas tree with all the fragile decorations for two reasons: Past experience would never allow me to use for this purpose the small amount of space available in a hospital room—space needed to carry out the necessary functions of healing. And again, it would mean pretending that this Christmas was like any other, which it definitely would not be. Instead, I would take one beautiful red rose in a small bud vase to put by her bedside table, from which the nurse could easily switch it to her tray or to a window ledge when extra room was needed. My friend could water it herself from her drinking glass.

For a Christmas gift it might be well to think of something that would bring hope—something to point to the day when the hospital sojourn would be over and life would be normal again—the January issue of *House Beautiful* (not the Christmas one); two tickets for a concert or play, dated a reasonable time ahead; a ski sweater instead of a bed jacket; a blouse or a soft wool sport shirt instead of another pair of pajamas. Any gift would have to be within the context of reason. It would be cruel to pretend that all would soon be well if I knew very well it wouldn't be. And if I didn't know, God forbid that the present I gave would bring pain—a sports magazine for a prospective amputee, or anything that might turn out to be equally as devastating.

And if total acceptance of grief and the resultant healing took place? Or if I had always been alone and liked being alone? How would I celebrate Christmas?

We become so bogged down in our own inconsequential quagmires; I'd like to study more and more ways to enjoy, *enjoy,* ENJOY the gifts that are ours. I'd like to try to compose a dance to be danced alone in praise of God's gift to the world; try more ways of accepting the gift of awareness, the gifts of touch, taste, smell. If I lived in a city apartment, I'd buy a plant, feel the dirt, smell it, then do the same with the leaves, the buds, the blossoms. I'd get on a bus and look at people's faces to see how beautiful they are, ride out into the country to watch the stars on Christmas Eve, walk in winter fields and really look at the sky on Christmas Day; pick up a seed pod to feel its roughness, marvel at its intricate design. I'd find a church where no service was going on and listen to silence, kneel alone to pray, to thank God for this wonderful Birthday being celebrated by so many different kinds of people in so many different places in the world.

"And if you didn't believe in God?"

If I didn't believe in God! I don't know what I would do. It wouldn't matter because it wouldn't really be Christmas.

"But the *day* would still be there. You'd have to pass it some way. What would you do?"

I'd have to pretend. I'd have to make believe that the world was all I wished it might be, that the heavens were opening, that a healing was pouring itself out upon all the evils I knew of; that somehow, every situation I'd been worrying about could be completely changed, redeemed—the boy we know who has lost the function of his brain due to drugs; the girl in our town who has walked out on her husband, taking their baby with her.

But if I saw this healing, I wouldn't be able to keep from calling it love. Would I? If I didn't believe in God? I could pretend it *was* love, pouring itself out on a whole country at war; trees would revive; people would find new homes and live normal lives.

And if I, as I am, could dream such a dream, mightn't it be possible that there *was* a God who had thought of it first?

A HANDY POCKET
Gift for a Bed Patient

Use a piece of bed ticking 32 inches long and 12 inches
wide (The new tickings are prettier than they used to be.
Try to find one of an unusual design and attractive colors.
Other washable materials may be used, but should be
sturdy.)

Turn up 8 inches at the bottom of the strip, stitching the
sides to form a pocket

Bind all the edges, including the top of the pocket, with
binding to match one of the colors in the design of the
ticking

The long flap slips under the mattress, at the side of
the bed, making the pocket a convenient place within reach of
the patient for all the little necessary articles.

You may want to include in your Handy Pocket a toothbrush
in a case, a small tube of toothpaste, a book of stamps, a small
pen, a pad for notes, some cuticle scissors, tweezers, a small
mirror, a package of Lifesavers (if the patient is allowed
sweets), and so forth.

122

SEVENTEEN

"What does one do about neighbors?" The question faced us when we returned to America. We moved into our new home in Stony Point in October. By Christmas we had only a nodding acquaintance with those in our neighborhood. Aside from Margaret and Howard Lent across the street, who helped us out of every difficulty, and the Dacres, who lived next door with their five wonderful, black-haired, brown-eyed children, we knew no one. We felt a need for community which those around us either had, did not want, or were too shy to seek; we couldn't be sure which.

Not only was this true of Stony Point; we sensed it wherever we went.

"Maybe it's because the world presses in on us so," said Fred. "They feel threatened, perhaps. Television brings us news of the danger we're in all the time. No man's home is sacred anymore."

"And maybe television brings them all the friends they feel they need," I suggested. "You know, their favorite commentator, the stars in the shows they always watch, the families they get to know through the soap operas . . ."

"And these friends you can turn off or on whenever you want them around," added Fred.

"You don't have to take care of their kids . . ."

"Or lend them your lawn mower or run them down to the garage . . ."

"But then, you miss all the fun," I said.

"People just don't want to get involved," said Fred. "You hear it everywhere. But I can't blame them entirely. I know something of how they feel. I see people all day long. When I get home at night, I want to sit down and relax and forget other people's troubles."

It was true, I had to admit. You can only take so much. But did this mean that the old idea of neighborhood was a thing of the past? Did it mean that even in our small town, each family would live in its own box, not knowing or caring about anyone else? Realizing how I felt when I got home from New York at night, it could be a danger, a real danger; because if we no longer cared, if we each went our own way, paying no attention to what happened to our neighbors, or what *would* happen to their children and ours, the human race was doomed. We had to care enough to live together and to work together for the good of one another and of our land, or we would perish.

Perhaps we felt this more deeply than others because of our life in the overseas mission of the church, where we few "foreigners," outsiders in every sense of the word, lived together in one compound. There we were more like a family than just friends. Like members of a family, we argued, became angry, apologized, took care of one another when ill, taught one another's children, argued, became angry . . . and so on. Together we celebrated all birthdays and anniversaries, the holidays of our own country and those of the country in which we lived.

To be sure, each of us had good friends and colleagues outside the clan whom we invited in to meet the "family." We did not in any way cut ourselves off from the Chinese or Indian communities in which we lived. However, it was a warm, loving, rich-in-experience haven from which we sallied forth each day into our separate worlds.

We found something very much like it in our Stony Point Presbyterian Church, but we still wanted to feel this much at home in our own neighborhood, especially at Christmas. It was a lot to expect, after only two months of living here, but something had to be done; a step had to be taken.

At the risk of "becoming involved" we decided to throw etiquette to the winds as to who should call on whom first. Though we were newcomers, we would start out on the afternoon of the day before Christmas and wish every family a Happy Holiday, taking some small gift for each child. (The children had *really* taken the first step in introducing themselves to us before we were even unpacked.)

To our delight we were received with warmth in every home to which we went. Rich friendships have developed over the years, and we have found that our privacy is not that much threatened; there are other busy people besides doctors and writers. Summers are a good time for calling to Mrs. O'Leary as she hangs out clothes, or to run in on Marie Allison or the McGuires as they do the yard work. Over a basket of vegetables from the Moores' garden, David and Fred exchange stamps; the Ehlers call out to ask how Vicki is; Mrs. Skinner and Connie arrive to show me the new aprons they're making; the Gamboli children sell us Girl Scout cookies.

Halloween is a riot when over a hundred children appear from nowhere and we find we do not recognize our nearest

125

neighbors. A few weeks later Peter Prideau will arrive to ask if the pictures Fred took have been developed. Come winter, Mr. Jones and young Pat Dacre try to beat Fred to the shoveling. Now the horns toot when I'm out for my walk. Everyone knows it is useless to stop to ask if I want a ride unless it is very cold or raining or my arms are full of groceries.

Some of the children have grown up and gone away, but they call on us whenever they return.

"I remember one Christmas you didn't come," said Nicki Te Bordo when he came home from college.

"We were probably in Boston," I said. "We thought it didn't matter."

"I was heartbroken. I thought you weren't ever coming again. But you gave us our presents later, when you got back."

The presents were never very much. We didn't think for a moment they'd be missed.

When possible, we try to choose gifts from another country —tiny baskets from Mexico; small wooden monkeys with long, leather-tail bookmarks from Germany; Christmas tree ornaments from Hong Kong; tops to spin or flowers to watch opening in a glass of water from Japan. Recently we chose little angels and stars and hearts made of braided straw from Sweden. We tie each child's name on the gift, then fill baskets, or red or green nut cups, with candies "so you'll have something to nibble while you're trimming the tree."

We are not the only giftgivers. The Nielsens will be waiting for us with a box of Danish cookies. (Nobody can make gingersnaps like Inge.) We ask to see the latest Christmas plate from their native Denmark. The walls of their guest room are covered with them and we enjoy their warm luster and soft blue color. The Russos will have ready a plate of Italian honeyballs, crisp and delicious; Marie, a homemade fruit cake, Mrs. Shaler, a box of candy or a pair of pillowcases with crotcheted edgings.

126

Just when I am most missing Myrtle Cray's visit and her Christmas morning Stollen, the McGuires step in to take her place, and the tradition goes on through these new friends.

And just when I have put the ceramic angels in their Indian baskets to give back to Judy and Vicki for their own homes, Maureen Stewart has made for us two lovely ceramic choristers to take their places. They even look a bit Indian in their bright red cassocks. The year before, her small brother, Gene, gave us a large shoe box with a few scribblings on scraps of paper. They turned out to be his version of the Manger scene. We immediately set them up on top of the piano—our *third* Holy Family that year.

Though we come home from our visits laden with gifts and aware of the little we have given, we know that to our friends, as well as to us, the gifts are not the important thing. The important thing is that we are a neighborhood.

It is good to see our children carrying on the neighborly tradition:

Saranac Lake, New York
December 28

Dear Mommy,

The other day when I was up in the attic getting out our Christmas decorations, I came across my old diaries. In reading back as far as 1947, *every* Christmas was "a perfect day," "God is so good to us," "a marvelous Christmas," "the best Christmas we ever had"; and the exaltations continue on through all the years. So before this Christmas gets to be just another ecstatic line in my diary, I'll tell you all about this one.

For us, more than half the fun of Christmas is preparing for it. A couple of weeks before, I start the baking—all those goodies we're supposed to avoid, cookies, coffee cakes, nut breads, fruit breads, and so forth. Of course, this year I didn't get as much done because we're in the midst of renovating the kitchen and you know how it is when you have two small babies and one big son, David. What would I do without him? He's such a help with the little ones. He loves the spicy aroma of the Lebkuchen when it's in the oven and so does John.

Then there are the extra church programs which add to the fun this time of year. Everyone enjoys the children's Sunday

128

school program. When Santa drops in with presents "un-expectedly," the adults are just as delighted as the smallest toddler.

And what is Christmas without a puppy for the children? Well, this year we even did that! There's a young girl at John's School who comes to him when she needs advice. Her dog had pups and they were all given away except one. She said they'd have to drown it if no one would take it. You know it just wasn't fair, telling us a thing like that. I mean, what choice did we have? Right? Right. So three days before Christmas we drove to her home and after one look at Prudence (their name for her), we adored her. She's the cutest, most affec-tionate little beagle we ever saw! The kids just love her.

I went wild shopping this year. I broke all the rules about "overindulging children." I'd buy things weeks ahead, then forget what I had for whom, and being afraid I didn't have enough for so-and-so, would get some more. But it was such fun and I figured I'd do it this one year.

About two days before Christmas, the children and I make our annual visits to our neighbors (not that we don't go other times, too). This year David, Andy, and I got bundled up, put our baked goods in a box on a sled, and started down the street. This is one of those pleasant traditions that you and Daddy gave us. The neighbors are so grateful for this very small gesture—just a visit and a cranberry loaf. We come home knowing that they've given us more than we have given them.

John and David rush out to do their shopping for me. I try to trick David into telling me what his father bought. But the bags and boxes are hidden and I'm given strict orders, "Don't you dare go into my room."

Christmas Eve and it's *snowing*! We've had a most unusual December with only a few inches of snow. Now we realize it will be a white Christmas. I get Lorraine and Andy into their yellow snuggly "sleepers" and off we go to the candlelight service at the church. It's packed, a real family night with everyone here from the oldsters down to the smallest babe. It's a wonderful feeling to sit with my darling and our three precious children with the candlelight flickering in their wondering eyes. I try not to think of the thousands in other lands who do not have this gift of Christmas. I say a prayer for them and express my overwhelming gratitude for all we have.

The carol singing begins, then the Bible story from Luke. It's so good to have time to sit here and enjoy this service. We all sing "Silent Night" as our candles are extinguished; and soon, after wishing everyone a "Merry Christmas," we drive home in a white fairyland.

Now is the time John and I sit by our tree. When the gifts are all laid out and the stockings filled, we have a mug of Grandmother's hot spiced orange juice. Our eyes are already drooping, so we go to bed, knowing we'll be up early.

The first sound I hear on Christmas Day is Lorraine's murmurings. (She never cries.) I tuck her in bed with me and as I nurse her, I find myself wondering about the lonely old people in a home we recently visited. What kind of a day will they have? Will anyone see that something special is done for them? I have the fleeting idea of taking the baby to see them. Wouldn't they love to see her and touch her?

And what about those two dear people who lost both their sons three years ago? They were drowned when one tried to save the other. How painful Christmas must be as they think of past years. "Oh, dear God, who are we to have so much!"

As the boys call me, I try to shake off the melancholy. Andy's eyes are big as saucers when he realizes that "Santa did come." We all open our stockings; no, Lorraine chews hers. We have devotions around our big red Advent candle, breakfast, and then the excitement of opening presents, with the usual "before" and "after" snapshots of the living room. Wait till you see the "after" one this year—wall-to-wall papers, ribbons, chil-

130

dren, toys, one puppy, one cat, one mother in bathrobe with hand on head! Wow!

Oh, it was a lovely Christmas—"the best Christmas we ever had!"

Now it is two weeks later. The tree is stripped and out in the yard, stuck in a snowbank, as so many of us desert Christ as soon as His Birthday is over. Maybe this coming year, with God's help, we can do better.

Love to you both,
Anne (Scovel Fitch)

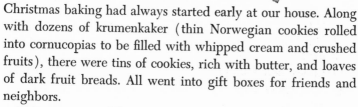

CHRISTMAS BAKING WITH A DIFFERENCE

by Dixie Lee Clifford Scovel

Christmas baking had always started early at our house. Along with dozens of krumenkaker (thin Norwegian cookies rolled into cornucopias to be filled with whipped cream and crushed fruits), there were tins of cookies, rich with butter, and loaves of dark fruit breads. All went into gift boxes for friends and neighbors.

This year was different. Six months before Christmas, our family gave up refined foods and decided to give nutrition and natural foods a whirl. All went well at first; we came through Thanksgiving dinner minus four butter-drenched courses and pumpkin pie.

But as Christmas drew near, my determination faltered. Our tradition of gift boxes was not easy to drop. But neither was our new way of eating.

Our compromise was a different contents for our boxes,

using—along with loaves of fresh whole wheat bread—the
following recipes:

FRUIT COOKIES

½ pound each
   sun-dried raisins
   natural figs
   sun-dried apricots
   walnut meats
   almond meats

Prepare fruit by removing seeds and stem ends. Put the
fruits and nuts through a meat grinder with the coarsest cutter.
Mix well. Form into a roll and wrap in wax paper. Refrigerate
overnight. Slice into ¼-inch slices with a sharp knife.

A DIFFERENT SUGAR COOKIE

1 cup butter
1 cup sugar
2 eggs
1 tablespoon vanilla
½ cup wheat germ
1 cup ground walnuts
1 cup whole wheat pastry flour
1 cup soy flour
2 teaspoons baking powder
½ teaspoon salt

Cream together the butter and sugar. Add eggs, vanilla,
wheat germ and walnuts. Mix well. Sift together the remaining dry ingredients. Stir only enough to mix well. Form into
a roll. Wrap in wax paper and refrigerate overnight. Cut into

¼-inch slices and place on baking sheet covered with foil. Bake 8 to 10 minutes at 350°.

Before baking, the tops of the cookies may be sprinkled with coconut, chopped citron or candied pineapple, chopped nut meats, sesame or anise seeds. Press lightly into dough with a fork.

The
Spirit
   of
Christmas
 Yet To Come

EIGHTEEN

What will the Christmas of the future be like?

In no time at all, Christmas cards will become obsolete, not only because, ecologically, they use up too many trees and pile up waste, but because they will no longer be needed.

Almost any year now, we will program our home computers to give us a print-off of the names of those we most want to remember at this blessed time of year. We will choose a quiet hour, perhaps our listening-to-music hour, and by new methods of extrasensory perception, tune in on several of our friends and eventually, all of them at once. We will think them our love, feel their greetings return and flow into us. We will rise refreshed and conscious of how great a blessing friendship is.

How different from the frustration and exhaustion of addressing cards, knowing that time is running out and we're only at the "S's"! But even in these backward times of having technology and not knowing how to use it, there is still a way. We may not have a family computer or a high degree of ESP, but we do have prayer and thought transference. Perhaps we should try getting out the address book and going down the list, a few pages a day, in restful, loving intercession for those we care about. Their Christmas and ours would be filled with peace and through all the days of Christmas, we would feel each other's presence.

But what of the future Future? Let's travel farther with the Spirit of Christmas Yet to Come and tune in on the young son of a Future family.

"Will there be snow?" we ask, and hear a voice reply:

"Oh, yes, we always have snow. We have it piped in from the Arctic regions by the same system of pipes that brings us our baths from the geysers, our body lotions from our favorite perfumers, our drinking water from our favorite springs. On the night before Christmas, we all stand in our patios and let the snow blow over us. It feels good having the snow sprayed over our bodies. We take up handfuls of it and throw it at each other and have lots of fun. We always look forward to Snow Night. Father and Mother say the snow used to be colder when they were young; then, on Snow Night, you could make it into balls or even, if it came fast enough, into snow-men. They say the Arctic Cap is melting and someday we won't have any snow at all. I wish I could make a snowman just once before that happens."

"Do you have Christmas trees?"

"Trees? Oh, now I remember. The Sage told us all about them. They were green and prickly—some of them were prickly, the ones they used to decorate with colored balls. But that was before primitive man of the twentieth century denuded the hillsides by cutting them all down. The Sage told us that the idea of the tree may be the reason why the Atomic Kaleidoscopic Pictures at Christmas time are apt to come into our minds in cone shapes."

"Pictures? Into your minds?"

"Well, they *come* into our minds, then we all work on them together, arrange the colors and the designs in the color tubes, then we flash them across the picture wall, changing them to bring out our ideas best. We love their movement and the way the light and color combine in unusual forms we never really planned, so that everything we create goes on creating itself and becomes more beautiful than we'd thought it would be. Of course, we have to meditate first and feel the Divine Spirit flowing through us. Some of us are better than others at Wall Pictures because some are closer to the Divine Mind."

"Do you have other Christmas pictures besides the ones with cones?"

"Oh, yes. We have all kinds of pictures, not only for Christmas, but for other days, almost all the days."

"Doesn't it take a lot of time to make them?"

"What is time?"

"Never mind. Tell us more about the pictures."

"Our family is working on one now. It's going to be on the Great Star, the one we hear about after the Snow on Christmas Eve when we gather in our love group to listen to the Sage tell us about when the Star appeared in the sky."

"What happened?"

"It's a strange story about the birth of a child in the manner children used to be born—in pain and many times in poverty— in a land where there were living things called animals, that watched his birth. The telling seems to draw us very close to one another."

"How long will it take you to make the Star picture?"

"Until it is finished. We want our telling of the Star, through the picture, to bring the creative feeling to all who see it. If we do it well enough, perhaps He-Who-Leads will choose it to hang in the Science Building to inspire those who work there. It's the building in which our uncle used to work."

"Your uncle? Where is he now?"

"He's helping the colonists on Mercury to make their last adjustments to their new atmosphere. Uncle was one of the men who found a way to regulate the atmosphere on all the planets. Mercury was the most difficult, but now that one is working well, too."

"Does he ever get back to Earth?"

"Of course. Distance is no problem anymore. But Uncle doesn't like Earth much. He thinks we're awfully backward here. He doesn't like our Wall Pictures, especially what we've shown him of our first attempts on the Star picture. 'You don't know anything about stars,' says Uncle. 'Stars have to be seen from far away, as the Wise Men saw them.'"

"Wise Men?"

"It's a Christmas Telling that is told on Mercury—about three kings who brought gifts to a little Boy that was born. Wouldn't it be wonderful if it turned out to be the same Baby who came to bring peace so long ago? The very one our Sage tells us about?"

"Perhaps it is."

"Uncle is sure that it is He. This I know—we feel the same warm glow inside us when we hear both stories."

"Do you ever travel to the other planets?"

"No, but someday I'd like to go to the cities under the sea, where most of Earth's inhabitants live now."

"Why isn't *your* family there?"

"Well, you see, our grandfathers were among those who could never accommodate to gill-breathing, so our family has remained on Earth. But we hear a lot about the Undersea People. We know they don't have snow there; that Wall Pictures are never used because the houses are all made of glass and the ever-changing beauties of the ocean floor are open for all to see.

"At Christmas time there are Tellings there, too, of course. Underwater sound vibrations from their Sages are translated by a system which turns them into words. It's all done right there in their homes, so they don't have to go even the short distance to where their Sage lives. But I'd miss the traveling to see the Sage, and I'd want to see his face during the Telling. Those under the sea say they like to be together in their own homes as a family for the Telling. So they gather from their work cities and from their play cities and listen to the story of a people who were on Earth long ago and who loved the Divine Spirit who walked on Earth then. After He left them, these people lived underground in catacombs; but strange as it may seem, their symbol was a small lake fish.

"Father would like to try again to see if he could now adapt to gill-breathing. But Mother says, 'If we go, who will feed the birds?'"

Roads Still Lead to Bethlehem

We, your children,
    have never heard a sleighbell.
We have never gone
    over-the-river-and-through-the-woods
    to Grandmother's house.
Ours is not your generation.

But good heavy-duty tires
    pull us through the same snow
    to places of our own
    where we sing of ancient things.

We have never decorated a tree with popcorn
    nor felt the one orange
    in the toe of a stocking.

But we have seen beauty, have known want.
And though the way for us is uncharted,
we follow a star.

NINETEEN

Meanwhile, we are here, living on Earth in a time which has been hopelessly bad but is getting hopefully better. However inadequate our solutions, the vast majority of the world's people now know that, for settling disputes, war is as obsolete as dueling. Our thinking and our planning is firmly set in the direction of "Peace on earth, goodwill among men."

We are willing at last to listen to our own shepherds keeping watch over their flocks on the plains of the West and are at least beginning an attempt to right the wrongs we have done to these Indian Americans from whom we took the country. We can no longer say that one of the three Wise Men, inquiring where the young Child lay, would be turned away from the Inn today.

And thousands of our young people (some say the figure is nearer the millions) are finding that the Man who was born in Bethlehem has the power to redeem their every situation,

143

including loosening them from the captivity of drugs. (It is interesting that some of them call themselves Jesus People—a direct translation of the word Christ-ians, the term used in derision of the same group years ago in Antioch.) For all our present sophistication, we are nearer to the first Christians than we were.

But we are not that up-to-date on how to celebrate the Birthday of this Man, Christ Jesus. Our preparations for it reduce the nation's population to frenzied desperation. We worry over how the piled-up bills will be paid, are frustrated because of lack of time to do all we make ourselves do. Instead of being renewed by Christmas, we collapse, a quivering pulp of fatigue. Ask any sales person, any airlines employee, any mother, any couple who have worked to within a few hours of Christmas Eve and must be back on the job the morning of the 26th.

In China Christmas was easier and it was harder than this. It was easier because it was simply a Holy Day for the church. It was harder because, for most of the twenty-one years there, we were in the midst of war. I would worry for months in fear that there would be no gifts for the children, or that, having them, the house would be searched again and the gifts confiscated. We lost other things during the war—two complete households of everything we owned, including furniture; but we never lost the Christmas presents. I thanked God fervently each Christmas morning when we wakened to find the tree, the presents, our home, just as we'd hoped they would be on Christmas and not bombed out of existence.

The difficulties brought a blessing that has carried over. I still begin to pray for Christmas early in the summer—that all our preparations will be according to what God wants our Christmas to be. The urgency and the fear are gone, now. (How I wish that could be said by every mother in the world!) It is pleasant to pray for the preparations without fear—that we will spend the holiday where He wants us to be;

that we will be guided to buy the right things for the right people, something that will be pure joy to look at or to use.

If this prayer brings no other balm, it at least spares you that awful moment when the presents are all wrapped and ready to be placed under the tree and you *know* you've given too little and nothing seems right for anybody. "Well, I prayed," you can say to yourself. "I prayed and I've tried my best. Nobody can do more." You can go to bed and not have to run out to buy a lot more stuff you can't afford.

Some year *soon* I'm going back to the old China plan of buying in the summer and setting the deadline for having all gifts wrapped by Thanksgiving Day instead of the night before Christmas. With that much behind me, I can enjoy the baking and the decorating. And, knowing that everything is ready, I can feel to the full the beauty of our church's Christmas Eve candlelight service. I can pray for each child and grandchild during the Communion without the intrusion of cataloguing what order to follow as soon as that last hymn is sung and I can hurry Fred away from all the people he has to see and get busy on what is yet to be done.

Meanwhile, back at the Christmas cards . . .

Until we have two-way ESP, this is the only way most of us keep in touch with our friends. But I am convinced that Christmas cards are self-proliferating. When I mentioned addressing six hundred, Faith said, "So that's where Carl gets the feeling he has to send a card to every person he meets on an airplane!"

Right, Faith. Sorry.

But I enjoy receiving Christmas cards, too—even those without a personal message. Myrtle Cray, while we were in India, gave me the idea of choosing special ones to use in making small arrangements for the top of a bookcase, the corner of a table or desk. Each year I begin with a card depicting the Annunciation, and put with it a candle and a small ceramic angel or a tiny carved wooden one. As the season progresses, on through the Birth, the Shepherds, and the Wise Men, I change the cards and the decorated candles to match colors, adding a carved wooden reindeer which Fred once brought me from Tübingen, or some other small treasure such as a bell. Sometimes I make several arrangements, upstairs and down. I also use Christmas cards and other beautiful ones, such as those from museums, for bookmarks all year long. I use our cards, I enjoy them, but oh, that list! How to choose one friend to cross out! Technology, hurry! Help! Six hundred Think-O-Grams, please.

One of our friends solved her card problem by enlarging her birthday list. She liked spreading out her silent conversations with friends to cover a whole year and thought we would enjoy the card on our own day instead of amid the plethora of Christmas. I like her idea.

And I would cast a vote for printed letters at some time other than Christmas, too. There isn't leisure enough, really, even to dash through them. Over seventy of them coming in at once, each one from a dear friend whose news you've been looking forward to hearing—here it is in your lap and you can't take time to read it!

It occurs to me that spreading birthday gifts over the year might help some families to solve the too-many-for-Christmas problem. Not ours! We have nine birthdays in the immediate family between November 29 and January 10. I once said to Judy and Vicki, "Now, girls, whenever a boy wants you to go out with him, ask first when his birthday is. If he says December, just say, 'Sorry.'" Jim Harris, Vicki's husband, barely got in under the wire, November 29.

I sometimes give "un-birthday, un-Christmas" presents, but our friend, Muriel Thorne, does the loveliest thing of all—she gives Advent presents. I can't think of another time of year when it is so much fun to receive a gift. You're just beginning to get excited about Christmas and feel you can hardly wait for its surprises and suddenly, right then, you find a package in the mailbox! Muriel has a talent for finding appropriate and unusual things for her friends. I know she shops all year long. She once gave us our own gargoyle on the Washington Cathedral. Someday we are going down there just to see it. Usually she gives us things from her travels—an olive-wood bell from Bethlehem, two exquisite cups and saucers decorated with dainty sprigs of holly from England, a Danish cheese knife perfect for slicing and of good design, an unusual ceramic angel she found in a shop in Alexandria. And the pin, which is perfect on the lapel of my old green suit, I bring out every year to wear to church on the first Sunday in Advent. It is an authentic reproduction of the Angel Gabriel, Flemish, fifteenth century, from the original in the National Gallery of Art in Washington, D.C. (where Muriel was formerly a lecturer). It is long after Epiphany before I can bear to put my angel back into its box.

Perhaps by simplifying our last-minute preparations or spreading them out over the year, we may find the leisure to give thought to new ways of celebrating the Birthday of Christ. We are caught in the same old wheel, year after year. For instance, from the standpoint of ecology, something has to be done *soon* about Christmas trees. We have better uses for the comparatively few acres of land left to us.

We might begin Christmas on Arbor Day and, having asked permission of the town fathers, gather the neighbors together and plant evergreens along our sidewalks, or in the town park, to be decorated by us all at Christmas time. We might even make a Christmas mini-park. Or, we might as a family plant a small evergreen in a tub each year to decorate for our own use the following Christmas; then plant it outside the next

147

Arbor Day, with a new one in the tub for the coming Christmas, and so on. If we planted a tree each year for each member of the family, our clan could reforest a hill in no time; and have our inside Christmas trees besides.

Or, we might try some secret tree planting as a year-round Christmas gift to a shut-in—say a dogwood in the side yard near a window. This, too, could be done on Arbor Day, with perhaps a note mentioning it, in some way, at Christmas time.

A couple we know decorate an outside evergreen near their living-room window for the winter birds. They hang it with apples, bright red and blue bags of woven string filled with peanuts or suet. These "decorations" attract the cardinals, nuthatches, blue jays, sparrows, purple finches, titmouses, and chickadees, making a veritable carrousel of a Christmas tree.

Many of us will want some living green inside our homes at Christmas. Cousins of ours in Beacon, New York, had a lovely planted bowl given them by their daughter-in-law, which they showed us with delight.

Fred and I look forward each year to our
own daughter-in-law's gift—Faith's partridge
berry wreath:

A PARTRIDGE BERRY WREATH

Tall pines rose skyward overhead,
  And dropped soft needles for my bed,
Where, glossy green and cheery red,
  My lowly fruit and leaves were spread.
Now in a wreath I come to you,
  As living friends are wont to do,
My Christmas wishes to renew,
  Accept please my devotion too.

Will keep indefinitely. Put in shallow dish of water.
Moisten top occasionally. Soak overnight once a week.

My grandfather, Hollis Webster, wrote this poem and had
the cards made up for his wife, Helen Noyes, to accompany
the small wreaths she made at Christmas time to give as gifts

149

of cheer. But the cheer was in the making as well as in the receiving and this, too, she gave to her friends.

As a child, I remember the dining room at Christmas time, smelling of woods and swamps, the dark wood sideboard covered with greenery, the brass samovar poking its cover through the cut branches; the dining-room table filled with cut sprigs of yew, spruce, and cedar, and with little bowls and trays of pine cones, gold-painted seed pods, partridge berries, black elder and juniper berries; spools of green twine, mosses in low waterfilled-dishes—what soothing confusion it all was!

This room was always cozily but expandably full. Greenery and people got pushed around with equally loving goodwill, to make room for more people or hot tea for a caller, in from the cold, or bowls of just-made applesauce for children in need of a break. Someone would move a chair and then you could squeeze past the sideboard where a little place was carefully cleared for you at the edge of the table. An aunt or maybe a neighbor who had just learned wreath-making would help you find a piece of wire, slide a few greens in your direction, then let you forage about for whatever you chose to put in your wreath.

I work a little more quickly now, after many years of this seasonal ritual, but it was very slow-going at first. This is how I was taught to make

A PARTRIDGE BERRY WREATH

I. Gather sphagnum moss, reindeer moss (really a lichen), partridge berries, and a little princess pine or other soft greenery in the fall or early winter. The berries should be gathered after the first cold snap has turned them red and before it is so deep in winter that the birds and deer have eaten them.

All these come from the northern piney woods with acid soil. The sphagnum moss grows best in moist areas; the reindeer moss likes the sides of rocks and grows taller as you go farther north.

The partridge berries grow in piney woods throughout New England. To collect them is arduous fun. You find the berries in patches under, and poking through, the pines and snow of the forest floor. With your fingers, break off four or five inches at the end of the growth. Try to get stems with berries, but stems without berries can be useful, too, as filler. Please don't pull up the root. It is needed for next year's supply.

In addition to the three basic ingredients—a moss (sphagnum) to hold moisture, a lichen (reindeer moss) for white color, and the berry sprigs—it's fun to have a few extra bits from the woods to tuck into your wreath.

There are three very important things to remember when you go:
1. Check the use and ownership of the property where you're going to pick.
2. It will be close to, if not in, hunting season, so wear some red or orange to warn hunters, just in case. If the berries are growing there, it is probably good deer country.
3. Dress warmly and wear boots or rubbers. Take a piece of old rug or something waterproof to kneel on. It can get very cold, squatting in damp, shady woods.

The greenery you have collected will keep in a cool

151

place for several weeks if it is made just barely moist and sealed in a plastic bag.

Now back to the second step in the *directions:*

II. Soak the mosses for several minutes or longer, till they become spongy. Take a piece of copper wire long enough to circle into your wreath when it is finished. (Do not circle it now.) Take an egg-sized piece of damp sphagnum moss and roll it between your hands till it's about the width of your thumb (as you used to do with modeling clay to make "snakes"). Using one hand, hold the sphagnum moss as a bed along the wire; lay bits of berry sprigs, reindeer moss, and princess pine on top of it, securing them with that same thumb until, with your free hand, you have wound string over the stem to hold them in place. Lay on a bit at a time, winding with the string as you go, working down the length of the wire. Arrange the tops of your greenery as you want the wreath to look. Don't worry about straggling stems, just hold them with the sphagnum moss as you go along and let them serve as bedding for the coming tops.

When it is long enough to make the size of a wreath you want, bend it into a circle and twist the ends of the wire together. As you do this, you will probably have to cut off the remaining stem ends or sew them into the moss. Bare and bunchy spots can be covered by gently pushing some of the greens to close the gap or by sewing a few sprigs into place with thread and needle.

III. Have fun; relax and enjoy the smell and feel of the wreath as you work. What it does for you is more important than what you do for it.

IV. To keep the wreath fresh, it should be set in a shallow dish of water so the moss will remain soft. (A soup plate works rather well.) Every few days either spray the top or soak the wreath upside down in a bowl of deeper water for a few minutes. Once a week submerge it completely in cold water and let it soak overnight.

Christmas is much more than this and Christmases have included much less, but making wreaths in my grandparents' home, in my parents' and now in our own, has become a very special part of the season for me.

Faith Greeley Scovel

Boston, Massachusetts

TWENTY

Meanwhile, what about the commercialism of Christmas?

Carl once wrote in a King's Chapel Bulletin for Advent:

"'Happy New Year' is an appropriate greeting for this season, since Advent marks the beginning of the Christian year. The church has its own year and the church has its own sense of time, indifferent to the calendar year and the fiscal year and even the commercial year. (The commercial Christmas now begins, I am told, just after Halloween.) The church keeps its own time, deliberately out of step with store and state and season, and this deliberate 'mistiming' shows that the church has its own identity and its own authority, independent of the voices of culture.

"We would do well *not* to cry and complain about the commercialization of Christmas, especially if we purchase our gifts and decorations at this time of year as everyone else does. . . . Commercialization cannot hurt our celebration of Christ's birth and His significance, so long as *we* do not con-

154

fuse the two. The commercial Christmas (perhaps we should use the proper pagan name, 'Yuletide,' will not affect our worship or devotions, so long as *we* keep our sense of what we are about when we celebrate the Christian Christmas.

"We solemnize our expectation of God's kingdom; we give thanks for God's inestimable love in the redemption of the world by our Lord Jesus Christ: we think upon and celebrate these things. We begin anew. Happy New Year!"

And a Happy New Year to all you who are behind the counters, driving delivery trucks, trudging the postal routes, answering the mail orders—all you who are involved in the commercialization of Christmas. It would be folly to wish you a Merry Christmas. Christmas to you must be a numb, exhausted body carried around by two aching legs and two sore feet. And I say, "A Happier New Year than you have ever had before," because this present situation does not have to be and must not be.

Our methods of shopping for Christmas are obsolete. Stores are inadequately built to handle the increase of population and its resultant flow of traffic through aisles in front of and behind counters which were built for our grandmothers. Such crowding brings out the worst in us shoppers. Our shouts of impatience drown the *God-Rest-You-Merry's* of the piped-in music.

It does not have to be so. A little thought and planning can leave you, the downtrodden-by-Christmas, with the relatively few who actually enjoy a last-minute rush. The rest of us will keep our own time, "deliberately out of step with store and state and season." Time does not control us; we control time by setting our priorities, by choosing what we will do with time. It can't be that difficult to shop early.

Have you ever noticed that immediately after Christmas, ideas for gifts seem to flood into your mind? Ads in magazines leap out at you. "That Teddy Bear will be just the thing for

155

Lorrie," we say. "I must remember it." I, for one, never do.

After Christmas, I made out a list of those to whom we usually give presents. Now, when I see such an ad, I vow to order at once, or clip it, label it for whomever, and put it in a pile until I have enough money to buy the article. And I think I'll stash away a few extra dollars in what I shall call my Christmas purse in case I see something while shopping that would take one more name off the list for later. If there still remain a few friends unprovided for, say by Halloween, I resolve to think through what I want *before* I go on my shopping expedition. So much for New Year's resolutions.

But if I waver, I shall keep saying to myself, "This does not have to be and I am the one to help to change it." For I rebel against our injustice to those who must work before, during, and after Christmas. I am perfectly serious about such people starting a CRUSADE FOR AN 8-DAY CHRISTMAS HOLIDAY! Until this is accomplished, why not, as individuals, declare your own Christmas week, say in April, the month in which some scholars believe Christ was born? It might be fun to think up new ways of decorating for that time of year. Trim a tree on the patio. Decorate for Christmas inside with the colors madonna blue, white, and gold, instead of the December reds and greens.

A Christmas tree for the center of the table could be made of white nylon net balls, for instance. For each ball, buy ¼ yd. net, which comes folded double on the bolt.

The directions are:

Cut in 3 three-inch-wide strips

Lay them one on top of the other, making 3 double strips of the folded nylon or six layers deep

Shirr them together down the middle of the strips with a fine mercerized crotcheting cotton

Then pull the thread tight to draw the material up into a fluffy ball and tie securely

Sew a ribbon with a small plastic flower into the top for
added decoration (optional)

Set up in a pyramid, the balls would make a lovely white
Christmas tree. Invite friends in for dinner. They'll think you
are crazy, celebrating Christmas at this time of year, and will
be sure of it when you give each one of them a fluffy nylon ball
to take home to use for scouring pots and pans. I didn't believe
it would work until I tried one; but it did. They are even on
sale for that purpose in some stores.

Why not set a date and give yourself a wonderful present
—like a cruise to . . . would you like to try the Holy Land?
It might make a difference in your celebration of Christmas
forever after. If you decide to go, do read Paul L. Maier's book,
The First Christmas (Harper & Row), and *In the Steps of the
Master* by H. V. Morton (Dodd, Mead & Co.) which Muriel
Thorne gave us for Lent one year. If you can't afford the trip,
treat yourself to the books anyway.

My heart goes out especially to clerks in large department
stores. You could take mini-Christmas-breaks during lunch
hours, I suppose, to sit in a quiet library or church, or go to a
museum, even if you had time for only one picture. I think I'd
choose a favorite, see if I could buy a postcard of it at the
museum shop, and carry it in my pocket to look at when the
going got rough.

I once knew a nurse who, when things piled too high, would
buy herself a new perfume, put a drop or two on a handker-

157

chief, and take a whiff now and then to remind her that "the world *can* be beautiful, fragrant, and lovely."

Is it possible for you salespeople to realize what a vital part you play in bringing joy to hundreds at this blessed time of year? Can you feel, throughout the store, the joy and glory of Christmas? Or are you so tired you cannot even pretend that Christmas is wonderful and you are about to give the woman tearing at your sleeve "one big fist sandwich" (to quote Judy)?

The true meaning of Christmas has nothing to do with the mob of faces swimming before your eyes. It cannot touch the real you, who are alone, in a simple hut, with the Holy Family. If we have taken this away from you, how can we celebrate Christmas ourselves?

He who knew what it was like to be hemmed in by crowds, came to redeem the world. And that includes department stores.

There will always be those of us who, at one time or another, will have to work on Christmas Day. Having been a nurse and having a doctor for a husband, I know it well. I know, too, how the Day can be gloriously brightened when one is shown appreciation and concern.

Someday, when the picky little worries start picking and one needs to think of something to take them off one's mind, it might be fun to try to write a few dialogues for those who help us to keep Christmas but cannot do so themselves. I have one in mind that I haven't had the courage to try out yet, for fear of a forced sojourn in a mental hospital. It is called:

HOW TO MAKE A SALESGIRL DROP IN HER TRACKS
or
Show a Clerk a Miracle

She: Which one do you want?
Me: I don't know. Which one do *you* like?

158

She: This one.

Me: Do you really like this one? Would you wear a scarf like this yourself?

She: Yes, it's my favorite color.

Me: Okay, I'll take it. And I want it gift wrapped.

She (*coming back with gift*): Do you have a card for it?

Me: Thanks, but I won't need one. Here (*handing her the gift*), take this home and open it when you wake up on Christmas afternoon.

    (*Disappear into crowd while she is still stunned*)

One such real-life dialogue used to take place in Fred's home and I recall hearing it again the Christmas of 1952, when we had our last Christmas celebration in America before leaving for India. It was at the home of our cousins, The Reverend George H. Allen, Jr., and his wife, Harriet, at the manse in Bath, New York:

Cousin Harriet: George, where are you going? You haven't finished opening your presents.

Cousin George: I'll be right back. I want to call the operator before I forget it.

Cousin George (*on the phone*): Good morning, Operator. I just want to wish you a Merry Christmas and to thank you for working today so we can have the pleasure of calling our family and friends. (*Silence*) No, Operator, I don't want to place a call. I just want to wish you a Merry Christmas. (*Returns, chuckling*)

One of us: What did she say?

Cousin George: She said, "Thank you, the same to you."

Cousin Harriet: What else did she say, George?

Cousin George (*still chuckling*): Just what they always say every year: "In all the times I've had to work on Christmas Day, no one has ever done this before."

❧⚬❧

Cousin George is no longer with us here on earth, but Harriet continues to mother (and sister!) us all. If you were to ask our children, "Who is the best cook in the immediate family," without question they would answer, "Aunt Harriet."

"*Cousin* Harriet sounds so distant," they all agreed. "Can't we call her 'Aunt' instead?"

She is much closer to us than cousin *or* aunt. She would be the matriarch of the family, if she were at all matriarchal. She is, rather, our children's eighty-seven-year-old contemporary.

Here is one of Cousin Harriet's recipes which we all like very much. I serve it with cold ham and a salad on Christmas Eve, or for a late supper on Christmas night. It's a good change from the fowl we usually have for Christmas dinner:

SCALLOPED OYSTERS

1 pint oysters
½ cup bread, crumbled loosely in *small* pieces
1 cup saltine crackers, also crumbled loosely
½ cup melted butter
½ teaspoon salt
⅓ teaspoon pepper
4 tablespoons oyster liquid (about)
½ cup rich milk or cream

Rinse oysters just a little under the cold-water faucet. Set them into a drainer cup for awhile where quite a bit of the heavier liquid will collect. Mix the bread and crackers with the melted butter. In a shallow baking dish, put a layer of the buttered crumbs. Cover with the oysters and seasoning. Add the rest of the crumbs and sprinkle lightly with the oyster liquid and cream. Bake, uncovered, in hot oven (425°) for 30 to 35 minutes until brown.

TWENTY-ONE

Meanwhile, what of Santa Claus?

Santa was not part of the Chinese or Indian celebrations of Christmas. It was strange to come back to the United States and find the major emphasis on His Jollyness. As one friend said, "It's all very well for you to talk about Christmas being Jesus' Birthday, but remember, our children here know very little about that <u>side</u> of it, unless they happen to be members of that small minority who go to Sunday school. The Christmas story is no longer read from the Bible in public schools; the carols aren't sung. The children do hear them on television, of course, but they are just another song like 'Rudolph, the Red-nosed Reindeer' and 'White Christmas.'"

Do you believe in Santa Claus? I was ten years old before the question even entered my mind. I believed in him because I knew that my parents would never lie to me. One day when my mother was brushing my long hair in front of her mirror, she asked, "Myra, do you mean to say you *still* believe in Santa Claus?"

"Of course," I told her.

She threw back her head and laughed one of her long, beautiful laughs—"the kind of a laugh Santa Claus has," I thought. Their handwriting was similar, too.

Santa is just as real as elves and fairies and leprechauns and hobbits, and everybody believes in *them*. Santa is the jolly old elf of Christmas surprises. He comes and you never see him. He leaves the gifts under the tree; sometimes he signs them, sometimes he doesn't. Sometimes the packages only say, "Guess Who?" You know he's been there because the piece of cake you leave for him is always eaten. Why, Santa Claus wouldn't miss celebrating Jesus' Birthday by making other people happy for all the snow at the North Pole. Santa Claus is the Spirit-of-Christmas-Giving.

Making other people happy—perhaps this is the test of what is a right thing to do for Christmas. Will our preparations bring joy and renewal in our own lives? For surely one way to *give* happiness at Christmas is to be happy ourselves (especially mothers!). Will what we do bring joy and renewal to others? If so, we may find those around us drawing closer to the message of the Manger.

And the dear old saint has given me a way to entertain our grandchildren while talking to my husband, two sons, two daughters-in-law, a daughter, a son-in-law, and a neighbor:

(*Aside, to the children:*) Bring me a piece of white paper, the scissors, and a box of crayons.

Children: How big do you want the paper?

Me: Typewriter-size. You'll find some in my study, the old paper you can draw on. Remember?

163

Children: Come on, I know where it is. On the bottom shelf
of that little white bench near her red chair.

Me: And the scissors and crayons are in the top drawer of the
table by the window. Right-hand side.

HOW TO MAKE
A CIRCLE OF SANTAS

Cut a sheet of 8½″ × 11″ typewriter paper down the middle
lengthwise (This will provide two sets of Santas.)

Fold one of the strips in 2-inch-wide folds, folding first one
way, then the other, as you would for a fan

If you need to, cut off a piece from the last fold to make it
even with the others

Hold folds   Fold again
together

Fold

Trace off this pattern on another
piece of paper and cut out

Fold it down the middle

Place fold of Santa
on fold of paper
and trace around it

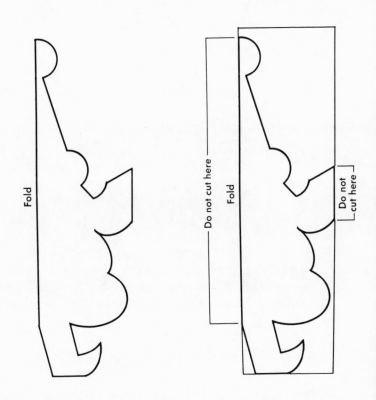

Cut out Santa, being careful not to cut the hands where
they meet the edge of the folded paper
Open the folds

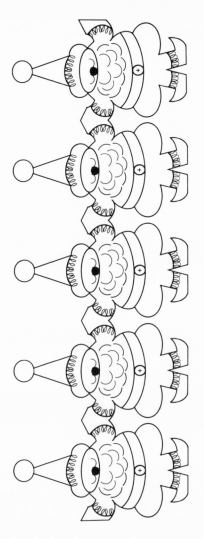

Draw in the face, beard, belt, etc., letting the children color
    them to suit their fancy

Leave them in a row, or paste the first and the last hands
    together to make a circle

TWENTY-TWO

The Christmas Story
that Should Never have to be Told

I was in a large room, I will not say where. Everything about the room was satisfying—its proportions, its furnishings, its atmosphere. I liked this room, lit now by the dazzling sun of Christmas morning.

Gathered around a glowing tree were those who loved me. They made it seem as if the whole celebration was meant for me alone. One of them came up and laid a present in my lap. It was a small thing, not worth much, but I liked it and expressed my thanks. There were other gifts—some I didn't like at all, some I thought I would never use and found later that I could not do without them. All these gifts I accepted as if they were my due and I responded with the necessary gratitude.

Then one came with a gift which I knew had cost him everything he had. I could guess what it might be, but I didn't really know and had no desire to find out.

168

"I don't want it," I said. "I don't want your gift at all."

I knew that if I looked up, I would see the hurt in his eyes, but I didn't even care enough to look up.

"Please take it," he said. "It is everything you've always wanted and never thought you'd have."

I might have felt his pleading, sensed the deep disappointment, but I didn't. His sacrifice meant nothing to me.

"Please take it," he said again, and knew at last that all he'd planned to make this the happiest Christmas of my life had been in vain.

"Maybe some other time," I replied. "I don't really need it now. I'll let you know when I want it."

Was it a dream or did it really happen?

It is happening every day. We accept the beautiful room, our world, its dazzling sun, its healing rain—our environment perfected to meet our every need. We accept all the smaller gifts, which are not really small—the roof over our heads, the love of those around us, the push-button conveniences that leave us free to do whatever we choose—these we take as our due.

But we have been offered a greater gift, a gift whose cost we cannot estimate—the one gift that is "everything you've always wanted and never thought you'd have."

Blessed are we if we accept the Gift of Christmas. As Vicki has said, "Christ was born! . . . Welcome, Saviour."

CHRISTMAS WISH

God give you blessings at Christmas time—
stars for your darkness, sun for your day,
light on the path as you search for the way,
and a mountain to climb.

God grant you courage this coming year,
fruit for your striving, friends as you roam,
joy in your labor, love in your home,
and a summit to clear.

With love,

Myra Scovel

170

FAMILY CHRISTMAS TRADITIONS

FAMILY CHRISTMAS RECIPES

RECIPES continued

RECIPES continued

CHRISTMAS CRAFTS

CRAFTS continued

CHRISTMAS ART AND POEMS

ART AND POEMS continued

ART AND POEMS continued

72 73 74 75 10 9 8 7 6 5 4 3 2 1